BARRON'S

HOW TO PREPARE FOR THE

AP®

EXAM IN HUMAN GEOGRAPHY

Peter S. Alagona

Meredith Marsh

BARRON'S

Acknowledgments

In the two years that it took to complete this book, I had the distinct pleasure of working with several outstanding individuals, without each of whom this project may never have reached fruition. Bob O'Sullivan, the editor of this volume, served as an excellent resource and an efficient manager. UC Santa Barbara Lecturer Alex Keuper, contributed numerous sample test questions from his own extensive files. Jessica Liberman offered encouragement, inspiration, perspective, and a source of distraction when I needed it most. My parents, Judy and Dr. Pete, and my sister, Robyn, continually amaze me with the kind of steadfast familial support that everyone hopes for in life but few people actually receive. The many undergraduate students that I have worked with at UC Santa Barbara, UCLA, San Francisco State, and Santa Monica College have made teaching geography a true learning experience. Finally, I would like to thank my co-author, Meri Marsh, who joined this project mid-stream, at a point when I seriously doubted whether the book would ever get done. I could not have hoped for a more able colleague or a better friend.

Peter S. Alagona
Venice, CA
December 2002

I could not have helped Pete successfully complete this project and maintain some level of sanity without the help and encouragement of some wonderful people. First and foremost, I have tremendous gratitude for Pete Alagona, for giving me this opportunity, and for providing an unbelievable amount of encouragement in some of my desperate moments. Secondly, Michael Vergeer patiently inspired me throughout the entire project with his pride, enthusiasm, and much-needed smiles during my many cranky moments! My intelligent colleagues at the University of California at Santa Barbara, namely Adrienne Domas and Jeff Howarth, helped maintain geographic accuracy, and finally, the love, support, and encouragement that I constantly depend on and too often take for granted from my wonderful family: Jimbo, Jackie, Jeremy, and Becky, made this challenge enjoyable and completely worthwhile.

Meredith J. Marsh
Santa Barbara, CA
January 2003

About the Authors

Peter S. Alagona received his bachelor's degree from Northwestern University in 1995 and his master's degree, in geography, from the University of California at Santa Barbara in 2000. He is currently a doctoral student in environmental history at the University of California at Los Angeles. Pete has worked as a lecturer in geography, both at UCSB and at Santa Monica College, and as a field instructor in San Francisco State University's Wildlands Studies Program. He is a co-author of *Physical Geography Laboratory Manual*, published by Kendall/Hunt in 1999.

Meredith J. Marsh received her bachelor's degree in geography from Calvin College in 1999. She is currently completing a Master's Degree in geography at the University of California at Santa Barbara. Meri has worked as a teaching assistant for the Introductory Human Geography course at UCSB from 1999–2002.

All inquiries should be addressed to:
Barron's Educational Series, Inc.
250 Wireless Boulevard
Hauppauge, New York 11788
http://www.barronseduc.com

Library of Congress Catalog Card No. 2003044420

International Standard Book No. 0-7641-2094-8

Library of Congress Cataloging-in-Publication Data
Alagona, Peter.
    How to prepare for the AP exam in human geography / Peter Alagona, Meri Marsh.
        p. cm.
Includes bibliographical references and index.
    ISBN 0-7641-2094-8
    1. Human geography—Examinations—Study guides.
I. Marsh, Meri. II. Title.
    GF26.5.A43   2002
    304.2′076—dc21   2003044420

Printed in the United States of America
9 8 7 6 5 4 3 2 1

Contents

Introduction

In This Chapter

- Introduction and About the Book
- The Structure of the Test
- Strategies for Studying for the AP Human Geography Exam
- Taking the Practice Exams

Introduction and About the Book

Description and Purpose of the AP Human Geography Exam

The AP Human Geography Exam covers a range of material that would normally be included in a semester-long college-level course in Introductory Human Geography. Typical Introductory Human Geography courses cover a wide variety of topics, with the basic goal of understanding patterns and processes that have shaped human relationships on earth over space and time. This overarching goal can be further divided into five main goals derived from the National Geography World Literacy Standards, introduced in 1994. According to the College Board, which adheres to these standards, upon completion of an Introductory Human Geography course, students should be able to:

- Use and think about maps and spatial data sets,
- Understand and interpret the implications of associations among phenomena in places,
- Recognize and interpret at different scales the relationships among patterns and processes,
- Define regions and evaluate the regionalization process,
- Characterize and analyze changing interconnections among places.

The Advanced Placement Exam covers seven major content areas. Each content area, described later in this chapter, will be covered by a percentage of the exam. *How to Prepare for the AP Exam in Human Geography* has been designed to correspond with the College Board's objectives, and one chapter is dedicated to each of the Board's seven major content areas.

If you have decided to take the AP Human Geography Exam and you do well on it, you will have demonstrated exceptional understanding of the objectives and goals of the course, and a general mastery of the subjects taught in an introductory college-level course. Each college has its own standards for accepting advanced placement credit. If you score high enough, you will earn course credit at the college you choose to attend. Depending on the core requirements of that school, you may never be required to encounter geography again.

However, if you find human geography interesting, you may be able to jump right into upper-division course work in the field! Thus, this book not only should prepare you for the Advanced Placement Exam but also give you a sound basis upon which to build, with future courses you might take in human geography.

Suggested Uses for the Book

This book was designed to prepare students for the Advanced Placement Exam in Human Geography. Each of the seven chapters devoted to major content areas on the exam also contains a list of important key terms, definitions, practice multiple-choice and free-response questions, and explanations to all questions provided. This text can stand on its own as the sole guide for an AP course in Human Geography; it can be used as a supplemental text to a more commonly used textbook for introductory courses; and it can also be used by individuals, not enrolled in an Advanced Placement course, to prepare independently for the exam. You need not be enrolled in an AP course to take the exam.

If this book is being read as the main text in an Advanced Placement course, students should read each chapter completely, and the instructor should use the sample questions at the end of each chapter as guidelines when evaluating students' knowledge of each major subject area. Additionally, instructors should develop activities or labs that strengthen students' understanding of the basic concepts. Included with each chapter is a list of additional text and web references that provide further resources on each of the subareas of human geography discussed throughout the book. Each web or text reference includes a brief description of the material, and the supplemental resources range from resources to purchase classroom maps, to ideas for lesson plans, to web pages for specific countries, to data sets helpful in understanding various concepts. These resources should provide added value to explanations and exercises provided in the book and should help to provide comprehensive preparation for students taking the exam.

Even if you are a high school teacher and you decide not to use this as the main text for your AP course, this volume still provides helpful tools for teaching, not found in any other introductory text, such as practice AP exams. Students enrolled in your course should be encouraged to purchase their own copy of the book and to use it as a source for reviewing the material they will encounter on the exam. The content in each chapter provides a means for students to review their knowledge of the information most relevant to the test. Additionally, students can use the key terms listed at the beginning of each chapter to ensure their knowledge of the various concepts, models, and personalities of human geography. Perhaps the most important tool this guide provides for the student using it as a supplementary text is the two full-length practice exams included near the end of the volume. These tests will help students identify their strong and weak points in the field, as well as help them develop strategies to successfully complete the exam in the time allotted.

If you have purchased this book and are planning to take the exam without any course work in the subject, it should serve you well as long as you are sure to follow the guidelines described later on in this chapter under the heading, "Strategies for Studying for the AP Human Geography Exam." If you follow those guidelines; read this book carefully; study the key concepts, personalities, and models listed at the beginning of each chapter; and use some of the additional resources to supplement and strengthen your understanding of the material, you will be ready to succeed on the exam.

Note to Teachers

If you have purchased this book to get a general idea of the exam but are not planning to use it in your classroom, please encourage your students to purchase the text. By using it as a supplemental study guide, students will be comprehensively prepared for what they will encounter on the exam. The chapters provide the basic material students must understand for successfully completing the exam, thus providing an easy review tool. In addition, both the practice questions at the end of each chapter, and the two practice exams at the end of the book will allow them to determine their strengths and weaknesses and to better prepare themselves for the exam.

If your plans are to use this text either on its own or as a supplemental text in your class, then make sure to familiarize yourself with all the various resources the book contains. The key terms provided at the beginning of each chapter can be used to help you in your lecture design. Additionally, the text and web sources provided at the end of each chapter suggest all sorts of different information, activities, and data sets that can be incorporated into your classroom to strengthen students' comprehension of each major content area. Finally, the practice questions for each content area and the two full-length practice exams provide helpful tools for you to evaluate the students' understanding of the material.

Note to Students

Whether you have bought this book as the main text or supplemental text of an AP class you are currently enrolled in or you have bought it and are planning on using it as your sole source to prepare for the exam, make sure to read this entire introductory chapter before moving on in the text. This chapter will provide answers to most of the questions you might have about the exam. If you have remaining questions, it will provide helpful information that should enable you to find the answers you are looking for. This chapter also explains how to use this book to ensure that you are best prepared for the exam. If you follow the guidelines in this chapter, specifically in the section on strategies for studying for the exam, you should be well prepared for the AP Human Geography Exam.

Commonly Asked Questions About the AP Human Geography Exam

Why Should I Take this Exam?

First, in preparing for this exam, you will be introduced to interesting material that you probably have not yet encountered during your high school experience. Preparation for the exam exposes you to an exciting discipline that explains many of the processes occurring on the earth that you encounter on a daily basis. Second, if you do well on the exam, you will be given Advanced Placement Credit that may exempt you from having to take this course at a college or university. If you find the subject material interesting, and you have completed this course, you can quickly move on in the field. Or, if human geography isn't up your alley, you will have a head start in pursuing whatever truly interests you.

How Much Does It Cost to Take the Exam?

The fee for every AP exam is $80.00. Many states and schools pay for students to take these exams. Be sure to check with your AP coordinator or high school counselor before paying the fee yourself. Fee reductions of $22.00 per exam are available to students who are at a financial disadvantage.

Do All Colleges Accept the Scores?

Advanced Placement is awarded to you by colleges or universities, not by the College Board. The best way to find out about a college's policy is to look in that institution's catalog or website, or by contacting the registrar's office at the particular college or university you are interested in attending. Additionally, you can use the College Board website *(www.collegeboard.com)* to investigate different university's policies. The College Board performs an annual survey and reports each college's policies on their website.

What Materials Should I Bring with Me to the Exam?

1. Several sharpened #2 pencils (with erasers) for the multiple-choice answer sheet.
2. Black or dark blue ballpoint pens for the free-response questions.
3. Your school code—Ask your AP coordinator if you are unsure. If you are homeschooled, you will be given a code at the exam.
4. A watch to keep track of time. Make sure all beepers and alarms are turned off.
5. Your social security number for identification purposes.
6. A photo I.D. if you do not attend the school where the test is being administered.

When Will I Get My Score?

Test scores will be mailed to you in July. However, the College Board has just begun a new program that allows you to call for your grades beginning July 1, 2003. Grades will be available for students from the United States and Canada by phone, 24 hours a day six weeks after the exam for a $15 fee. The phone number is 888-308-0013.

Should I Guess on the Test?

If you are completely unsure of an answer it is not a good idea to guess on the test, since ¼ of a point penalty is given for multiple-choice questions with five possible responses, and ⅓ of a point penalty for multiple-choice questions with four possible responses. If you have eliminated one or two possibilities and feel somewhat confident of your guess, go ahead and choose the option you are most comfortable with.

If I Do Poorly, Can I Cancel the Test Score?

It is possible to cancel an AP grade. The grade reports sent to you and your high school will list the exam and indicate that the score has been cancelled, but on the report sent to colleges, there will be no indication that you took the exam. After you ask the College Board to cancel your grade, it is permanently removed from the records. If you are sure that you wish to cancel your record, then write to

The AP Program
P.O. Box 6671
Princeton, NJ 08541-6671

You must include your full name, home address, the year in which you took the exam, the name, city, and state of your college, and the name of the exam for which you want the grade to be canceled. This request carries no fee, but you still must pay the full exam fee. All requests for exam cancellations must be received by June 15 of the year in which the exam was taken.

How Do I Register to Take the Test?

The AP coordinator at your school is your best source for registering for the test and getting all the specific details of test date and location. If you do not have this resource, contact the College Board *(www.collegeboard.com),* and they will guide you to the nearest location to register for the exam.

When Is the Exam Offered?

All AP exams, including the AP Human Geography Exam, are offered in May. Check with the College Board website *(www.collegeboard.com)* to find out the exact date of the exam as it is subject to change.

How Many Times Can I Take the Exam?

You can take the exam every year it is offered, but your grade report will include grades for every AP exam you have taken, including scores for any repeated exams.

Are Any of the Old Exams Available?

The College Board has just released a copy of the 2001 AP Human Geography Exam. The exam costs $25.00 and can be purchased by phone (1-800-323-7155), or over the Internet *(http://store.collegeboard.com).* Additionally, if you go to the College Board website and navigate to the Human

Geography Exam page, sample multiple-choice questions along with the actual free-response questions from both the 2000 and 2001 exam are available for free.

What If I Have More Questions?

If you still have questions about the exam, the best source is the College Board website. If you cannot find the information you are looking for within the site, it is easy to contact the Board with any questions or concerns you might have about the exam.

The Structure of the Test

Time and Format

The AP Human Geography exam contains two sections and lasts for two hours. The first section includes 75 multiple-choice questions; students are given 60 minutes to complete this portion of the exam. These questions are structured such that the first questions are less difficult than the questions that follow. In the remaining 60 minutes, students will answer three free-response essay questions.

The test covers seven different content areas.

1. Geography, Its Nature and Perspectives, covers 5 to 10% of the exam. Topics to focus on in this section include geography as a field of inquiry; the evolution of key concepts and models within the field of human geography; the importance of space, place, and scale as underlying concepts in geography; sources of geographical ideas; and data such as field data or census data. Students must be familiar with key geographical skills such as the ability to use and think about maps and spatial data sets, to interpret implications of associations among phenomena in places, to recognize and interpret the relationships among patterns and processes at different scales, to define regions and evaluate the regionalization process, and to characterize and analyze changing interconnections between places.

2. Population issues comprise 13 to 17% of the test. This section focuses on how geographers analyze population patterns, population growth and decline in both time and space, and population movement. Students should understand density, distribution, and scale, as well as the resulting consequences of various densities and distributions. Students should also be able to describe population in terms of its composition including age, sex, race, and ethnicity. Finally, they should understand how natural hazards affect population.

3. Cultural Patterns and Processes comprise 13 to 17% of the exam. In this section, students must demonstrate complete understanding of specific cultural concepts including traits, complexes, diffusion, acculturation, and culture regions and realms. Additionally, they must be able to describe cultural differences in terms of language, religion, ethnicity, and gender, as well as the differences between folk and popular culture. Students will be examined on their knowledge of the impact of cultural attitudes and practices on

the environment and how cultural landscapes contribute to and define cultural identity.

4. Political Organization of Space also covers 13 to 17% of the exam. Students must understand the territorial dimensions of politics, the evolution of the contemporary political pattern, and both historical and current challenges to inherited political-territorial arrangements. Students should be able to describe the concept of territoriality; the nature and meaning of boundaries; how boundaries contribute to identity, interaction, and exchange; the types of assumptions underlying the nation-state ideal; how colonialism and imperialism affect the current political pattern; the designation of internal boundaries; the changing nature of sovereignty, political fragmentation, unification, and alliance; and finally the spatial relationships between political patterns and patterns of ethnicity, economy, and environment.

5. Agricultural and Rural Land Use covers 13 to 17% of the exam and focuses on four main components: the development and diffusion of agriculture, major agricultural production regions, rural land use and settlement patterns, and modern commercial agriculture (the third Agricultural Revolution). Students must demonstrate proficiency on all three agricultural revolutions, they should be able to describe agricultural systems associated with specific climates, variations within these zones, and how they affect markets, linkages, and flows among regions of food production and consumption. They should also be able to describe models of land use and localization of economic activities, settlement patterns associated with major agricultural types, the details of the Green Revolution and how it signified the beginning of the biotechnologic revolution, spatial organization and diffusion of industrial agriculture, future food supplies, and environmental impacts of agriculture.

6. Industrialization and Economic Development also covers 13 to 17% of the exam. Students must understand key concepts of industrialization and development, growth and diffusion of industrialization, and contemporary patterns and impacts of industrialization and development in order to do well on the questions pertaining to this subject. To demonstrate their proficiency in the three components just mentioned, students should be able to describe the changing roles of energy and technology, the Industrial Revolution and its impacts, the diffusion of economic cores and peripheries, geographic critiques of models of industrial location, economic development, world systems theory, the current spatial organization of the world economy, variations in levels of development, deindustrialization, pollution and quality of life issues, industrialization and environmental change, sustainable development, and economic development initiatives.

7. Urbanization covers the remaining 13 to 17% of the exam and consists of definitions of urbanism, the origin and evolution of cities, functional character of contemporary cities, and the built environment and social space. Students must understand historical patterns of urbanization; the cultural context of urban forms; urban growth; rural to urban migration; global cities and megacities; models of urban systems; comparative models of internal city structure; changing employment mix within cities; changing demographic and employment structures; transportation and infrastructure

in urban areas; political organization of urban spaces; urban planning and design; patterns of race, ethnicity, gender, and class; uneven development; ghettoization and gentrification; and the impacts of suburbanization and edge cities.

As you can see, the test covers quite a bit of material! However, the authors of this book had all these guidelines in mind as they wrote. You will soon discover that even though it looks like quite a bit of information, you may already be familiar with some of it. Geography deals with many aspects of everyday life: where you live, the food you eat, how you get between places, and how you and your family make a living. However, geography brings a new perspective to all these activities as it investigates how these daily patterns have changed and continue to change over time and space. Do not be alarmed by everything you will need to know to do well on the exam! As you find ways to relate much of what you learn to your life, you will find that all this information is actually not that hard to remember.

How the Test Is Scored

The first section of multiple-choice questions is graded by computer, and students are penalized for answering or guessing incorrectly. One fourth of each point given for a correct answer will be subtracted for each incorrect answer when multiple-choice questions contain five options. The free-response essays will be scored at the AP Reading in June by a group of faculty consultants, college professors, and AP teachers. A chief faculty consultant—a college professor who both sits in with the development committee and directs the June Reading—develops the initial scoring standards for each free-response question. Then, the question leader, who is in charge of monitoring the scoring of a particular question, meets with the other question leaders several days prior to the grading meeting to outline more detailed criteria for each essay question. When all the graders arrive at the meeting, they are carefully trained to apply the grading standards consistently to all questions and all tests. Throughout the grading process, consistency is ensured through several faculty members grading each response without prior knowledge of scores the response may have received from other graders.

The score from the multiple-choice section will be combined with the scores you receive for your free-response questions, and the total raw score will be converted to the AP's five-point scale:

AP Grade	Qualification
5	Extremely well qualified
4	Well qualified
3	Qualified
2	Possibly qualified
1	No recommendation

Most colleges or universities accept a score of 4 or 5 for credit and placement. Many schools accept a score of 3 for credit and/or placement. It's usually quite difficult to get placement with a score of 2, and nearly impossible if you score 1. In general, as you take the practice tests, if you consistently answer 50 to 60% of the questions correctly, you can expect a minimum score of a 3; if you answer 65 to 75% correctly, you can expect a minimum score of a 4; and if you correctly answer between 80 and 100% of the questions, you should be able to score a 5 on the exam. These scores, of course, assume that you do well on the free-response questions.

Strategies for Studying for the AP Human Geography Exam

How to Read and Analyze the Material

1. *Familiarize yourself with the layout of the book.* Before you begin reading the text, look through the entire book, investigating its organization. You may want to devise a timeline for yourself, dedicating a week or two for studying each chapter. You will also need to make a schedule of when you plan to take each of the two practice exams, allowing yourself a couple of weeks between each exam, and a couple of weeks between the second practice exam and the real exam in May.

2. *Read the summary at the beginning of each chapter.* The summary at the beginning of each chapter provides an overview of what will be discussed within the body of that chapter. By reading all the summaries before reading any of the chapters, you will get an overview of an entire Introductory Human Geography course. All the major content areas contain numerous connections with other subfields of human geography. If you have carefully read each summary, you will be able to begin making connections between different subfields of human geography as you read each chapter.

3. *Look over the list of key terms.* Before you read each chapter, look over the list of key terms. You may want to make flashcards of each term using your own words to define them based on your reading. At the end of every chapter, use the definitions given to make sure that your own definitions are correct. To help you remember the key concepts, models, and processes mentioned in these lists, include on your flashcards some examples of each term.

4. *Carefully read the chapter.* As you are reading, explore the material for key principles and concepts by asking yourself these questions: What are the general principles? What examples are used to illustrate key concepts and principles? Can I think of any other examples? Who are the main personalities? Why are their contributions important? After you have read the chapter, look back at the key terms and quiz yourself, making sure that you know the definition of each term as well as any examples used to illustrate it. Next, you can test your understanding by completing the practice questions at the end of the chapter. As you grade yourself, be careful to note what you got wrong. You may want to highlight the concepts you struggled with in order to remind yourself to spend more time focusing on those terms before taking the first practice exam.

5. *Pay attention to the figures.* Readers often ignore the material presented as figures within the body of the text. However, it will work to your detriment if you choose to ignore this information. The figures provided describe many of the concepts, models, and processes presented throughout the text. Additionally, many figures will appear in both multiple-choice and free-response questions of the actual Advanced Placement Exam. Consequently, your familiarity with them will greatly enhance your success in answering these types of questions.

Taking the Practice Exams

Two practice tests have been included within this text. Each exam includes 75 multiple-choice questions and 3 free-response questions, as on the actual exam. These exams are an extremely important tool in getting you ready for the real thing. Take them seriously! Before taking the first exam, make sure that you have read each chapter completely and thoroughly, that you are able to define all of the key terms, and that you can provide examples of the concepts, models, and processes presented within each chapter. After you have done this for all seven chapters, you should be ready to take the first practice exam.

When you feel prepared to take the first practice exam, find a quiet place where you will not be interrupted or distracted for two hours. Also make sure to have a clock with you to keep accurate time. If you cannot complete either section in the 60-minute time slot, do not allow yourself any extra time. Make the practice exam situation as close to the real testing situation as possible. After you've scored the test, carefully read the explanations given for the correct answers on the questions you missed. As you do this, try to recognize patterns in areas where you might have struggled. This will help you focus your studies before taking the second practice exam.

In studying for the second practice exam, you do not need to reread the text. Instead, carefully reread each summary and thoroughly review the key terms and concepts. If, in the first practice exam, you struggled in a particular content area, take the time to reread that chapter. To absorb the material completely, think of your own examples for the key concepts, models, and processes described. This technique is extremely helpful. If you have your own experience to draw on, chances are much greater that you will remember the material when you take the exam. As you prepare for taking the second practice test, pretend you are preparing for the actual exam. In other words, do not allow yourself to take it until you feel absolutely prepared. Also, leave a couple of weeks between the practice exam and the real exam for last minute preparation and review. Find an environment similar to the one where you took the first exam, and follow the same process. Again, make sure to read carefully the explanations given on any questions you might have missed, and make notes of concepts you still need to review. At this point, you should be just about completely prepared for the real exam. Before the exam, read over the summaries one more time; review the key terms, concepts, models, and processes, making sure you have some examples at your disposal to support them, and reread the strategies for answering both multiple-choice and free-response questions.

It is important to remember that, no matter how well prepared you are, some of the questions you encounter on the actual Advaned Placement Exam will be unfamiliar. However, if you draw on the wide range of material presented in this book, and use the general strategies presented next—you will greatly enhance your chances of arriving at the correct answer.

Strategies for Answering Exam Questions: Multiple-Choice

1. *Read the entire question.* Underline any key works in the question and check for correspondence between key words used in the question and key words in the correct answer.
2. *Use the process of elimination.* If the correct answer does not immediately pop out at you, eliminate all possibilities that you know are incorrect. If you still have trouble, circle that question, and come back to it later on.
3. *Beware of negative questions.* Negative multiple-choice questions contain statements such as "All of the following are true *except* . . ." or "Which of the following does *not* fit . . . ." When you face these types of questions, beware of the negative, and make sure that your choice represents the option that does not fit with the question or statement.
4. *Do not guess wildly.* If you are absolutely unsure about a question, leave it blank. You get a ¼-point penalty for every question answered incorrectly if the question has five options. If you are completely unsure of an answer, leave it blank rather than risk a penalty. However, if you are able to eliminate a couple of choices and can make a relatively educated guess, then you should choose that option.
5. *Go with your first instinct.* More often than not your first instinct proves to be the correct answer.
6. *Always be aware of your time limit.* Bring a clock or watch with you, and be sure to pace yourself. You have 75 multiple-choice questions to answer in 60 minutes, that's less than a minute per question. If you find yourself struggling with a particular question, circle it and come back to it when you have gone through all 75 questions. Additionally, do not spend a lot of your time answering the first questions. The questions will increase in difficulty, so you want to save extra time for answering the more difficult questions later on.

Different Types of Multiple-Choice Questions

Definitional

1. Which of the following best defines a functional region?

   (A) The boundary including all areas within the circulation of a particular newspaper
   (B) The boundary including all people who speak Creole in Louisiana
   (C) The boundary around gerrymandered voting districts
   (D) The boundary that includes the American "Deep South"

Cause-and-Effect Relationships

2. As a country becomes increasingly developed, economic activities become dominant in which sector?

(A) Primary sector
(B) Tertiary sector
(C) Non-basic sector
(D) Secondary sector
(E) Basic sector

Sequencing or Series of Related Events or Ideas

3. Place the following agricultural events in the correct order

I. Biotechnologic Revolution begins genetically modifying plants and animals.
II. Mechanization takes hold allowing much more work to be done with much less human labor.
III. Developed countries extend certain agricultural innovations to the Third World during the Green Revolution.
IV. Rachel Carson writes *Silent Spring*.

(A) II, III, IV, I
(B) II, IV, II, I
(C) IV, II, III, I
(D) III, II, IV, I
(E) None of the above

Generalization

4. The von Thunen model describes agricultural activity as it takes place in relation to the market. Which of the following statements generally represents the agricultural landscape according to the model?

(A) Agricultural activity is solely determined by the longevity of the agricultural product.
(B) Goods that are expensive to transport and spoil quickly must be located closer to the market.
(C) Smaller agricultural goods like beans, herbs, and berries will be grown closer to the market than bigger goods like pumpkins.
(D) Animals, like grazing cattle and hens, will be located closer to the market, because they are difficult to move.

Solution to a Problem

5. Which of the following economic enterprises is the best example of a footloose industry?

(A) Shoe store
(B) Jewelry store
(C) Dance company
(D) Cheese factory

Hypothetical Situation

6. You decide to eat dinner at the local diner and get there right during the dinner rush when the restaurant is full of people. What is the most likely makeup of the group of diners?

   (A) You don't recognize many of them so they must be mainly tourists, with a couple of familiar faces from the local area.
   (B) You don't recognize too many faces, but they seem very neighborly so most of them probably come from the neighboring town because they don't have a local diner, and the rest are from around town.
   (C) It's probably about an equal mix of tourists, locals, and people from the neighboring towns.
   (D) You recognize most faces, but there are a few you don't know, that are probably from the neighboring towns, and possibly a couple of tourists stopping through.

Chronological Problem

7. When did the Industrial Revolution take hold in England?

   (A) Late 20th century
   (B) Late 19th century
   (C) Late 18th century
   (D) Early 20th century
   (E) Early 18th century

Comparing/Contrasting Concepts and Events

8. India's population policy differs from China's in that

   (A) They aren't different; they both strictly enforce a one-child-per-couple policy.
   (B) India's is much more stringent, forcefully implementing their population policy.
   (C) China strictly adheres to their one-child-per-couple policy with benefits for those who conform and punishments for those who don't, while India does not really have a policy.
   (D) India encourages rather than forces couples to limit the number of children they have.

Multiple Correct Answers

9. Which of the following are characteristic of American suburbs?

   (A) Many suburban developments are eating up agricultural land.
   (B) Some suburban areas have developed small cities within themselves.
   (C) Many of the inhabitants of suburban areas participate in gentrification as they flee cities for quieter lifestyles.
   (D) Both (A) and (B)
   (E) All of the above

Negative Questions

10. Which of the following is not a characteristic of agribusiness?

(A) It in large part has led to the demise of the American family farm.
(B) It has incorporated production, consumption, and marketing into an integrated whole.
(C) It has allowed for increased family market gardening.
(D) It has transformed agricultural productivity such that agricultural activities yield much more than they have historically.

Stimulus-Response Questions

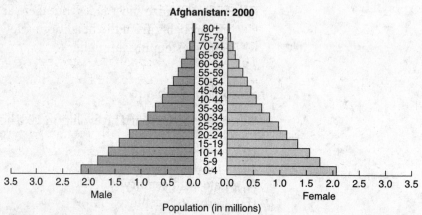

Afghanistan: 2000

Population (in millions)

Source: U.S. Census Bureau, International Data Base.

11. Based on this population pyramid, which of the following statements accurately describes Afghanistan's most likely population pyramid in 20 years.

(A) While growth is currently very rapid, in 20 years it will have begun to stabilize, causing the base to narrow.
(B) Most likely, the population pyramid will resemble the current figure, as the current large base will begin to reproduce, causing an even larger base.
(C) The top of the pyramid will begin to widen as the death rate begins to decrease.
(D) The pyramid will look less like a pyramid and more like a rectangle as the larger base moves up and fills in the middle.

Answers and Explanations

1. In this question, you are tested on how well you can define a functional region. As you noticed, the choices were not strict definitions but rather examples of different types of regions. To be prepared for these types of questions, as you study, make sure that you know several different types of examples of each of the key terms. This will strengthen your understanding of each concept, and ability to identify the correct answer in this type of situation. The correct answer is (A) because it best demonstrates the functional nature of a particular area.

2. In this question, you are given a cause and must determine the effect. The cause, increasing development in certain countries, has a certain effect on those countrys' economies. In this case, a transition into the tertiary sector or service-based activities characterizes many developed countries across the globe today; thus (B) is the correct answer.

3. In a sequence question, you are generally given a list of events or parts of processes, and you must be able to put them in the correct order. In this case, the correct answer is (A), which places all four agricultural events in their correct historical sequence.

4. In a generalization question, you will be given a specific event, process, or model, and you must be able to identify the general principle that came about as a result of that event, process, or model. The von Thunen model stated that agricultural activities that produce goods that spoil quickly and are expensive to transport, in general, will be located closer to the market, thus, (B) is the correct answer.

5. This question is actually a combination of two types of questions; you must first know the definition of a footloose industry before you can determine the best example of the specific term. If you don't know the definition, you are liable to be tricked by options (A) and (C) as you might associate both of those choices with the term "footloose." However, by knowing the correct definition, the problem becomes quite easy. Jewelry stores represent the only footloose industry on the list, as cost of transportation plays no role in industrial location.

6. Here you are asked to put yourself in a hypothetical situation and use your knowledge of certain principles to determine the correct answer. This question is tricky because it does not explicitly tell you that you are dealing with the phenomena of distance decay. You must figure that out from reading all four options and apply your knowledge of this trend to choose (D) as the correct answer. Distance decay states that you interact much more with people near you than people farther away; thus, most people at the local diner will be from the local area.

7. Chronological problems are simply those that draw on your memory of the time period of certain notable events. In this case, you must remember exactly when the Industrial Revolution occurred. It's virtually impossible to guess on these types of questions. The correct answer is (B). When you read the chapters on industry and agriculture, you will learn (if you haven't already) that the Industrial Revolution occurred in England during the late 1800s.

8. In these types of questions you are asked to compare two events, processes, models, or concepts. As you answer these types of questions, define the two terms, processes, or events you are comparing before even looking at your options. Often, in comparative situations, it's easy to get confused by options that switch the defining factors of the items you are comparing. In this case you are asked to compare the population policy of India with that of China. If you recall both countries' policies before looking at the possible choices, it will be easier to determine the correct response as (D). India does not adhere to nearly as stringent a policy as China.

9. These types of questions can be kind of tricky because it isn't as easy to use process of elimination if you aren't completely sure of the correct

answer. The best strategy is to think through each of the options. If option (A) is correct, put a plus by it and continue this process for all three of your options. After you have read the chapter on urbanization thoroughly, you will quickly recognize that both (A) and (B) are true characteristics of suburbs. You should put pluses by both options. Option (C) is false, gentrification is the process of individuals moving back into cities; thus, you should put a negative sign next to this option. Knowing that both (A) and (B) are true and that (C) is false makes it easy to choose the correct answer, (D).

10. When answering negative questions, which are easily identified through use of the terms "not" or "except," it is sometimes easier to identify all the true statements which have to be incorrect, leaving you with the one false statement. In this example, you can eliminate (A), (B), and (D), as all three options characterize modern agribusiness, leaving you with option (C), which is actually quite opposite from this trend.

11. In stimulus-response questions, you are given a graph, cartoon, figure, quote, or other bit of information that you must interpret in order to answer the question. These kinds of questions emphasize the importance of paying attention to the figures included within the text. Population pyramids are discussed in much greater depth in the accompanying figure description than in the body of the chapter. When you encounter these types of questions, take a moment to study whatever it is you are asked to analyze and make sure that you understand it before trying to answer the question. In investigating the population pyramid of Afghanistan, you should quickly notice that it depicts a very rapidly growing population, as most of the population is concentrated in very young cohorts. In thinking about future growth, it's safe to assume that the country will continue this dynamic for at least the next 20 years as the young cohorts enter reproducing age. Thus, (B) is the correct answer.

Strategies for Answering Questions: Free-Response

1. *Identify your task.* Identify what is required of you in the essay by looking for one of these types of terms: list, identify, describe, explain, evaluate, analyze, assess, or compare. Most free-response questions will ask you to do one of these, and by initially identifying the type of task, you can structure your essay accordingly. For example, evaluating a concept or process will look much different than listing or identifying it, and the structure of your essay must correspond to what it is that is being asked of you.

2. *Read the entire question and underline key terms.* After you have identified your task, you should identify and underline the key concepts, models, or processes relating to your task. By underlining these terms, you can easily determine if you have included all of them in your outline, in turn, ensuring that you don't leave any important details out of your essay.

3. *Make an outline.* The structure of your outline will depend on the type of question you are asked. Some questions have more than one component, and you need to dedicate a section of your outline to each of the main components. Begin your outline by defining the premise of your essay and then identify each of the tasks you must complete to support your premise. If

there are multiple tasks, you should devote a section of your outline to each task, including the supporting claims, arguments, or examples you will use to complete each of these tasks. Organizing your thoughts and arguments into a cohesive outline will make the actual writing of the essay quite simple, and the final product should be a well thought-out and organized statement or argument.

4. *Use a solid thesis statement and specific examples to support your thesis statement.* The thesis statement will grab your readers' attention so make it solid and make sure to choose a statement that you can support comprehensively and powerfully. It is helpful to design your introductory statement before designing your outline to ensure that all your main points and arguments support your introductory claim.

5. *Summary should reiterate your thesis statement.* Your thesis is basically the premise of your essay. After you have explained and supported your tasks with good examples, you must summarize your essay. The best way to do this is first to reiterate your thesis statement in different words and then to emphasize the main points you used to support your claims.

Things to Avoid When Writing the Free-Response Essays

1. If you are not sure of the facts of possible examples, don't use them. The readers of your essays will recognize poor examples or misrepresentation of facts. You are being tested on your ability to communicate your understanding of a particular process, concept, or model. Supporting evidence and examples strengthen your ability to communicate effectively; however, they only increase effectiveness when they are relevant and accurate. Weak factual support may cause your readers to question your understanding of whatever you are discussing.

2. Do not use statements that are implausible, can't be proven, or don't relate to the question. Be careful to stay on track and be careful not to make claims that have not been proven or that are based on opinion rather than fact.

3. Do not make unsubstantiated generalizations in the body of the essay. Avoid making general claims about processes, events, or concepts, without supporting evidence or examples. To validate the arguments or points you make in your essay, you must use supporting evidence or examples. Any claims you make without them will be considered unsubstantiated.

4. Do not impose your own opinion. This might be difficult in questions that ask you to evaluate a certain model or theory; however, it is entirely possible and desirable that you answer these questions from an unbiased standpoint. Evaluating simply means pointing out both the positive and negative contributions or aspects of a particular theory, process, or model. As tempting as it may be to interject your personal opinion, your validity and credibility will be stronger if you don't.

5. Avoid lengthening your essay with excessive wordiness. Often students do not realize that readers recognize this strategy. The length of your response does not matter as long as you have comprehensively answered all aspects of the question. Readers would much prefer reading a short, concise organized essay, than a long, excessively wordy argument.

Example Outline and Free-Response Essay

In the final section of this chapter, we will follow the process of writing a free-response essay step by step, beginning with a question similar to the types of questions you will encounter on the exam. Then, we will discuss outlining techniques and, finally, demonstrate the transition from the outline to the essay.

Free-Response Question

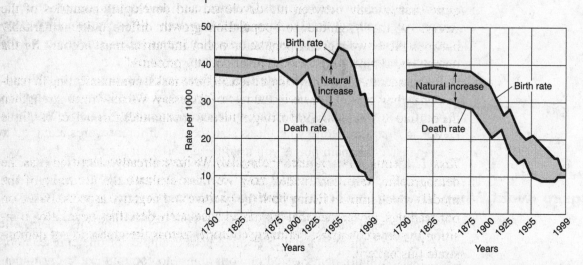

1. The figure on the left represents the demographic transition model typical for developing countries of the globe, the figure on the right for developed countries.
   (a) Identify and evaluate the model that these two figures represent.
   (b) Name specific parts of the globe that could correspond to each of the two figures.
   (c) Describe how population policy might differ in the parts of the world represented by each figure.

Following the strategies just described for answering free-response questions, we begin by identifying the main tasks we must complete by looking for key words in the question. "Identify and evaluate," "name," and "describe" are our three main tasks. We should begin by spending a few minutes investigating the figure, quickly recognizing it as the demographic transition model presented in Chapter 5. Next, we must read the entire question carefully, underlining key terms. We have already underlined our key tasks; now we underline the terms: "model," "parts of the globe," and "population policy" which correspond to each of our tasks:

Identify and evaluate: model
Name: parts of the globe
Describe: population policy

These three tasks will comprise the main structure of the outline. At this point, we should brainstorm some ideas for our introductory statement, which will be the premise of our argument. If we decide on our thesis statement first, we can ensure correspondence between it and our tasks. In this statement, we want to cover all three aspects of the question, thereby including the name of the model, where it applies, and its implications for population policy. We've identified it as the demographic transition model, and upon investigation of the two figures, it's clear that the first corresponds to developing countries, and the second, to developed countries. Furthermore, we know that population policy looks quite different in these two parts of the globe. Combining all these factors, we form a thesis statement:

"The demographic transition model describes population growth as a country develops in terms of changes in birth and death rates. As such, it differs quite dramatically between the developed and developing countries of the world. As the magnitude of population growth differs quite remarkably between these two regions, population policy initiatives must account for the unique population issues each type of country presents."

In this statement, we have identified all three tasks, communicating to readers what they can anticipate in the rest of the essay. We now must strengthen the outline by including supporting evidence or examples for each of our three tasks.

Task 1: Identify and evaluate the model. We have already identified it as the demographic transition model; now we must evaluate the accuracy of the model, which implies listing both the positive and negative aspects. Based on our readings, we learned that the model adequately describes population transition in some countries, but many countries across the globe do not demonstrate this pattern.

Task 2: Name parts of the globe that correspond to each of the two figures. In our thesis statement, we generally identified correspondence between the model and the globe; in the essay, specific names will strengthen this task. Thus, we could use the United States as an example of a developed country that follows the model describing population transition since European colonization. For developing countries, we could use any number of African countries, discussing how the formidable growth rate depicted in the figure demonstrates that they have not yet transitioned through the entire model.

Task 3: Describe population policy. In this step, we move back toward general differences between developed and developing countries of the globe. As we've just discussed, population growth presents a looming issue in developing countries; consequently, policy initiatives must focus on curbing growth. In developed countries, unsustainable consumption of resources to maintain an excessive standard of living presents a much greater issue than growth, thus policy initiatives should focus on curbing consumption rates.

After developing the tasks and incorporating the thesis statement, the outline should resemble:

I. Thesis statement: The demographic transition model describes population growth as a country develops in terms of changes in birth and death rates. As such, it differs quite dramatically between the developed and developing countries of the world. As the magnitude of population growth differs quite remarkably between these two regions, population policy initiatives must account for the unique population issues each type of country presents.

II. Demographic transition model: Evaluation
   A. Positive aspects: Accurately describes some countries

    B. Negative aspects: Leaves out too many important factors (culture, religion, world economics, etc.) to describe the whole globe

III. Name parts of the globe each figure corresponds to

    A. First figure: developing countries such as many countries in Africa

    B. Second figure: developed countries such as the United States

IV. Population policy in each part of the globe

    A. Developing countries: initiatives to curb growth

    B. Developed countries: initiatives to curb consumption

V. Conclusion/summary

    A. Restate thesis

    B. Reiterate three main points

Transforming the Outline into the Essay

The demographic transition model describes population growth as a country develops in terms of changing birth and death rates. As such, it differs quite dramatically between the developed and developing countries of the world. Because the magnitude of population growth differs quite remarkably between these two regions, population policy initiatives must account for the unique population issues each type of country presents.

The demographic transition model, represented by these figures, describes developmental transitions in a country through birth and death rates. In its initial stages, a country experiences both high birth and death rates and, as it becomes increasingly developed, progresses through four stages, ending in stable growth comprised of both low birth and death rates. It is true that many developed countries of the world exhibit stable population growth with comparatively low birth and death rates. It is also true that many developing countries experience rapid population growth as birth and death rates remain comparatively high because certain forces more prevalent in developed countries, such as education, access to contraception, and increased medical technology do not fully exist in developing countries. However, to propose that all countries progress sequentially through all four stages cannot be historically proven. Many geographers argue that the simplicity of the model neglects numerous factors that also play into demographic transition. Factors such as culture, religion, geopolitics, migration, and the structure of the global economic system may prevent many of today's less-developed countries from ever taking the path described. Thus, while the model may accurately depict the development path of some countries, it leaves out too many factors to be used as an accurate predictor of numerous countries' population transitions.

Because most developing countries of the world currently experience comparatively high birth and death rates with a rapid population growth rate, the figure on the left more accurately describes demographic characteristics of these countries. The figure on the right, which portrays stable population growth with low birth and death rates, depicts the final stage of transition of a developed country of the world. The United States historically exemplifies these transitions from European colonization until the present day. When the first settlers arrived, in an effort to populate the land, birth rates were quite high, but death rates corresponded as the country experienced much warfare and the population interacted with new kinds of diseases and bacteria. As the people adapted to the environment, and as warfare decreased, the death rate dropped. Finally, as the country became increasingly technologically developed, the birth rate also began to drop such that, over time, both rates somewhat converged, resulting in rather stable population growth. Conversely, many African countries of the world demonstrate a pattern more similar to the first figure. Birth and death rates were initially quite high, but a certain level of adaptation and medical technology has allowed death rates to decrease, and perhaps, through increased exposure to certain forms of contraception, birth rates have also begun to decrease. However, at the present stage, both rates are much higher than those in the developed world, and birth rates must drop considerably to temper the extremely high rates of natural increase; thus many of these countries have one or two more stages to progress through until they resemble the figure on the left.

As just described, population growth in developed countries is quite stable, but it is very rapid in the developing countries of the world. Additionally, the level of development enjoyed by highly developed countries of the globe implies very high consumption rates of natural resources, significantly disproportionate to consumption of resources by developing countries of the globe. Although developing countries don't consume nearly as much as developed ones, they contribute most of the world's global population, consequently introducing many sticky issues regarding the number of people the earth can sufficiently sustain. In order to achieve a balance, policy initiatives should focus on curbing consumption rates in the developed world while curbing growth rates in the developing world.

The demographic transition model simplistically describes a country's hypothetical transition through changes in birth and death rates that gradually converge, allowing stable population growth. While it describes the development path of several countries, it ignores too many factors to be globally applicable. However, in general, it does provide a poignant illustration of the demographic differences between developed and developing countries of the globe. Those places experiencing stable growth, but high levels of development, consume a disproportionate amount of the world's resources. However, the countries that have not yet achieved stable population growth disproportionately contribute to the numbers the earth must support. As such, policy makers must focus policy initiatives on curbing consumption rates in the developed world while curbing growth rates in the developing world.

Discussing the Essay

The essay consists of five paragraphs: the first contains the premise or thesis and introduces your readers to the three issues you will be discussing in the essay. The second paragraph is dedicated to the first task of identifying and evaluating the model. The third corresponds to the second task in which we named parts of the globe that represent each of the two figures. In the fourth paragraph we discussed how population policy initiatives differ in the two parts of the globe depicted by the figures. Finally, in the last paragraph, we rephrased the thesis statement and reiterated the three main points. Essentially, the first and last paragraphs look very similar. In paragraph one, you told your readers what you planned to accomplish in your essay; in the final paragraph, you told them what you did accomplish in your essay.

The example essay should have demonstrated to you the importance of making an outline before writing the essay. We knew what the thesis statement would be, we knew what to discuss in every paragraph, and we knew how to summarize our arguments making the actual writing of the essay quite simple. Use the practice free-response essays at the end of each chapter to get used to this process so that by the time you are ready to take the first practice exam, you will be familiar with all the steps. The answers given for each free-response question within the chapters simply provide the main points that should be discussed within your essay. Use them to ensure that you covered all aspects of the question in your response.

Conclusion

This chapter has provided all of the basic tools you need to succeed on the Advanced Placement Exam in Human Geography. Be careful to follow the strategies given to you as you begin reading the content chapters. It will be helpful to come back to this chapter and review both the multiple-choice strategies and the free-response strategies before answering the practice questions provided at the end of each chapter. Additionally, review the section on taking the practice exams when you reach that stage. You now have all the tools you need to read the book carefully, and the book presents most of the information you will encounter on the test. If you diligently apply the tools as you progress through the book, you should experience complete success on exam day. Good Luck!

CHAPTER 1
What Is Human Geography?

Summary

Human geography is the study of human activities on the earth's surface. Since the first scholars began studying geography some 3,000 years ago, the field has matured into an important and wide-ranging area of academic and applied research. Today, geographers in all the discipline's three major fields—human geography, physical geography, and environmental geography—use high-tech tools to study spatial patterns, from local places to the entire earth system. One thing that binds them all together is the spatial perspective. Looking at the earth from a spatial perspective means looking at how objects and processes vary over the earth's surface. While historians look at how the world has changed through time, geographers look at how the world changes over space. Whether they study physical systems or cultural landscapes, whether they use qualitative or quantitative methodologies, whether they study unique places or universal processes, all geographers use the spatial perspective to better understand the world in which we live.

In This Chapter

- History and Development of the Discipline
- Geography Today
- Thinking Geographically
- Applications of Geography

Key Terms

Anthropogenic	George Perkins Marsh
Cartography	Natural landscape
Cultural ecology	Nomothetic
Cultural landscape	W. D. Pattison
Earth system science	Physical geography
Environmental geography	Ptolemy
Eratosthenes	Qualitative data
Fertile Crescent	Quantitative data
Geographical Information Systems	Quantitative revolution
Global Positioning System	Region
Idiographic	Regional geography

Remote sensing   **Sustainability**
Carl Sauer   **Systematic geography**
Sense of place   **Thematic layers**
Spatial perspective

History and Development of the Discipline

During the last 3,000 years, geography has evolved from a speculative philo-
sophical endeavor into a vigorous area of academic research and applied science. The first geographers studied places and regions for an entirely practical
purpose. They were interested in learning about geography primarily for
developing trade routes to distant, and often dangerous, lands. Without knowledge of geography, travelers were literally lost. During the early centuries of
geographic research, Chinese, Greek, and North African scholars took the
lead. Their amazingly accurate measurements and detailed maps laid the
foundations for what later became the art and science of map-making, or **cartography**. Cartography has been central to the study of geography ever since,
and perhaps you automatically associate maps with geography, as one of its
most defining characteristics. As you continue reading, you will find that cartography is indeed an important aspect of this field, but geography encompasses much more than the art of map-making.

   Eratosthenes, who served as the head librarian at Alexandria during the
third century B.C., was one of these early cartographers. One of his greatest
accomplishments was a remarkably accurate computation of the earth's circumference, which he based on the sun's angle at the summer solstice and the

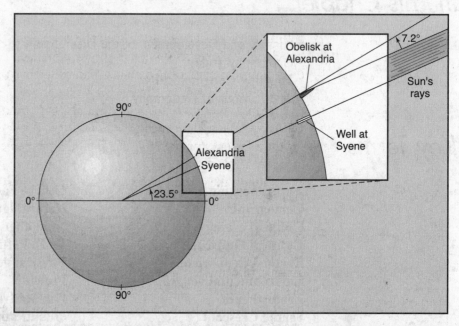

Figure 1.1. In 247 B.C., Eratosthenes calculated the circumference of the earth by measuring the
sun's angles on June 21st at Alexandria and Syene in modern-day Egypt. He measured the distance
between the two cities and then, using basic geometry, computed the earth's circumference to be
46,250 km, only about 175 km too long.

distance between the two Egyptian cities of Alexandria and Syene. He is also credited with coining the term "geography," which literally means "earth-writing." About 500 years later, in the second century A.D., **Ptolemy** published his *Guide to Geography*, which included rough maps of the landmasses, as he understood them at the time, and a global grid system. Eratosthenes' and Ptolemy's efforts represent significant early contributions, both to the technical aspects of cartography and to our general understanding of geography.

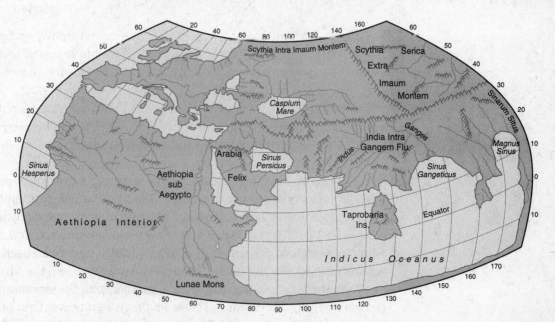

Figure 1.2. This early world map was created by Ptolemy in the second century A.D., more than 1200 years before Europeans reached the New World.

Beginning in about 1400 A.D., scholars from Western Europe arrived at the cutting edge of geographic thought. It was during this period that explorers traveled the globe mapping landforms, climates, indigenous cultures, and the distribution of plants and animals. Names such as Bartholomeu Dias, Christopher Columbus, and Ferdinand Magellan are representative of this period of European exploration and colonization. Later, explorers such as Alexander von Humboldt and the men of the Lewis and Clark expedition became famous for their adventures traveling the globe in the name of geography and natural history.

Although these men were certainly not the first humans to see the places they "discovered"—European explorers encountered native peoples in almost every corner of the globe—their efforts did contribute much to the integration of geographic knowledge and to our understanding of spatial relationships. During the 18th, 19th, and early 20th centuries, scholars began to use the geographic information that was pouring into European museums and universities to synthesize theories about people and nature. This period saw the development of many modern academic disciplines, such as anthropology, geology, and ecology. Many key theories that rely heavily on geographic information were also proposed during this period, such as Charles Darwin's theory of evolution through natural selection and Alfred Wegner's theory of continental drift.

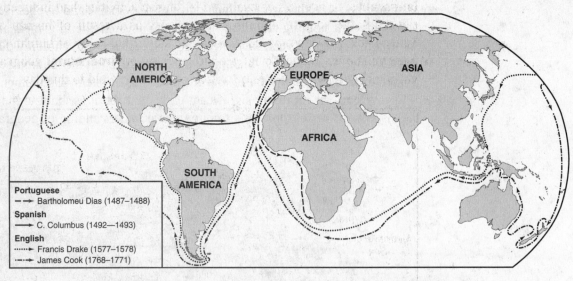

Portuguese
— —▸ Bartholomeu Dias (1487–1488)
Spanish
——▸ C. Columbus (1492—1493)
English
······▸ Francis Drake (1577–1578)
—·—·▸ James Cook (1768–1771)

Figure 1.3. Routes of four European sailors during the Age of Exploration.

An important step in the development of geographic theories regarding people and the environment was taken in 1864 by the inventor, diplomat, politician, and scholar **George Perkins Marsh**. Marsh's classic work, *Man and Nature, or Physical Geography as Modified by Human Action*, provided the first description of the extent to which natural systems had been impacted by human actions. Marsh traveled extensively in Europe and the Middle East and was also profoundly influenced by the transcendentalist movement, which was centered in his home region of New England. This movement, popularized by Ralph Waldo Emerson, held that reality must be sought through spiritual intuition; in other words, understanding reality involves going beyond the senses and investigating the processes of the mind or thought. In *Man and Nature*, Marsh warned that people's willful destruction of the environment could have potentially disastrous consequences, such as the desertification that he had witnessed in what had formerly been the **Fertile Crescent**. This area, located in the Middle East in the vicinity of modern-day Iraq, was one of the first areas of sedentary agriculture and urban society. However, climate changes and overuse of this environment radically transformed it over the centuries into the dry desert that exists there today. Based on his observations of places like the Fertile Crescent, Marsh advocated a conservationist approach to natural resources. Today he is remembered as a great scientist, humanist, and writer; many scholars also consider him to be the first modern environmentalist.

Despite advances made by Marsh and others, by the beginning of the 20th century, geographers had proposed few testable hypotheses and generated no real unifying theories. But in 1925, a geographer from the University of California at Berkeley named **Carl Sauer** charted a new course for generations of geographers. Sauer argued that **cultural landscapes**, which are the products of complex interactions between humans and their environments, should be the fundamental focus of geographic inquiry. Humans interact with their environments in complex ways and, with his methods of landscape analysis, Sauer offered geographers a means of interpreting those relationships. Sauer's work was in large part historical, and in his concept of a cultural landscape, he implied that most places, even those that outwardly appeared to be **natural**

landscapes, or landscapes unaltered by human activities, had indirectly experienced some sort of alteration over history as a result of human activity. Sauer's new paradigm paved the way for the formal study of human-environment relations, frequently referred to as either **environmental geography** or **cultural ecology**, which characterizes much of the field to this day.

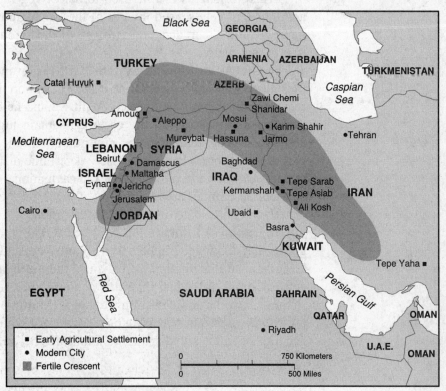

Figure 1.4. The Fertile Crescent.

Some 40 years after Carl Sauer's groundbreaking work, geographers at the University of Washington and elsewhere once again altered the direction of professional geography by joining a greater movement throughout the social sciences known as the **quantitative revolution**. The quantitative revolution stressed the use of empirical measurements, the use of hypothesis testing, the development of mathematical models, and the use of computer programs to explain geographic patterns. This approach reflected the influences of both modernist philosophy and technological innovation in the social sciences during this period. Although many geographers credit the quantitative revolution with bringing geography into the mainstream of modern science, others have criticized the quantitative approach for limiting the types of questions that are deemed important and for ignoring a myriad of cultural issues inherent in scholarly research.

Since the 1970s, geography has undergone a new revolution. Geographers now use high-tech tools such as remote sensing, the Global Positioning System, and Geographical Information Systems to collect and analyze spatial data. Since spatial data includes any type of information that is associated with a particular location on the earth's surface, these technologies have radically changed the methodologies many geographers use.

Remote sensing is the process of capturing images of the earth's surface from air-borne platforms, such as satellites or airplanes. Remotely sensed images can be digital, such as those taken by satellites, or analog photographs. All remotely sensed images are snapshots that record spatial data on the earth's surface at a particular point in time. One neat aspect of remote sensing is the use of multispectral bands to collect images of various landscapes. Each band detects different features of the physical environment. For example, infrared wavelengths can be used to detect vegetation on the earth's surface and thus remotely sensed images of the Brazilian rainforest at different time intervals provide an accurate measure of the amount of deforestation occurring in that region.

The **Global Positioning System (GPS)** is an integrated network of satellites that orbit the earth, broadcasting location information to hand-held receivers on the earth's surface. With a hand-held GPS receiver, a person standing at any point on the earth can obtain highly accurate information about their geographic location in terms of latitude and longitude. This accuracy allows geographers to precisely determine distances between two points making GPS a very valuable tool for navigational purposes. In fact, several automobiles come fitted with GPS systems on the dashboard providing the driver with up-to-date directional information.

Geographical Information Systems (GIS) are a family of software programs that allow geographers to map, analyze, and model spatial data. Most Geographical Information Systems use **thematic layers**. Each thematic layer consists of an individual map that contains specific features, such as roads, stream networks, or elevation contours. Multiple thematic layers may be united into one comprehensive map combining many useful features that help geographers understand spatial relationships between different phenomena.

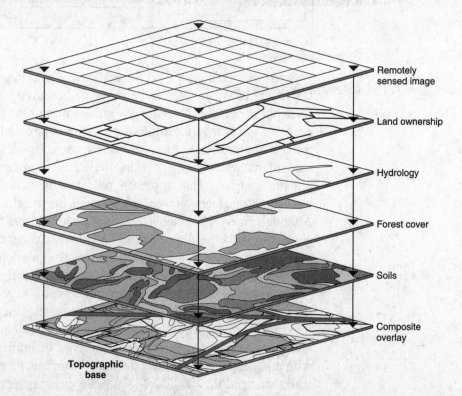

Figure 1.5. Geographical Information Systems unite multiple thematic layers to create one data-rich map.

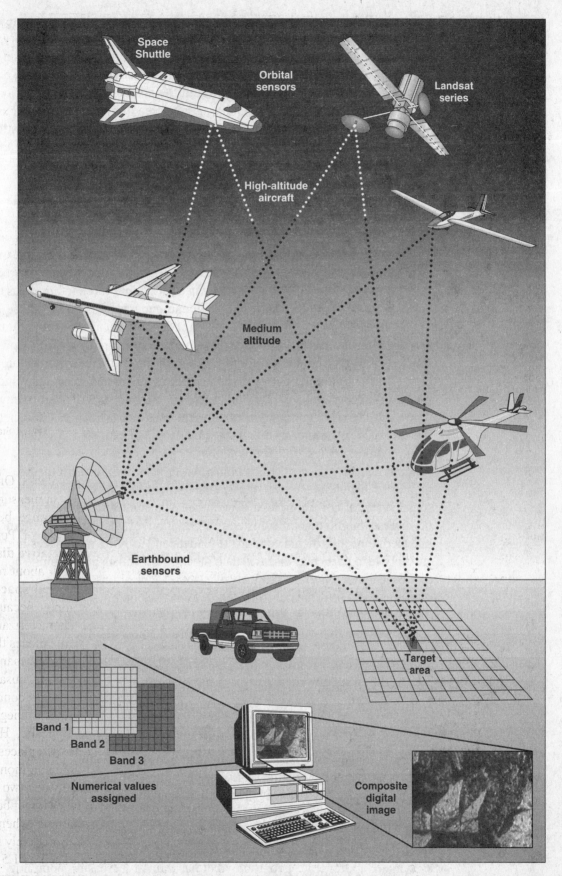

Figure 1.6. Remote sensing includes the use of both airplanes and satellites to capture images of the earth's surface.

For example, if geographers wanted to understand why a particular area of a city demonstrated higher property values than other areas within the city, they might overlap thematic layers, each with different types of information such as locations of certain amenities (beaches, schools, or recreation areas), income levels, and employment opportunities to see if a spatial relationship existed between those three variables and the area of higher-priced real estate. With the development of increasingly powerful computers and sophisticated software packages, GIS has become a tremendously powerful tool for understanding spatial processes on the earth's surface.

Geography Today

Today, geography is an extremely diverse discipline covering several major areas of study and involving researchers with different backgrounds from all over the world. The field of geography is divided into three major areas, each consisting of several subdisciplines. Human geography is one of those three major areas. Human geography can be broadly defined as the study of human activities on the earth's surface. That does sound pretty broad! However, people who study human geography generally focus their work in more specific subdisciplines. The major subdisciplines of human geography include population geography, cultural geography, economic geography, urban geography, agricultural geography, and political geography. Each of these fields is the subject of a chapter in this book, and each has its own theoretical framework, methodologies, and applications.

Many human geographers combine two or more subfields in their research, hoping to better understand the spatial dimensions of complex, interlinked social systems. For example, a geographer who studies the diffusion or spread of disease might combine his/her information of that spatial pattern with knowledge of a particular culture to understand why certain places are more susceptible to particular diseases than others. The Amish, a Mennonite community concentrated in rural Pennsylvania, shun vaccinations because of their religious beliefs. Unfortunately, this led to a measles outbreak that affected many Amish communities in 1987 and 1988. The spatial pattern of the spread of measles during that time period cannot be fully understood without knowledge of particular aspects of cultural geography. This is the nature of many geographic problems. A geographer cannot understand a problem fully without examining all the possible spatial relationships at work in a particular place.

The other major areas of geography are physical geography and environmental geography. Natural scientists, many of whom have been trained as meteorologists, climatologists, ecologists, oceanographers, geologists, soil scientists, or hydrologists, study **physical geography**. Physical geographers study spatial characteristics of the earth's physical and biological systems. During the past few decades, a new field, called **earth system science**, has arisen as a way to study the interactions between physical systems on a global scale. As you could probably guess, physical geographers have been at the forefront of this emerging discipline. Earth system science is also part of a systematic approach to geography that has gained increasing popularity over the last several decades. In **systematic geography**, researchers study the earth's integrated systems as a whole, instead of focusing on particular processes in a single place. A researcher may study a particular phenomenon as it occurs across the globe, instead of focusing on the many phenomena occurring in one unique place. This approach allows them to apply their knowledge of a specific spatial process broadly beyond unique places to other areas across the globe. Physical geographers have also been instrumental in understanding phenomena such as climate change, biodiversity loss, desertification, and the El Niño Southern Oscillation, all of which have tremendous importance for people around the world.

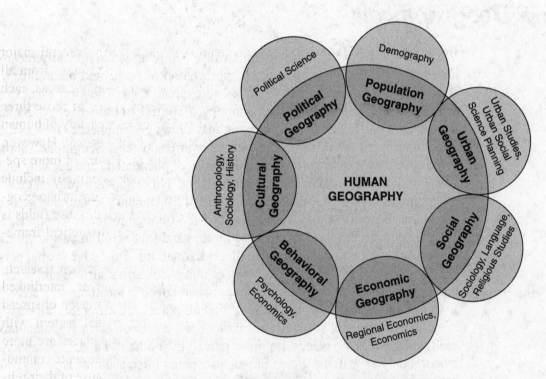

Figure 1.7. The discipline of human geography combines many subfields.

Where physical and human geography meet—and they often do—one enters the realm of **environmental geography**. Environmental geographers come from almost every academic discipline and frequently occupy prominent positions at the forefront of debates regarding **anthropogenic**, or human-induced, environmental change; conservation planning; and sustainability. **Sustainability** means many things to many people and, accordingly, is mentioned at several different points in this book. Generally, sustainability implies an approach to the environment that emphasizes restraint in the use of natural resources to ensure enough resources for future generations. As we will see later, even simple definitions of sustainability like this one have proven highly contentious. Environmental geographers may be concerned with anything from the history of a given landscape, to the effects of pollution on impoverished neighborhoods, to the creation of nature reserves for endangered species. The thing that ties this diverse group of people together is their need to think geographically in order to understand complex problems at the intersection between social science, natural science, and the humanities.

A slightly different way of thinking about the discipline of geography was outlined in 1964 by the University of Chicago geographer **W. D. Pattison**. Pattison claimed that geography drew from four distinct traditions: the earth-science tradition, the culture-environment tradition, the locational tradition, and the area-analysis tradition. Pattison's earth-science tradition is clearly another name for physical geography, his culture-environment tradition is what we now call environmental geography, and his locational tradition relates to the analysis of spatial data through cartography. The area-analysis tradition, which refers to regional geography, is covered in the next section.

Thinking Geographically

What does it mean to think geographically? Thinking geographically means developing a spatial perspective, an appreciation of scale, and the ability to analyze and interpret varied forms of geographic data. The first aspect of thinking geographically involves adopting a **spatial perspective**. A spatial perspective is an intellectual framework that allows geographers to look at the earth in terms of the relationships between various places. Geographers look at the spatial distribution of all different types of phenomena and ask why and how certain phenomena occur in certain places. For example, a cultural geographer might look at the spatial distribution of McDonald's restaurants across the globe. Beyond simply noting the fast-food conglomerate's locations, a geographer asks *why* McDonald's are located and successful in various parts of the world and *how* they spread to those destinations. This is the spatial perspective: observing the spatial location of things on earth's surface and determining why and how those things occupy their specific locations.

Geography is based on the premise that all places are different, but many places have important similarities. Likewise, all places on earth are related to each other, but some places are more related than others. Thus, geographers look not only at spatial patterns but also at spatial interrelations. How do two places interact economically, socially, and culturally? Why do some places have more in common than others? And how are social phenomena conveyed over time and space? These questions require a spatial perspective.

Thinking geographically also requires an understanding of scale. Map scale, which is covered in Chapter 4, is simply the ratio between distance on a map and actual distance on the earth's surface. Geographic scale, however, is a more general concept that refers to a conceptual hierarchy of spaces, from small to large, that reflects actual levels of organization in the real world. Examples of characteristic scales in human geography, from small to large, include the neighborhood, the urban area, the metropolitan area, and the region. Other frequently cited geographic scales include the watershed, ecosystem, landscape, and biome. A geographer seeks to understand how processes occurring at one scale may affect activities on other scales. For example, pollution sources that cause acid rain occur at very local scales, but the implications these point sources incur on other parts of the earth's surface may be national, continental, or even global in their scope.

One of the most important and hotly contested topics in all of geography is the **region**. As discussed earlier, no two places on the earth are exactly the same. However, the shared characteristics between places provide a means for geographers to group places together into a more manageable unit of study, the region. A region is generally defined as an area larger than a single city that contains unifying social or physical characteristics. However, a unifying characteristic of a particular region may be anything that defines that place for the purpose of the particular question being asked. Regions do not exist as well-defined units in the landscape; instead, they are conceptual constructions that geographers use for convenience and comparison. Every region can be described by its unique area, location, and set of boundaries. A region's area may be small or large, such as Little Italy in New York City or all of Western Europe. Its location may be based on physical characteristics such as mountain ranges or climate patterns, or cultural characteristics such as language or religious practices. Its boundary may be physical such as a river, social such as a political border or division between two languages, or even imagined such as a boundary line perceived to contain the "Midwest." Such is the shifting nature of the concept of region in geography. Despite much debate about what exactly makes a region, the concept itself remains important because regions often form the basic units of geographic research. **Regional geography**, or Pattison's area-analysis tradition, is the study of regions. Courses such as the "Geography of the United States" or the "Geography of California" take a regional approach to geography and explore the common characteristics unique to those particular regions.

Geographers have described several different types of regions. Functional regions have special identities because of the social and economic relationships that tie them together. They are often also referred to as nodal regions because they are defined by the connections and interactions that occur between them and surrounding areas. For example, the San Francisco Bay area depends on its heart or the actual city of San Francisco to generate economic activity for the entire region. The boundary around this region encompasses all of the connections between the economic heart and the various economic functions within the surrounding area. Formal regions have specific characteristics that are relatively uniform from one place to another within the designated region. These properties may include physical features, such as rolling hills or redwood trees, or cultural properties, such as religion or ethnicity. Tibet, for example, is a region of high mountains and plateaus, where most people have a common culture and observe the religious practices of Buddhism. This example might lead you to think that any country can be categorized as a formal region. However, despite most people's conceptions of this area, Tibet is not actually a state and thus provides a good example of a region for its boundaries are determined by a set of common cultural and physical variables rather than a political line. Perceptual regions exist in the minds of people. A common example used to illustrate this concept is that of the American "Deep South." When individuals are asked to draw a boundary around this region, their boundary line is most likely based on both physical and cultural characteristics, and possibly stereotypes they associate with the Deep South. These characteristics might include a muggy climate, magnolia trees, a distinct accent, culinary traditions such as fried chicken, and religious practices such as Southern Baptist. The boundaries of this region, as with all perceptual regions, will be necessarily fuzzy at their borders, but frequently involve important issues of identity. People's attachment to the region that they perceive as their home is what geographers call a **sense of place**. The characteristics just mentioned to describe the American South are the same types of characteristics southerners associate with "home" and thus give them a special attachment to that particular geographic place.

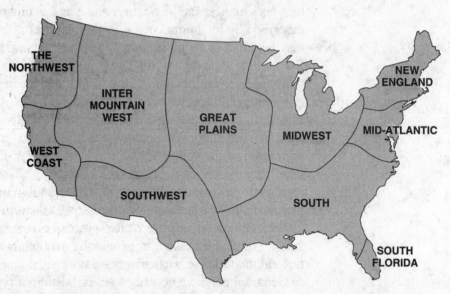

Figure 1.8. The United States is commonly divided into about ten major regions.

One example of a distinctive region is South Florida. South Florida is bounded by the Gulf of Mexico to the west, the Florida Strait to the south, the Atlantic Ocean to the east, and Interstate 4 to the north. It is distinctive because of its humid subtropical, monsoonal climate, its sprawling urban centers, its high proportion of Caribbean immigrants and retirees, and its unique and expansive wetland system known as the Everglades. Miami is an important city that spawns numerous social and economic interactions throughout the region. Thus, South Florida is a unique place tied together by both social and natural factors.

Thinking geographically also requires the ability to understand and synthesize various types of data. Human geographers work with two main forms of data: qualitative and quantitative. **Qualitative data** approaches are often associated with cultural or regional geography because they tend to be more unique to and descriptive of particular places and processes. Qualitative data are not well suited to statistical analyses and modeling and are often collected through interviews, empirical observations, or the interpretation of texts, artwork, old maps, and other archives. **Quantitative data** approaches use rigorous mathematical techniques and are particularly important in economic, political, and population geography, where hard, numerical data abounds. Most physical geography is also based on quantitative methods.

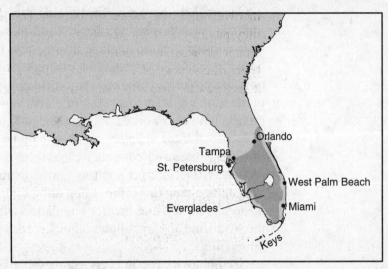

Figure 1.9. South Florida is a relatively well-defined region, with recognizable borders and cohesive geographical characteristics.

Another important distinction involving geographic information is the difference between the **idiographic** and the **nomothetic**. In human geography, idiographic refers to facts or features that are unique to a particular place or region, such as its history or ethnic composition. Nomothetic refers to concepts that are universally applicable. This contrast is similar to the regional/systematic distinction in approaches to human geography. A regional approach tends to be more idiographic, looking at the particular characteristics that make a region unique. In contrast, systematic geography takes a nomothetic approach by seeking universal laws that can be applied broadly to numerous places on the earth's surface. This distinction is particularly important in geography because geographers recognize that every place is different, but that no matter where you are many of the same processes are at work. The world is full of distinctive places, but even unique places are formed by a set of universal underlying processes. Although the canyonlands region of southern Utah is a spectacularly unique landscape, the erosional processes that created Utah's canyons, buttes, reefs, and arches are at work in similar climates across the world. And although the history of industry in central England may be unique, lessons learned about the use of capital and the adoption of technology may be applicable to industrialization more generally.

Applications of Geography

In recent years geographers have moved to the forefront of debates regarding the world's social and environmental problems. This is, in part, because all such problems have spatial characteristics. For example, human populations have exploded during the last half century, leading to social strife and ecological degradation in many areas of the world. But because this growth has been limited primarily to less-developed countries in the tropics and southern hemisphere, the world's wealthiest countries have been largely isolated from its effects. Geographic analyses of population data can help policy makers pinpoint areas of rapid growth and design policies to deal with the consequences of an increasing population.

Geographers have also benefited from technological advances, such as improved remote sensing imagery and increased computer capability, which have allowed them to analyze information in complex ways that were never before possible. One important example of this involves climatologists, who now use powerful computers to create models that predict potential changes in the earth's climate as a result of global warming. These same physical geographers have also worked with human geographers to predict some of the possible effects these changes could have on people. Another important example involving increased computer capability, is the greater availability of information on the Internet such as United Nations demographic statistics. The ease of obtaining this information allows population geographers greater ability to understand and predict population patterns and concentrations around the world and, in turn, allows a quicker response in both population and planning policy.

Geographers work in every conceivable field, from consulting to retailing, and from teaching to government. For more information on applications of human geography and careers in the field, check out some of the websites described in the "Additional Resources" section.

Key Terms Defined

Anthropogenic Human-induced changes on the natural environment.

Cartography Theory and practice of making visual representations of the earth's surface in the form of maps.

Cultural ecology The study of the interactions between societies and the natural environments they live in.

Cultural landscape The human-modified natural landscape specifically containing the imprint of a particular culture or society.

Earth system science Systematic approach to physical geography that looks at the interaction between the earth's physical systems and processes on a global scale.

Environmental geography The intersection between human and physical geography, which explores the spatial impacts humans have on the physical environment and vice versa.

Eratosthenes The head librarian at Alexandria during the third century B.C.; he was one of the first cartographers. Performed a remarkably accurate computation of the earth's circumference. He is also credited with coining the term "geography."

Fertile Crescent Name given to crescent-shaped area of fertile land stretching from the lower Nile valley, along the east Mediterranean coast, and into Syria and present-day Iraq where agriculture and early civilization first began about 8000 B.C.

Geographical Information Systems A set of computer tools used to capture, store, transform, analyze, and display geographic data.

Global Positioning System A set of satellites used to help determine location anywhere on the earth's surface with a portable electronic device.

Idiographic Pertaining to the unique facts or characteristics of a particular place.

George Perkins Marsh Inventor, diplomat, politician, and scholar, his classic work, *Man and Nature, or Physical Geography as Modified by Human Action*, provided the first description of the extent to which natural systems had been impacted by human actions.

Natural landscape The physical landscape or environment that has not been affected by human activities.

Nomothetic Concepts or rules that can be applied universally.

W. D. Pattison He claimed that geography drew from four distinct traditions: the earth-science tradition, the culture-environment tradition, the locational tradition, and the area-analysis tradition.

Physical geography The realm of geography that studies the structures, processes, distributions, and change through time of the natural phenomena of the earth's surface.

Ptolemy Roman geographer-astronomer and author of *Guide to Geography* which included maps containing a grid system of latitude and longitude.

Qualitative data Data associated with a more humanistic approach to geography, often collected through interviews, empirical observations, or the interpretation of texts, artwork, old maps, and other archives.

Quantitative data Data associated with mathematical models and statistical techniques used to analyze spatial location and association.

Quantitative revolution A period in human geography associated with the widespread adoption of mathematical models and statistical techniques.

Region A territory that encompasses many places that share similar attributes (may be physical, cultural, or both) in comparison with the attributes of places elsewhere.

Regional geography The study of geographic regions.

Remote sensing Observation and mathematical measurement of the earth's surface using aircraft and satellites. The sensors include both photographic images, thermal images, multispectral scanners, and radar images.

Carl Sauer Geographer from the University of California at Berkeley who defined the concept of cultural landscape as the fundamental unit of geographical analysis. This landscape results from interaction between humans and the physical environment. Sauer argued that virtually no landscape has escaped alteration by human activities.

Sense of place Feelings evoked by people as a result of certain experiences and memories associated with a particular place.

Spatial perspective An intellectual framework that looks at the particular locations of specific phenomena, how and why that phenomena is where it is, and, finally, how it is spatially related to phenomena in other places.

Sustainability The concept of using the earth's resources in such a way that they provide for people's needs in the present without diminishing the earth's ability to provide for future generations.

Systematic geography The study of the earth's integrated systems as a whole, instead of focusing on particular phenomena in a single place.

Thematic layers Individual maps of specific features that are overlaid on one another in a Geographical Information System to understand and analyze a spatial relationship.

Sample Questions and Answers

Section 1: History and Development of the Discipline

Multiple-Choice Questions

1. Which of the following is the oldest field of geography?

    (A) Cultural ecology
    (B) Conservation biology
    (C) Cartography
    (D) Environmental geography
    (E) Physical geography

2. _____ argued that cultural landscapes should form the basic unit of geographic inquiry.

    (A) Ptolemy
    (B) George Perkins Marsh
    (C) Eratosthenes
    (D) Carl Sauer
    (E) W. D. Pattison

3. During the quantitative revolution, geographers

   (A) focused mainly on measuring physical processes.
   (B) stressed the use of empirical measurements, hypothesis testing, and mathematical models.
   (C) abandoned older, speculative notions of the cultural landscape and human-environment interactions.
   (D) adopted powerful new technologies, such as remote sensing and GIS.
   (E) began studying the region as the fundamental unit in human geography.

4. Which of the following is comprised of an integrated system of satellites?

   (A) The Global Positioning System
   (B) remote sensing
   (C) Geographical Informational System
   (D) thematic map
   (E) Haptic Navigation systems

5. A thematic layer is

   (A) a method used in cartography to produce mathematically accurate map projections.
   (B) a map portraying a particular feature that is used in a GIS.
   (C) used in GPS systems to provide more accurate navigational information.
   (D) a map used by early explorers to find particular resources in new regions of the earth.
   (E) used as a method to analyze thematic regions.

Free-Response Questions

1. The discipline of geography has evolved over the last 3,000 years to become a wide-ranging field of both academic research and applied science.

   (a) Discuss the contributions different individuals have made to the development of the discipline and how their contributions may have shaped current geographic thought.
   (b) How has geography been influenced by trends in other academic fields?
   (c) Describe some of the overarching themes of the current trends in the discipline.

2. Technological innovations have greatly influenced the methods in which geography can be done today.

   (a) Describe the three technological advances that have dramatically changed the capabilities of the discipline of geography.
   (b) Provide an application for each type of technology.

Section 2: Geography Today

Multiple-Choice Questions

1. Which of the following is not one of the four traditions of geography according to W. D. Pattison's definition?

    (A) Area-analysis tradition
    (B) Field studies tradition
    (C) Culture-environment relations
    (D) Earth-science tradition
    (E) Locational tradition

2. Today, physical geographers tend to focus on

    (A) the ecumene.
    (B) places and regions.
    (C) large-scale systems.
    (D) sustainability.
    (E) cultural landscapes.

3. Human-induced environmental change is often referred to as

    (A) anthropomorphic.
    (B) anthropocentric.
    (C) anthropogenic.
    (D) nonsustainable.
    (E) environmental determinism.

4. Conserving resources to ensure enough for future generations is called

    (A) subsistence agriculture.
    (B) sustainability.
    (C) cultural ecology.
    (D) environmental determinism.
    (E) the organic movement.

5. The following is a true statement regarding the nature of environmental geography:

    (A) It studies processes and problems at the intersection of human and physical geography.
    (B) It takes a regional approach, looking at the particular environmental characteristics of specific places.
    (C) It is one of the four traditions of geography described by W. D. Pattison.
    (D) It studies the areal differentiation of human activities on the earth's surface.
    (E) It studies the earth's environment outside of human activity.

Free-Response Question

1. If you were to become a geographer, you would choose an emphasis in one of three areas characteristic of this field: human geography, physical geography, and environmental geography.

    (a) Define each of these types of geography.
    (b) Provide an example of a research problem characterizing each of the three areas of geography.
    (c) Describe the different research methods that might be used within each approach.

Section 3: Thinking Geographically

Multiple-Choice Questions

1. Geographic scale refers to

    (A) the ratio between distance on a map and distance on the earth's surface.
    (B) a conceptual hierarchy of spaces.
    (C) a notion of place, based on an individual's perception of space.
    (D) the many ways that people define regions.
    (E) the level of aggregation at which geographers investigate a particular process.

2. Which of the following is true concerning regions?

    (A) They are strict, functional units.
    (B) They are usually defined by a standard mathematical formula.
    (C) They are figments of the imagination.
    (D) They are conceptual units.
    (E) They all have well-defined boundaries.

3. _____ refers to concepts that are universally applicable.

    (A) Nomothetic
    (B) Qualitative
    (C) Idiographic
    (D) Idiocentric
    (E) Quantitative

4. If a geographer performs a study on people's perceptions of the Deep South using interviews as his primary data source, his method is

    _____.

    (A) quantitative
    (B) systematic
    (C) anthropogenic
    (D) qualitative
    (E) idiographic

5. A perceptual region's boundaries are

(A) determined by a set of uniform physical or cultural characteristics across a particular area.

(B) drawn around the functions that occur between a particular place and the surrounding area.

(C) determined by the portion of a particular area that has been modified by human activities.

(D) fuzzy because they allow for individual interpretation.

(E) designated by the inclusion of a particular cultural characteristic.

Free-Response Questions

1. Geography is unique from other disciplines in that it applies a spatial perspective to different phenomena and processes that occur on the earth's surface.

   (a) Define the spatial perspective. Include in your definition what it means to think geographically and include descriptions of the types of data that geographers analyze.

   (b) Provide an example of a problem that can only be solved from a spatial perspective.

2. The region is a highly contested yet critical concept in the study of human geography.

   (a) Why and how do geographers perform the regionalization process?

   (b) What is regional geography?

   (c) Discuss the different types of regions that human geographers study, and provide an example of each type.

Answers for Multiple-Choice Questions

Section 1: History and Development of the Discipline

1. **(C)** The first geographers were primarily interested in exploration. Cartography allowed these first geographers to map the information gleaned from their expeditions.

2. **(D)** Carl Sauer developed the notion of a cultural landscape to describe the parts of the earth's surface that have been modified by human activities. He also argued that virtually all of earth's surface has in some way been affected by human activity and thus paved the way for environmental geography.

3. **(B)** The quantitative revolution in geography occurred in response to changes in the social sciences in an effort to make them more scientific. These new methods allowed geography to enter the realm of a rigorous scientific discipline with theories, laws, and methods that could be applied across geographical spaces. Soon after the quantitative revolution, geographers began implementing high-tech tools into their research.

4. **(A)**   A portable hand-held device (a GPS) allows you to determine your near accurate location based on an integrated system of satellites transmitting locational information.

5. **(B)**   The purpose of GIS is to provide a tool to better understand spatial relationships between different phenomena. This goal is accomplished by overlaying different thematic layers, or maps with different geographic information, on top of one another to determine whether a spatial relationship occurs between the various phenomena represented on each of the thematic layers.

Section 2: Geography Today

1. **(B)**   Although field studies are very important to the study of geography, they are not one of the main traditions of geography according to Pattison. However, field studies are an important component of one of his four traditions, the earth-science or physical-geography tradition.

2. **(C)**   Today, physical geographers are beginning to take a systematic approach to their field by looking at the earth's integrated physical systems as a whole instead of focusing on particular phenomena in a single place.

3. **(C)**   Anthropogenic, by definition, means human-induced changes on the physical environment. The other options are only tricky because they look similar to this term.

4. **(B)**   Sustainability is the idea of using the earth's resources in such a way that you are able to provide for current populations while also thinking of the resource needs of future generations.

5. **(A)**   Carl Sauer's notion of the cultural landscape paved the way for environmental geography. This unit of analysis was defined as areas that had been altered by human activities. Human geography looks at the distribution of human activities on the earth's surface, physical geography studies the processes of the earth's physical systems, and environmental geography studies how each of these two forces influence and counteract one another.

Section 3: Thinking Geographically

1. **(B)**   The one other option that might be confusing is (A), which refers to map scale. Geographic scale pertains to a scale of analysis, thus looking at phenomena through a hierarchy of scales such as neighborhood, city, state, nation.

2. **(D)**   Regions are an organizing tool that allow geographers to combine areas with similar features into one conceptual unit that provides them with a more manageable unit for analysis.

3. **(A)**   A nomothetic approach to geography seeks to find theories, rules, and laws that can be systematically applied across the globe. It is the opposite of

an idiographic approach, which describes the unique characteristics of particular places.

4. **(D)** Qualitative data are more humanistic, often collected through interviews, empirical observations, the interpretation of texts, artwork, old maps, and other archives. Quantitative data are mathematical, and these methods can be used to analyze quantitative data in different settings.

5. **(D)** The first two options define formal regions and functional regions respectively. The third option defines a cultural landscape, whereas the fifth defines a thematic region, leaving option (D). Perceptual regions are determined by commonly perceived characteristics of particular places on the earth's surface. Different individuals have different ideas about where these characteristics begin and end, thus the boundaries are necessarily "fuzzy."

Answers for Free-Response Questions

Section 1: History and Development of the Discipline

1. Main points:
   - Eratosthenes performed a remarkably accurate computation of the earth's circumference and is also credited with coining the term "geography," which literally means "earth writing." About 500 years later, in the second century A.D., Ptolemy published his *Guide to Geography*, which included rough maps of the landmasses, as he understood them at the time, and a global grid system. Both contributed greatly to the methods of cartography.
   - George Perkins Marsh wrote extensively on the effects of man's destruction of the environment particularly focusing on the Fertile Crescent. His contributions to early geographic thought consist of a conservation approach to the environment as well as an emphasis on the importance of the interaction between humans and the environment.
   - Carl Sauer's notion of the cultural landscape provided a unit of study that incorporated both the physical environment and human actions on the physical environment to basically begin a new branch of geography, environmental geography.
   - W. D. Pattison formalized the main fields of geography as the area-analysis tradition, the earth-science tradition, the culture-environment tradition, and the locational tradition, and has thus provided a somewhat unifying definition of the discipline.
   - The quantitative revolution that occurred in the social sciences in the 1960s had a great impact on geography. The changes in geography reflected the technological innovations and rise of modernist philosophy that were occurring in the social sciences. The quantitative revolution stressed the use of empirical measurements, hypothesis testing, the development of mathematical models, and the use of computer programs to explain geographic patterns.

WHAT IS HUMAN GEOGRAPHY? 45

• Current trends in the discipline include a relatively recent emphasis on a systematic approach, which allows geographers to apply their information and methods to more areas. There is an increasing use of technology, which is having a dramatic effect on how geographers can do geography today.

2. Main points:
   • Three technological innovations that have dramatically changed the methods of geography are remote sensing, the Global Positioning System, and Geographical Information Systems.
   • Remote sensing is mostly used to determine land use change. It is one of the most-effective tools for quantifying the amount of tropical rainforest being deforested. GPS is a geographical tool used by geographers as well as the general public. It is a very useful tool for navigational purposes; it comes as a feature in many automobiles and provides accurate up-to-date directional information. Geographical Information Systems are an extremely important tool for geographers today. GIS allow geographers to apply the spatial perspective to different phenomena more quickly through the overlay of thematic maps each containing information about different spatial features. The map overlay allows geographers to determine quickly whether a spatial relationship exists between different spatial phenomena. A GIS of New York City with thematic layers of street systems, fire hydrants, and hospital locations would provide a useful tool for deciding upon evacuation routes and getting people to hospitals as quickly as possible.

Section 2: Geography Today

1. Main points:
   • Human geography is the study of human activities across space. This field of geography is divided into several main subfields such as cultural geography, population geography, economic geography, political geography, behavioral geography, urban geography, and agricultural geography. Each of these subfields studies some aspect of human activities and how these activities manifest themselves on the earth's surface.
   • Physical geography is concerned with the earth's physical systems and how they vary across space.
   • Environmental geography is at the intersection of human and physical geography; it looks at how humans alter the physical environment and vice versa.
   • Human geographers might study the transportation habits of a particular population (i.e., how many people drive cars, how many use the bus, what types of cars they are driving). A physical geographer might study the various climate dynamics that occur across the globe such as rainfall patterns and temperature patterns. Finally, the environmental geographer might combine these two and study how human behavior affects global climate change by way of increased carbon emissions from automobiles and the reverse, the types of implications global climate change has on both current and future populations.

- Human geography can use both a systematic and regional approach in its research. Human geographers use quantitative data both to describe the unique characteristics of particular places and to analyze human activities on the earth's surface. One such example is in population geography where mathematical calculations are used to predict population change in particular places. Both physical and environmental geography are well suited towards a systematic approach where each of the earth's various systems are studied as a whole. This approach allows them to apply their knowledge of how the earth's systems interact with each other in places where similar types of interactions take place. Generally, both of these types of geographers work with quantitative data since the type of research they do is quite scientific and mathematic.

Section 3: Thinking Geographically

1. Main points:
   - The spatial perspective is an intellectual framework in which the spatial characteristic of particular phenomena are analyzed in terms of location and relationships with other spatial phenomena. Thinking geographically involves recognizing the location of particular processes or features and also understanding how and why those processes occur at specific locations.
   - Spatial data are any type of data that pertain to a particular location and can be either quantitative or qualitative. Quantitative data are usually numerical and manipulated through mathematical or statistical models. Qualitative data are more descriptive and are usually obtained from interviews, texts, or archives of particular places or phenomena.
   - Any problem that is spatial in nature is best solved using a spatial perspective. An example that was given in this chapter was that of the Amish community and the measles epidemic in the United States in the mid-1980s. The Amish, because of their belief system, refused to get measles vaccinations; as a result, the disease ran rampant through this community and the surrounding Amish communities of the eastern United States. Understanding the spread of this disease could not be done without understanding the spatial relationship between the Amish communities and the areas of outbreak.

2. Main points:
   - The regionalization process involves grouping similar characteristics of different places into a more manageable unit of study, which is the region. The region is a conceptual unit that is bounded based on whatever feature a particular geographer wants to include within a particular region. These features can be either physical or cultural.
   - Regional geography is concerned with the study of regions and the characteristics of those particular regions that make them different from other places on the earth's surface. Generally, regional geography takes an idiographic approach because it looks at the unique characteristics of particular places without generalizing the processes occurring within those regions beyond their boundaries.

- Functional regions are defined by the connections and interactions that occur between a central place and its surrounding area. An example could be Chicago (or any other large city) and all the various transportation, economic, cultural, and recreational connections that exist within that area.
- The boundary of a formal region contains an area of similar cultural or physical characteristics. An example of a formal region would be Friesland in the Netherlands. In this part of the country, the people speak a different language and perceive themselves quite differently from the other citizens of the Netherlands.
- Perceptual regions are based on people's perceptions of various places. They are based on certain physical and cultural characteristics perceived as unique within a particular place. The United States can be divided into several perceptual regions that each has defining characteristics to determine their usually quite fuzzy boundaries. Some examples include the Midwest, the Deep South, the Northeast, and the Southwest.

Additional Resources

Text

Agnew, John, David Livingstone, Alisdair Rogers (eds). 1996. *Human Geography: An Essential Anthology*. Cambridge, Massachusetts: Blackwell.

This text contains numerous essays written by academic human geographers, both in the past and the present, describing many different facets of human geography. The essays are organized into five main sections: Recounting Geography's History; The Enterprise; Nature, Culture and Landscape; Region, Place and Locality; and Space, Time and Space-Time.

Johnston, R. J. 1997. *Geography and Geographers: Anglo-American Human Geography since 1945*. New York: Arnold.

Johnston discusses the history of the discipline of human geography beginning in 1945. He begins by discussing the nature of an academic discipline and then discusses geography's many different foci and some of the difficulty the discipline has encountered in struggling to both define itself and maintain academic rigor.

Web

Association of American Geographers: *www.aag.org/*

This is the website for the largest academic society of geographers. Once you arrive at the opening page, you are presented with a variety of options. One of which, "Jobs/Careers," will tell you a little bit more about the types of work geographers do. Additionally, the "Education" link will connect you to some excellent educational resources pertaining to different topics in geography.

Earthworks: *http://www.earthworks-jobs.com*

This website contains a directory of all the various jobs available for people with geography degrees. Some of the jobs described pertain more to physical geography, and some to human geography. Many of the jobs involve using either remote sensing or GIS technology.

The National Geographic Society: *www.nationalgeographic.com*
An excellent and comprehensive resource of geographic information. The data available on this site ranges from maps of places all over the globe, to lesson plans, to issues and processes covered in recent editions of the magazine, to geographic games and quizzes you can take on-line.

University of Edinburgh Department of Geography: *www.geo.ed.ac.uk/home/giswww.html*
This site houses hundreds of links relating to GIS listed in alphabetical order. It is a great source for finding an interesting case study to make GIS more relevant and interesting for both students and teachers.

Internet Resources for Geography and Geology: *http://www.uwsp.edu/geo/internet/geog_geol_resources.html*
This site contains an extensive directory of numerous Internet resources for geography. The resources are categorized into numerous topics including links to cartography and GIS, career information, environmental information, government resources, points of interest, multimedia resources, resources for teaching and learning geography, world regional geography, human geography, and virtual field trips.

CHAPTER 2
Maps, Scale, Space, and Place

Summary

Human geographers describe human activities on earth by creating visual representations of spatial data in the form of maps. All maps are based on a projection, all maps have a characteristic scale and resolution, and all maps use symbols to depict spatial information. Geographers use a diverse set of concepts, tools, technologies, and mathematical equations to study places, regions, and the processes that link them. In general, places that are closer to each other in absolute distance tend to interact more. However, the interaction between places is also determined by their size, their level of connectivity, and the diffusion processes that carry information and cultural traditions from one place to another.

In This Chapter

- Map Fundamentals
- Cognitive Maps
- Describing Location
- Space and Spatial Processes

Key Terms

Absolute distance	Fuller projection
Absolute location	Geoid
Accessibility	Gravity model
Azimuthal projection	Hazards
Breaking point	Hierarchical diffusion
Cartograms	International Date Line
Choropleth maps	Intervening opportunities
Cognitive maps	Isolines
Complementarity	Large-scale
Connectivity	Latitude
Contagious diffusion	Law of retail gravitation
Coordinate system	Location charts
Distance decay effect	Longitude
Dot maps	Map projections
Expansion diffusion	Mercator projection
Friction of distance	Meridian

Parallel	**Site**
Preference map	**Situation**
Prime meridian	**Small-scale**
Proportional symbols map	**Spatial diffusion**
Reference map	**Thematic map**
Relative distance	**Time-space convergence**
Relative location	**Topographic maps**
Relocation diffusion	**Topological space**
Resolution	**Transferability**
Robinson projection	**Visualization**
Scale	

Map Fundamentals

In Chapter 1, we learned that some of the first contributions to geography were made in the field of cartography, or map-making. Since geography's early beginnings, map-making has persisted as one of the main techniques geographers use to display spatial information. Even if you are not a geographer or are not at all interested in geography, you still probably encounter maps on a daily basis. Whether it be a weather map on the evening news, a political map in the newspaper depicting an area of the world in turmoil, or a sketch map you draw for a friend when giving directions to your house, maps are a pervasive aspect of society.

Maps come in all different shapes and sizes. Maps of your city's local bus system look quite different from a map depicting average income in your city, and a map of national voting patterns will probably not help you find the nearest public library. Consequently, the ways that different maps look largely depends on their purpose. When choosing the type of map they want to make, cartographers base their scientific and artistic decisions on what they are trying to communicate and on what data they have available. They must choose between types of projections, levels of simplification, levels of aggregation, map scale, and what symbols to use to depict information.

All maps are created by projecting the earth's three-dimensional shape, which in reality is a bumpy oblate spheroid, or **geoid,** onto a two-dimensional surface. Transforming something spherical into something flat necessarily means that the two-dimensional representation will never exactly represent what is visible in three dimensions. Originally, maps were produced by placing a light source, such as a candle or bulb, inside of a translucent globe and then projecting the globe's features onto another shape surrounding it—such as a cylinder or cone, which could later be unrolled into a flat map. Now, geographers use numerous different mathematical equations to produce **map projections.** No matter the method or the equation used, it is important to remember that three-dimensional shapes can never be transferred to two-dimensional surfaces without losing some detail or distorting some features. As a result, all flat maps have some distortion in their representation of distance, shape, area, or direction.

The **Mercator projection**, which preserves accurate compass direction, distorts the area of landmasses relative to each other. In the Mercator projection landmasses become increasingly distorted, or large in size, at high latitudes near the North and South Poles. The Mercator projection was originally created by projecting the earth's features onto a cylinder. Unfortunately, when a geoid is projected onto a cylinder and then unrolled, lines of longitude, which all normally intersect at the North and South Poles, all become parallel. This distortion causes space to get increasingly "stretched out" the closer you get to the poles, which is why, on Mercator projections, Greenland, Alaska, Antarctica, and other high-latitude landmasses look so big.

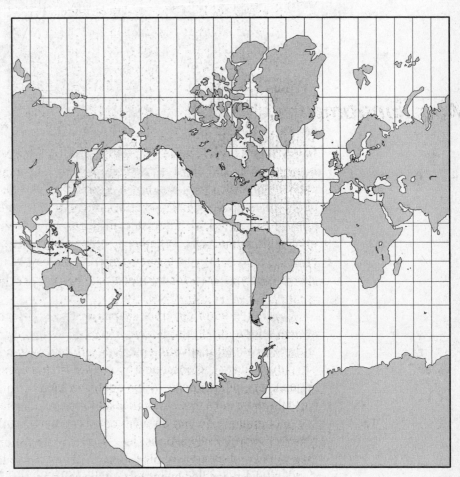

Figure 2.1. Mercator projection.

The **Fuller projection** strikes a different compromise. It maintains the accurate size and shape of landmasses but completely rearranges direction, so that the cardinal directions—north, south, east, and west—no longer have any meaning. The **Robinson projection** is an example of an attempt to balance projection errors. It does not maintain accurate area, shape, distance, or direction, but it minimizes errors in each. The Robinson projection provides an aesthetically pleasing balance and, as a result, is frequently used by cartographers at organizations such as the National Geographic Society. **Azimuthal projections** provide a different perspective than most people are used to seeing. Azimuthal projections are *planar*, meaning they are formed when a flat piece of paper is placed on top of the globe and, as described earlier, a light source projects the surrounding areas onto the map. Thus, in an azimuthal projection, either the North Pole or the South Pole is oriented at the center of the map, giving the viewer an impression of looking up or down at the earth. It is important to remember that there is no *best* type of map projection—the type of projection you should use depends on your data and the purpose of your map.

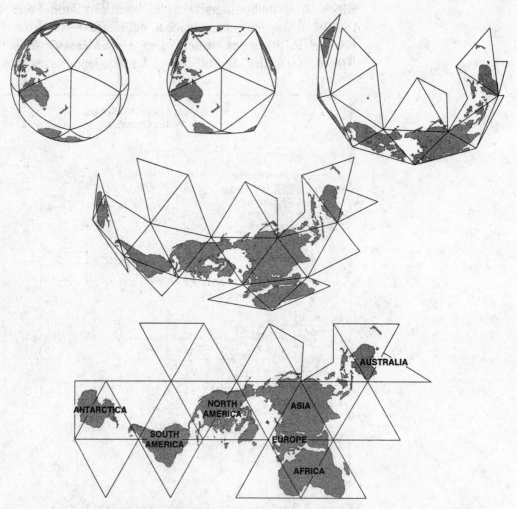

Figure 2.2. Fuller projection.

After cartographers choose which type of projection to use, they must decide on the level of simplification portrayed on the map. This simply refers to the level of detail included. If you are designing a map of the entire United States, you probably will not include minute details such as the locations of towns smaller than 50,000 people. If, however, you are designing a map of a shopping mall, you will probably include such details as the location of the nearest restroom. Again, what cartographers choose to display on a map depends on the overall purpose of the map and the size of the area covered, and they will choose the level of simplification necessary to accomplish their goals. Similarly, the level of aggregation cartographers choose to show on a map will largely depend on the map's purpose. Level of aggregation just refers to the size of the unit under investigation such as cities, counties, states, or countries. When showing population patterns across the United States, cartographers probably would not depict the population concentrations of counties within states. However, if showing the population of the state of Illinois, geographers might divide the data into population density per county. Very different pictures of population density result as the level of aggregation varies. In the map of the entire United States, Illinois would probably be represented with a uniform population density across the entire state. However, when just looking at Illinois by county, we would discover that a large proportion of the state's population is actually concentrated in the northeast, near the city of Chicago. Again, the level of aggregation depicted will depend on the overall purpose of the map.

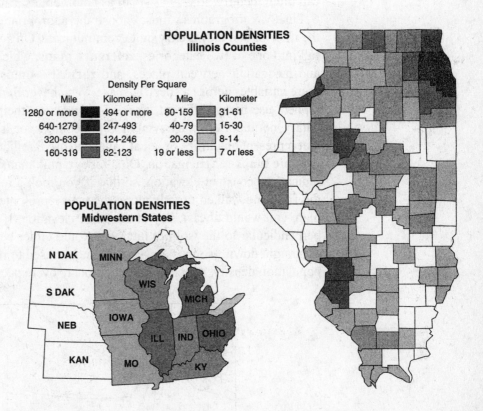

POPULATION DENSITIES
Illinois Counties

Density Per Square

Mile	Kilometer	Mile	Kilometer
1280 or more	494 or more	80-159	31-61
640-1279	247-493	40-79	15-30
320-639	124-246	20-39	8-14
160-319	62-123	19 or less	7 or less

POPULATION DENSITIES
Midwestern States

Figure 2.3. Population densities of midwestern states and Illinois by county. Notice that state level categories obscure differences by county.

All maps have a particular map scale and resolution. Map **scale** refers to the ratio between the distance on a map and the actual distance on the earth's surface. The U.S. Geological Survey (USGS), for example, produces standard quadrangle maps at the scale of 1:24,000, pronounced "one-to-twenty-four thousand." On these maps, one unit—an inch, a foot, a finger, whatever—equals exactly 24,000 of those same units on the ground. In a **small-scale** map, the ratio between map units and ground units is small, such as 1:100,000. Since one map unit equals so many of those same units on the earth's surface, these maps tend to cover large regions. Maps of the entire world are necessarily small-scale maps because they cover such an enormous area. **Large-scale** maps have large-scale ratios, such as 1:5,000, and cover much smaller regions. A large-scale map, at a one-to-five thousand scale, might depict a farm or a neighborhood.

Resolution is another extremely important concept. Resolution refers to a map's smallest discernable unit. For our purposes, you can also think of resolution as the smallest thing you can see on a map. If, for example, an object has to be 100 meters long in order to show up on a map, then that map's resolution is 100 meters. For many world maps, the smallest discernable detail may be the size of a large city, such as New York. If you have a globe or a world atlas, take a look at New York City—can you see Manhattan Island? How about San Francisco Bay? These spaces are pretty close to the resolution of a standard globe. At the other extreme, some highly accurate, large-scale satellite photos have a resolution of less than one meter. In these images, which can act as maps, you can often identify objects as small as automobiles, cattle troughs, and shrubs.

Finally, cartographers must choose the appropriate map type according to the information they are trying to communicate. On a very general level, maps fall into one of two categories: **reference maps,** which work well for locating and navigating between places, and **thematic maps**, which display one or more variables across a specific space. Whichever the map type, human geographers use many different types of symbols on their maps to depict spatial data. One important map symbol is the contour, or **isoline**. Isolines are lines that represent quantities of equal value and are familiar to those who use **topographic maps** for navigation. On a topographic map, the path of each isoline indicates a constant elevation, so that if you took a topographic map out into the field and walked exactly along the path represented by an isoline on your map, you would always stay at the same elevation. If you turned and walked perpendicular to the isolines then you would either be walking straight uphill or straight down. Isolines are also commonly used to represent values, such as population density, which vary continuously over space.

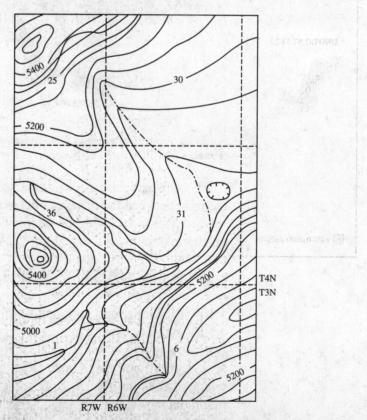

Figure 2.4. Topographic maps use isolines to represent points of common elevation.

Several other types of map symbols are common in thematic maps. In a **proportional symbols** map, the size of the chosen symbol—such as a circle or triangle—indicates the relative magnitude of some value for a given geographic region. Bigger circles, stars, dots, or icons represent more of some feature, such as churches, crimes, or baseball fans. **Location charts** convey a large amount of information by associating charts with specific mapped locations. In a map of Canada, each province may have a chart within it depicting number of native French speakers versus number of native English speakers. **Dot maps** use points to show the precise locations of specific observations or occurrences, such as crimes, car accidents, or births. If two car accidents occurred at the corner of Main and Horizon Streets, then two dots will show up there. **Choropleth maps** use colors or tonal shadings to represent categories of data for given geographic areas. A choropleth map of Africa may use five different colors to show levels of literacy, by country. And **cartograms** transform space, such that the political unit—a state, or a country, for example—with the greatest value for some type of data is represented by the largest relative area. In a population cartogram of Asia, China would be the largest country on the map and India the second largest, because of their populations, even though Russia has the most land area. These are just a few examples of the many different types of maps and the many ways spatial information can be portrayed.

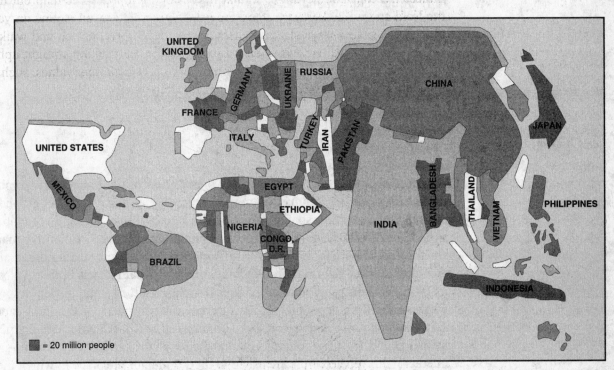

Figure 2.5. A cartogram of world population. Countries that have the greatest populations are also depicted as being the largest in size.

Technological innovations in the area of map-making are radically changing the methods of modern cartography. (The powerful implications of GIS were introduced in Chapter 1.) Another interesting class of maps that have become increasingly popular in recent years is called **visualizations**. Visualizations use sophisticated software to create dynamic computer maps, some of which are three-dimensional or interactive. Some visualizations allow geographers to investigate features that cannot be seen with the naked eye. Others use models to show how landscapes change over time. And in others, you can even walk through or fly over the landscape. Visualizations are also extremely helpful learning tools for aspiring young geographers. To see some interesting visualizations from the NASA Goddard Space Flight Center, go to *http://svs.gsfc.nasa.gov/index.html*.

Maps can be powerful tools. If a geographer makes even one error on his or her map, it can have dramatic implications. In this sense, it is useful to think of maps as texts, with tremendous power to communicate ideas and information. Maps can be powerful tools for examining spatial processes. Many spatial epidemiologists, or geographers who study the spread of disease, use maps to investigate the correlation between the incidence of disease and proximity to harmful environmental factors. The movies *Erin Brokovich* and *A Civil Action* provide excellent examples of this process. In both films, each of which was based on a true story, the incidence of diseases—cancer in *Erin Brokovich* and leukemia in *A Civil Action*—was correlated with toxic industrial chemicals in the environment. In both films, the defendants, their lawyers, and a cadre of scientists were able to make positive correlations between disease and toxic waste to win monumental lawsuits. No amount of money can make up for the tragedies that occurred to the families and communities involved, but hopefully in the future spatial analysis will help to identify such problems earlier and save lives and protect the environment in the process. As you can see, mapping can help geographers understand all sorts of spatial processes at a variety of different scales. In this example, mapping was useful at the community level, but maps are useful even at the individual level; maps can also help geographers understand the psychology of human spatial behavior.

Cognitive Maps

An entire class of maps falls outside of the purview of traditional cartography, as described earlier. **Cognitive maps**, which many behavioral geographers believe guide people's spatial behavior, are one example. A cognitive map is an individual's internal, geographic understanding of a place. Cognitive maps are formed when people perceive information about their surroundings and then process that information into a mental image that reflects both the physical environment and that individual's social, cultural, and psychological framework. In essence, people are internal cartographers of the landscapes they encounter on a daily basis. They organize streets, landmarks, and districts in their mind to form coherent mental maps of the places they live in and interact with. When people are asked to draw a map of the place in which they live, they necessarily include some details that they personally deem important but leave out many others. Consequently, no two cognitive maps of the same place will look exactly alike. What people include on their maps can be quite revealing, in terms of their perception of place. Cognitive maps are extremely informative because they give us important clues for understanding how people interpret and understand the places in which they live.

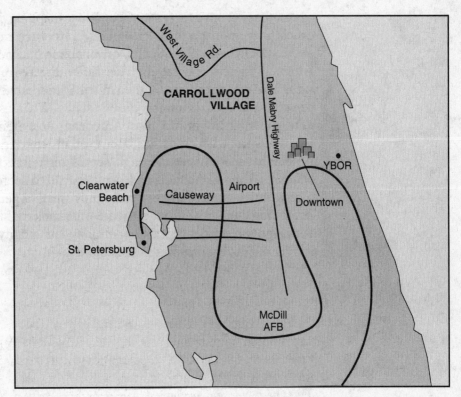

Figure 2.6. Cognitive map of Tampa, Florida, drawn by a former resident.

Cognitive maps also serve several other functions. For instance, someone's cognitive map may include **hazards** that that person avoids during their daily activities. Hazards such as jammed intersections or dangerous parts of town are imprinted into people's cognitive maps and, in general, people tend to avoid such places. Interestingly, human spatial behavior does not always reflect the presence of *real* natural hazards. Housing developments in fire-prone, flood-prone, or exposed coastal areas are an example. Cognitive maps also guide navigation. Every day, millions of people wrestle with the question: "What's the fastest way to get to work?" The answer may depend on the individual's geographic knowledge of their hometown and their understanding of traffic patterns, potential obstacles, and the effects of variables such as weather, time of day, and day of the week.

Cognitive maps reflect much about the person who draws them. Different people's cognitive maps show different levels of engagement with the landscape. For example, Eskimos living in the North American arctic have drawn amazingly detailed maps of the regions in which they live without ever seeing professionally produced maps of the area. One can only assume that this knowledge is essential for their daily lives, which often include long distance travel in remote areas with few stationary landmarks. Cognitive maps also give clues to different people's levels of access to things like education, language, and transportation. In Los Angeles, affluent college students living in Westwood are often able to draw quite detailed maps of the city, while poor Latinos in East LA, many of whom do not speak English, frequently only possess spatial information about the neighborhoods in their immediate vicinity. These urban disparities speak volumes about the relationship between geographic knowledge, economics, and access.

Another interesting type of cognitive mapping involves people's preferences for certain places over others. **Preference maps** show people's ideas about the environmental, social, or economic quality of life in various places. Although these maps are not necessarily directly related to spatial behavior, there is some correlation in the United States between growth rates and perceived quality of life among various states. When asked to rate certain states in terms of quality of life, most Americans give their home state a high ranking, no matter where they live. However, the states of California, Florida, and Colorado generally receive high scores regardless of where the individual being surveyed actually lives. Big cities tend to score higher than rural areas; places with beautiful scenery and sunny weather get high marks as well. It is interesting to note that not only are high-ranking states mentally associated with high levels of economic opportunity and quality of life, but they are also among the fastest growing in the country.

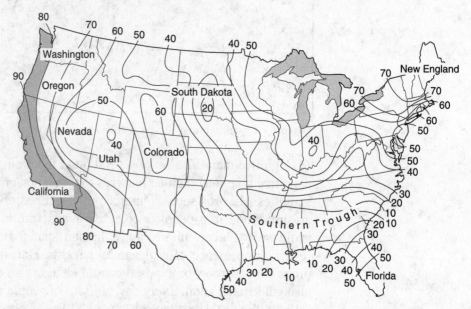

Figure 2.7. This preference map of the United States shows that most people would generally prefer to live on the West Coast or in New England.

As you are now aware, there are many different kinds of maps and many different ways to design them—this makes the profession of cartography much more complicated than it otherwise might seem. Furthermore, the act of mapping—whether it is a cartographer making decisions in producing a population map of a specific region or an individual developing a cognitive map of a new neighborhood—requires a thorough understanding of the dynamics of space. Geographers must also understand the importance of location, distance between locations, and the interactions that occur across space.

Describing Location

One of the basic tasks of human geography is to describe places in terms of both their location and their relationship to other places. Some features on the earth's surface are commonly represented as points, some as lines, and some as areas, making the concepts of location, distance, and scale critical concepts for describing earth's features.

The precise location of any object on the earth's surface can be pinpointed on a standard grid, or **coordinate system**, upon which you can designate and describe a place's **absolute location.** Coordinates are made up of lines of **longitude** and **latitude.** Lines of longitude, or **meridians**, originate at the **prime meridian** (0°), which passes through Greenwich, England, and end at the **International Date Line** (180°), in the Pacific Ocean. All lines of longitude also meet at the poles. Unlike meridians, lines of latitude never touch, as a result they are often referred to as **parallels.** Lines of latitude originate at the equator (0°) and terminate at the poles (90°). An example of a well-known parallel is 49°N latitude, which marks the boundary between the western United States and Canada.

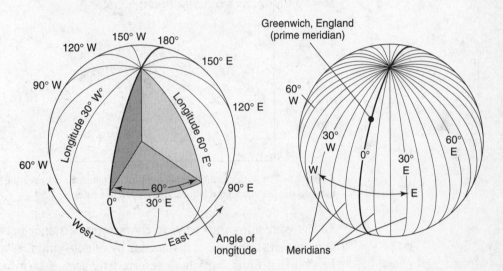

Figure 2.8. The Cartesian coordinate system uses both parallels and meridians. Meridians, or lines of longitude, originate at the prime meridian centered on Greenwich, England.

In addition to describing places in terms of their coordinates, geographers also use other methods to describe location. One way to describe a place's location is by its site. **Site** refers to the physical and cultural features of a place, independent of that place's relationship to other places around it. For instance, the city of San Francisco is located at about 37°N latitude and 123°W longitude, on a windswept peninsula separating the San Francisco Bay from the Pacific Ocean. San Francisco is characterized by diverse ethnic neighborhoods; a large harbor, fine Victorian-era architecture; a cool, foggy climate; and hilly topography. **Situation**, or **relative location**, describes a place's relationship to other places around it. San Francisco is the economic capitol of northern California and the center of a large metropolitan area containing more than 6 million people. To its east lie the San Francisco Bay and the cities of Oakland and Berkeley, to its west is the Pacific Ocean, to the north is Marin County, and to the south is the sprawling South Bay metropolis. The city of San Francisco forms a boundary between the culturally and climatically distinct regions of central and northern California.

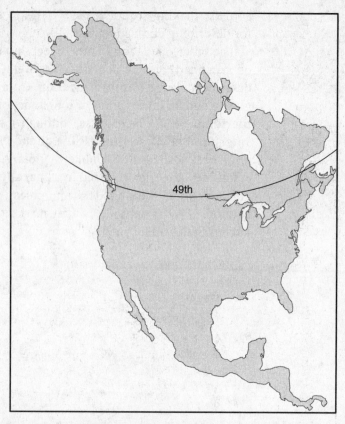

49th

Figure 2.9. The 49th parallel forms a political boundary between the western United States and Canada, though it has no relationship to natural features.

There are numerous ways to characterize distance between places. One way geographers think about distance is by quantifying it as an exact measurement in standard units, which is referred to as the **absolute distance** between places. Bangor, Maine, for example, is 130 miles northeast of Portland, Maine. Although it is important to know absolute distances, **relative distance** measures are often much more meaningful. One way to think about relative distance is through the concept of **connectivity**, or **topological space**. The notion of topological space is important in human geography because the absolute distance between places is often not an accurate characterization of their social, cultural, political, or economic connectivity. Some places that are close together in absolute distance are actually less *connected* than other places that are farther apart. For example, Honolulu, Hawaii, is thousands of miles away from the American mainland and yet it is very closely connected, culturally and economically, to cities like Los Angeles and San Diego, and with the larger American culture in general. Quite the opposite, Havana, Cuba, is less than 200 miles from Key West, Florida; yet the two places could hardly seem more remote. Two other distance measures, time and money, are related to this notion of connectivity. Often, the distances between two places are described in terms of the amount of time or money it takes to get between them rather than by a standard unit of measurement. For example, when asked how far it is from your home to your school, you might be more likely to give a time unit such as 10 minutes, rather than a distance unit such as 1.5 miles. Another important concept surrounding current conversations of relative distance measures is that of **time-space convergence.** This idea states that with

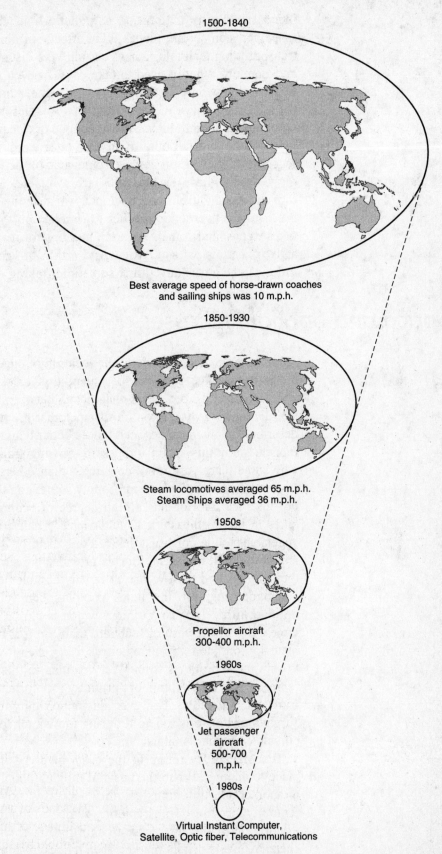

1500-1840

Best average speed of horse-drawn coaches
and sailing ships was 10 m.p.h.

1850-1930

Steam locomotives averaged 65 m.p.h.
Steam Ships averaged 36 m.p.h.

1950s

Propellor aircraft
300-400 m.p.h.

1960s

Jet passenger
aircraft
500-700
m.p.h.

1980s

Virtual Instant Computer,
Satellite, Optic fiber, Telecommunications

Figure 2.10. Throughout history, improvements in technology have "shrunk" the size of the earth in terms of the amount of time it takes to travel to distant places and communicate with distant people.

increasing transportation and communication technology, the absolute distance between certain places is, in effect, shrinking. For example, increased transportation technology has "shrunk" the distance between New York City and London. When it used to take days, or even weeks, to cross the Atlantic by boat, it now only takes half a day by plane. And while it used to take weeks for a letter to arrive in Paris from Los Angeles, residents in these cities can now instantly communicate via telephone or e-mail. Thus, certain places *seem* much closer to each other than they once were. However, it is important to recognize that this process is somewhat limited to developed parts of the globe where these technologies are available. Many developing countries remain "distant" from the developed world, in the sense that absolute distance must still be overcome in order for interaction to occur. For example, it still takes weeks, and sometimes even months, for mail originating in America to arrive in certain parts of Africa. And within Africa, traveling a couple hundred miles can be a true adventure, sometimes taking days to complete.

Space and Spatial Processes

After geographers understand the location of specific features and places on the earth's surface, they can then spend time investigating the spatial associations and spatial processes that occur between places at different scales. Recall from the discussion on distance that the notion of connectivity often describes the distance between places better than an absolute measure. Geographers study this spatial process borrowing from economics to understand why some places are more connected than others. **Complementarity** is the degree to which one place can supply something that another place demands. For instance, Florida has a high degree of economic complementarity with cities in the northeastern United States because it supplies fresh fruits and vegetables to the northeast that can only be grown in Florida's warm subtropical climate. In this case, Florida provides the supply, the northeast provides the demand, and the two are extremely complementary. A second idea from economic geography that helps to explain connectivity is that of **intervening opportunities**. If West Virginia, which is closer in absolute distance to the large cities of the eastern seaboard than Florida, had a warm subtropical climate appropriate for growing citrus fruits, then it would probably make sense to ship those products from West Virginia. In this case, West Virginia would represent an intervening opportunity for northeasterners to acquire fresh fruits and vegetables. However, this opportunity does not exist because West Virginia's climate is too cold during the winter for the production of warm-climate crops like oranges.

Transferability refers to the costs involved in moving goods from one place to another. When the costs of moving people or goods from one place to another are high, transferability decreases, but when costs are low, transferability increases. Transferability can be a function of the product itself. For example, it makes less sense to ship fertilizer, which is heavy to move and cheap to buy, to distant markets then it does to ship computer chips, which are small, lightweight, and expensive to purchase. Computer chips are cheap to ship and profitable to sell. This, in part, explains why so many computer chips can be made in one place, like California's Silicon Valley, and then shipped all over the world, while fertilizer is usually produced and sold locally. Transferability also relates to other factors like transportation. Interstate highways, railroads, and shipping routes make some places highly accessible and decrease the transferability costs of transporting products to those places. People who live in Alaska often complain that food in their grocery stores is more expensive than in the contiguous United States. The fact that food in Alaska is expensive is partly due to the high costs associated with transporting goods over great distances to "the last frontier." Thus, **accessibility** is an important factor in the cost of goods and services and in the interaction between places.

The concepts discussed in this section help to describe connectivity between places, independent of their absolute distance apart. One should not forget, however, that absolute distance is *the* single most important overarching determinant of spatial interaction.

Tobler's First Law of Geography
Everything is related to everything else, but near things are more related than distant things.

Tobler's first law of geography describes a concept referred to as the **friction of distance**. In other words, distance itself hinders interaction between places. The farther two places are apart, the greater the hindrance. For example, you might walk a couple of blocks to grab a sandwich, but you probably would not walk all the way across town. You might drive to the neighboring town to see a concert of your favorite band, but you probably would not drive across the country.

The friction of distance causes what geographers call a **distance decay effect**. Consider a group of people eating in a restaurant in your hometown. If you did a survey, you would probably find that a large number of these people lived relatively close to the restaurant. There would also be several people who did not live too close but were from the same region. Maybe they live in a neighboring town. There would probably be fewer people who lived far away in another state—perhaps they were in town on business or visiting friends and family. Finally, if you were lucky, you might find a few people who lived very far away, in another country in another part of the world. Although this example might not work in some places, such as inner city neighborhoods full of recent immigrants, it does work in most cases, and it exemplifies the concept of distance decay. You have less of a chance of eating dinner in a restaurant next to someone who lives far away than next to someone who lives close by.

One interesting twist on this concept of spatial interaction is the **gravity model**, which was first described in the 1850s and is based on Isaac Newton's law of universal gravitation. According to Newton, the degree to which objects are attracted to each other by gravity is a result of the product of their respective masses, divided the square of their distance apart. The gravity model in geography applies this exact formulation to the spatial interaction of various population centers. In the gravity model, population substitutes for gravity. Thus, the interaction between two places is equal to the product of the places' populations, divided by the square of their distance apart.

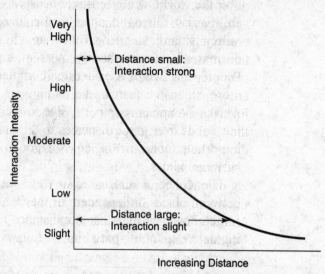

Figure 2.11. Generally, when phenomena are close together in absolute distance, they tend to interact closely, whereas objects farther apart interact less. Of course, this general rule has many exceptions.

The Gravity Model

$$I_{ij} = \frac{P_i P_j}{D_{ij}^2}$$

where

I_{ij} = the interaction between places i and j

P_i = the population of place i

P_j = the population of place j

D_{ij}^2 = the distance between places i and j, squared

One implication of this equation is that large cities may still have extensive and important interactions, despite being separated by great distances. Los Angeles and New York are excellent examples of two highly connected large cities that are on opposite sides of a continent. Their extremely large populations, when multiplied together in the numerator, are large enough to overcome the distance between them, represented in the denominator.

Another insight that arises from this general line of thinking is that large cities seem to have a greater "gravitational pull" for individual people than small ones. This makes intuitive sense because large cities provide diverse opportunities for employment, education, products, and services, which smaller towns usually cannot provide. This phenomenon was described formally in 1931 in the **law of retail gravitation**. This law basically states that people will be drawn to larger cities to conduct their business because larger cities have a wider influence on the hinterlands that surround them. The outer edge of a city's sphere of influence is called the **breaking point**. Beyond the breaking point, another city's sphere of influence begins.

Spatial diffusion is an extremely important concept in human geography for it describes the ways in which phenomena, such as technological innovations, cultural trends, or even outbreaks of disease, travel over space. Geographers have identified two main types of spatial diffusion processes. In **expansion**

diffusion, the thing or process being spread remains in the area of origin as well as spreads to surrounding areas. Expansion diffusion takes two main forms: contagious and hierarchical diffusion. In **contagious diffusion**, something is transmitted over space because people who carry it are close to each other. The common cold is transmitted from place to place simply because people are close enough to each other to pass along air-borne germs. **Hierarchical diffusion** involves the transmission of a phenomenon from one place to another because the level of interaction between places overcomes the actual distance between them. Hierarchical diffusion processes strongly correlate with interaction levels calculated in the gravity model in the previous section. Places with higher levels of interaction, such as New York and Los Angeles, are the first to adopt trends in music, fashion, and art. Not far behind are those who live in other cosmopolitan urban centers, such as Chicago, San Francisco, Seattle, and Boston. These cities have much in common, including large populations of young people, diverse ethnic neighborhoods, and high concentrations of theaters, concert halls, recording studios, museums, and universities, which may explain why they are the first to adopt new cultural trends. Finally, the other major diffusion type, **relocation diffusion** occurs when people migrate from one place to another, bringing with them cultural traditions from their previous homelands. In the early 1900s, millions of people migrated to the United States from Europe, bringing with them the diverse languages, culinary delights, and social traditions that characterize the American cultural landscape today.

The concepts of distance decay and friction of distance discussed earlier, play a large role in the rate of acceptance of certain trends and innovations as they diffuse across space. Additionally, certain physical and social barriers prohibit the adoption of particular traits in particular areas. Some religious traditions, such as Islam, have strong regulations regarding dress and thus the latest fashion trends are not diffused into dominantly Muslim areas. Also, many countries strive to maintain a common, unified culture and limit the acceptance of certain innovations that harm their unique cultural heritage and language system. Similarly, physical barriers such as mountains or rivers might prohibit the transmission of new innovations to isolated areas. These impediments to diffusion help explain why some places on the earth's surface that have few regulations or barriers interfering with diffusion processes appear so socially and culturally diverse, while other areas remain rather homogenous in their social and ethnic makeup.

Geographers, as scientists and researchers of all the processes that occur on the earth's surface, have a tremendous and wildly varied amount of information to investigate, explain, and communicate. To do their job effectively, they must make difficult cartographical decisions and have a complete understanding of the organization of space. In this chapter, you have explored how space is described in terms of location and distance and how these two concepts help to determine the interactions that occur between places.

Key Terms Defined

Absolute distance The distance that can be measured with a standard unit of length, such as a mile or kilometer.

Absolute location The exact position of an object or place, measured within the spatial coordinates of a grid system.

Accessibility The relative ease with which a destination may be reached from some other place.

Azimuthal projection A map projection in which the plane is the most developable surface.

Breaking point The outer edge of a city's sphere of influence, used in the law of retail gravitation to describe the area of a city's hinterlands that depend on that city for its retail supply.

Cartograms A type of thematic map that transforms space such that the political unit with the greatest value for some type of data is represented by the largest relative area.

Choropleth map A thematic map that uses tones or colors to represent spatial data as average values per unit area.

Cognitive map An image of a portion of the earth's surface that an individual creates in his or her mind. Cognitive maps can include knowledge of actual locations and relationships between locations as well as personal perceptions and preferences of particular places.

Complementarity The actual or potential relationship between two places, usually referring to economic interactions.

Connectivity The degree of economic, social, cultural, or political connection between two places.

Contagious diffusion The spread of a disease, innovation, or cultural traits through direct contact with another person or another place.

Coordinate system A standard grid, composed of lines of latitude and longitude, used to determine the absolute location of any object, place, or feature on the earth's surface.

Distance decay effect The decrease in interaction between two phenomena, places, or people as the distance between them increases.

Dot maps Thematic maps that use points to show the precise locations of specific observations or occurrences, such as crimes, car accidents, or births.

MAPS, SCALE, SPACE, AND PLACE 67

Expansion diffusion The spread of ideas, innovations, fashion, or other phenomena to surrounding areas through contact and exchange.

Friction of distance A measure of how much absolute distance affects the interaction between two places.

Fuller projection A type of map projection that maintains the accurate size and shape of landmasses but completely rearranges direction such that the four cardinal directions—north, south, east, and west—no longer have any meaning.

Geoid The actual shape of the earth, which is rough and oblate, or slightly squashed; the earth's circumference is longer around the equator then it is along the meridians, from north-south circumference.

Gravity model A mathematical formula that describes the level of interaction between two places, based on the size of their populations and their distance from each other.

Hazards Anything in the landscape, real or perceived, that is potentially threatening. Hazards are usually avoided in spatial behavior.

Hierarchical diffusion A type of diffusion in which something is transmitted between places because of something the two places have in common.

International Date Line The line of longitude that marks where each new day begins, centered on the 180th meridian.

Intervening opportunities The idea that one place has a demand for some good or service and two places have a supply of equal price and quality, then the closer of the two suppliers to the buyer will represent an intervening opportunity, thereby blocking the third from being able to share its supply of goods or services. Intervening opportunities are frequently utilized because transportation costs usually decrease with proximity.

Isoline Map line that connects points of equal or very similar values.

Large-scale A relatively small ratio between map units and ground units. Large-scale maps usually have higher resolution and cover much smaller regions than small-scale maps.

Latitude The angular distance north or south of the equator, defined by lines of latitude, or parallels.

Law of retail gravitation Law that states that people will be drawn to larger cities to conduct their business because larger cities have a wider influence on the hinterlands that surround them.

Location charts On a map, a chart or graph that gives specific statistical information of a particular political unit or jurisdiction.

Longitude The angular distance east or west of the prime meridian, defined by lines of longitude, or meridians.

Map projection A mathematical method that involves transferring the earth's sphere onto a flat surface. This term can also be used to describe the type of map that results from the process of projecting. All map projections have distortions in either area, direction, distance, or shape.

Mercator projection A true conformal cylindrical map projection, the Mercator projection is particularly useful for navigation because it maintains accurate direction. Mercator projections are famous for their distortion in area that makes landmasses at the poles appear oversized.

Meridian A line of longitude that runs north-south. All lines of longitude are equal in length and intersect at the poles.

Parallel An east-west line of latitude that runs parallel to the equator and that marks distance north or south of the equator.

Preference map A map that displays individual preferences for certain places.

Prime meridian An imaginary line passing through the Royal Observatory in Greenwich, England, which marks the 0° line of longitude.

Proportional symbols map A thematic map in which the size of a chosen symbol—such as a circle or triangle—indicates the relative magnitude of some statistical value for a given geographic region.

Reference map A map type that shows reference information for a particular place, making it useful for finding landmarks and for navigating.

Relative distance A measure of distance that includes the costs of overcoming the friction of absolute distance separating two places. Often relative distance describes the amount of social, cultural, or economic connectivity between two places.

Relative location The position of a place relative to places around it.

Relocation diffusion The diffusion of ideas, innovations, behaviors, and the like from one place to another through migration.

Resolution A map's smallest discernable unit. If, for example, an object has to be one kilometer long in order to show up on a map, then that map's resolution is one kilometer.

Robinson projection Projection that attempts to balance several possible projection errors. It does not maintain completely accurate area, shape, distance, or direction, but it minimizes errors in each.

MAPS, SCALE, SPACE, AND PLACE 69

Scale The ratio between the size of an area on a map and the actual size of that same area on the earth's surface.

Site The absolute location of a place, described by local relief, landforms, and other cultural or physical characteristics.

Situation The relative location of a place in relation to the physical and cultural characteristics of the surrounding area and the connections and interdependencies within that system; a place's spatial context.

Small-scale Map scale ratio in which the ratio of units on the map to units on the earth is quite small. Small-scale maps usually depict large areas.

Spatial diffusion Spatial diffusion refers to the ways in which phenomena, such as technological innovations, cultural trends, or even outbreaks of disease, travel over space.

Thematic map A type of map that displays one or more variables—such as population, or income level—within a specific area.

Time-space convergence The idea that distance between some places is actually shrinking as technology enables more rapid communication and increased interaction between those places.

Topographic maps Maps that use isolines to represent constant elevations. If you took a topographic map out into the field and walked exactly along the path of an isoline on your map, you would always stay at the same elevation.

Topological space The amount of connectivity between places, regardless of the absolute distance separating them.

Transferability The costs involved in moving goods from one place to another.

Visualization Use of sophisticated software to create dynamic computer maps, some of which are three-dimensional or interactive.

Sample Questions and Answers

Section 1: Map Fundamentals

Multiple-Choice Questions

1. The ratio between distance on a map and distance on the earth's surface is called the

   (A) projection.
   (B) resolution.
   (C) scale.
   (D) azimuth.
   (E) aggregation.

2. Cartography is the science of

   (A) demographics.
   (B) map-making.
   (C) spatial orientation.
   (D) cognitive imagery.
   (E) making visualizations.

3. Map projections attempt to correct for errors in

   (A) transferability.
   (B) area, distance, scale, and proportion.
   (C) area, distance, shape, and direction.
   (D) distance, proximity, and topology.
   (E) distance, shape, and lines of latitude and longitude.

4. The Mercator projection preserves

   (A) direction.
   (B) area.
   (C) shape.
   (D) scale.
   (E) distance.

5. Topographic maps must use which of the following symbols?

   (A) Tonal shadings
   (B) Isolines
   (C) Proportional symbols
   (D) Location charts
   (E) Cartograms

6. Which of the following map projections preserves the correct shape of the earth's landmasses?

   (A) Fuller's Dymaxion
   (B) Mercator
   (C) Robinson
   (D) Mollewide
   (E) Smithsonian

7. The size of a map's smallest discernable unit is its

   (A) scale.
   (B) density.
   (C) region.
   (D) resolution.
   (E) projection.

Free-Response Question

1. Scale is an extremely important concept in geography because spatial relationships appear to vary depending upon the scale at which they are measured.

   (a) Define scale, and discuss the relationship of scale to resolution.
   (b) Discuss the role of scale in interpreting geographical information.
   (c) In the 2000 election, George W. Bush won the electoral votes of every southern state. Explain how an analysis of these results at the county level could yield valuable additional information about voting patterns at finer geographic scales.

Section 2: Cognitive Maps

Multiple-Choice Questions

1. Which of the following is false regarding cognitive maps?

   (A) They accurately reflect mapped hazards.
   (B) They guide spatial behavior.
   (C) They vary between people of different social and educational backgrounds.
   (D) They enable people to navigate through space.
   (E) No two cognitive maps look the same.

   2. Preference maps of the United States tend to show that

   (A) people prefer the Old South.
   (B) people dislike crowded West Coast cities.
   (C) people tend to dislike states or regions bordering their own.
   (D) people look unfavorably upon their own home towns.
   (E) people prefer humid climates.

   3. Which of the following features would NOT be included on a cognitive map?

   (A) Areas where traffic jams are common
   (B) Landmarks
   (C) Distribution of universities
   (D) Location of the nearest gas station
   (E) Location of places commonly visited

   4. According to most preference maps of the United States, which state of the five would be least preferred by the overall U.S. population?

   (A) California
   (B) Colorado
   (C) South Carolina
   (D) Florida
   (E) New York

Free-Response Question

   1. What makes some places more attractive to live in than others? Are certain types of places more attractive for certain types of people? Use your knowledge of preference maps in your answer.

Section 3: Describing Location

Multiple-Choice Questions

   1. Seattle is located on Puget Sound in northwestern Washington. It has a moist, marine climate, a large university, and a famous downtown market. Seattle's primary economic activities include ship and aircraft construction and high-technology enterprises. This information gives us a description of Seattle's

   (A) situation.
   (B) cognitive image.
   (C) site.
   (D) landscape.
   (E) relative distance.

2. Lines of longitude

   (A) never meet.
   (B) begin at the equator.
   (C) are referred to as parallels.
   (D) intersect at the poles.
   (E) contain the two tropics.

3. Even though some cities are far apart in terms of absolute distance, they are actually quite connected economically and socially. This is representative of

   (A) topographic space.
   (B) cognitive space.
   (C) topological space.
   (D) relative location.
   (E) situation.

4. Which of the following is a true statement regarding time-space convergence?

   (A) Places seem to all look the same.
   (B) Places seem to be getting closer together.
   (C) Places are increasingly concentrated on maintaining their histories.
   (D) Places are making more of an effort to converge activities to save time.
   (E) Places are implementing more rapid forms of transportation.

5. Which of the following is not a measure of relative distance?

   (A) 2,339 centimeters
   (B) 35 seconds
   (C) Two dollars and fifty cents
   (D) 216 footsteps
   (E) 15 minutes

Free-Response Question

1. The notion of time-space convergence has had dramatic impacts on how geographers think of distance.

   (a) Define time-space convergence, and give examples of this process at work in the world today.
   (b) Describe the effects of this convergence on the level of connectivity between places. Does the process connect all areas of the globe?
   (c) Discuss Tobler's first law of geography as it relates to the notion of time-space convergence? Does this law still apply and/or will it apply in the future?

Section 4: Space and Spatial Processes

Multiple-Choice Questions

1. Tobler's first law of geography states that "Everything is related to everything else, but

   (A) distant things are generally unrelated."
   (B) near things are more closely related than you might think."
   (C) distance is always a factor."
   (D) near things are more related than distant things."
   (E) distance is relative."

2. Rap music first appeared in New York in the 1970s. Later, it spread to large cities with vibrant African-American populations—such as Los Angeles, Oakland, Chicago and Detroit—without being absorbed by the smaller cities and rural areas in between. This type of spatial diffusion is called

   (A) relocation potential.
   (B) hierarchical diffusion.
   (C) contagious diffusion.
   (D) cultural diffusion.
   (E) cascade diffusion.

3. Stores and restaurants in Oregon that find it cheaper to buy fresh vegetables grown in California than those grown in Florida are taking advantage of

   (A) expansion diffusion.
   (B) distance decay.
   (C) economies of scale.
   (D) intervening opportunities.
   (E) retail gravitation.

4. According to the gravity model, which two places are most likely to have a high level of interaction?

   (A) Two cities with very large populations but separated by the Atlantic Ocean like New York and London
   (B) Two cities with medium populations separated by a whole continent like Grand Rapids, Michigan, and Gulf Shores, Alabama
   (C) Two cities with small populations that are relatively close together like Richmond and Winchester, Kentucky
   (D) Two cities, one with a large population and the other with a medium population, that are very close in distance, like Seattle and Tacoma, Washington
   (E) Two cities with medium populations that are relatively close to each other like Akron, Ohio, and Springfield, Missouri

5. Which of the following is NOT a good example of a barrier to spatial diffusion?

(A) A mountain range
(B) A different language
(C) A different dietary preference
(D) A highway system
(E) A strict religious system

Free-Response Question

1. Geographers define space, location, and distance according to both absolute and relative measures.

(a) Describe the difference between absolute and relative measures of distance.
(b) Give two examples of instances where the degree of interaction between places is more related to connectivity than to absolute distance.
(c) Describe the difference between absolute and relative measures of location. Give examples.

Answers for Multiple-Choice Questions

Section 1: Map Fundamentals

1. **(C)** In cartography, scale refers to the ratio of map distance to distance on the earth surface. Large-scale maps have a large ratio, such as 1:2,000, and small-scale maps have a small ratio, such as 1:200,000.

2. **(B)** Cartography is the science of map-making and cartographers are the scientists who make maps. Geographers who make maps are cartographers as well.

3. **(C)** Map projections represent attempts by cartographers to correct for the simple geometrical fact that a spherical or geoidal surface, such as the earth, cannot be accurately depicted on a two-dimensional surface. Map projections attempt to correct for errors in the area and shape of features on the earth's surface, errors in the distance between places, and errors in the compass direction from one place to another.

4. **(A)** The Mercator projection accurately preserves compass direction. However, because the lines of longitude do not meet at the poles in the Mercator projection as they do on the surface of the earth, area is distorted, with increasing inaccuracy at high latitudes.

5. **(B)** Isolines, or contours, are lines of equal value. Isolines are used on topographic maps to show the locations of places with equal elevation. Isolines are also commonly used for maps that represent spatial densities, such as population density or pollution concentration.

6. **(A)**   The Fuller projection correctly preserves area and shape, although distance and direction are distorted severely.

7. **(D)**   Resolution is important in geography since the smallest discernable unit is directly related both to the map's scale and to the amount of spatial data that can be displayed. Generally, large-scale maps have a greater resolution, although this is not always the case.

Section 2: Cognitive Maps

1. **(A)**   Cognitive maps reflect the presence of *perceived* hazards, such as dangerous intersections or high-crime neighborhoods. Such hazards may be real or imaginary.

2. **(C)**   Most people's preference maps of the United States tend to show a "border effect." Regions neighboring the subject's home region tend to score low, while the home region itself scores high. It appears that people will differentiate their own home regions from the ones next door. This differentiation indicates the formation of a regional identity.

3. **(C)**   The cognitive map is an individual's representation of a particular place that exists in that individual's mind. The individual uses the cognitive map to navigate between places and, as such, will not calculate the distributions of particular features (such as universities) over a particular space.

4. **(C)**   While most people when asked which state they prefer the most are likely to answer with the state they live in, preference maps tend to show a strong preference for California, Colorado, Florida, and New York regardless of the location of the individual being questioned.

Section 3: Describing Location

1. **(C)**   Site is a description of the qualities of a place, independent of that place's relationship to other places around it. Situation refers to a place's relationship to the other places around it.

2. **(D)**   All latitudes are parallel, but all lines of longitude converge at the North and South Poles. In many map projections—such as the Mercator projection—longitude lines do not converge at the poles as they do on the globe; this causes geographical features at high latitudes to be warped and to appear larger than they actually are.

3. **(C)**   Topological space describes the level of connectivity between places. While some places may be quite far from each other, in actuality they might be quite close in terms of the economic, social, and cultural relationships between them. New York and Los Angeles are much more connected in terms of economic and cultural relationships than Los Angeles and Lincoln, Nebraska even though Nebraska is much closer in absolute distance.

4. **(B)** Time-space convergence is the notion that distance between places seems to be "shrinking" with increased transportation and communication technology.

5. **(A)** The centimeter is an absolute distance measure with a standard unit of measurement. All the other options are relative measures, including the footstep option. While footsteps are a distance measure, they are not a standard unit of measure in use across the globe.

Section 4: Space and Spatial Processes

1. **(D)** Tobler's *First Law of Geography* expresses the concept of distance decay. Generally, things are less related the farther they are away from each other in absolute space.

2. **(B)** Hierarchical diffusion is the form of spatial diffusion that occurs when a phenomenon spreads from one place to another because the places have something in common. Large cities were the first to adopt rap music. Rap later spread to medium and small cities across the United States, but it has yet to be fully absorbed into many rural areas.

3. **(D)** An intervening opportunity exists when a closer source is available for the supply of some desired good or service. All else being equal, people tend to prefer closer sources of goods and services to those farther away.

4. **(D)** The gravity model predicts the level of interaction between two cities in terms of their populations and distances apart from one another. The correct option has a very large numerator (product of both populations) and a very small denominator (distance between Seattle and Tacoma) thus the resulting level of interaction will be quite high.

5. **(D)** A highway system facilitates diffusion because it connects places, whereas the other four options prevent certain innovations and cultural traits from spreading.

Answers for Free-Response Questions

Section 1: Map Fundamentals

1. Main points:
   • Map scale is the ratio between distance on a map and distance on the earth's surface. Small-scale maps have a small distance ratio and tend to represent larger geographical areas. Large-scale maps have a larger distance ratio and tend to depict smaller areas.
   • Resolution, which is the smallest discernable unit on a map, tends to decrease in smaller-scale maps and increase in larger-scale maps. This is why larger-scale maps, which tend to cover smaller regions also have more detail. Small-scale maps that cover large regions tend to have lower resolution and, as a result, less detail.

- Scale is very important in interpreting geographical information for several reasons. One example of the importance of scale in geography involves the relationship between scale and resolution. If you analyze geographical information from too small a scale, you might lose valuable information only apparent at smaller scales and higher resolution. Conversely, by looking at geographical information from too large a scale, you can lose sight of the bigger context. Consider a map of the dominant regional religions drawn at a relatively small scale and depicting the entire United States. This map will show that, in much of southern California, Catholicism is the dominant regional religion. However, a larger-scale, higher-resolution map of religion in southern California will show that the region contains an extremely diverse population with a multitude of religious beliefs and practices displaying significant spatial variation. In this way the larger-scale, higher-resolution map gives more detailed information, while the smaller-scale, lower-resolution map places that information within a more general regional context.
- In the United States, electoral votes are apportioned by state. When a candidate wins a state, all of that state's electoral votes are given to the single winning candidate, no matter how close the total vote count or how significant the spatial variation in voting patterns across the state. An examination of voting patterns in the southeastern states by county renders some extremely interesting geographical information. First, Al Gore won many urban counties in and around large metropolitan areas such as Miami, Atlanta, Memphis, and Raleigh-Durham. Second, Gore won many rural counties with predominantly African-American populations. Although George W. Bush won all the southern states, voting patterns within those states was quite irregular, and Gore succeeded in many urban and minority-dominated districts. A closer look at the southeastern states by county reveals that some geographic patterns in voting are not evident at the level of the state; this is an example of the importance of geographic scale in voting representation.

Section 2: Cognitive Maps

1. Main points:
   - Several factors; including economic, recreational, and educational opportunities; cultural attractions; and climate combine to make some places more attractive to live in than others.
   - Most people tend to like the place in which they live. However, most people also usually rate the areas neighboring their own low in terms of desirability. This is called a boundary effect and is part of a sense of place.
   - In the United States, people also tend to rate certain regions high, no matter where they live. The West Coast states of California, Oregon, Washington usually rank high, as do Colorado, Arizona, Texas, Florida, and New York.
   - Young people also tend to rate urban areas higher because they offer more jobs and cultural amenities.

Section 3: Describing Location

1. Main points:
   - Time-space convergence is the idea that distance between places is, in effect, shrinking due to certain transportation and communications technologies. In today's world, instant communication with many parts of the globe is possible thanks to the telephone and computer. If you ask individuals in developed parts of the world where they have traveled, it is not nearly as uncommon as it once was to hear that people are traveling all across their countries, and even all across the globe. When it once took days and even months to travel to other continents, it can now happen at very rapid speeds.
   - Connectivity between places increases rapidly as the result of the development of better mechanisms for establishing connections between places. Communications technologies such as telephone, Internet, and fax machines allow cities all across the globe to connect with one another instantaneously, thereby increasing and strengthening the level of interaction and connectivity between places. Furthermore, distance between places used to inhibit interaction between them. Rapid transportation removes this obstacle, allowing greater connectivity between places. However, it is important to recognize that only a certain network of places is, in fact, converging. Large parts of the developing world do not have access to these technologies making it difficult for interaction to occur.
   - Tobler's first law states that everything is related but near things are more closely related than far things. With the increased levels of connectivity occurring between certain places as a result of time-reducing technologies, certain places that are far apart are becoming more related than some places that might be closer together. As the world becomes increasingly interconnected, we will probably see this law continue to lose potency as distance loses its ability to impede interactions between certain places.

Section 4: Space and Spatial Processes

1. Main points:
   - Absolute measures of distance involve numerical computations in units such as meters or miles.
   - Connectivity, often referred to as topological space, describes the degree of interaction between places, independent of their absolute distance apart.
   - It is possible for two places that are relatively far apart in absolute distance to have a high degree of connectivity. Connectivity can result from the easy transferability of goods and services, from economic complementarity, or from the absence of intervening opportunities for economic interaction. Other cultural, historical, or political factors also contribute to connectivity.
   - One example of the interaction between places being more related to connectivity than to absolute distance involves the production and dis-

tribution of agricultural products. Historically, the vast agricultural regions of the Midwest and Great Plains have had a high degree of economic complementarity with the city of Chicago. This is due to the fact that, during the 19th century, Chicago became the primary center for the sale, processing, and distribution of agricultural products grown in the rural hinterlands—the region that was then called the Great West. In this way, Chicago had a high degree of connectivity with agricultural regions that were quite far away in absolute distance.

• A second example of high connectivity independent of absolute distance is the establishment of ethnic enclaves in cities such as New York and Boston during the great period of immigration that occurred in America around the beginning of the 20th century. New York, for instance, had large neighborhoods dominated by immigrants of common ethnicity, heritage and national origin, such as Chinatown and Little Italy. The people living in these neighborhoods often retained a high degree of social, cultural, and economic connectivity with the families and friends they had left behind in Europe and Asia.

• A place's absolute location, or site, is defined by its characteristics, independent of the place's relationship to other places around it. For example, Mexico City is located in south-central Mexico at approximately 19°N latitude and about 7,200 ft. elevation. Mexico City is a large, sprawling, and crowded metropolis; it is the center of Mexico's economic activities and the capital of the Mexican federal government.

• Situation refers to a place's location and function relative to other places around it. Tijuana, Mexico, is located in Baja California Norte on the Pacific Ocean directly south of the United States/Mexico border. As a major center of international trade and manufacturing, Tijuana serves as the industrial capital of northwestern Mexico, with close economic ties to large U.S. cities such as Los Angeles, San Diego, and Phoenix.

Additional Resources

Text

Hanson, Susan (ed.). 1997. *Ten Geographic Ideas That Changed the World*. New Brunswick, New Jersey: Rutgers University Press.

An excellent book that covers various types of maps and various types of map-making. Consisting of ten chapters, by ten different authors, a wide variety of perspectives discuss a range of cartographic issues from reading weather maps to understanding GIS.

Monmonier, Mark. 1995. *Drawing the Line: Tales of Maps and Cartocontroversy*. New York: Henry Holt.

Monmonier loves to discuss the deceptive powers of maps. In this book, he looks at some historical decisions based on maps that had false details. He discusses how the cartographer's bias manifests itself in many different historically popular maps, and how many political decisions have been made using maps that portrayed information in an inaccurate manner.

Monmonier, Mark. 1991. *How to Lie With Maps*. Chicago: University of Chicago Press.

Similar to his other book, *Drawing the Line: Tales of Maps and Cartocontroversy,* Monmonier, discusses how people accept maps as objective models of reality, when in actuality they present many forms of deception that most map-readers never recognize. He encourages a healthy skepticism of maps, and discusses how to be a critical evaluator of cartographical information.

Web

Hammond, Inc. *On Map Projections: http://www.hammondmap.com.*

If you are a teacher looking for maps for your classroom, this provides all different types of maps for all places across the globe. If you do not yet have a good world map in your classroom, it would be a good idea to purchase one before teaching this class, and you can even get an educator's discount on the website.

National Geographic Society. *Round Earth, Flat Maps: http://www.nationalgeographic.com/maps/*

This is an excellent site for finding all kinds of maps, including maps that will be useful for understanding other subjects discussed in this book. The search engine allows you to find maps of specific places, printer-friendly maps of every continent, topographic maps, and lesson plans on map skills for educators. The best feature is the Atlas of the World in which you have several different options, one of which is to look at various thematic maps of the United States showing different political and cultural features such as toxic waste sites.

The Great Gallery (of Maps): *http://hum.amu.edu.pl/~zbzw/glob/glob1.htm*

This site provides numerous links to all different kinds of maps, with several excellent links on different types of map projections. Many of the maps relate to physical geography, but they also have good maps of human geography (i.e., the diffusion of the Internet). The site also contains a link to websites for educators that specifically provides lesson plans and activity ideas for teachers, does not strictly apply to geography, but does contain some geography-related sites.

U.S. Geological Survey. *Map Projections*: *http://mac.usgs.gov/mac/isb/pubs/MapProjections/projections.html*

One of the best sources on projections, it tells you all about different types of map projections, how they are made, what they preserve and distort, and what types of projections are good for what purposes.

University of Texas Digital Map Library:*www.lib.utexas.edu/Libs/PCL/ Map_collection/map_sites/map_sites.html*

This site contains an exhaustive listing of general map sites with options to additional pages on city, state, country, historical, and weather map sites, and "cartographic references" contains different projection types. In general, it is an excellent site that could be used at any time during the course to access maps on different subjects related to each of the content areas.

Cartography Lab, University of Utrecht: *http://oddens.geog.uu.nl/index.html*

This site provides links to all different kinds of maps and cartographic resources including map sellers, cartographic societies, and universities with cartography departments. If you are looking for different kinds of maps, the library at the University of Texas is a better source.

GIS links: *www.geo.ed.ac.uk/home/giswww.html*

This site houses hundreds of links relating to GIS listed in alphabetical order. It is a great source for finding an interesting case study to make GIS more relevant and interesting for both students and teachers.

CHAPTER 3
Population Geography

Summary

During the past two centuries, the world's human population has exploded. The causes, mechanisms, and consequences of this tremendous increase are multifaceted. Population geographers collect demographic data and use mathematical equations to understand trends in population growth and to make predictions about the future. Population growth and population density both vary dramatically over space—some countries are not growing at all while others are doubling their populations every couple decades. The fastest growing countries are also among the poorest, and in many cases rapid population growth has led to severe environmental degradation and human suffering. However, environmental problems are not simply a function of population growth; they also result from the overconsumption of resources. Consequently, issues regarding population, consumption, social justice, and environmental sustainability provide geographers with many fascinating and complex questions.

In This Chapter

- Human Population: A Global Perspective
- Population Parameters and Processes
- Human Migration
- Population Structure and Composition
- Population Sustainability

Key Terms

Age-sex distribution	Demography
Baby boom	Dependency ratio
Baby bust	Doubling time
Carrying capacity	Emigration
Chain migration	Exponential growth
Cohort	Forced migration
Cotton Belt	Generation X
Crude birth rate	Immigration
Crude death rate	Infant mortality rate
Demographic accounting equation	Internal migration
Demographic transition model	Life expectancy

Thomas Malthus

Migration

Natural increase rate

Neo-Malthusian

Overpopulation

Population density

Population geography

Population pyramid

Pull factor

Push factor

Refugees

Rust Belt

Sun Belt

Total fertility rate

Voluntary migration

Zero population growth

Human Population: A Global Perspective

Sometime in October of 1999 the world's population reached 6 billion people. It is hard to comprehend a number like 6 billion, but even dizzying numbers do little to illustrate the immensity and diversity of the human endeavor here on earth. Perhaps even more astounding than the sheer number of people alive today is the rate at which human population has increased during the past 200 years. According to the United Nations Population Division, it wasn't until 1804 that world population reached 1 billion. It took just 123 years for that population to double, reaching 2 billion by 1927. Forty-seven years later, in 1974, the population had once again doubled, and by 2000, 6 billion people inhabited the earth. Projections indicate that the world population will reach 7 billion by 2013.

Staggering human population growth is one of the defining characteristics of our present era in world history; it is also one of the most important issues in all of human geography. To explain this amazing and rapid growth, and to begin to understand its implications, we must ask difficult questions about politics, culture, economics, and history. Why is the population growing so quickly? Which areas are growing fastest? What effects has this growth had on social and ecological systems? And what can we expect in terms of future growth? These questions all lie at the heart of **population geography**.

On a global scale, human population shows several distinct geographic characteristics. First, approximately 80% of the world's population lives in the less-developed countries, which includes all of Africa, Asia (excluding Japan), Latin America, and the island nations of the Caribbean and Pacific. Two countries, China and India, each have over a billion people and together hold one-third of the world's current population! Less-developed countries also contain the fastest growing populations. Of the approximately 80 million people that were being added to the world's population each year during the 1990s, 95% lived in the less-developed world. People are also living longer. During the past 50 years, the global average life expectancy has increased by 20 years, from 45 to 65. In the less-developed countries, where most people reside, the basic equation is relatively simple—more babies are being born and people are living longer.

When people read news reports about growth rates in the less-developed countries, they often see figures like 3% and think, "Hey, that's not too much." However, if you look a little more closely at the math, you will quickly realize that even growth rates that seem low can cause rapid population increases over

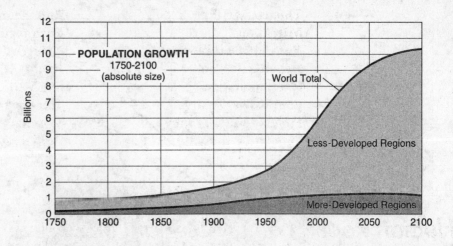

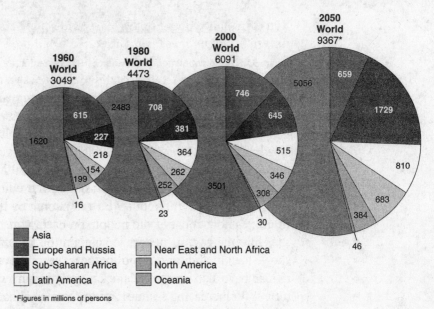

Figure 3.1. The world population began growing exponentially during the late 20th century, with particularly high rates of growth in the world's less-developed countries. Global population will probably plateau off around 2010.

time. Like interest in a bank, population growth is *compounded*. In other words, if a population grows by 3% both this year and next year, then next year's 3% will actually include more people than this year's. This is because next year's growth will be 3% of a population that is bigger than it was just a year ago. For example, if you live in a country with a population of 1 million people, after one year, the population will grow by 3% for a total of 1,030,000. You've added 30,000 more people to your country in one year. The next year, when you apply a 3% growth rate to your current population of 1,030,000, you get a new total of 1,060,900. In year two, 3% ended by including 900 more people than in year one! You can now see how, at a 3% rate of increase, it would not take long for your country to grow dramatically. In fact, one of the most surprising implications of this concept is that, at a 3% growth rate, the time it will take for a population to double, known simply as **doubling time**, is less than 25 years! Growth rates currently exceed 3% in parts of sub-Saharan and tropical Africa, the Middle East, and Central America.

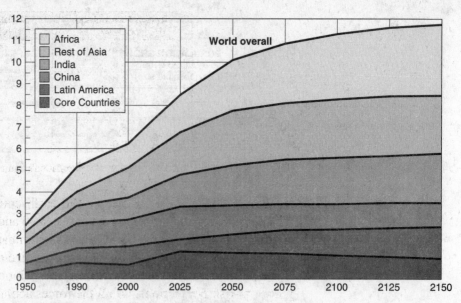

Figure 3.2. World population growth since 1950 by region.

The study of human populations, or **demography,** is not static because the world's population will not keep growing forever. Most **demographers,** or people who study population, agree that growth is already showing signs of slowing down. Many current models based on demographic data predict that the world's population will plateau at around 12 billion people some time in the 21st century. Some of the most recent predictions have population leveling off even lower, at about 9 billion people by the end of this century. In the future, as now, most of the people on earth will be living in Africa or Asia.

While the overall pattern of population growth throughout human history shows steady and even rapid increase, certain events and environmental limitations have also served to check population growth at different periods in history. With increasing technology, the human species has enabled itself to adapt to many of these constraints, explaining why the number of people on earth is continually growing. The innovations that occurred as a result of the domestication of plants and animals and the Industrial Revolution had dramatic

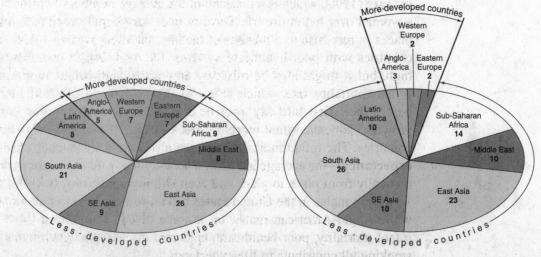

Figure 3.3. Population distribution by world region.

Annual Percentage Increase	Doubling Time (years)
0.5	140
1.0	70
2.0	35
3.0	24
4.0	17
5.0	14
10.0	7

Figure 3.4. Doubling time as a function of a population's annual percentage increase.

impacts on the number of people the earth could sustain. However, in the 1300s, the Black Plague wiped out between 30 and 40% of the entire European continent. The Irish potato famine in 1845 eliminated half of the country's population in just 50 years as millions of people died of starvation or left the country. Natural disasters such as earthquakes, floods, and hurricanes regularly reduce at-risk populations. Of all the forces acting to check world population, none has been more effective than epidemic disease. When European explorers and settlers arrived in the Americas and the Pacific Islands, they introduced devastating diseases, such as smallpox, that formerly had only been known in the Old World. Indeed, disease—not war—was the main factor that led to the toppling of native cultures throughout the New World. Today, in many African countries, AIDS is contributing to an escalating death rate and constraining population growth within those nations. In 1999 in sub-Saharan Africa, 23.20 million people were living with the AIDS virus, and over 4 million were becoming infected each year. While this part of the world is one of the areas mentioned as experiencing rapid growth, in the future we may see its growth severely limited by the devastating effects of this virus.

Population Parameters and Processes

All the population processes that have been discussed so far can be broken down into a set of parameters, each of which holds vital information about the history and future of a given population. One such statistic is the **total fertility rate** (TFR), which is a measure of the average number of children born to a woman over her entire life. Fertility rates vary both over time and between places in response to a number of factors that affect women's lives. In some countries with poor healthcare systems, the total fertility rate may be very high, but it might also be offset by an equally high **infant mortality rate.** Infant mortality rate, which refers to the percentage of children who die before their first birthday, may be a significant factor limiting population growth. Sadly, the infant mortality rate exceeds 10% in some less-developed countries. The infant mortality rate can also have a significant effect on **life expectancy**—the average length of a person's life. Life expectancy varies dramatically from place to place and even within populations. In 1996, African-American males in the United States had a life expectancy of about 66 years, while Anglo-American males, on average, lived to be almost 74. Violence, infant mortality, poor healthcare, epidemic disease, and risk factors such as smoking all contribute to life expectancy.

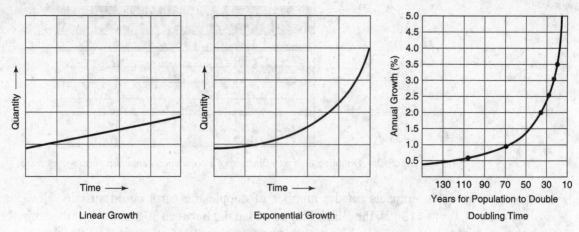

Figure 3.5. When a population is growing exponentially, the rate of growth increases over time, whereas linear growth connotes a steady rate.

Each of the parameters described here can be encapsulated within two aggregate variables, the **crude birth rate** (CBR) and **crude death rate** (CDR), which are statistical terms that refer to the number of live births and deaths, respectively, per thousand people. The difference between the CBR and CDR is called the **natural increase rate** (NIR). This term is a bit misleading because there is nothing really "natural" about natural increase and because natural "increase" can be either positive or negative. A negative increase rate indicates that the number of babies being born is not high enough to make up for deaths and, as a result, the population is declining. It is also important to recognize that the NIR is an internal measure that does not account for migration into or out of a country.

Year	Estimated Population	Doubling Time (years)
1	250 million	
1650	500 million	1650
1804	1 billion	154
1927	2 billion	123
1974	4 billion	47
World population may reach		
2021	8 billion	47[a]

[a]The leveling of doubling time reflects assumptions of decreasing and stabilizing fertility rates. No current projections contemplate a further doubling to 16 billion people.

Source: United Nations.

Figure 3.6. The earth's human population is currently growing exponentially. However, there are already signs that the global growth rate is slowing down, which confirms the predictions of many demographers.

A few countries are currently showing negative rates of natural increase. In the more developed regions of the world, which include North America, Japan, Europe, and Australia/New Zealand, the natural increase rate has decreased markedly, in some cases actually leading to a stable or even declining population. This is particularly evident in some European countries with aging populations, where death rates now outpace birth rates. As a result, much of the growth occurring in the more-developed world is associated with immigration from less-developed countries. In the United States, natural rates of increase are low; however, immigration and high fertility rates among some groups of newer immigrants are causing the overall population to continue growing. It is also interesting to note that, in the many developing countries, such as Mexico, Brazil, and Indonesia, rates of natural increase are actually beginning to decline. Although the populations of these countries are still growing, they are no longer growing as fast as they once were.

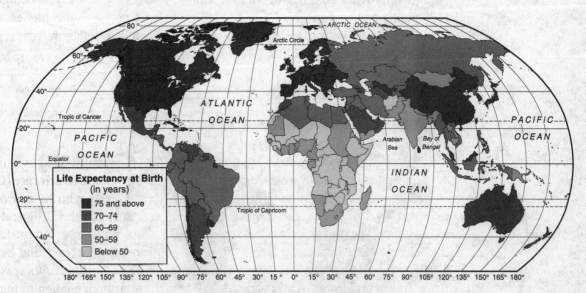

Figure 3.7. Life expectancy by country.

What determines a population's natural increase rate? Several factors have been identified as affecting this rate, most of which are related to economic development, culture, or public policy. The following factors are considered important in determining a population's rate of natural increase.

- *Economic development* has profound implications on the quality of available healthcare, employment opportunities, nutrition, and many other factors that affect population growth. Generally, increases in economic development lead to decreases in fertility and growth rate.
- *Education* affects every aspect of population growth, from fertility rates to prenatal care to the use of contraception. Populations with better education tend to have lower fertility rates and lower rates of natural increase.
- *Gender empowerment* refers to the relative status and opportunities available to women in a given population. When women have more economic and political access, power, and education, fertility rates inevitably drop.
- *Healthcare* can have contradictory effects on the rate of natural increase. Improved healthcare in the less-developed countries has decreased the infant mortality rate and increased the life expectancy, thus contributing to population growth. Conversely, the same healthcare services are often effective at providing desperately needed contraception and family planning education.
- *Cultural traditions* in many parts of the world encourage high fertility rates by limiting women's employment opportunities outside of the home, by elevating motherhood to a high post and deterring women from doing anything else, or by discouraging the use of contraception.

- *Public policy* can have important implications for population growth in places like China, where the "one couple, one child" program, initiated in 1979, provides economic incentives favoring families who have fewer children and legal penalties for those who have too many.

Countries that have low levels of economic development, education, and gender empowerment, as well as newly reduced infant mortality rates because of improving healthcare, cultural traditions favoring fertility, and little or no public policy limiting population growth tend to have the highest growth rates. These countries, again, are found mainly in sub-Saharan Africa, parts of the Middle East, and Latin America.

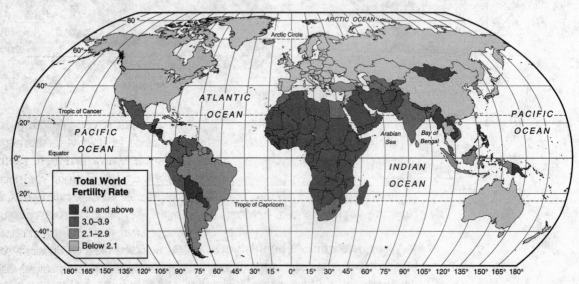

Figure 3.8. World fertility rate by country.

Will a given population continue to grow indefinitely? If not, why, when and at what level will it stabilize? An enormous body of research surrounds these questions, and many careers have been dedicated to projecting and planning for population growth. To predict how much a population will grow, population geographers start with a single, basic formula called the **demographic accounting equation**.

$$P(t + 1) = P(t) \ldots$$

$$+ B\,(t, t + 1) - D\,(t, t + 1) \qquad \text{(natural change)}$$

$$+ I\,(t, t + 1) - E\,(t, t + 1) \qquad \text{(net migration)}$$

Where
P = population
B = births
D = deaths
I = immigration
E = emigration
t = time now
$t + 1$ = some time in the future

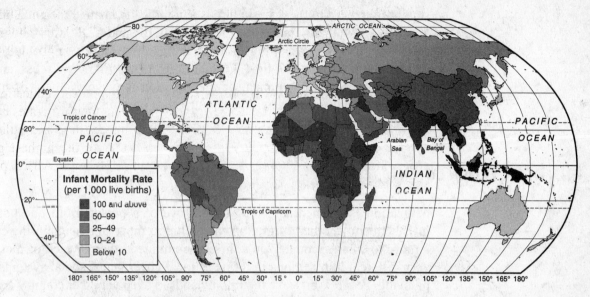

Figure 3.9. Infant mortality rate by country.

The demographic accounting equation says that if you want to predict the population at some time in the future, you need to start with the population now, add the amount of births you expect between now and then, subtract the number of deaths, add immigration, and subtract emigration. The part of the equation regarding births and deaths is the natural increase rate and is, in large part, the subject of this chapter. The part of the equation that computes net migration is covered in the next section. For now, just remember that immigration refers to people moving into some place and emigration refers to people moving out of some place. In the demographic accounting equation, you add people coming in and subtract people leaving.

The demographic accounting equation offers what, at first, appears to be a very simple way of predicting future population. Unfortunately, as we have already seen, many factors affect the parameters that go into the equation, and

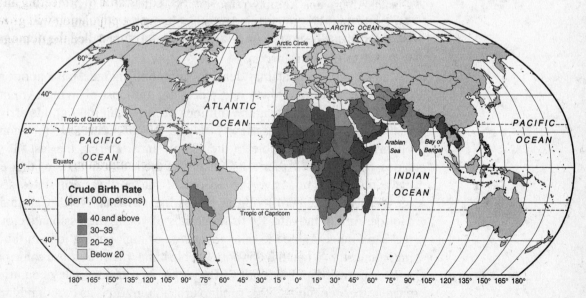

Figure 3.10. Crude birth rate by country.

small differences in these basic inputs can radically change the final answer. You now know that parameters, such as the CBR and CDR, vary geographically from place to place, but to make things even more complicated, these variables also change over time. Furthermore, as we will now discuss, another critically important component of the equation is the movement of human populations between and within countries, or migration, which also varies dramatically over both space and time.

Human Migration

Migration is defined as a long-term move of a person from one political jurisdiction to another. Migration can include a move to a neighboring city or a move to another country on a different continent, though each of these has very different implications in terms of local governance, social systems, and planning. People who leave their homelands to live in another country are said to **emigrate**, while people who move into a country **immigrate**. Immigrants from the less-developed world form an increasingly large portion of the populations of many more-developed countries. The difference between immigration and emigration is considered in the demographic accounting equation. As was already mentioned, the accuracy of this equation tends to be somewhat compromised as population rates change over time. With increasing immigration from developing countries into developed countries, it becomes harder to predict future population growth.

Several factors cause people to migrate. The following list outlines some of the main reasons why people might leave homelands for new places.

- *Political issues*, such as armed conflict and the policies of oppressive regimes, have been important historical forces leading to migration. The pilgrims, who sailed on the *Mayflower* to America, fled oppressive governments that had imposed limitations on their religious freedom in Europe. Later, as the United States expanded westward toward the Pacific Ocean, Americans forcibly removed thousands of Native Americans from the lands that their ancestors had inhabited for millennia, relocating them to far-off reservations. Both of these migrations occurred largely in response to political forces.
- *Economic factors* that may lead to migration include job opportunities, economic cycles of growth and recession, and cost of living. Around the beginning of the 20th century, millions of European immigrants arrived in east coast cities, such as New York and Boston, searching for economic opportunities not available in their homelands. During the last 40 years, thousands of older Americans—many of them descendants of that earlier wave of migration—have moved out of the northeastern states seeking inexpensive retirement living in places like Arizona, North Carolina, and Florida. And in the mid-1990s thousands of young professionals moved to the San Francisco area to take advantage of high-paying jobs in the computer industry. When the dot-com bubble burst, many of those same people left the crowded and overpriced Bay Area. In addition, many countries are currently experiencing large rural to urban migrations as corporate farming and increased technology have reduced the number of agricultural laborers

needed in rural areas. Many of these former farm workers have migrated to cities in hope of finding new economic opportunities.

- *Environmental issues* can be an important cause of migration in both the less-developed and the more-developed world. For example, in African countries such as Ethiopia, Sudan, and Kenya, many nomadic herders have been forced to breach the boundaries of their former rangelands, searching for more fertile areas that have not been adversely impacted by drought or overgrazing. In the United States, regions such as the Sierra Nevada range in California have experienced dramatic population growth as people living in the state's crowded coastal cities have sought cleaner air, cheaper houses, less traffic, and a perceived higher quality of life in the mountains. The irony is that, as urbanites leave places like Los Angeles and San Francisco in favor of smaller towns and rural areas, they frequently bring big city problems—like crime, pollution, traffic, and high costs of living—with them.

- *Cultural issues* can also cause people to move to places where they feel more at home or where they are able to take advantage of certain institutions. For example, after World War II, many Jews from Europe, the Americas, and elsewhere relocated to the newly formed state of Israel. Israel was the ancestral hearth of Jewish culture and religion, and many Jews feel a strong sense of attachment to it. Israel also served as a place where the Jewish people could regroup in safety, reestablish social ties, and create a sense of political unity after the tragedy of the Holocaust.

- *Transportation routes* can enable and entice people to migrate to new areas. Throughout history, improved transportation technology and improved routes between places have allowed many people to move within countries and across borders. During the 17th and 18th centuries, better ships and more reliable navigation systems made safe travel across the Atlantic Ocean to the Americas a real possibility for many aspiring European immigrants. Similarly, during the 19th century, new stagecoach routes enabled many white settlers to move westward across the American Great Plains and Rocky Mountains to California and Oregon. Finally, new roads into the Amazon constructed by the Brazilian government during the second half of the 20th century, encouraged thousands of people to leave Brazil's densely populated southeastern coast for a life of farming the country's largely unsettled interior.

As you can see, many factors cause people to migrate, despite the inherent costs involved with picking up and moving one's entire life to a different place.

Another way that geographers have sought to understand the nature of these motivating factors behind migration is by dividing them up into push factors and pull factors. **Push factors** include anything that would cause someone to want to move *from* somewhere, such as an economic recession or a lack of religious freedom. The political issues faced by the Pilgrims and Native Americans are excellent examples of push factors. **Pull factors** induce people to move *to* someplace because that place has something enticing to offer them, such as a pleasant climate or an abundance of jobs in their chosen field. One important pull factor that is probably on your mind right now is educational opportunity. If you go away to college, then the prospect of getting an education will have "pulled" you from your current home to a new place.

Geographers also think of migration as being either voluntary or forced. **Voluntary migration** occurs when someone chooses to leave a place, either as a result of push factors or pull factors. For example, most of the Mexican immigrants who have come to the United States over the decades have done so voluntarily, in order to take advantage of the economic opportunities available north of the border. One type of migratory pattern that is usually voluntary is called **chain migration.** In chain migration, people follow others in succession from one place to another. Distinct ethnic neighborhoods in American cities are often the result of this process because new immigrants often move to places where family members and friends from their home country have already established themselves. In **forced migration**, someone is removed from his or her home without any choice. Forced migration is often the result of dire political, economic, social, or environmental causes.

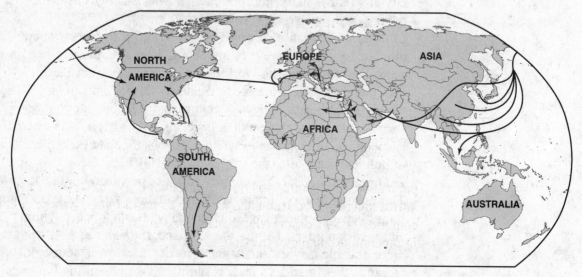

Figure 3.11. Recent global flows of voluntary migration.

The removal of Native Americans from their traditional homelands in the eastern United States and the African slave trade of the Colonial Period, are two particularly tragic examples of forced migration. In 1830, the U.S. Congress, under the direction of President Andrew Jackson, passed the Indian Removal Act, which forced about 100,000 Cherokees, Chickasaws, Choctaws, Creeks, and Seminoles to move west of the Mississippi. Their route of forced migration is now known as the Trail of Tears. Another dreadful example of forced migration was the African slave trade, which, between the 15th and 18th centuries, removed hundreds of thousands of Africans from their homelands and transported them against their will to the Americas. Those who survived the voyage were condemned to a life of bondage.

People who leave their homes because they are forced out, but not because they are being officially relocated or enslaved, are said to be **refugees**. The 1951 Convention Relating to the Status of Refugees defined a refugee as someone who, "owing to a well-founded fear of being persecuted for reasons of race, religion, nationality, membership in a particular social group, or political opinion, is outside the country of his nationality, and is unable to or, owing to such fear, is unwilling to avail himself of the protection of that country." According to the United Nations High Commissioner for Refugees, the global refugee

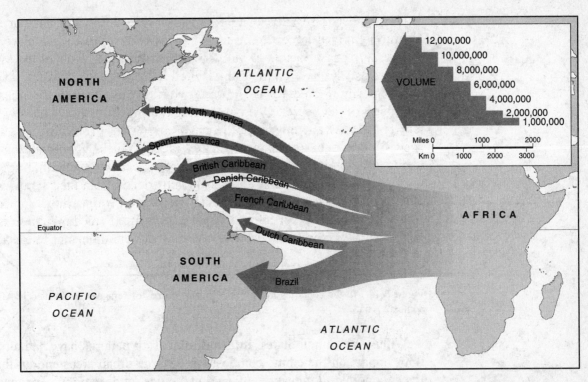

Figure 3.12. The slave trade of the Colonial Period resulted in a mass forced migration of Africans to the New World.

population, as of 2002, was over 21 million people. In recent years, Asia and Africa together have accounted for more than two-thirds of those people, with countries like Pakistan, Afghanistan, Sri Lanka, Colombia, Angola, and the Democratic Republic of the Congo heading up the list.

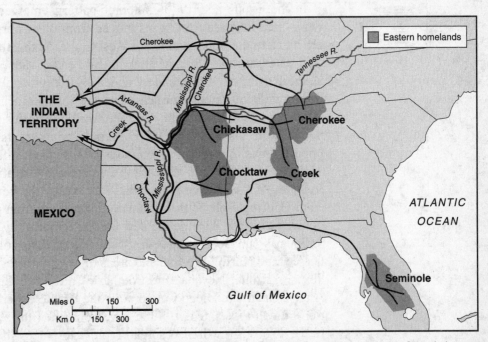

Figure 3.13. In the 1830s, thousands of Native Americans were forced to migrate from their ancestral homelands in the southeastern United States to the High Plains. Their route is remembered as the Trail of Tears.

Figure 3.14. All the countries that are significant sources of refugees are located in Africa and southern Asia.

Within the United States, **internal migration** patterns have had a tremendous impact on the ethnic composition of large urban areas and on the relative economic dominance of various cities and regions. For example, beginning in the early 20th century, large numbers of African-Americans moved from the rural South to large cities in the Northeast and Midwest to join the growing industrial workforces located in places like Chicago, Detroit, and New York. For African-Americans, the South had offered racial oppression and little economic opportunity, whereas the North promised a new start and a better way of life. The social effects of this particular migration event are discussed further in Chapter 8.

In the 1960s and 1970s, another pattern emerged, as large numbers of white, middle-class Americans moved from older northeastern and midwestern cities to the South and to the West Coast. At this time, the northern industrial states, such as Ohio, Michigan, and Pennsylvania, were becoming known as the **Rust Belt**. These states, which had previously been industrial powerhouses with vibrant economies, were now losing much of their economic base to other parts of the country and the world. Factories were closing down and people were losing their jobs. For would-be migrants, the South offered job opportunities in new high-tech industries, such as software development and aerospace engineering, a pleasant climate, and a relatively affordable cost of living. As a result, during the mid-20th century, the South ceased to be known as the **Cotton Belt**, with its connotations of agrarian poverty and backwardness, and instead became the new land of opportunity—the **Sun Belt**.

Today's Sun Belt includes the "New South" states of Florida, Georgia, Tennessee, and North Carolina, and areas of the Southwest, including portions of Texas, Arizona, Nevada, and Southern California. Cities like Houston, Los Angeles, and San Diego were among the first to experience the rapid population growth associated with the development of the Sun Belt, but beginning in the 1960s, growth also spread rapidly to places like Phoenix, Las Vegas, Dallas, Miami, Tampa, Austin, and Nashville. Some parts of the South and West, such as Louisiana, Mississippi, Alabama, and New Mexico have yet to

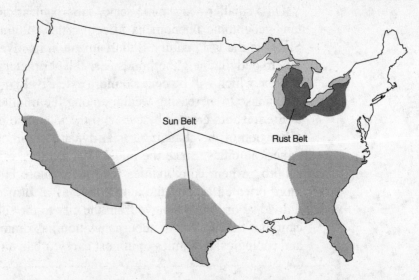

Figure 3.15. The Rust Belt of the Great Lakes region experienced economic woes during the 1970s and 1980s. Many migrants left the upper Midwest for a brighter future in the Sun Belt.

benefit significantly from the Sun Belt phenomenon. However, the economy, culture, and landscape of much of the southern and western United States have been dramatically transformed.

Internal migration patterns have also radically altered the balance of political and economic power. California, Texas, and Florida are now three of the four most populous states in the country (New York is the other). These states, all three of which are at least partly located in the Sun Belt, carry a disproportionate number of electoral votes, have large congressional delegations, and are dominant in many economic sectors, such as technology, energy production, and agriculture. One interesting side note is that the centroid, or geographic center of the U.S. population, is now much farther west and south than it was during the early part of the 20th century, indicating an overall change in the geographic distribution of the U.S. population.

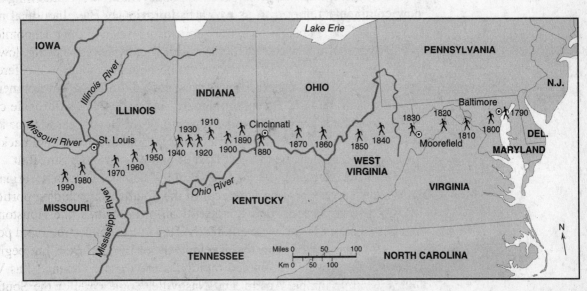

Figure 3.16. The centroid, or geographic center, of the U.S. population has moved progressively west during the past 200 years.

On a smaller geographic scale, suburbanization is one of the most important geographic phenomena affecting the cultural landscape of the United States in the last century. Suburbanization involves migration from the inner city to outlying neighborhoods near the perimeters of urban areas. Suburbanization, which will be covered more extensively in Chapters 7 and 8, is partly a response to increasing wealth among the middle classes, partly a response to the freedom created by cars and the interstate highway system, and partly a function of the changing social dynamics and ethnic composition of older American cities. Since the mid-1940s millions of Americans have moved to suburbs, where communities tend to be more ethnically homogeneous and more oriented around the automobile as a form of transportation. A single individual or family's move from the city to the suburb is relatively insignificant, but the process of suburbanization has dramatically affected the social and ecological dynamics of almost every urban area in the United States.

Population Structure and Composition

Now that the mechanisms controlling and describing populations within certain areas have been discussed, it is important to spend some time focusing on how geographers model population growth, as well as on the various implications population growth may have on the earth's ability to sustain itself. Several models have been developed to explain changes in population over time and to relate various social, economic, and environmental factors to population growth. The economist and demographer **Thomas Malthus,** in his *Essay on the Principle of Population,* published in 1798, developed the most famous of these models. Malthus based his argument on two claims: (1) people need food to survive, and (2) people have a natural desire to reproduce. He also noted that food production increases arithmetically but population increases geometrically. What he meant by this was that food production grows by the *addition* of more acreage into cultivation, whereas population grows by the *multiplication* of human beings. Malthus' geometric growth is now commonly referred to as **exponential growth**. Based in this premise,

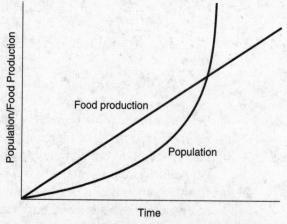

Figure 3.17. Thomas Malthus predicted the population, which grows geometrically (exponentially), would eventually outpace food production, which grows arthmetically (linearly).

Malthus argued that human population growth would eventually outpace people's ability to produce food, leading to widespread starvation and disease, what he called "negative checks" on the population. Malthus' theory has been revisited over the decades by many prominent scholars, most recently in 1968 by the **neo-Malthusian** Stanford ecologist Paul Ehrlich. In *The Population Bomb*, Ehrlich made a similar argument about the ability of the earth to sustainably provide resources for an exponentially growing population.

There are several problems with the Malthusian perspective. First, although Malthus foresaw the development of new agricultural technologies, he did not fully account for the ability of people to increase food production dramatically with these technologies. Second, Malthus assumed that humans have no control over their reproductive behavior. He did not foresee that population growth would slow down over time because of effective contraception, the changing roles of women in society, and individual people's reproductive decisions. Finally, he did not recognize that famine is usually related not to a lack of food, but to the unequal distribution of food. For example, famine struck various parts of Africa repeatedly throughout the 20th century, despite the fact that an abundance of food existed in other parts of the world. These problems have caused many people to discount Malthusian theory altogether. However, Malthus' theories have helped to bring attention to issues of sustainability and have informed the work of numerous other influential scholars, such as the great ecologist and evolutionary theorist Charles Darwin.

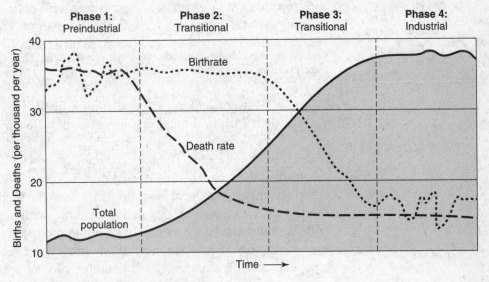

Figure 3.18. The demographic transition model.

The **demographic transition model**, which explains changes in the natural increase rate as a function of economic development, provides another interpretation of population growth. According to this model, at low levels of economic development, birth and death rates will both be high, but births will significantly outpace deaths. As a country progresses through several stages of economic development, birth rates and death rates will both decrease, ultimately flattening out at some low level. The total population, which increased markedly during the early and middle stages, eventually plateaus as birth rates and death rates converge. This model seems to describe accurately the paths taken by some countries that are already highly developed. It also effectively characterizes various states of population change and development currently existing in many countries across the world.

Whether this model is universally applicable is another matter. Many geographers have argued that the demographic transition model is too simplistic in its portrayal of the relationship between economic development and population and that factors such as culture, religion, geopolitics, migration, and the structure of the global economic system itself may prevent many of today's less developed countries from ever taking the path described. Thus, the relationship between national economics and population is complicated by other factors, such as the structure of the world economic system and cultural constraints.

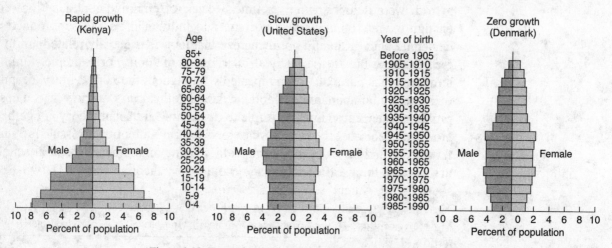

Figure 3.19. Population pyramids for three different countries: Kenya, the United States, and Denmark. Compare Kenya's rapidly growing, youthful population to Denmark's older, stable population.

Another way of looking at population growth is by analyzing a country's **age-sex distribution** through the use of **population pyramids**. A population pyramid shows how a country's populace is distributed between males and females of various ages. Population pyramids are useful because they explain much about the recent history of a country's population and because they present a convenient, graphical basis on which to make predictions about impending population change. A population pyramid with a triangular shape and a wide base depicts a country that has a high proportion of young people and is growing rapidly. A population pyramid with a more rectangular shape depicts a population with a relatively even number of young, middle-aged, and older people and is typical of highly developed countries with low growth rates.

The **baby boom** generation is an example of a population **cohort** that has had a tremendous influence on American culture, politics, and economics. A cohort is simply a group of people that all have something in common and are usually grouped together for statistical purposes. The baby boom generation includes all Americans born between 1946 and 1964. After World War II, which ended in 1945, the United States entered a period of relative peace and economic prosperity. Jobs were plentiful, and government aid programs, such as the G.I. Bill, helped many veterans reestablish themselves in the postwar economy. War veterans were able to begin a new life at home in the States with an education, a home, and a secure job. These conditions, combined with the relatively conservative social environment of the day, encouraged high rates of marriage and fertility. Although the total fertility rate had already peaked before 1950, the baby boom still produced the largest, best-educated, and most financially secure generation in all of American history.

The generation that followed the baby boom is another story. People born between the years of 1965 and 1980 are sometimes referred to as **Generation X**. The term "Generation X" was coined by the off-beat author and artist Douglas Coupland to describe a generation without the overwhelming numbers and unifying identity enjoyed by the baby boomers. By the mid-1970s the American psyche had been severely damaged by the tragedy of the Vietnam War and the debacle of the Watergate affair. In addition, the women of the baby boom generation, many of whom reached mothering age during this period, were seeking more education, pursuing more demanding careers, waiting longer to marry, and having fewer children than the generation that had come before them. As a result, the natural increase rate declined significantly during the 1960s and 1970s, in what some demographers have called a **baby bust**.

The baby boomers are currently leaving Generation X with another interesting problem. As they get older, they will place unprecedented pressure on healthcare, social security, and other services that will cost billions of dollars. As a result, the **dependency ratio**, which refers to the percentage of people in a population who are either too old or too young to work and, thus, must be supported by others, will increase dramatically over the next two decades. It remains to be seen what Gen-Xers will be able to do with the complex world they have inherited, as they come of age and emerge out of the shadow of the baby boom.

Population and Sustainability

To truly appreciate the impact of population on people and the landscape, geographers must also consider **population density**. Population density, defined as the number of people living in a given unit area, varies dramatically from place to place, tending to be greatest in large urban areas and least in regions with harsh environments, such as deserts and polar climates. On a global scale, the greatest population densities currently occur in eastern China, Japan, Southeast Asia, the Indian subcontinent, Western Europe, and the northeastern United States. The countries with the highest population densities on earth are generally considered to be Bangladesh and the Netherlands. Within the United States, the highest population densities occur in crowded cities such as New York and San Francisco.

In many of the world's most populous regions, population density has become so great that some people have raised the thorny issue of **carrying capacity**. In human geography, as in ecology, carrying capacity refers to the number of individuals a given area is capable of maintaining. Carrying capacity is a tricky subject because most people do not live exclusively off products produced locally. Average consumption of resources varies dramatically from place to place, and social and technological change constantly alters people's resource demands. These problems make carrying capacity a moving target that is impossible to ever really compute. One way of thinking about carrying capacity is to use the concept of the limiting factor. This concept, which was originally used to describe the way in which plants use resources in the environment, says that the only truly limiting resource is the one that is in the scarcest supply. Las Vegas, for example, may have an ample amount of electrical power and inexpensive land, but in a place that receives just a few inches of rain a year, water should guide planning and limit growth. By this rule, the population of Las Vegas, like so many other cities in arid and semiarid regions, has probably already surpassed its sustainable carrying capacity. The result of artificially surpassing such natural limits is almost always ecological degradation, loss of arable land, and harm to native ecosystems, not to mention the profound social and psychological impacts of living in an overcrowded, overused landscape. Yet, for the past 20 years, Las Vegas has been the fastest growing city in the United States.

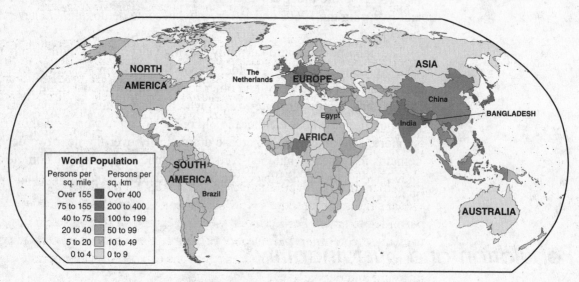

Figure 3.20. Population density by country.

With so many potential problems resulting from population growth, many countries and some international organizations have begun to think about and address **overpopulation**. Overpopulation is not easy to define because many of today's most pressing international problems related to overpopulation also involve a host of other issues, from overconsumption of resources, to the inefficient allocation of goods and services, to unsustainable land use practices. Generally, overpopulation in a particular area implies a breach of that area's carrying capacity. A given geographical area has the ability to sustainably support a specific population. As that population increases, the region may employ new agricultural techniques or cultivate more land to support more people. At some point, the area is no longer able to return enough goods to sustain a certain population; at this point, the area has extended beyond its carrying capacity. In addition, the mechanisms used to try to increase carrying capacity often have environmental and social repercussions. Many activists in the more-developed countries, who believe that overpopulation is the root cause of the world's social and environmental problems, support policies that they believe will lead to **zero population growth**. However, most leaders from the less-developed countries tend to lay blame on people in the wealthiest countries, who consume a disproportionate share of the earth's natural resources. The following statement—submitted by the Indian delegation to the United Nations International Conference on Population and Development, held in Cairo, Egypt, in 1994 – regarding the development of international population policy is representative of that sentiment.

> The Indian delegation agrees . . . that the draft document focuses disproportionately on the linkages of population and environment. There is little mention of the pattern of consumption in the industrialized nations which cannot long be supported without serious damage to the biosphere. The industrialized nations with approximately 20% of the world's people are currently responsible for three-quarters of the world's energy use, two-thirds of all greenhouse gases and 90 percent of the chlorofluorocarbons. Population growth alone is not responsible for environmental degradation. The inter-linkage between population, poverty, environment and sustainable development is complex.

As the world population swells and as urban areas and developing countries experience increasing population density, it is increasingly apparent that certain policy initiatives will be necessary to combat future problems stemming from overpopulation. Some population policies seek to limit population growth in particular countries either through fertility control or by imposing immigration restrictions. In both cases, the type of policy implemented is largely determined by the politics of public perception and by prevailing ideologies. Many seemingly unsolvable questions surround the design and implementation of population policy. Is it possible to humanely limit an individual's right to reproduce? How should a government determine who will be permitted to enter? Furthermore, when designing an appropriate policy, countries must determine the number of people they think they can sustain. Of course, this involves even trickier questions regarding an appropriate standard of living and people's level of consumption.

The world's two most populated countries, India and China, both have implemented policies to curb population growth within their borders. The policies implemented in each country reflect differing cultures and political situations. In communist-controlled China, families are "encouraged" to have only one child by rewards given to families who follow this dictate and punishments given to those who do not. In the more democratic India, individuals are also encouraged to limit the number of children they bear, but instead the means of encouragement come through education and improved access to family planning.

The numerous questions surrounding population policy illustrate that it is an issue that is continually fraught with controversy. Some leaders see international population policy as infringing upon the fundamental human right to reproduce. For others, fertility has special cultural or religious value, and any attempts to limit it are seen as cultural persecution. The Catholic Church officially believes that practices of birth control and abortion are sinful, thus implementing any form of fertility control can be difficult in predominantly Catholic countries. However, even in predominantly Catholic countries, where there is a high standard of living and plentiful opportunities for women, growth is always low. Italy, which has an extremely low growth rate, is a case in point.

Immigration policy is also frequently contentious. Many people are concerned that policies specifically limiting the number of immigrants into a particular area are inhumane and may be the product of racist desires to limit the population of particular types of people. Within a given state, it is hard to predict how citizens may react to seeing new immigrants move into their neighborhood. Whether or not you believe that the Indian delegation is correct in its assessment of the population debate, it is obvious that there are no easy solutions, and that the Indians do make an excellent point when they say that the "inter-linkage between population, poverty, environment and sustainable development is complex." They have firsthand experience as a country with over a billion people.

As you have probably surmised, population geography is a wide-ranging and multifaceted field, and one that keeps geographers extremely busy! Geographers know that it is critical to understand population dynamics and growth patterns throughout the world, in order both to provide for current populations and to plan for the future. At the same time, issues of mobility, healthcare, education, policy, and economics render making steadfast predictions extremely difficult. With these challenges in mind, geographers work to improve their models, to test their theories, and to better understand human populations throughout the world.

Key Terms Defined

Age-sex distribution A model used in population geography that describes the ages and number of males and females within a given population; also called a population pyramid.

Baby boom A cohort of individuals born in the United States between 1946 and 1964, which was just after World War II in a time of relative peace and prosperity. These conditions allowed for better education and job opportunities, encouraging high rates of both marriage and fertility.

Baby bust Period of time during the 1960s and 1970s when fertility rates in the United States dropped as large numbers of women from the baby boom generation sought higher levels of education and more competitive jobs, causing them to marry later in life. As such, the fertility rate dropped considerably, in contrast to the baby boom, in which fertility rates were quite high.

Carrying capacity The largest number of people that the environment of a particular area can sustainably support.

Chain migration The migration event in which individuals follow the migratory path of preceding friends or family members to an existing community.

Cohort A population group unified by a specific common characteristic, such as age, and subsequently treated as a statistical unit.

Cotton Belt The term by which the American South used to be known, as cotton historically dominated the agricultural economy of the region. The same area is now known as the New South or Sun Belt because people have migrated here from older cities in the industrial north for a better climate and new job opportunities.

Crude birth rate The number of live births per year per 1,000 people.

Crude death rate The number of deaths per year per 1,000 people.

Demographic accounting equation An equation that summarizes the amount of growth or decline in a population within a country during a particular time period taking into account both natural increase and net migration.

Demographic transition model A sequence of demographic changes in which a country moves from high birth and death rates to low birth and death rates through time.

Demography The study of human populations, including their temporal and spatial dynamics.

Dependency ratio The ratio of the number of people who are either too old or young to provide for themselves to the number of people who must support them through their own labor. This is usually expressed in the form $n:100$, where n equals the number of dependents.

Doubling time Time period required for a population experiencing exponential growth to double in size completely.

Emigration The process of moving out of a particular country, usually the individual person's country of origin.

Exponential growth Growth that occurs when a fixed percentage of new people is added to a population each year. Exponential growth is compound because the fixed growth rate applies to an ever-increasing population.

Forced migration The migration event in which individuals are forced to leave a country against their will.

Generation X A term coined by artist and author Douglas Coupland to describe people born in the United States between the years of 1965 and 1980. This post-baby-boom generation will have to support the baby-boom cohort as they head into their retirement years.

Immigration The process of individuals moving into a new country with the intentions of remaining there.

Infant mortality rate The percentage of children who die before their first birthday within a particular area or country.

Internal migration The permanent or semipermanent movement of individuals within a particular country.

Life expectancy The average age individuals are expected to live, which varies across space, between genders, and even between races.

Thomas Malthus Author of *Essay on the Principle of Population* (1798) who claimed that population grows at an exponential rate while food production increases arithmetically, and thereby that, eventually, population growth would outpace food production.

Migration A long-term move of a person from one political jurisdiction to another.

Natural increase rate The difference between the number of births and number of deaths within a particular country.

Neo-Malthusian Advocacy of population control programs to ensure enough resources for current and future populations.

Overpopulation A value judgment based on the notion that the resources of a particular area are not great enough to support that area's current population.

Population density A measurement of the number of persons per unit land area.

Population geography A division of human geography concerned with spatial variations in distribution, composition, growth, and movements of population.

Population pyramid A model used in population geography to show the age and sex distribution of a particular population.

Pull factors Attractions that draw migrants to a certain place, such as a pleasant climate and employment or educational opportunities.

Push factors Incentives for potential migrants to leave a place, such as a harsh climate, economic recession, or political turmoil.

Refugees People who leave their home because they are forced out, but not because they are being officially relocated or enslaved.

Rust Belt The northern industrial states of the United States, including Ohio, Michigan, and Pennsylvania, in which heavy industry was once the dominant economic activity. In the 1960s, 1970s, and 1980s, these states lost much of their economic base to economically attractive regions of the United States and to countries where labor was cheaper, leaving old machinery to rust in the moist northern climate.

Sun Belt U.S. region, mostly comprised of southeastern and southwestern states, which has grown most dramatically since World War II.

Total fertility rate The average number of children born to a woman during her childbearing years.

Voluntary migration Movement of an individual who consciously and voluntarily decides to locate to a new area—the opposite of forced migration.

Zero population growth Proposal to end population growth through a variety of official and nongovernmental family planning programs.

Sample Questions and Answers

Section 1: Human Population: A Global Perspective

Multiple-Choice Questions

1. Which of the following regions is currently experiencing the fastest population growth?

   (A) Northern Asia
   (B) Tropical Africa
   (C) Eastern Europe
   (D) Sun Belt
   (E) Northeast United States

2. Most of the world's people live in

   (A) the world's poorest countries.
   (B) the southern hemisphere.
   (C) the developed world.
   (D) China.
   (E) urban areas in the developed world.

3. Throughout human history, world population has

   (A) grown at a steady rate.
   (B) experienced numerous periods of dramatic decline.
   (C) been confined to countries in the southern hemisphere.
   (D) grown most rapidly over the last 200 years.
   (E) grown most rapidly in the developed world.

4. _____ occurs when a population is adding a fixed percentage of people to a growing population each year.

   (A) Doubling
   (B) Arithmetic growth
   (C) Overpopulation
   (D) Exponential growth
   (E) Demographic accounting

5. Life expectancy has increased

   (A) only in the most-developed countries.
   (B) only in the least-developed countries.
   (C) owing to increased food production.
   (D) worldwide.
   (E) owing to the Green Revolution.

Free-Response Question

1. Exponential world population growth is one of the defining characteristics of contemporary human geography. Explain this growth in terms of

   (a) historical trends
   (b) global geographic patterns
   (c) economic development

Section 2: Population Parameters and Processes

Multiple-Choice Questions

1. The number of live births per thousand people per year is called the

   (A) total fertility rate.
   (B) natural increase rate.
   (C) crude birth rate.
   (D) exponential growth rate.
   (E) infant growth rate.

2. Which of the following countries is most likely to be showing the lowest natural increase rate?

   (A) Afghanistan
   (B) Liechtenstein
   (C) United States
   (D) Japan
   (E) Chile

3. Total fertility rate is not closely correlated with which of the following?

   (A) Industrial output
   (B) Gender empowerment
   (C) Education
   (D) Economic development
   (E) Literacy

4. The demographic accounting equation does not take into account
_____ when calculating a country's population.

   (A) the death rates
   (B) emigration
   (C) natural increase over time
   (D) instances when natural increase is negative
   (E) immigration

5. Within the United States, overall life expectancy

   (A) is limited by a unusually high infant mortality rate.
   (B) varies between various cohorts within the larger population.
   (C) varies between regions, with people in the Southwest living longer
   on average.
   (D) All of the above
   (E) Both (B) and (C)

Section 3: Human Migration

Multiple-Choice Questions

1. Millions of _____ came to the United States during the early years
of the 20th century.

   (A) suburbanites
   (B) emigrants
   (C) immigrants
   (D) refugees
   (E) colonists

2. In the 1930s, thousands of "okies" fled the Dust Bowl of the southern
Great Plains and moved to the fertile agricultural regions of California
to start a new life. This is an example of

   (A) external migration.
   (B) eco-migration.
   (C) political migration.
   (D) economic migration.
   (E) forced migration.

3. Which of the following is the result of chain migration?

   (A) The African slave trade
   (B) French colonial rule
   (C) The formation of Israel
   (D) San Francisco's Chinatown
   (E) Colonization of the American frontier

4. Refugees are produced through

(A) cultural migration.
(B) forced migration.
(C) internal migration.
(D) economic migration.
(E) chain migration.

5. Many recent college graduates and young professionals move to large, vibrant cities—such as New York, Chicago, and Los Angeles—with nightlife, cultural amenities, and job opportunities. These attractions are examples of

(A) economic factors.
(B) mobility opportunities.
(C) suburban amenities.
(D) pull factors.
(E) push factors.

6. Suburbanization is most evident in

(A) older American cities like Boston.
(B) large European cities like Madrid.
(C) regionally planned Canadian cities like Toronto.
(D) newer American cities like Las Vegas.
(E) large South American cities like Sao Paulo.

7. The Sun Belt includes

(A) the Rocky Mountain States.
(B) Alabama and Louisiana.
(C) Texas and New Mexico.
(D) Southern Nevada, southern California, and South Florida.
(E) Florida, Georgia, Alabama, and South Carolina.

Section 4: Population Structure and Composition

Multiple-Choice Questions

1. Thomas Malthus predicted that

   (A) technology will offset population growth.
   (B) the distribution of resources would be a continuing problem.
   (C) population would outpace food production.
   (D) the environment would allow less food to be grown in the future.
   (E) the Green Revolution would provide agricultural technology to support increasing populations.

2. Which of the following countries is at stage two of the demographic transition model?

   (A) San Marino
   (B) Nigeria
   (C) Denmark
   (D) Russia
   (E) Finland

3. A rectangle-shaped population pyramid indicates a country that is

   (A) growing slowly or not at all.
   (B) growing rapidly.
   (C) experiencing high immigration rates.
   (D) composed mainly of the older age classes.
   (E) highly dependent on the economically productive generations.

4. The baby boom

   (A) occurred in the years following World War I.
   (B) was a result of free love during the late 1960s.
   (C) was fostered by economic prosperity and relative peace.
   (D) was limited to California and the West.
   (E) was described by the off-beat author Douglas Coupland.

5. When the baby boomers have reached retirement age, what will the population pyramid for the United States look like?

   (A) An hourglass, wide at both top and bottom but narrow in the middle
   (B) Relatively rectangular, with a slight bulge near the top
   (C) Carrot-shaped, a narrow bottom and wide top
   (D) Pear-shaped, wide at the bottom, but narrow at the top
   (E) None of these

Section 5: Population and Sustainability

Multiple-Choice Questions

1. Which of the following countries would you expect to have the densest population?

    (A) China
    (B) Peru
    (C) Mexico
    (D) Belgium
    (E) Colombia

2. Carrying capacity is a function of

    (A) technology.
    (B) natural resources.
    (C) resource allocation.
    (D) limiting factors.
    (E) (A), (B), and (D)

3. Population policy usually involves limitations on

    (A) fertility levels.
    (B) immigration levels.
    (C) education levels.
    (D) All of the above
    (E) Both (A) and (B)

4. India and China are the world's two most populous countries. While China has instituted a strict population policy, India

    (A) for cultural reasons, encourages women to continue to reproduce.
    (B) does not endorse birth control because of the Catholic majority.
    (C) encourages lower fertility through education and access to family planning.
    (D) has a similar policy as China.
    (E) because of their agricultural system, encourages reproduction.

Free-Response Question

1. According to the demographic transition model, population growth should slow down as a country becomes more developed. Although many of the world's most-developed countries have already made the transition to extremely low, or even negative growth rates, some have not. The United States, for example, experienced increased population growth during the 1990s. Explain recent population growth in the United States, compared to slow growth in other highly developed countries.

POPULATION GEOGRAPHY   113

2. At the United Nations International Conference on Population and Development, held in Cairo, Egypt, in 1994, the Indian delegation claimed that, although huge human populations in places like India do have detrimental effects on the environment, consumption of natural resources is also an important problem. Discuss the ways that population, technology, and affluence have affected the environments of three countries: Costa Rica, China, and Canada.

Answers for Multiple-Choice Questions

Section 1: Human Population: A Global Perspective

1. **(B)**   Tropical Africa is one of the fastest growing areas in the world. Increases in crop production and better access to medical care, combined with high fertility rates have caused tremendous population growth throughout the region. Cities, like Lagos, Nigeria, are also among the fastest growing urban areas anywhere. Although the Sun Belt region of the United States has grown rapidly since World War II, this growth is nowhere near as sudden or as dramatic as that of tropical Africa.

2. **(A)**   Approximately 80% of the world's population lives in the less-developed countries, which includes all of Africa, Asia (excluding Japan), Latin America, and the island nations of the Caribbean and Pacific.

3. **(D)**   Human population has demonstrated overall steady growth throughout human history; however, in the last 200 years, population has been growing at exponential rates with 1 billion more people expected in just over 10 years, which is only 14 years after the world passed the 6 billion marker.

4. **(D)**   When you add a fixed number of people to a growing population each year, it is called arithmetic growth, but when you add a fixed percentage of people each year, it is called exponential growth. Exponential growth is compound, since the same percentage is being added to an increasing population each year; if the population is growing, then the same percentage will include more people next year than it does this year.

5. **(D)**   Life expectancy varies both between countries and within countries and is related to many factors, including race, sex, and wealth. However, life expectancy has increased worldwide during the past 50 years, from 45 to 65.

Section 2: Population Parameters and Processes

1. **(C)**   Many people get total fertility rate (TFR) and the crude birth rate (CBR) mixed up. The TFR refers to the average number of children born to a woman over the course of her life.

2. **(B)** Liechtenstein is a small, wealthy, and highly developed country located in the European Alps between Switzerland and Austria. Like other wealthy European countries with aging populations, Liechtenstein's growth rate is currently less than 1%.

3. **(A)** Although the total fertility rate is correlated with overall development, its relationship to industrial output is less direct. Small, highly developed countries, like Liechtenstein may have little heavy industry but low fertility rates, while countries like Brazil may have much more industrial activity but much higher fertility rates. Gender empowerment, education, and general economic development are all closely correlated with fertility.

4. **(C)** The demographic accounting equation predicts a country's future population on the basis of current birth rates, death rates, immigration rates, and emigration rates. It is not always a very accurate prediction because these rates can change dramatically over time.

5. **(B)** On average, white American males live longer than males of other races within the United States. Generally, life expectancy is calculated for particular countries; thus, it would be hard to determine regional variations in this statistic.

Section 3: Human Migration

1. **(C)** During the late 19th and early 20th centuries, millions of immigrants came to the United States from all over the world. Many came from southern and Western Europe in search of new economic opportunities.

2. **(B)** The Dust Bowl refugees, often called okies, left the southern Great Plains because of the environmental disaster of the Dust Bowl. When people leave an area because of environmental factors, it is called eco-migration.

3. **(D)** Ethnic urban enclaves, like San Francisco's Chinatown, result when people follow those who went before them in migrating from one region to another. Chinatown has been an attractive place for many Chinese immigrants to settle after arriving in the United States because of the neighborhood's familiar language and customs.

4. **(B)** Refugees, by definition, are people who are forced to leave their homes and move to a new place. Refugees can be produced through any type of forced migration, such as religious persecution, environmental degradation, or even natural disasters.

5. **(D)** Pull factors include anything that draws someone from one place to another. Cities provide strong pull factors for young people looking for economic opportunities and recreational diversions.

6. **(D)** Most newer American cities, and newer areas of older American cities, have been designed to accommodate sprawling suburban housing communities and wide highways geared for automobile transportation. Although some European cities have been affected by sprawl, it is much less of a problem in countries like France and Germany, where people

tend to live in older neighborhoods and the car is less important for transportation. Some Canadian cities, such as Toronto, have limited sprawl through well-coordinated urban planning.

7. **(D)** Parts of the Rocky Mountains, the Old South, and the Southwest are all considered to be within the Sun Belt. However, each of these regions also contains areas that have not benefited from the economic growth associated from the Sun Belt phenomenon. Southern Nevada, southern California, and South Florida are all classic Sun Belt regions.

Section 4: Population Structure and Composition

1. **(C)** Thomas Malthus predicted that food production would grow arithmetically while population would grow geometrically (exponentially). Malthus' theory has been criticized because it does not account for other factors affecting food production and population such as technology, the distribution of food resources, personal choice, and environmental change.

2. **(B)** In stage two of the demographic transition model, a country's population growth is high because death rates have decreased but birth rates have not. Nigeria's explosive population growth is an example of this situation. Denmark, Russia, and San Marino are all advanced to stage three, in which fertility decreases and population growth slows down.

3. **(A)** A triangle-shaped population pyramid indicates that there are a high percentage of young people in the population and that it is growing rapidly. A rectangular-shaped age-sex distribution means that the population is composed of a more even range of older and younger people and that the population is growing slowly or not at all.

4. **(C)** The baby boom, which occurred during the years following World War II, was a national phenomenon in which economic prosperity and relative peace were accompanied by high fertility rates. Although fertility began to decline as early as the late 1940s, the baby boom generation became the most numerous, wealthiest, and most prosperous generation in American history.

5. **(B)** The baby boom is a large cohort of the American population, larger than the generation behind them. When they reach retirement age, their bracket, near the top of the pyramid, will most likely be larger that other segments of the pyramid. This demonstrates the magnitude of the dependency ratio, or number of individuals relying on younger, economically productive generations for support.

Section 5: Population Sustainability

1. **(D)** Small, northern European countries, like the Netherlands and Belgium are some of the most densely populated in the world. China has the largest population of any country on earth, yet its immense size allows for large, sparsely populated rural areas to remain.

2. **(E)**   The quality and quantity of natural resources available in an area and technological innovations that help people to use those resources both affect carrying capacity. The limiting factor describes the resource in scarcest supply within a region and thus provides a method for understanding how big a population an area can adequately sustain. However, the limiting factor within a region can be extended by use of technological innovations. Because of this, carrying capacity changes over time and is notoriously hard to pin down.

3. **(E)**   These two forces, births and immigration, are the largest contributors to population increase within a country. Humane population policy usually seeks to limit or decrease somehow the fertility level within a country, or it seeks to limit the number of individuals allowed into a particular country.

4. **(C)**   Population policies implemented within countries usually reflect the country's prevailing ideologies and thus, usually its political system. China is a communist-controlled country, which is demonstrated in their strict enforcement of their one-child policy. However, India is a democratic nation that encourages, rather than demands, lower fertility through increased education and access to family planning.

Answers for Free-Response Questions

Section 1: Human Population: A Global Perspective

1. Main points:
   - For the great majority of human history, population grew very slowly. It was not until the 19th century that world population reached 1 billion.
   - During the 19th and 20th centuries the world's human population grew exponentially because of increases in crop yields, advances in health care, and a variety of other factors.
   - During the 20th century, developing countries experienced the most dramatic population growth. Many of the least-developed countries are still among the fastest growing.
   - The current world population is over 6 billion. Most of the world's people live in poverty in the less-developed countries. Many of these people have inadequate access to health care, social services, and healthy environments with clean air and water.
   - Population growth is a gendered issue. In countries where women are given access to education, health care, family planning services, and employment opportunities, population growth always drops, independent of other cultural factors such as religion.
   - China and India alone account for about a third of the world's population. With less than 300 million people, the United States has about 5% of the world's population.

Section 5: Population Sustainability

1. Main points:
    - The demographic transition model (DTM) is based on a simplified, deterministic approach to population growth; it does not account for particular historical events, such as wars, international agreements, economic cycles, immigration, or a country's relations with its neighbors.
    - In the United States, population growth has fluctuated over time. In the 1990s, several factors that are not accounted for in the DTM, caused growth to increase.
    - The most important of these factors was immigration. During the 1990s, economic prosperity—in part associated with a boom in the high-tech economy—initiated a need for more workers. American companies recruited workers from overseas, and thousands of construction and service industry jobs opened for unskilled and semiskilled laborers from Mexico and other developing countries.
    - Another factor causing population growth in the United States during the 1990s is that many of the new immigrants to the United States had higher overall fertility rates than citizens whose families had been established in the United States for several generations.
    - Although the DTM was correct in predicting that fertility rates would drop within established American families, economics and immigration caused the rate of growth to increase in the United States during the 1990s.

2. Main points:
    - Environmental degradation is a nearly universal feature of today's world; however, its causes are difficult to quantify. Large-scale economic and social forces drive environmental change, yet most conservation efforts are aimed at the specific, proximate causes of environmental problems.
    - In addition, the relationships between population, consumption, and technology are extremely complex.
    - Malthusians think that overpopulation is the main cause of environmental problems. Indeed, countries such as China, India, and Indonesia, and other developing countries with their enormous human populations, place huge stresses on their environments and natural resources.
    - However, as the Indians have stated, overconsumption by the most-developed countries is also responsible for environmental problems. The United States, for example, consumes a disproportionately large share of the world's natural resources. Even though the United States has only about 300 million people, their impact is felt worldwide, through their consumption of resources such as oil and forest products.

Additional Resources

Text

Livi-Bacci, Massimo. 2001. *A Concise History of World Population*. Malden, Massachusetts: Blackwell.

This book provides a concise history of the world's population, primarily by looking at the intersection between nature, culture, and population. By examining historic checks on growth, and projections for future growth, Livi-Bacci proposes, using historical patterns, methods for preventing future environmental and human catastrophes that may result from overpopulation.

Weinstein, Jay, and Vijayan Pillai. 2001. *Demography: The Science of Population*. Needham Heights, Massachusetts: Allyn and Bacon.

The authors begin by talking about population in general, but then further explore different demographic measures across the globe including birth and fertility, mortality, and migration. They also look at several different models designed to understand population growth and change, and finally investigate population policy and some of the environmental repercussions of overpopulation.

Meadows, Dana. H., Dennis L. Meadows, and Jorgen Randers. 1992. *Beyond the Limits*. Post Mills, Vermont: Chelsea Green.

This book discusses some of the population limits the earth has already passed, forecasting global collapse if the trends do not change and people do not start living sustainably. The authors introduce a new model, called the World$_3$, which is computer-based and uses different policy initiatives to predict different scenarios for the future of the world's resources.

Web

Musee de L'homme. *6 Billion Human Beings: http://www.popexpo.net/eMain. html*

An excellent website that looks at current population growth with the opening page containing a counter illustrating how rapidly the earth adds to its numbers. From the opening page, you can choose from a number of options that allow you to explore the different factors that contribute to population growth and how they vary across the globe, as well as the different factors contributing to differing death rates across the globe, and finally, the site explores many questions relating to recent population explosion, population growth and demographic rates in the future, and the earth's ability to support an ever-expanding global population.

Population Council: *http://www.popcouncil.org*

This website reports on research conducted by the council on three fronts: biomedical, social sciences, and public health. The research is geared toward understanding reproductive health and population growth across the globe.

Some issues they currently investigate include access to reproductive health, particularly in the developing world; education and career opportunities for women; and the prevention of HIV/AIDS transmission.

UN Demographic and Social Statistics: *http://www.un.org/depts/unsd/*

This extremely extensive website includes numerous demographic statistics. While the data are an excellent source for understanding current demographic trends across the globe, most of what you will be interested in investigating requires a subscription to the website.

Census Bureau: *www.census.gov*

This excellent and extremely comprehensive website provides U.S. demographic statistics at all different scales. If you are a teacher, you could use this site to develop an activity in which students must compare demographic measures between two different census tracts within the local area.

Population Reference Bureau: *www.popnet.org*

This website is a directory that provides comprehensive data on global population issues such as demographic statistics, education, environment, economics, gender, and reproductive health. You can search for websites by organization, by region or country, or by topics within countries.

The World Health Organization: *www.who.int*

This site provides information on health threats from disease, environment, and lifestyle sources, many of which relate to population issues, specifically in the developing world.

The United Nations Population Fund: *www.unfpa.org/*

This website reports on the organization's goals to assist developing countries in reproductive health and family planning issues. It also includes access to the current "State of the World" population report which allows you to explore the connections between population growth and environmental impact across the globe, along with other issues such as women and the environment, health and the environment, and global agreements on human rights, reproductive health, and gender equity.

CHAPTER 4
Cultural Geography

Summary

Cultural geography is the study of how cultures vary over space. Cultural geographers also study the ways in which cultures interact with their environments. Possibilism, the notion that humans are the primary architects of culture and yet are limited somewhat by their environmental surroundings, is now a dominant paradigm in the field. Geographers study a wide diversity of cultural traits, including language, religion, and ethnicity. Geographers also study the everyday aspects of people's lives, such as folk traditions and popular culture, in order to better understand the many ways that diverse people make sense of a rapidly changing world.

In This Chapter

- Cultural Basics
- Language
- Religion
- Ethnicity
- Popular Culture

Key Terms

Acculturation	Denomination
Animism	Dialect
Artifact	Diaspora
Buddhism	Ecumene
Caste system	Environmental determinism
Christianity	Ethnic cleansing
Creole	Ethnic neighborhood
Cultural complex	Ethnic religion
Cultural extinction	Ethnicity
Cultural geography	Evangelical religions
Cultural hearth	Folk culture
Cultural imperialism	Fundamentalism
Cultural trait	Genocide
Culture	Ghetto
Custom	Global religion

Hinduism	Official language
Indo-European family	Pidgin
Islam	Pilgrimage
Judaism	Polytheism
Language extinction	Pop culture
Language family	Race
Language group	Romance languages
Lingua franca	Shaman
Literacy	Sino-Tibetan family
Local religion	Syncretic
Minority	Toponym
Missionary	Tradition
Monotheism	Universalizing religion
Multiculturalism	

Cultural Basics

Culture means many things to many people. Linguistically, the English word "culture" derives from the Latin word *cultus,* which means "to care about." The concept of culture dates back at least to the Enlightenment, when culture referred to a variety of endeavors that were essentially human, such as agri-*culture.* Later, the term came to connote differences between people's lifestyles in different areas of the world. The modern notion of culture, which includes all the ideas, practices, and material objects associated with a particular group of people, evolved from this notion of difference. The study of how cultures vary over space is called **cultural geography**. Cultural geographers use techniques from sociology, anthropology, psychology, history, and numerous other disciplines to better understand the spatial dimensions of human cultures throughout the inhabited world, known as the **ecumene**.

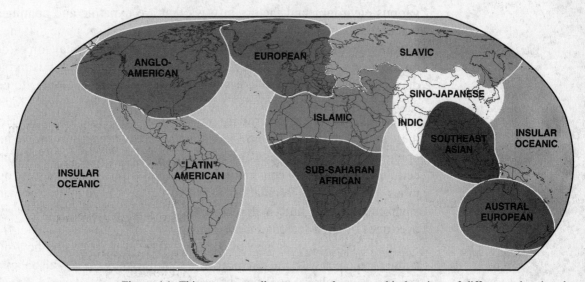

Figure 4.1. This map generally represents the geographic locations of different cultural realms across the globe.

When geographers think about culture, they include both the material things that a group of people cares for and the suite of beliefs, values, and characteristics that define their collective identity and set them apart from others. The material aspects of culture are called **artifacts** and include such things as clothing, tools, and artwork, whereas the practices followed by the people of a particular group are called **customs**. A cohesive collection of customs is called a **tradition**. Traditions are **syncretic**, meaning that they borrow from both the past and the present, and dynamic, since they are constantly changing over time. On a broader scale, **cultural traits** are specific customs that are part of everyday life, such as language, religion, ethnicity, social institutions, and aspects of popular culture. The group of traits that define a particular culture is called a **cultural complex**. Finally, all cultural traits have **cultural hearths**, or places where they first arose.

Cultural geographers study the spatial distribution of cultural traits and the intricate relationships between cultures and the natural environment. The doctrine of **environmental determinism**, which had enjoyed considerable popularity at several points in history, was a particularly important impediment in modern geographer's early efforts to study culture-environment relations. Environmental determinists claim that cultural traits are formed and controlled by environmental conditions. Certain types of people, who come from cultures that arose in certain physical environments, may be smarter, more attractive, or more able to govern themselves as a result. This doctrine, the racist implications of which are obvious, was often used by European states to justify their colonization of native peoples in Africa, South America, Australia, and elsewhere because the people who lived in those hot, muggy, and seemingly oppressive environments were deemed less intelligent and industrious than individuals coming from more temperate climates characteristic of the European continent.

In recent years, a new conception of culture-environment relations has found favor among geographers. In this version, called possibilism, different natural environments offer both restraints and opportunities to people in various regions. However, people control their own destinies and deal with these various environmental factors in ways that are dynamic and contingent and that unfold unpredictably over history. Many possibilists argue that the degree to which a particular culture is influenced by environmental forces depends on the level of technology prevalent within that society. Cultures in the more developed parts of the globe have designed various technologies to counteract environmental limitations. For instance, automobiles with four-wheel drive make traveling in virtually any weather condition possible. However, these and other similar types of technologies are not readily available in developing societies; thus, these cultures may encounter greater limitations from certain environmental constraints. Possibilism offers excellent new opportunities to explore the fascinating ways that cultures have interacted with their environments over time, without the intellectually limiting and clearly racist overtones of environmental determinism.

Finally, beyond studying how cultures vary over space and how different cultures interact with the environment, cultural geographers also explore the various ways cultural qualities diffuse to other parts of the world. Recall from Chapter 2, the discussion of the different ways certain phenomena diffuse across space. Cultural geographers study how language, religion, and other cultural artifacts such as fashion, music, and culinary traditions move from their areas of origin to other, very culturally different parts of the world. How is it that Americans can choose from pad thai, Indian curry, pasta primavera, or Japanese sushi for dinner on almost any given evening of the week? Or, why are Europeans wearing Levi's jeans as they walk into a Burger King in Amsterdam? In today's world, cities have become havens to numerous cultural diversities; cultural geographers study how and why specific cultural traits are so easily transmitted and accepted in other parts of the world.

Language

Language is one of the oldest, most geographically diverse, and most complex cultural traits on earth. Although language is basic to the human experience, it is clear that people from different parts of the world have found very different ways to express themselves. In the prehistoric past, there were probably at least 10,000 languages spoken throughout the world. Currently, about 5,000 to 7,000 languages remain, with Africa and Asia being the most linguistically rich continents. The world's greatest concentration of linguistic diversity is on the island of New Guinea. In New Guinea, rugged terrain and social mores limit interaction between different tribal groups, enabling some 900 languages to persist into the present day. The linguistic diversity of New Guinea provides a sharp contrast to the modern global trend, in which a few languages are becoming increasingly dominant across the world. A knowledge of the geography of language is essential for understanding larger spatial patterns in human societies and for piecing together the common histories of people who have spoken to, written to, and learned from each other over time.

On the broadest scale, all languages belong to a **language family**. A language family is a collection of many languages, all of which came from the same original tongue long ago, but have since evolved different characteristics. Although all languages in a language family have a common origin, two members of the same family may sound very different depending on how long ago the two languages branched off and on the historical events that have altered them since.

About 50% of the world's people speak languages belonging to the **Indo-European family.** Languages from this family are spoken on all continents but are dominant in Europe, Russia, North and South America, Australia, and parts of southwestern Asia and India. This language family includes the Germanic and Romance languages, as well as Slavic, Indic, Celtic and Iranic. Of the world's people, 20% speak languages from the **Sino-Tibetan family.** This language area spreads through most of Southeast Asia and China and is comprised of Chinese (which has the world's most speakers), Burmese, Tibetan, Japanese, and Korean. The final 30% of the world's populations speak languages from the Afro-Asiatic, Niger-Congo, Altaic, or Austronesian language families.

Language families can also be divided into smaller **language groups**. A language group is a set of languages with a relatively recent common origin and many similar characteristics. Spanish and Italian, for example, are both

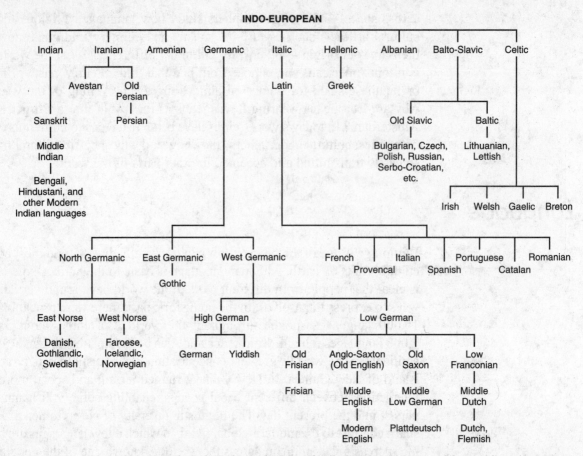

Figure 4.2. The Indo-European language family represents just one of the world's major language families, but its members include many of the languages spoken across the globe today.

part of the **Romance languages**—they are both derived from Latin, they have many related words, and they contain similar grammatical structures. Diversity also exists within individual languages. **Dialects** are geographically distinct versions of a single language that vary somewhat from the parent form. Italian and English are both languages that contain numerous dialects, reflecting the historical, social, and geographic differences between many diverse peoples. Anyone who has traveled to cities such as London, Toronto, New York, Houston, and Sydney is well aware of distinct variations in the English language. Different dialects may have different terms for the same thing, for example, an English speaker from the American South might call his friends "y'all," whereas an English speaker from Australia might call them "mates." Dialectical differences are, however, often more easily recognized through differences in accent.

Languages are carried over space by the same set of diffusion processes described in Chapter 2. Language diffusion occurs when migration, trade, war, or some other event exposes one group of people to the language of another. When two groups of people with different languages meet, a new language with some characteristics of each may result. This hodgepodge form is called a **pidgin.** If, over time, a pidgin evolves to the point at which it becomes the primary language of the people who speak it, then it is called a **Creole**. Interesting Creole languages have frequently developed in colonial settings where the linguistic traditions of indigenous peoples and colonizers have blended. Multiple other tongues have actually influenced some modern languages. Modern English, for example, contains aspects of half a dozen different languages because the British Isles have seen so many foreign conquerors and visitors over the centuries. The colonial history of West Africa offers a very different example of the ways in which linguistic interactions can affect other aspects of culture and economics. In Ghana, which was colonized by Britain during the late 1800s, many people speak English. In neighboring Togo, where the French exercised colonial control during the same period, most native people now speak French. In this case, patterns of colonial history have had important implications for trade, interpersonal interactions, power relationships, and international politics.

Many linguists believe that the development of alphabets and the resulting literary traditions have contributed to the complexity and dominance of particular cultures, and thus particular nations across the globe. Most likely the invention of agricultural societies, alphabets, and the resulting efficient record keeping, provided a means for these societies to dominate other illiterate societies more easily. Literacy is thus one of the critical tools that explains why countries such as the United Kingdom, France, the Netherlands, Belgium, Portugal, Spain, and the United States have had such a dramatic impact on the languages spoken around the world today. When these nations had colonial power over large numbers of African and South American countries, they imposed their languages on the native populations. The imposition was easily accomplished because the European nations had well-developed alphabets whereas many of the native languages were passed on solely through verbal transmission. Even after decolonization, the European languages remained as dominant languages spoken in these areas, as already demonstrated in the examples of Ghana and Togo. Another poignant example is evident in South America, where, in 1494, the Treaty of Tordesillas determined which portion of the continent would fall under Spanish control and which would fall under Portugal's sovereignty. The line divided the continent nearly equally from top to bottom, and the repercussions of this division are still evident today, even though Spain and Portugal no longer rule in this part of the world. The Portuguese-controlled side consists of what we know as Brazil, in which most residents still speak Portuguese; the remainder of the continent fell under Spanish rule, and Spanish remains the dominant language spoken by most of the population.

When people who speak different languages need to communicate quickly and efficiently, a **lingua franca** frequently results. A lingua franca is an extremely simple language that combines aspects of two or more complex languages. For example, in Southeast Asia, where the residents of hundreds of little islands and mountain valleys each speak their own unique language or dialect, simple trade languages are used at ports and central markets. Lingua francas are usually very simple, often lacking fundamental features common to most full-fledged languages, like verb tense. However, they provide an efficient and easy-to-learn means for diverse people to engage in trade despite the great distances and significant cultural barriers that normally separate them.

Although many countries have established one or more **official languages**, in which all government business occurs, most countries also contain significant linguistic diversity. In the United States, which has no official language, dozens of native tongues are in common usage. In many urban areas, like Los

Angeles, New York, Chicago, and San Francisco, a significant portion of the resident population speaks a first language other than English. A few countries, such as Switzerland and Belgium, have formally recognized their cultural diversity by establishing multiple official languages. In Canada, language and the cultural heritage associated with it has been a source of conflict between secession activists from French-speaking Quebec and the majority English-speaking Canadian population.

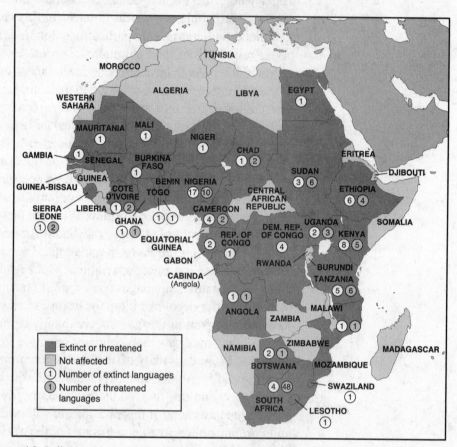

Figure 4.3. Indigenous languages are rapidly dying out across the globe, particularly in formerly colonized countries, like Africa, where colonial languages wiped out many native tongues.

An important topic in the current scholarship surrounding linguistic diversity is **language extinction**. Language extinction occurs when a language is no longer in use by any living people. Thousands of languages have become extinct over the eons since language first developed, but the process of language extinction has accelerated greatly during the past 300 years. Colonialism in the 18th and 19th centuries and economic globalization in the 20th century have driven many languages to premature extinction. As in the examples of Ghana and Togo, languages such as English and French have replaced dozens of native tongues all over the world. Although languages can be lost through the extinction of an entire people or through linguistic evolution over time, the pressures of economic and social **acculturation** are responsible for most of today's losses. Acculturation refers to the adoption of cultural traits, such as language, by one group under the influence of another. Many of the languages that have been lost over the past few hundred years were spoken in now defunct Native American societies. It is important to note that some languages have also been lost as part of a greater **cultural extinction** in which an entire culture was obliterated by war, disease, acculturation, or a combination of the three. When a culture and its linguistic tradition disappear, it takes with it a tremendous amount of history and knowledge that might never be regained. For instance, language can provide clues to various historical human migration patterns through the study of the assimilation of certain words across differing historical cultural groups.

Today, movements have begun to revive lost aspects of culture and, in particular, native languages. In parts of Scotland, Ireland, and Wales, Celtic is being brought back from near extinction, Hebrew was revived after World War II when Israel became an independent state, and Native Americans from Alaska to the tip of South America have begun to reestablish their distinct and unique linguistic heritage. Although it is economically important for many people to speak the languages that are widely used for international trade, such as English, Russian, and Chinese, the world's thousands of other languages all hold priceless secrets to human history and important insights into our relationships with other people and with the environments in which we live.

Another important issue having to do with the geography of language that was mentioned earlier is **literacy**. Literacy, or the ability to read and write, varies dramatically between and even within countries. Literacy also varies between genders, especially in countries where social mores prohibit women from receiving a formal education. While many of the world's wealthiest countries have literacy rates approaching 100%, in some African and Asian states, fewer than half of the population can read. According to a study published in 2000 by the United Nations Statistics Division, in the African country of Niger less than 24% of the adult men and less than 9% of the adult women can read and write. In Afghanistan, the Taliban regime, which ruled the country from 1996 to 2001, instituted measures to limit women's educational opportunities. As a result, in 2000, only about 22% of Afghani women could read and write, compared to about 52% of men. The Taliban, like many other tyrannical regimes, used illiteracy as a tool of oppression.

One final aspect of language of interest to cultural geographers is that of how language manifests itself in the landscape. The names different cultures give to various features of the earth such as settlements, terrain features, streams, and other land features are called **toponyms** and can reveal interesting aspects of the spatial patterns of different languages and dialects. In the United States, many of the names given to American cities reveal the dominant cultures of their first inhabitants: "New York," "Baton Rouge," and "San Diego" reveal the English, French, and Spanish influence of some of the first settlers in these parts of the country. Many of the states in the United States were named after royalty in the settlers' countries of origin: Georgia for an English King, Louisiana for a French king, and Virginia for the Virgin Queen Elizabeth. Most place names in any culture contain two parts: the generic and the specific. The generic classifies whatever is being described such as a lake, river, mountain, or street, while the specific term modifies the classification: Lake *Erie*, *Mississippi* River, Mount *Whitney*, *Wall* Street. The various ways different cultures have named the land throughout history can provide insights into historical cultural migration patterns and diffusion processes across the globe.

Religion

For many people, religion, more than any other cultural trait, defines who they are and how they understand the world around them. Because religion is tied to all aspects of human culture and social systems, studying the geography of religion can help us understand everything from population growth, to international politics, to the design and structure of cities. For these reasons, religion occupies a central place in the field of cultural geography.

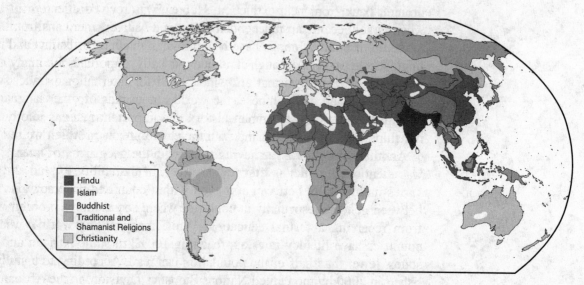

Figure 4.4. The geographic distribution of the world's major religions.

There are many commonalities between the world's many religious traditions. First, all religions share some set of teachings that imply a value system. Second, all religions include some notion of the sacred, whether the sacred be a single divine being, a set of texts, or some powerful symbol. And third, all religions include some ideas about the place of human beings in the universe. Many religions also have a creation story to explain the origins of humans and the physical universe. Some religions also include teachings on law, politics, social mores, sexual relations, physical fitness, cleanliness, eating habits, and even interior decorating!

In thinking about the geography of religion, it is useful to first consider why some religions may have spread far from their hearths, while others have remained primarily local or regional in distribution. One explanation for this is that some religions, through their teachings, seek to unite people from diverse backgrounds, while others seek to ground people in local traditions or landscapes. While Buddhism seeks to explain ultimate realities for all people—such as the nature of suffering and the path toward self-realization—many Native American religions center around local environmental phenomena and use locally occurring plants and animals as religious figures or in religious ceremonies. Religions that seek to unite are called **universalizing religions,** and those that are more spiritually bound to particular regions are called **local religions**. Another useful distinction that may help to explain the global distribution of religions is that some religions are explicitly evangelical, while others are not. **Evangelical religions**, such as Christianity, expand their membership by using **missionaries** to recruit new followers actively. However, some nonevangelical religions, like Buddhism, are also widespread.

Most scholars think of religions as being divided into a few main categories. Some religions are **monotheistic**, meaning that they teach the primacy of a single god, whereas other religions are **polytheistic**, teaching that there are numerous gods or spiritual powers. Christianity, Islam, and Buddhism are **global religions** in the sense that their members are numerous and widespread and that their doctrines might appeal to different people from any region of the globe. **Ethnic religions** tend to appeal to smaller groups of people with a common heritage or to large groups of people living in a single region. Local religions, which were mentioned earlier, are also associated with particular places; tend to attract small, localized followings; and are often invested in the powers of particular living people or local natural phenomena. **Shamanism** is the term for a local religion in which a single person takes on the roles of priest, counselor, and physician and claims a conduit to the supernatural world. **Animism** is another class of local religious traditions, mostly from Africa and the Americas, in which the world is seen as being infused with spiritual and even supernatural powers. Although there are many other ways to classify the world's diverse religions, these distinctions can help us to understand the spatial distribution of religious belief and participation.

Now let's look at the three global religions already mentioned because they affect the daily lives of so many people. With about 2 billion believers, **Christianity** is the world's most widespread religion. Christianity is a monotheistic religion with its origins in Judaism. Christians believe in one God and that his son Jesus was the promised Messiah, delivering salvation to all people, not just the chosen people of Israel. Although Christianity is practiced on every continent and in almost every country, the forms it takes vary significantly between places. The three major categories of Christianity are Roman Catholic, Protestant, and Eastern Orthodox. The Roman Catholic Church, based at Vatican City in Rome, is the most important religion in large parts of Western Europe and North America and is overwhelmingly dominant in Central and South America. Pockets of Catholicism also exist in Asia, Australia, and Africa. In 1517, the Protestant tradition began when Martin Luther broke away from the Catholic Church and began a different type of Christian church, which had a similar belief system to Catholicism but with much less emphasis on many of the rituals that were characteristic of the Catholic Church during that time. Protestantism includes a large group of distinct **denominations**, some of which differ considerably from Catholicism in their beliefs and practices. In the United States, Baptists, Episcopalians, Lutherans, Methodists, Mormons, and Presbyterians all comprise important Protestant denominations. The American Frontier provided individualistic new settlers an atmosphere in which to freely express whatever type of faith they desired. While certain regionalizations of different denominations exist in America today, such as the Mormons in Utah or the Baptists in the South, in many American cities, you can find a diversity of different worship centers for different types of Protestant faiths. Finally, Eastern Orthodox is dominant only in Eastern Europe and Russia, although its adherents also live in smaller populations throughout the world.

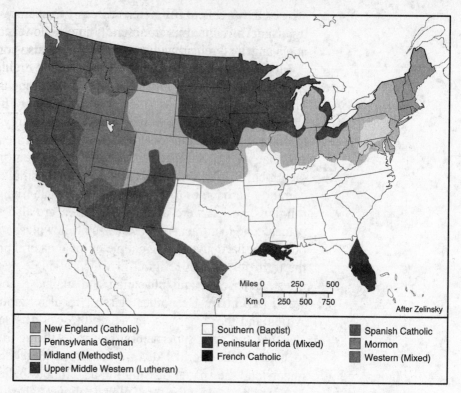

New England (Catholic)
Pennsylvania German
Midland (Methodist)
Upper Middle Western (Lutheran)

Southern (Baptist)
Peninsular Florida (Mixed)
French Catholic

Spanish Catholic
Mormon
Western (Mixed)

Miles 0   250   500
Km 0   250   500   750

After Zelinsky

Figure 4.5. The geographic spread of Protestant denominations across the United States.

Islam claims about 1 billion members worldwide. Although its distribution is centered in North Africa and the Middle East, Muslims (practitioners of Islam) are found throughout the world, including Europe, Southeast Asia, and the United States. Islam is a monotheistic religion, also stemming from Judaism, which is based on the belief that there is one God, Allah, and that Muhammad was Allah's prophet. Mecca, Saudi Arabia, is the birthplace of Muhammad and serves as the base for the nation of Islam. Observance of the Koran, or word of Allah revealed to Mohammed, along with the observation of the five pillars of the faith unite Muslims across the globe. The five pillars consist of repeated recital of the basic creed; prayers five times daily, facing Mecca; the observance of Ramadan, which is a month of daytime fasting; almsgiving; and if possible, a **pilgrimage,** or journey, to the holy city of Mecca, the birthplace of Mohammed.

In recent years, a surge in radical **fundamentalism** has caused division and conflict between Muslims throughout the world. It is important to understand this distinction in the wake of the September 11 terrorist attacks in the United States. The individuals participating in these attacks were all fundamentalist Muslims. Most fundamentalists take the Koran as an unquestioned guide on both religious and secular matters. Consequently, most fundamentalists adamantly avoid any sort of western influence on their culture or belief system to maintain purity of faith. The Taliban of Afghanistan is also comprised of Islamic fundamentalists who strongly oppose Western culture. As discussed earlier, this oppressive regime limited the educational opportunities of women in their society. Islamic fundamentalism provides an illustrative example of the various manifestations a belief system can have within its own society and across the globe. Islam is not the only religion experiencing a rise in fundamentalism. Many other religions have fundamentalist sects, or groups that strictly and intensely adhere to the basic tenets of their religion. Similar to Islam, fundamentalism in other religions can contribute to intense conflict. Later, we will look at more examples of how religion contributes to various political tensions and territorial conflicts on the earth's surface.

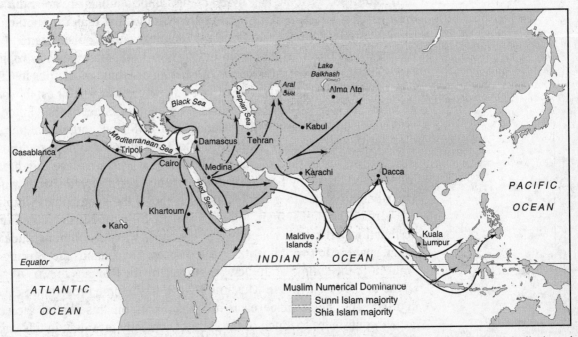

Figure 4.6. Islam originated in Saudi Arabia near Mecca and Medina and diffused originally through expansion diffusion to surrounding areas and then by relocation diffusion to Malaysia, Indonesia.

With more than 300 million adherents worldwide, **Buddhism** is the third great world religion. Buddhism, which originated in the 6th century B.C. in northern India, traces its origins and many of its traditions from Hinduism. Founded by Siddhartha Gautama (or, simply, the Buddha), Buddhism teaches that suffering originates from our attachment to life and to our worldly possessions. According to Buddhism, a state of Nirvana, or ultimate purification and happiness, can be achieved through an eight-step process. Although Buddhism is still centered in its ancient East Asian hearth, it has gained an increasingly large following in Europe and North America since the 1950s. This pattern can be attributed in part to emigration by Asian people to Western nations and in part to Buddhism's teachings, which seem to resonate with many westerners. Nearly half of the Buddhists in the United States live in southern California.

Although they are not truly global religions, Hinduism and Judaism are important ethnic religions that deserve to be mentioned briefly here. **Hinduism** is a religion closely tied to Indian culture. For over 4,000 years, people living on the Indian subcontinent have developed a cohesive and unique society that integrates their spiritual beliefs with their daily practices and official institutions. One important aspect of the Hindu culture is the **caste system**, which gives every Indian a particular place in the social hierarchy from birth. Each caste defines individuals' occupations along with their social connections, where they can live, the clothes they wear, and the food they eat. Individuals may improve the position they inherit in the caste system in their next life through their actions, or karma. After many lives of good karma, they may be relieved from the cycle of life and achieve salvation and eternal peace through union with the universal soul known as the Brahman. Hindus worship in temples or shrines that can be found in every Hindu village. Additionally, Hindus follow the doctrine of ahimsa, as do Buddhists, which instructs them to refrain from harming any living being. Thus, animals are an enduring presence in most Hindu societies. **Judaism** was the first major monotheistic religion. It is based on a sense of ethnic identity, and its adherents tend to form tight-knit communities wherever they live. In 1948, after the catastrophe of the Holocaust and almost 2,000 years of existing as ethnic minorities in Christian- and Muslim-dominated countries, the Jewish people finally established their own state in Israel. Today, most Jews live in either Israel or the United States.

Beyond understanding the location and diffusion patterns of the world's major religions, geographers are also interested in how religious traditions manifest themselves in the landscape. The fact that Muslims face the direction of Mecca each time they pray provides an example of a sacred space, which is of special significance to geographers for it shows the geographical implications of a particular belief system. Another example from the Muslim community can be found in Jerusalem, where two of the world's major religions, Judaism and Islam, share, often with hostility, sacred space. Here stands the Wailing Wall, a remnant of the temple of the Jews destroyed by the Romans in A.D. 70, with the Dome of the Rock, where Muslims believe Mohammed rose into heaven, just in front. The significance each religion places on this shared sacred space largely contributes to much of the conflict currently prevalent in this part of the world. Other examples of sacred spaces in the landscape include places of worship such as temples, synagogues, churches, mosques, or cathedrals. The spatial distribution of these buildings provides geographers with an understanding of the prevalence of particular religions in particular places; they also provide clues about the belief system simply through architectural style. If you have ever driven by a Mormon temple, you probably noted the near-regality of these establishments. It is obvious from the lighting, the gates, the stone, and the detail, that these places are sacred houses of worship. In fact, you may not completely enter one of these temples or tabernacles unless you are a Mormon.

One final important topic regarding the geography of religion is how it contributes to various territorial tensions and conflicts across the globe. An extreme level of violence that relates to religion and territory currently plagues the Middle East. The Palestinians, who are predominantly Muslim, are working hard to establish their own state including the territories of the West Bank, Gaza strip, and East Jerusalem in Israel. However, their requests conflict with the predominantly Jewish Israelites who currently have control over the land. This tension has caused major bloodshed between the two culturally and religiously different groups, particularly in the past few years, although the conflict has existed for almost a century. Another example of current territorial conflict is that of Northern Ireland. This country is under British rule, but a large portion of the Irish Catholic population wishes to be under the sovereignty of culturally and religiously similar Ireland. This conflict manifests itself most poignantly in the city of Belfast where a wall separates the two culturally and religiously different groups. In addition, flags from each country are displayed predominantly through the city, murals of Irish nationalists are painted on walls in the Irish-Catholic part of town, and even cemeteries choose the nationalities of those they will hold. As mentioned earlier, religion can be one of the most defining characteristics of a culture and, as such, it becomes a unifying and sometimes violent force in securing a place where a particular culture can freely celebrate and maintain its belief system.

Ethnicity

The word "**ethnicity**" originates from the ancient Greek root *ethnos*, which referred to a unique and cohesive group of people. Currently, the term refers to a group of people who share a common *identity*. The term first came into popular usage during the 1940s as an alternative to the term "**race**," which had become negatively associated with Hitler's Nazi regime, but the two terms do not mean exactly the same thing. Ethnicity involves more than simply the physical characteristics commonly associated with race—it also involves a person's perceived social and cultural identity. The meaning of the concept continues to be debated, however, because individual people express their common ethnicities in different ways because the lines that divide ethnic groups are almost always blurry, and the cultural traditions that characterize particular ethnic groups are notoriously flexible.

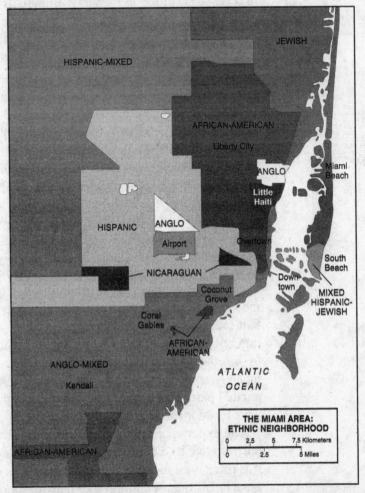

Figure 4.7. Miami, like many large coastal cities in the United States, demonstrates a strong ethnic diversity in the various ethnic neighborhoods comprising the urban landscape.

Today many place great value on ethnic diversity, realizing that communities are made richer by a variety of perspectives. However, disagreements between people of differing ethnic identities are also at the heart of many social and political conflicts throughout the world. Over 90% of the world's countries contain more than one ethnicity, all countries share borders with people of foreign ethnicities, and many otherwise cohesive ethnic groups have been artificially divided by political boundaries. Places where particularly sharp ethnic boundaries characterize the cultural landscape or where people of various ethnic identities lay claim to the same lands or resources are often marred by political unrest and violence. In recent years, the Middle East, the Balkans of Eastern Europe, eastern Africa, and Kashmir (on the border between India and Pakistan) have all experienced devastating ethnic violence. In the worst cases, this violence has taken the form of **ethnic cleansing,** which is the effort to rid a country or region of everyone of a particular ethnicity either through forced migration, or through **genocide**, which is a premeditated effort to kill everyone from a particular ethnic group.

Back in the United States, the 2000 census showed in dramatic fashion the extent to which the American cultural landscape has become truly **multicultural**. Hispanic-Americans, Asian-Americans, and other once "**minority**" ethnic groups are now part of a culturally diverse, polyglot nation in which a clear ethnic majority simply no longer exists. Geographers are now hard at work making sense of the tremendous amount of cultural data collected through the 2000 census. Perhaps the most striking ethnic pattern to emerge from early analyses of the 2000 census is that the population of Hispanic-Americans, particularly Latinos of Mexican origin, has increased dramatically during the past ten years. Of particular interest was the discovery that Latino populations have increased not only in areas traditionally associated with Hispanic-American culture—such as California, Texas, Florida, New York, and Illinois—but also in large cities and rural regions across the country. The relative openness of the U.S. borders during the 1990s, combined with economic globalization, has literally changed the face of America. The American populace looks very different now than it did just ten years ago; it increasingly looks like a representative sample of the world's diverse population.

American cities are the best representatives of this diversity of ethnicities. The process of migration, particularly chain migration (discussed in Chapter 3), makes America's ethnic mosaic possible. Many American cities display their ethnic diversity in **ethnic neighborhoods**, or concentrations of people from the same ethnicity in certain pockets of the city. Common examples are the various "Chinatowns" that exist in cities such as New York, Chicago, and San Francisco. These clusterings result from friends and relatives who have immigrated to the United States, encouraging friends and relatives back home to join them where opportunities or freedom may be more abundant. Unfortunately, sometimes ethnic groups are essentially forced to live in certain segregated parts of the city. These ethnic neighborhoods are called **ghettos**, and their locations tend to be some of the least desirable within the city.

The experiences of people who come from a common ethnic background but who live in different regions or ethnic neighborhoods is called **diaspora**. It is often used to refer to Jews or to blacks of African descent, who maintain aspects of their common heritage despite living in diverse communities

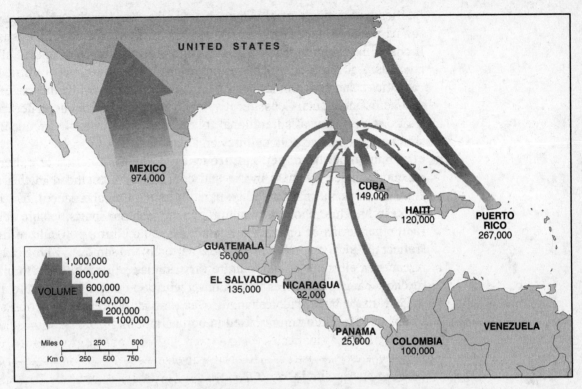

Figure 4.8. This map depicts legal immigration into the United States from 1981–1990. As shown, the majority of immigrants from Central and South America come from Mexico.

throughout the world. Although blacks in the United States may be integrated into American culture, many also identify with a common African heritage, and this might be illustrated through music, food, or religious traditions that allow these individuals to celebrate and maintain their common heritage outside of their native culture region.

Popular Culture

Folk and popular culture are also active areas of geographic research. **Folk culture** refers to a constellation of cultural practices that form the sights, smells, sounds, and rituals of everyday existence in the traditional societies in which they developed. A folk culture is usually rural, with strong family ties and strong interpersonal relationships leading to a cohesive group identity. They usually form a subsistence economy, where most goods are handmade, and most individuals perform a variety of tasks rather than specializing in any one area. Buildings representative of folk culture are built without blueprints but tend to a follow a similar plan and use similar materials as those used by other members of the same culture group. Along with their distinct architectural patterns, other material artifacts such as tools, musical instruments, and clothing physically set folk cultures apart from one another and other culture groups. Additionally, nonmaterial aspects of folk culture, such as songs, stories, philosophies, and belief systems set these traditional societies apart from much of the world's current population. Very few traditional folk societies exist today, specifically in North America, but many of the traditions are perpetuated, both materially and nonmaterially, through collections of songs and stories, and through art, needlework, and other handcrafts. Additionally, relics of past folk cultures exist in the present in the form of different types of houses like shotgun cottages in the South, different types of foods and drinks such as hush puppies and moonshine whisky, different types of music such as bluegrass, and different kinds of medicines or remedies like the use of different herbs and plants. Consequently, while you many never encounter the physical establishment of a traditional folk culture, you probably encounter many remnants of various folk cultures on a daily basis.

On the other hand, **pop culture** tends to convey a notion of cultural productions fueled by mass media and consumerism. Included in this are the visual and performing arts (e.g., painting, sculpture, and dance), the culinary arts, architecture and city planning, music, fashion, sports, leisure activities, and other forms of entertainment. Unlike folk culture, pop culture does not reflect the local environment; it looks virtually the same anywhere it appears. Generally, elements of folk culture vary dramatically from place to place but do not change much over time. Conversely, pop culture is relatively uniform across space but rapidly changes over time as conveyed by terms such as "fad" or "trend" commonly used in pop culture lingo.

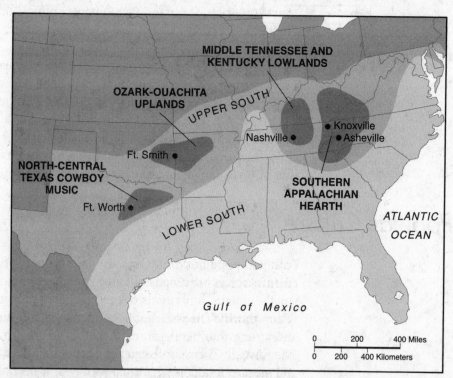

Figure 4.9. Country music has its origins in folk music which began in the southeast United States, with different regions producing different types of music.

Artifacts of popular culture are those things that can be produced, transmitted, and accepted virtually anywhere on the earth's surface. They include music, food, entertainment, fashion, recreation, and various forms of art. Popular culture is easily diffused across national boundaries, primarily through advertising and now through the Internet, enabling individuals all across the globe access to Big Macs, Levi's jeans, Madonna, and other various exports of American pop culture. The increasingly globalized world system allows for the rapid diffusion and acceptance of elements of pop culture. In some cases, this process has led to increased access and improved economic and educational opportunities. However, in many instances, the invasion of Americanized pop culture has been seen by many as just another example of **cultural imperialism**, causing people to lose their traditional ways of life in favor of cheap entertainment and disposable goods. In many less-developed countries, television sets, fast food restaurants, and other emblems of American economic power are causing troublesome social changes.

Language, religion, ethnicity, and popular culture are just some of the subjects that researchers study within the field of cultural geography. By mapping the distribution and diffusion of cultural traits, geographers can gain both a broad understanding of the ways in which aspects of culture are expressed over space and a deeper understanding of the relationship between various cultural groups. In addition, geographers can analyze the ways cultures have interacted with the environment, resulting in the creation of unique cultural landscapes.

Key Terms Defined

Acculturation The adoption of cultural traits, such as language, by one group under the influence of another.

Animism Most prevalent in Africa and the Americas, doctrine in which the world is seen as being infused with spiritual and even supernatural powers.

Artifact Any item that represents a material aspect of culture.

Buddhism System of belief that seeks to explain ultimate realities for all people—such as the nature of suffering and the path toward self-realization.

Caste system System in India that gives every Indian a particular place in the social hierarchy from birth. Individuals may improve the position they inherit in the caste system in their next life through their actions, or karma. After many lives of good karma, they may be relieved from cycle of life and win their place in heaven.

Christianity The world's most widespread religion. Christianity is a monotheistic, universal religion that uses missionaries to expand its members worldwide. The three major categories of Christianity are Roman Catholic, Protestant, and Eastern Orthodox.

Creole A pidgin language that evolves to the point at which it becomes the primary language of the people who speak it.

Cultural complex The group of traits that define a particular culture.

Cultural extinction Obliteration of an entire culture by war, disease, acculturation, or a combination of the three.

Cultural geography The subfield of human geography that looks at how cultures vary over space.

Cultural hearth Locations on earth's surface where specific cultures first arose.

Cultural imperialism The dominance of one culture over another.

Cultural trait The specific customs that are part of the everyday life of a particular culture, such as language, religion, ethnicity, social institutions, and aspects of popular culture.

Culture A total way of life held in common by a group of people, including learned features such as language, ideology, behavior, technology, and government.

Custom Practices followed by the people of a particular cultural group.

Denomination A particular religious group, usually associated with differing Protestant belief systems.

Dialect Geographically distinct versions of a single language that vary somewhat from the parent form.

Diaspora People who come from a common ethnic background but who live in different regions outside of the home of their ethnicity.

Ecumene The proportion of the earth inhabited by humans.

Environmental determinism A doctrine that claims that cultural traits are formed and controlled by environmental conditions.

Ethnic cleansing The systematic attempt to remove all people of a particular ethnicity from a country or region either by forced migration or genocide.

Ethnic neighborhood An area within a city containing members of the same ethnic background.

Ethnic religion Religion that is identified with a particular ethnic or tribal group and that does not seek new converts.

Ethnicity Refers to a group of people who share a common identity.

Evangelical religions Religion in which an effort is made to spread a particular belief system.

Folk culture Refers to a constellation of cultural practices that form the sights, smells, sounds, and rituals of everyday existence in the traditional societies in which they developed.

Fundamentalism The strict adherence to a particular doctrine.

Genocide A premeditated effort to kill everyone from a particular ethnic group.

Ghetto A segregated ethnic area within a city.

Global religion Religion in which members are numerous and widespread and their doctrines might appeal to different people from any region of the globe.

Hinduism A cohesive and unique society, most prevalent in India, that integrates spiritual beliefs with daily practices and official institutions such as the caste system.

Indo-European family Language family including the Germanic and Romance languages that is spoken by about 50% of the world's people.

Islam A monotheistic religion based on the belief that there is one God, Allah, and that Muhammad was Allah's prophet. Islam is based in the ancient city of Mecca, Saudi Arabia, the birthplace of Muhammad.

Judaism The first major monotheistic religion. It is based on a sense of ethnic identity, and its adherents tend to form tight-knit communities wherever they live.

Language extinction This occurs when a language is no longer in use by any living people. Thousands of languages have become extinct over the eons since language first developed, but the process of language extinction has accelerated greatly during the past 300 years.

Language family A collection of many languages, all of which came from the same original tongue long ago, that have since evolved different characteristics.

Language group A set of languages with a relatively recent common origin and many similar characteristics.

Lingua franca An extremely simple language that combines aspects of two or more other, more-complex languages usually used for quick and efficient communication.

Literacy The ability to read and write.

Local religion Religions that are spiritually bound to particular regions.

Minority A racial or ethnic group smaller than and differing from the majority race or ethnicity in a particular area or region.

Missionary A person of a particular faith that travels in order to recruit new members into the faith represented.

Monotheism The worship of only one god.

Multicultural Having to do with many cultures.

Official language Language in which all government business occurs in a country.

Pidgin Language that may develop when two groups of people with different languages meet. The pidgin has some characteristics of each language.

Pilgrimage A journey to a place of religious importance.

Polytheism The worship of more than one god.

Pop culture (or popular culture) Dynamic culture based in large, heterogeneous societies permitting considerable individualism, innovation, and change; having a money-based economy, division of labor into professions, secular institutions of control, and weak interpersonal ties; and producing and consuming machine-made goods.

Race A group of human beings distinguished by physical traits, blood types, genetic code patterns or genetically inherited characteristics.

Romance languages Any of the languages derived from Latin including Italian, Spanish, French, and Romanian.

Shaman The single person who takes on the roles of priest, counselor, and physician and acts as a conduit to the supernatural world in a shamanist culture.

Sino-Tibetan family Language area that spreads through most of Southeast Asia and China and is comprised of Chinese, Burmese, Tibetan, Japanese, and Korean.

Syncretic Traditions that borrow from both the past and present.

Toponym Place names given to certain features on the land such as settlements, terrain features, and streams.

Tradition A cohesive collection of customs within a cultural group.

Universalizing religion Religion that seeks to unite people from all over the globe.

Sample Questions and Answers

Section 1: Cultural Basics

Multiple-Choice Questions

1. Cultural geography is the study of

   (A) global customs and artifacts.
   (B) cultural complexes.
   (C) the spatial distribution of cultural traits.
   (D) human-environment relationships.
   (E) how cultures change through time.

2. Throughout history, numerous colonial powers have argued that certain types of people, living in certain areas of the world, are less able to govern themselves because of the qualities they have developed due to their interactions with natural factors, such as climate. This is an example of

   (A) environmental determinism.
   (B) cultural ecology.
   (C) possibilism.
   (D) ecumenism.
   (E) positivism.

3. Cultural traditions, such as Christmas, are _____ since they borrow from the past and are continually reinvented in the present.

   (A) erratic
   (B) inauthentic
   (C) complex
   (D) syncretic
   (E) ecumenical

4. The cultural hearth of Christianity is in

   (A) New York.
   (B) Rome.
   (C) Israel.
   (D) South Carolina.
   (E) Turkey.

5. Wooden shoes characteristic of the Dutch culture are an example of a(n)

   (A) mentifact.
   (B) artifact.
   (C) custom.
   (D) syncretism.
   (E) complex.

Free-Response Question

1. Consider the impacts of colonialism on the world's cultural geography. Explain how colonialism affected global patterns of language and religion, using specific examples to support your argument.

Section 2: Language

Multiple-Choice Questions

1. The most widespread language family on earth is the

   (A) Sino-Tibetan.
   (B) Romance.
   (C) Germanic.
   (D) Indo-European.
   (E) Mandarin Chinese.

2. People in London, Melbourne, Vancouver, and Mumbai all speak

   (A) a pidgin language.
   (B) lingua francas.
   (C) different dialects.
   (D) official languages.
   (E) different creoles.

3. Acculturation is a common cause of

   (A) illiteracy.
   (B) language extinction.
   (C) assimilation.
   (D) creolization.
   (E) cultural diffusion.

4. A simple trade language is called a

   (A) lingua franca.
   (B) pidgin.
   (C) dialect.
   (D) Creole.
   (E) syncretic.

5. Literacy rates vary by

   (A) sex.
   (B) location.
   (C) education.
   (D) economic development.
   (E) All of the above

Free-Response Question

1. Language extinction, both currently and throughout history, has been a major concern for cultural geographers, linguists, anthropologists, and other academics. What are some of the causes of language extinction? What kind of repercussions exist as a result of the loss of linguistic diversity? Finally, discuss some current trends to revive endangered or extinct languages around the world.

Section 3: Religion

Multiple-Choice Questions

1. All evangelical religions are also

   (A) local religions.
   (B) universal religions.
   (C) animist religions.
   (D) ethnic religions.
   (E) polytheistic religions.

2. Local Native American and African religions that teach a belief in a natural world full of spiritual beings and supernatural powers are often referred to as

   (A) animist.
   (B) shamanistic.
   (C) missionary.
   (D) denominational.
   (E) local religions.

3. The world's most widespread religion is

   (A) Islam.
   (B) Animism.
   (C) Christianity.
   (D) Hinduism.
   (E) Buddhism.

4. The hearth and spiritual center of Islam is at

   (A) Baghdad.
   (B) Cairo.
   (C) Jakarta.
   (D) Mecca.
   (E) Jerusalem.

5. _____ is an excellent example of a nonevangelical, universalizing religion.

    (A) Christianity
    (B) Buddhism
    (C) Protestantism
    (D) Polytheism
    (E) Hinduism

6. In _____ religions, community, common history, and social relations are inextricably intertwined with spiritual beliefs.

    (A) monotheistic
    (B) local
    (C) evangelical
    (D) ethnic
    (E) universal

Free-Response Question

1. Christianity has spread in large part through evangelism, but Buddhism is a widespread religion that has no evangelical aspect. How has this difference affected the current distribution of these two religious traditions?

Sections 4 and 5: Ethnicity and Popular Culture

Multiple-Choice Questions

1. An ethnicity is defined as

    (A) a group of people with a common history.
    (B) a group of people with similar physical characteristics.
    (C) a group of people who share a common identity.
    (D) a group of people united against a common enemy.
    (E) a group of people with a similar religion.

2. In the 1990s the United States

    (A) became less ethnically diverse.
    (B) decreased in overall population.
    (C) saw few changes in its ethnic composition.
    (D) saw dramatic changes in its ethnic composition.
    (E) remained relatively homogenous in its ethnic makeup.

3. A group of people, all of the same ethnicity, live in the same area of a city near a nuclear waste facility. This is an example of a(n)

   (A) diaspora.
   (B) ghetto.
   (C) cultural landscape.
   (D) ethnic neighborhood.
   (E) gentrified neighborhood.

4. Which is the most characteristic statement of a folk culture?

   (A) They look virtually the same anywhere on the globe.
   (B) Individuals within the culture specialize in producing specific goods for the community.
   (C) They quickly adopt new techniques useful for their community.
   (D) They have a subsistence economy.
   (E) They have weak ties to friends and family.

Free-Response Question

1. Define cultural imperialism. What are some of the global effects of the spread of Western popular culture to the rest of the world?

Answers for Multiple-Choice Questions

Section 1: Cultural Basics

1. **(C)** Cultural geographers do study customs, artifacts, cultural complexes, and human-environment relationships; however, what makes cultural geography different from other disciplines, like anthropology, is its focus on the spatial distribution and diffusion of human cultures.

2. **(A)** Environmental determinism is the notion that human traits or historical events are directly attributable to environmental factors, that people's actions are determined by environmental factors. This idea has been discredited as simplistic and racist. Possibilism, the notion that humans have agency and yet are limited somewhat by the environmental surroundings, provides an attractive alternative to environmental determinism.

3. **(D)** The term syncretic refers to something, such as a cultural tradition, that borrows from multiple sources.

4. **(C)** Rome is the center and headquarters of the Catholicism, which is the largest wing of Christianity. However, the hearth, or birthplace, of Christianity is in Israel, where Jesus was born and lived his life.

5. **(B)** Artifacts are the material aspects of a particular culture and would include such things as wooden shoes or other fashion apparel, along with artwork, or tools.

Section 2: Language

1. **(D)** The Indo-European family includes the Romance and Germanic groups. About 50% of the world's people speak Indo-European languages.

2. **(C)** Although many people in all of these cities speak English, the versions of English that they speak all vary somewhat in pronunciation, spelling, and other characteristics.

3. **(B)** Literally thousands of languages are currently in danger of going extinct. Reasons for language extinctions include genocide, cultural collapse, and acculturation.

4. **(A)** Simple trade languages are called lingua francas and use terms developed and understood by both cultures to complete economic transactions.

5. **(E)** Sex, geographic location, education, and economic development are all factors affecting literacy rates. In many countries where women are prevented from attaining education, women's literacy rates are considerably lower then men's.

Section 3: Religion

1. **(B)** A universal religion is one that seeks to unite people from different backgrounds under one, all-encompassing faith. Christianity is the best example of an evangelical, universalizing religion.

2. **(A)** Many animist religions also include a shamanistic aspect. However, shamanism itself refers specifically to beliefs in which a single person takes on supernatural and healing powers.

3. **(C)** With about 2 billion believers, Christianity is the most widespread world religion. Islam is the second largest, and Buddhism is the third.

4. **(D)** Mecca is the hearth and holy city of Islam. Many Muslims face Mecca and pray several times each day.

5. **(B)** Buddhism teaches beliefs about the nature of life and human suffering that are universally applicable, yet its adherents generally do not attempt to recruit followers.

6. **(D)** In ethnic religions, culture, history, public life, and spiritual beliefs are interwoven. Examples of ethnic religions include Judaism and Hinduism.

Sections 4 and 5: Ethnicity and Pop Culture

1. **(C)** Whereas race connotes common physical characteristics, ethnicity connotes a common identity. Because people's outward traits do not necessarily say anything about their personal identities, and because the notion of race is associated with prejudice and superficiality, ethnicity has largely replaced it as a way of grouping people.

2. **(D)**   During the 1990s, large-scale immigration from Asia and Latin America dramatically changed the ethnic composition of the United States, making it a truly polyglot nation. In some areas, whites are no longer a majority.

3. **(B)**   A ghetto is a form of an ethnic neighborhood where individuals of a particular ethnicity are essentially forced to live. They usually exist in areas of a city where most individuals would rather not live, such as a nuclear waste facility.

4. **(D)**   Folk cultures vary significantly over space as opposed to pop culture, which looks similar everywhere you encounter it. Also pop culture is characterized by a consumer economy, whereas folk cultures practice a subsistence economy; individuals usually do not specialize in any one activity but instead provide multiple goods and skills for the community.

Answers for Free-Response Questions

Section 1: Cultural Basics

1. Main points:
   - Colonialism has had dramatic impacts on the cultural geography of language and religion.
   - Acculturation under colonial rule has led to the disappearance of hundreds of indigenous languages and has created dominant world languages, such as French, Spanish, English, Russian, and Chinese that are now spoken across the globe. In many of the former colonies of Africa and Latin America, a few European languages have largely replaced diverse native tongues.
   - Christianity, in particular, has benefited from colonialism. In many formerly colonized regions of the world, local, animist religions have been either replaced or reconfigured to accommodate Christian beliefs. Christianity is now the dominant religion throughout the Americas.
   - In general, colonialism has led to the homogenization of linguistic and religious geography. However, interesting and diverse new pidgin languages, in places like Southeast Asia and the Caribbean, and hybrid religions, in the American Southwest, have also resulted.

Section 2: Language

1. Main points:
   - Language extinction can occur as a result of a variety of different factors. The most common cause is that of colonialism. European powers took control over numerous countries in Africa and South America during the colonization era and imposed their languages on these Native American and native African societies. Many of these societies had well-developed languages but did not have established alphabets; thus, the obliteration of their languages was relatively easy. Other causes of language extinction include diseases that wipe out entire populations

and acculturation, which is when one culture dominates another culture and the dominating culture's language prevails.

- Language provides many insights and helpful clues for understanding both historic cultures and historic migration patterns. When a language becomes extinct, the world essentially loses the means to learn about an entire culture and whatever that culture had to offer the world. It also means the loss of important clues for understanding historic migration patterns.

- Today, in parts of Scotland, Ireland, and Wales, Celtic is being brought back from near-extinction. Hebrew was revived after World War II when Israel became an independent state and Native Americans from Alaska to the tip of South America have begun to reestablish their distinct and unique linguistic heritage. The revival of these languages provides these cultures with a means to reestablish a very important aspect of their cultural identities.

Section 3: Religion

1. Main points:
   - Christianity is an evangelical religion, meaning that its practitioners have a mandate to spread the gospel. Buddhists have no such mandate.
   - Christians have been extremely successful at spreading their beliefs. Christianity is now the most widespread world religion, with practitioners in every corner of the globe, particularly in the former mission lands and colonized regions of North and South America.
   - Christian missionaries spread the gospel through relocation diffusion; they purposefully moved to new regions of the world to convert native peoples.
   - Until relatively recently, Buddhism was mostly limited to central and eastern Asia. Historically, Buddhism has spread through contagious diffusion, meaning that it was passed on to people because of their proximity to other practitioners.
   - In recent years, Buddhism has gained a foothold with Americans and Europeans, due to their increasing exposure to Eastern cultures and to Buddhism's peaceful and individualistic teachings.

Sections 4 and 5: Ethnicity and Pop Culture

1. Main points:
   - Cultural imperialism is dominance by one culture over another. For example, American fast food chains, pop music, and films have infiltrated other countries across the world. Traditional British, French, Japanese, Spanish, and Russian cultures have also been widely disseminated.
   - Although many people in these places enjoy their access to Western popular culture, others claim that new ways of life are diluting traditional cultural practices and social systems.
   - Cultural extinction is one potential consequence of imperialism. In cultural extinction, traditional ways of life are lost as new, dominant ways are adopted. Linguistic diversity, in particular, is affected by cultural imperialism, as more and more people abandon native tongues in favor of widespread world languages like English and French.

Additional Resources

Text

Conzen, M. 1990. (ed.) *The Making of the American Landscape*. Boston Massachusetts: Unwin Hyman.

This text presents a comprehensive view of the cultural evolution of the American landscape. Written by a team of leading scholars, each essay examines how historical forces of human settlement have shaped the land over the past 10,000 years, focusing most on the past three centuries. With meticulous illustrations, the authors show the reader how to analyze the historical transformations in today's landscapes. They investigate ethnic and cultural movements along with environmental challenges and urbanization trends as the dominant forces behind the shaping of America's landscapes.

Lane, Belden C. 2001. *Landscapes of the Sacred: Geography and Narrative in American Spirituality*. Baltimore Maryland: Johns Hopkins University Press.

Lane explores the connections between spirituality and place evidenced in Native American, early French and Spanish, Puritan New England, and Catholic worker traditions. He also addresses how to analyze the landscape to understand the symbol-making processes of religious tradition and experience.

Mitchell, D. 2000. *Cultural Geography: A Critical Introduction*. Malden, Massachusetts: Blackwell Publishers.

Mitchell takes a less traditional approach to cultural geography. Instead of focusing on the geography of language, religion, and ethnicity (as was done in this chapter), he looks at cultural change in everyday settings, specifically examining cultural politics. The book is divided into three parts: first, Mitchell discusses the development of cultural geography and examines cultural theory both within the discipline of geography and other disciplines. Second, he explores the landscape, which is the fundamental unit of analysis for the cultural geographer, and what it means and how to understand its production and use. Finally, he explores different aspects of cultural politics by discussing aspects of control and resistance within and across different cultural groups.

Rayburn, Alan. 1994. *Naming Canada: Stories about Place Names from Canadian Geographic*. Toronto, Canada: University of Toronto Press.

This book contains a compilation 61 articles of a few pages each, published in *Canadian Geographic* from December 1983/January 1984 to November/December 1993. Each article explores such aspects of toponymy as the name Canada itself, names and pronunciations of local places, war commemorations, native names, the borderless land of Acadia, Spanish and Portuguese names, and the trail of names left by the Mackenzie expeditions.

Web

The Summer Institute of Linguistics: *www.sil.org/ethnologue*

This organization is connected to the International Linguistics Center in Dallas; it focuses on the study of languages and cultures around the world. Its greatest feature is the "Ethnologue: Languages of the world" which is a detailed catalog of more than 6,700 languages including an index of language names, dialects, and multilingualism.

The American Dialect Society: *www.americandialect.org/*

This organization researches the English language in North America and other languages or dialects related to it. The website provides an index to current volumes of the society's journals as well as links to other language- and dialect-related sites.

The Geographic Names Information System (GNIS): *http://geonames.usgs. gov/*

This site links to an organization that has been developed by the U.S. Geological Survey and the U.S. Board on Geographic Names. It contains information on almost 2 million physical and human geography features in the United States with features described in terms of location by state, country, and geographic coordinates.

Michigan State University's page, Diversity and Pluralism: *www.msue.msu. edu/msue/imp/moddp/masterdp.html*

This site contains a database of articles searchable by key word. For example, if you were interested in researching more on "race" you would find numerous articles relating to that topic. However, for the site to be beneficial, you must have a clearly defined idea of the topics you are interested in researching.

Library of Congress' The American Folklife Center: *http://lcweb.loc.gov/ folklife/afc.html*

The Library of Congress created the American Folklife Center in 1976 to preserve artifacts of American folklife. The center and its collections have grown to encompass all aspects of folklore and folklife from this country and around the world. The website presents activities at the center along with a valuable link to other websites related to ethnographic studies.

Bowling Green University's Department of Popular Culture website at*: http:// www.bgsu.edu/departments/popc/*

This site links to an academic department, located at Bowling Green University, which is dedicated to the study of popular culture. The most useful information will be found on the "research and resource" link that leads you to more links including a pop culture library, a sound recordings archive, and link to the homepage for the Popular Culture Association.

Home page of the Popular Culture Association/American Culture Association at: *http://h-net2.msu.edu/~pcaaca/*

Here you can access the table of contents for both the *Journal of Pop Culture* and the *Journal of American Culture.*

Sara Zupko's cultural studies center: *www.popcultures.com*

This site contains a collection of annotated links to popular culture and cultural studies, including journals, articles, academic programs, bibliographic references, film, television, and theorists and critics.

Academic Information, Religion Gateway: *http://www.academicinfo.net/religindex.html*

This site provides a directory of academic Internet resources for numerous religions across the world, including every religion discussed in this chapter.

CHAPTER 5
Political Geography

Summary

Political geography is one of the oldest fields in the discipline of geography. Political geographers use the spatial perspective to study political systems from local and regional politics, to national politics, to international politics. At local scales, political geographers study issues like territorial organization, representation, and voting patterns. At national and international scales, geographers study the relationship between physical geography and politics, the historical geography of colonialism and imperialism, the formation of international alliances, and the current political tensions between the wealthy countries of the industrialized north and the poorer countries of the less-developed south.

In This Chapter

- What Is Political Geography?
- The Geography of Local and Regional Politics
- Territory, Borders, and the Geography of Nations
- International Political Geography
- Spatial Conflict

Key Terms

Antecedent boundaries	Federalism
Centrifugal forces	Fragmented state
Centripetal forces	Frontier
Colonialism	Geometric boundary
Commonwealth of Independent States	Geopolitics
	Gerrymandering
Compact state	Heartland theory
Confederation	Imperialism
Domino theory	International organization
East/west divide	Landlocked state
Electoral College	Law of the sea
Electoral vote	Lebensraum
Elongated state	Microstate
European Union	Nation
Exclaves	Nationalism

Nation-state	Rectangular state
North American Free Trade Agreement	Redistricting
	Rimland theory
North Atlantic Treaty Organization	Self-determination
North/south divide	State
Organic theory	States' rights
Organization of Petroleum Exporting Countries	Subsequent boundaries
	Superimposed boundaries
Perforated state	Supranational organization
Physical boundary	Territorial dispute
Political geography	Territorial organization
Popular vote	Theocracy
Prorupted state	United Nations
Reapportionment	

What Is Political Geography?

Political geography is one of the oldest fields in the discipline of human geography. Political geographers use the spatial perspective to study political systems at all geographic scales, from local governments to international political systems. According to the geographers Paul Knox and Sallie Marston, political geography can be considered within the context of two complementary perspectives. The first perspective focuses on the impacts of economic, cultural, and physical geography on political systems. For example, some Middle Eastern governments owe their organizational structures to the teachings of Islam. Governments controlled through divine guidance or religious leadership such as these are called **theocracies,** and they provide an excellent illustration of the impact of culture on politics. The second perspective flips this around and views political systems as the driving force behind different country's economic and cultural systems. In Kashmir, a region that lies on the border between India and Pakistan, many Muslims who have more in common with their Pakistani neighbors live on the Indian side of the border, while many Hindus who have more in common with their Indian neighbors live in Pakistan. The official border between these two countries, drawn by a political agreement in 1972, has been disputed for many years, and outbreaks of violence occur regularly in the region. This example shows how political structures can have important implications for culture. In recent years, political geographers contributed many important insights to the study of issues involving poverty, war, culture, ethnicity, and environmental change.

The Geography of Local and Regional Politics

Most political geographers focus their studies on one or more of the following geographic scales: local politics, national politics, and international politics. The country is the fundamental unit of political geography. A country, more formally called a **state**, may be composed of more than one nation.

A **nation** consists of a group of people with a common political identity, but every nation does not have its own state. For example, the Palestinians have been fighting to establish their own state for decades but have yet to achieve their goal. Israel, however, has achieved statehood designated by an internationally recognized government and territorial borders. Ideally, political boundaries define **nation-states,** which consist of relatively cohesive populations with similar identities and political goals.

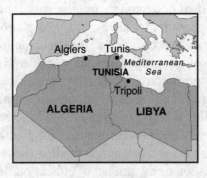

Figure 5.1. Relationships between states and nations. Japan contains a relatively uniform nation within state boundaries, Canada exemplifies a multinational state with two official languages, the Arab nation extends across many states in northern Africa and the Middle East, and the Kurds have no state they can claim as their own, and thus exemplify a stateless nation.

It is interesting to note that our current notion of the nation-state is, itself, a relatively new idea. Our modern concept of the nation-state arose in 18th-century Europe, demonstrated for the first time in the French and American Revolutions. The modern nation-state differs from older political ideologies in that the citizens of a modern state are members of a country composed of people and their institutions, not subjects to a king or queen. Unfortunately, many states created over the past 200 years contain political boundaries left over from a colonial system that failed to recognize preexisting ethnic and religious boundaries. Because of this, many of today's states must constantly represent themselves as unified nations, despite the tremendous historic and cultural divides they contain. For countries like Afghanistan, Indonesia, and Rwanda, this task has proven extremely difficult, and internal ethnic conflict is an ongoing problem.

Most countries are organized into a geographically based hierarchy of local government agencies. This division of land, or **territorial organization** into more easily governable units, serves several important functions. First, territorially organized governments have a basis for efficiently delegating administrative functions in what may otherwise be a large and unwieldy area. Second, territorially organized governments can allocate resources through local agencies that may be more in touch with the needs of the people under their jurisdiction. Third, national governments organized by territory usually give their local territories some degree of autonomy, such as the ability to enact laws, police their lands, and tax local citizens. However, the degree to which power is distributed between local and national agencies causes much political debate. In the United States, the issue of **states' rights** arose in the early days of the republic, divided the country during the Civil War, resurfaced during the Civil Rights Movement, and even today surrounds issues of environmental regulation and management of natural resources.

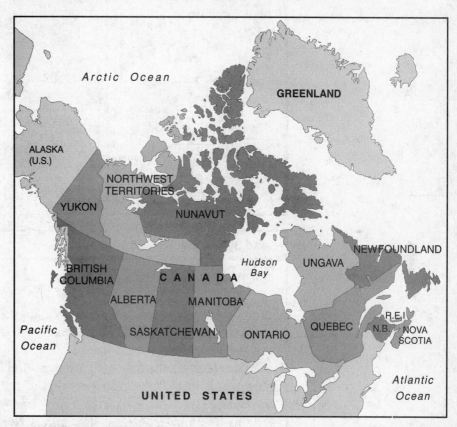

Figure 5.2. Canada, like the United States and Mexico, is organized by territory. Canada's provinces are the rough equivalent of U.S. states.

Under **federalism,** governments bestow autonomous powers upon their local territories rather than centrally controlling the entire country. These governments are called federal states. However, some federal states do have strong central governments—for example, the United States—but all such countries give some power to their constituent local territories. The United States, Canada, and Mexico, all federal states organized into territories (called states in the United States, *estados* in Mexico, and provinces in Canada) designate a certain level of political power to local areas allowing voting individuals greater influence in political processes. Territories within states are usually subdivided even further into smaller areas such as counties, cities, school districts, and voting precincts. As a result, local government agencies may have overlapping functions, and several agencies may have jurisdiction over the same geographical areas. In such cases, local government agencies must work to delegate services and authority efficiently. Some cities, such as Toronto, Canada, and Jacksonville, Florida, have worked to eliminate this problem by consolidating their government functions into a limited number of agencies that have authority over the entire metropolitan area.

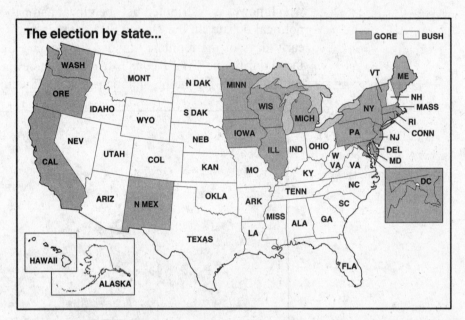

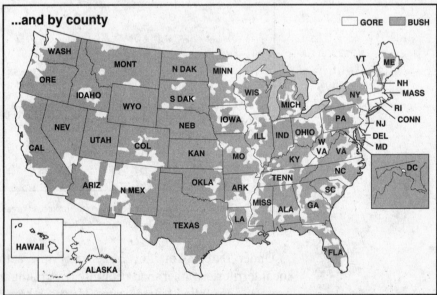

Figure 5.3. In the 2000 election, George Bush won most of the states but Al Gore picked up a few of the most populous states, including New York and California. At the county level the pattern looks different and we can see that many states were nearly evenly divided. What other interesting patterns can you detect?

Geographic organization of the state into locally governed areas has dramatic implications for individual representation. In a democracy like the United States, voters elect officials to posts that are associated with specific geographic areas. Congressional representatives, for instance, serve the people from their own home district. As all Americans learned in the aftermath of the 2000 election, even our presidents are chosen on a state-by-state basis, and the individual who captures the popular vote does not necessarily win the election. In 2000, Al Gore won the **popular vote**, which includes all the votes cast in all the states, by a slim margin but lost the **electoral vote** to George W. Bush. The **Electoral College** consists of a specific number of electors from each state, proportional to that state's population. Each elector chooses a candidate believing they are representing their constituency's choice. The candidate who receives a higher proportion of electoral votes within a state receives all the electoral votes for that state, explaining why, in 2000, it was determined that George W. Bush won the electoral vote when the key state of Florida finally cast its electoral votes for the Republican candidate.

In most federal states, officials represent citizens from their locale in a congress or parliament. Thus, the political and ethnic composition of a district may be a significant factor determining where district lines are drawn, in turn having a large effect on who gets elected. In the United States, congressional districts are redrawn after every census to reflect changes in the population of various states. This geographic exercise, called **reapportionment** or **redistricting**, has often been fraught with political turmoil. In 1993, a divided U.S. Supreme Court ruled that North Carolina's proposed 12th Congressional District violated the rights of white voters guaranteed in the Voting Rights Act. Plaintiffs in the case argued that the 12th District had been **gerrymandered**, or purposely drawn to favor one set of candidates over another. As you have probably determined by now, the inherent geographic organization of government in democratic states may have profound effects on who represents the people.

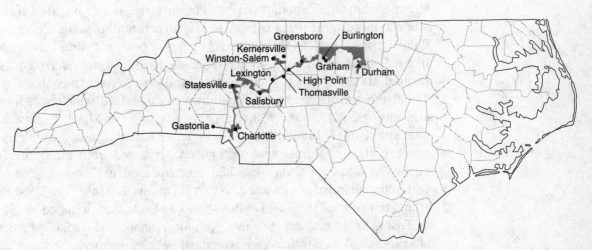

Figure 5.4. North Carolina's proposed 12th Congressional District was the subject of a 1996 Supreme Court case in which white voters claimed that the district was drawn specifically to consolidate the African-American vote.

Territory, Borders, and the Geography of Nations

Chances are that the majority of maps you have looked at of the earth's surface are political maps depicting the boundaries separating unique territories across the globe. In fact, most people's impression of the earth's surface involves a near innate understanding of the political division of space as almost all globes and world maps contain these designations. One of the main tasks of a political geographer involves understanding the evolution of these bounded territories. The geographic location and designation of political boundaries and the size and shape of the territories they contain play an extremely significant role in a state's economy, its political stability, its relations with other nations, and its culture.

When thinking on the scale of a country, the first thing that should be obvious to any student of political geography is that each country has a unique land base, and a particular set of physical properties and natural resources. The world's largest country, in terms of land area, is Russia, which occupies some 17 million square kilometers, or about 11% of the earth's land surface. Tiny countries, such as Vatican City and San Marino, both of which are located within the larger borders of Italy, are known as **microstates**. In general, larger countries tend to have larger pools of natural resources, but this is not always the case. Despite Canada's immense size and abundance of fresh water, agriculture is limited to the far southern portion of the country where a reasonably long growing season permits the cultivation of crops. Australia has abundant minerals and much sunshine but is dominated by arid deserts. Brazil's great rainforests, which have tremendous stores of minerals, water, and timber, also tend to have highly leached, infertile soils. Thus, the size of the country does not necessarily guarantee greater levels of natural resources.

Countries also take a wide variety of shapes and sizes. Fiji, with its many small islands, is what geographers call a **fragmented state.** Chile, which is stretched thin along South America's Pacific coast, is an **elongated state**, and Angola, in western Africa is more or less a **rectangular state**. Countries like Poland that have relatively rounded shapes, are **compact states**, and countries like Italy that completely surround other smaller states, are referred to as **perforated states**. Nepal is a completely **landlocked state**, meaning that it is completely surrounded by other countries, and Thailand, which has a long thin arm jutting out from the rest of its territory into the Malay Peninsula, is a **prorupted state**. In addition to these general shapes, many countries have small, outlying holdings that are entirely separated from the bulk of their landmass. Some of these detached pieces called **exclaves** lie completely within the boundaries of another country. During the Cold War, West Berlin, at that time owned by West Germany, was an exclave surrounded on all sides by East German territory. In short, the unique shape and size of each country is a product of its physical geography and political history.

Each country's unique shape and location offers it both advantages and disadvantages in the scope of global politics. Countries with extremely large land bases, such as Russia and Canada, must deal with a unique set of problems related to the administration of vast physical landscapes. Countries that have proruptions or exclaves must be able to incorporate effectively areas that are physically detached into the national mainstream. And fragmented states must determine ways to create a cohesive national fabric out of many little swatches of land.

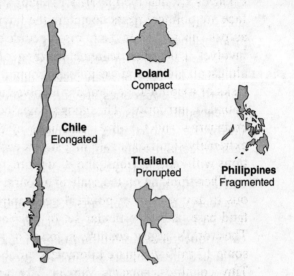

Figure 5.5. The various shapes of countries.

Some countries also occupy extremely strategic sites. Israel, the Korean Peninsula, and Panama, all relatively small areas, loom large on the world political scene because of their strategically important locations. Hawaii, at the center of the Pacific Basin, and Istanbul, Turkey, at the crossroads of Europe and Asia also occupy key positions in the geopolitical landscape. What counts as key, of course, changes through time. For most of American history after European colonization, New Orleans held an extremely important site at mouth of the Mississippi. Thomas Jefferson once remarked that whoever controls New Orelans controls the entire Mississippi River, which at the time was the main artery for transporting goods and services into the central part of the North American continent. Although New Orleans today remains an important port city, it no longer seems as economically essential as it did in the early 19th century.

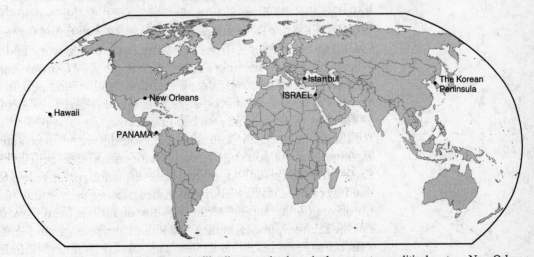

Figure 5.6. Politically and militarily strategic places in the current geopolitical system. New Orleans has lost much of the geopolitical significance it had during the 18th century.

Another important geographic feature of a country is its border. **Physical boundaries** follow important features in the natural landscape such as rivers or mountain ridges. Some borders do not follow any significant features in the landscape, but are purely based on political decisions. However, some political areas are defined by **geometric boundaries**—meaning that they follow straight lines and have little to do with the natural or cultural landscape, and some are marked with well-defined landmarks, such as the wall that separates Tijuana, Mexico, from San Diego County, California. The origin and evolution of particular boundaries provide extremely important clues for understanding current political tensions within certain countries. **Subsequent boundaries** are drawn after a population has established itself and respect existing spatial patterns of certain social, cultural, and ethnic groups. When a boundary is given to a region before it is populated, it is called an **antecedent boundary**, which carries little significance until the area becomes more populated. The western boundary between the United States and Canada was designated by treaty in 1846, when very few people occupied that region so the boundary did not carry much social or cultural significance. As the area became increasingly populated the boundary became an important division between countries. The opposite of antecedent boundaries, **superimposed boundaries** are drawn after a population has been settled in an area and do not pay much attention to the social, cultural, and ethnic compositions of the populations they divide. These types of boundaries prevailed in Africa during colonialism and still remain, causing much of the political tensions prevalent in this continent.

Within their boundaries, countries must contend with forces that work to pull them apart, while promoting the forces that bind them together. **Centrifugal forces** pull countries apart and include regionalism, ethnic strife, and **territorial disputes**. By the late 1980s, the central government of the Soviet Union had become weak, and the country was being pulled apart by powerful centrifugal forces, including the nationalist aspirations of its many republics. **Centripetal forces** bind countries together and include strong national institutions, a sense of common history, and a reliance on strong central government. Sometimes even negative external forces or threats can pull a nation together. The September 11 attacks on the United States, while extremely devastating, joined many Americans in a time of great vulnerability. Certain symbols in the landscape provide evidence of the loyalty of a country's population. After these attacks, many Americans started displaying the American flag prominently, from the windows of their cars and homes to pins placed on lapels or backpacks. Other symbols of strong centripetal forces include good institutions, strong traditions and values, and an effective circulation and communication system connecting all parts of a country.

Centripetal forces can also become destructive. The feeling that one's country should be internally cohesive and should have political autonomy is called **nationalism**. At controlled levels, nationalism can be a healthy centripetal force binding a nation together. However, some nations elevate themselves to such an extent that they adopt doctrines placing their individual nations above all others on the earth's surface. Nationalism has been associated with militaristic regimes, power-hungry leaders, dangerous group mentalities that prevent introspection, and racist ideologies. Nazi Germany is the classic example of nationalism run amuck.

Concise political boundaries do not define all geographic spaces. Certain areas of the earth's surface have yet to be officially designated with political boundaries and as such are more accurately described as poorly defined frontiers. Although the meaning of the term "**frontier**" has been debated for more than 100 years by geographers and historians, it generally connotes an area where borders are shifting and weak, and where peoples of different cultures or nationalities meet and lay claim to the land. One example of a modern frontier is the western Amazon Basin. In this remote region, the national borders between Brazil, Peru, Bolivia, Colombia, and Venezuela mean very little on the ground. Instead, the Amazon is characterized by weak administrative powers, lush rain forests, and rugged terrain. Another interesting example of a frontier is Antarctica. Australia, Norway, France, Argentina, Chile, New Zealand, and the United Kingdom have all made territorial claims on Antarctica; however, their borders have no meaning whatsoever on the ground.

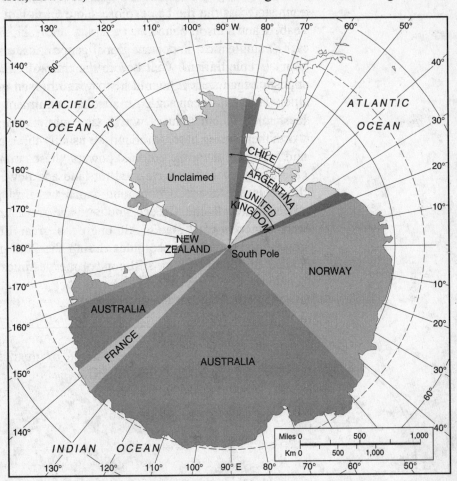

Figure 5.7. Nebulous land claims on Antarctica conform to lines of longitude and have little relationship to physical features or human impacts.

Another important and highly contested frontier, the world's oceans, cause boundary confusion and disputes that have largely been resolved through the **law of the sea**. Countries with coastal access have historically claimed sovereignty over certain strips of adjacent waters. Centuries ago, uneven and very country-specific designations of territorial waters caused little international conflict; however, as discovery of particular resources ranging from fish to oil from continental shelves increased, states across the globe scrambled to claim certain areas of the "high seas" as their own. Legislation controlling the designation of coastal waters quickly became necessary to avoid international conflict. In 1958, the United Nations Conference on the Law of the Sea (UNCLOS I) met for the first time to decide on uniform laws to govern the ownership of one of the world's most giant frontiers. The first two meetings of this group proved unsuccessful, and it was not until their third meeting ending in 1983, that they devised a coherent system of laws to govern this vast and resource-rich area. The provisions of this law have been generally adopted across the globe and include two important clauses. The first one describes the restriction of territorial seas to 12 nautical miles (19 km) from a specific shoreline, in which ships of other countries have right of passage. The second designates an exclusive economic zone (EEZ), which recognizes a state's economic rights to 200 nautical miles (370 km) from shore. Within this zone, each state has the right to explore and exploit natural resources in the water, seabed, and subsoil below.

The single most important global geopolitical phenomenon of the past 500 years is **colonialism**. Well before the time of Christopher Columbus, colonialism began shaping world history and human geography in ways that are difficult to overemphasize. An adequate treatment of the role of colonialism in shaping global politics would take many volumes, but a few points are worth mentioning here. Although we usually think of Britain, Spain, Portugal, and France as the great colonial powers, these countries are only a few of the colonizing forces that have vied for land and power in modern history. Sweden, Russia, Austria, China, and Japan were all great colonial powers. In ancient times, Rome, Greece, and even the great Aztec civilization of Mexico were all colonialist states. Although the great European colonial empires largely disbanded their colonies during the 20th century, countries like the United States and China still control the destinies of millions of colonized people throughout the world.

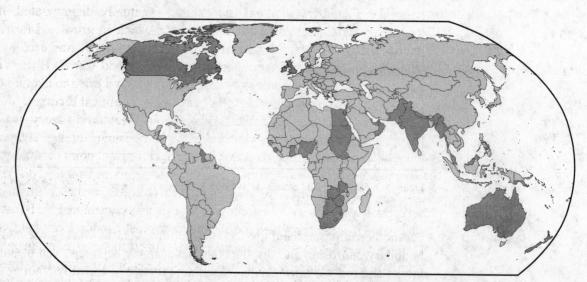

Figure 5.8. The shaded areas represent the British Empire at its colonial apex.

In many cases, imperialism has arisen where colonialism once flourished. While colonialism involves the official government rule of one state over another, **imperialism** describes a situation in which one country exerts cultural or economic dominance over another without the aid of official government institutions. Many South American and African countries that were European colonies during the 18th and 19th centuries are still dominated by Spanish, French, or British culture, even though their former colonizers no longer officially govern them. For example, Kenya, which gained independence from Britain in 1963, still retains a legacy of British language, religion, and administrative systems. The United States is a particularly dominant imperial power in the sense that American popular culture and economics affect the lives of millions of people throughout the world.

Countries under imperialist domination have one very significant feature that people living under colonial powers do not, self-determination. **Self-determination** is the right of a nation to govern itself autonomously and thus to determine its own destiny. Imperialist powers may dominate the cultural and economic relations of a less-powerful country, but that country still maintains autonomous political power. Although self-determination represents a great advantage for newly independent countries, former colonies frequently remain dominated by their historic colonizers. As a result, imperialism has become an insidious and long-term problem for many African, Asian, and South American countries.

International Political Geography

Three early theories of international political geography are worth mentioning here, before moving on to a discussion of current global politics. First, in the late 19th century, Friedrich Ratzel proposed his **organic theory** of the evolution of nations, which was later developed by the Swedish political scientist Rudolf Kjéllen into the field of **geopolitics**. Geopolitical theorists believed that nations must expand their land base in order to maintain vibrancy. Countries that did not expand eventually disintegrated, like an organism that fails to find food sources on which to grow and thrive. This theory was completely discarded by geographers after it was used by Adolf Hitler to justify his military aggression during World War II. Hitler's expansionist theory of **lebensraum**, which was based on a drive to acquire "living space" for the German people, was based on geopolitical theory.

Another important and related concept is the **Heartland theory**, which was developed by Sir Halford Mackinder in the beginning of the 20th century. According to Mackinder, the great geographical "pivot" point of all human history was in northern and central Asia, the most populous landmass on earth, and he who rules the heartland, rules the world. However, many geographers took exception to this theory. First, most of Mackinder's contemporaries believed that the world's oceans provided the avenue to colonial conquest, not land. Second, history did not hold sufficient evidence to support this area as the geographical basis of world conquest. One dissenter, Nicholas Spykman, in fact argued that the **rimland**, the area surrounding the heartland, was most important for world political power. Although these theories provide political geography with a rich history, they have little importance in the scope of the modern field.

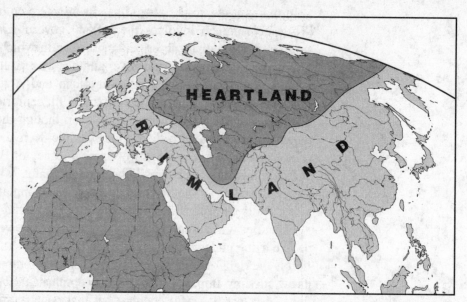

Figure 5.9. The heartland of Sir Halford Mackinder and the rimland of Nicholas Spykman.

One of the most important trends in current global politics is the development of international alliances. International alliances take several forms, one of which is the **international organization**. An international organization is an alliance of two or more countries seeking cooperation with each other without giving up either's autonomy or self-determination. The **United Nations** (UN) and the **North American Free Trade Agreement** (NAFTA) are both international organizations, but they encompass much different geographic scales. The United Nations, a global international organization, includes most of the world's autonomous states and is specifically focused on international peace and security. Because almost every country enjoys membership, the UN presents a powerful global force ensuring internationally approved standards of behavior. With collective action, this organization can enforce certain political decisions such as economic sanctions to isolate misbehaving countries forcing them to comply with UN standards. On the other hand, NAFTA is a regional accord that links the United States, Canada, and Mexico through economic arrangements aimed at opening borders and promoting trade. The **European Union** (EU) represents a good example of a **supranational organization.** These types of organizations are similar to international organizations, but to some extent member nations must relinquish some level of state sovereignty in favor of group interests. The European Union includes over a dozen European states, has a central administrative center in Brussels, Belgium, and a new unified currency, the Euro. Joining this union does require giving up some autonomy, but for a greater good. If strength comes in numbers, then the unification of Europe into a single cooperative community has surely produced a great world power.

The **Organization of Petroleum Exporting Countries** (OPEC) is an international economic organization whose member countries all have a single thing in common—they all produce and export oil. This exemplifies an economic alliance. Certain countries also join together for military purposes. NATO or the **North Atlantic Treaty Organization** is one such union. These types of organizations may require member states to allow other members to establish military bases within their territories and thus can be quite internationally significant. **Confederations** are similar to international organizations in that they bring several autonomous states together for a common purpose. The **Commonwealth of Independent States** (CIS) is a confederacy made up of independent states of the former Soviet Union who have united because of their common economic and administrative needs. The confederation of southern states that seceded from the United States before the Civil War is another classic example of this type of alliance.

Figure 5.10. The European Union.

An important point to remember about international alliances is that they have changed dramatically since the late 1980s. From 1945 to 1989, the Cold War defined the global geopolitical situation. During this period, an **east/west divide** separated the largely democratic and free-market countries of Western Europe and the Americas from the communist and socialist countries of Eastern Europe and Asia. Some Western leaders were concerned that, if communism caught on in a few key countries that were in close proximity to the sphere of Soviet influence, then many others would fall in quick succession, tipping the scales of political power. This idea was called the **domino theory**. Of course, the east/west divide was a gross generalization with many exceptions, capitalist Japan and communist Cuba being the most obvious examples, and the domino effect never occurred. However, these are the ways that many people thought of world politics during the Cold War.

Since the dismantling of the U.S.S.R. and the European revolutions of the late 1980s, the world's global geopolitical axis has shifted. Now, the most obvious division of world power lies in the disparity between the north and south. The **north/south divide** describes the division between the wealthy countries of Europe and North America (as well as Japan and Australia) and the generally poorer countries of Asia, Africa, and Latin America. Whereas the east/west divide was mainly ideological and political, the north/south divide is mainly economic. This economic inequality was created by a long history of colonization and dominance. Now, the formerly colonized countries of the south are struggling to lift themselves from the crushing poverty and disorder that has characterized the postcolonial period.

Spatial Conflict

It should be quite evident by now that a large component of political geography involves the investigation of historical and current conflicts over territory at all scales, all across the globe. Whether it be the designation of waters to specific countries, the effects of imposed boundaries on many of the colonized countries throughout the developing world, or tensions in choosing voting districts within the United States, space ownership has proven one of the most volatile issues throughout human history. Spatial conflict occurs at all geographic scales. Currently in Los Angeles, the San Fernando Valley is seeking secession from the city. The citizens of the valley think that Los Angeles does an inadequate job supplying their civic needs, and that if given authority to spend their own tax money, they would do a better job providing for their citizens. On a different scale, Spain and Morocco are currently disputing ownership of a tiny island off the coast of Morocco called Perejil (and Leila in Morocco). Both countries are working to establish an agreement without using military force. Finally, on a global scale, in recent decades, debate and regulation over environmental problems that cross national boundaries have moved to the top of the agenda in international policy discussions. Issues such as ozone depletion, biodiversity loss, and climate change will eventually affect all people, but certain, quite often, advanced countries contribute more to these global problems making universal legislation difficult to unilaterally enforce.

Political geography may be one of the most controversial subfields within human geography. The designation and demarcation of space to particular unified populations constantly causes political turmoil. Even as you read this chapter, different counties within your state, different countries within continents, and different continents across the globe discuss, debate, and fight over territory. As such, political geographers contribute great understanding of the evolution and constant changes in political boundaries, as well as an understanding of how individuals and groups within in these boundaries successfully interact with other countries across the globe.

Key Terms Defined

Antecedent boundaries A boundary line established before an area is populated.

Centrifugal forces Forces that tend to divide a country.

Centripetal forces Forces that tend to unite or bind a country together.

Colonialism the expansion and perpetuation of an empire.

Commonwealth of Independent States Confederacy of independent states of the former Soviet Union that have united because of their common economic and administrative needs.

Compact state A state that possesses a roughly circular, oval, or rectangular territory in which the distance from the geometric center is relatively equal in all directions.

Confederation A form of an international organization that brings several autonomous states together for a common purpose.

Domino theory The idea that political destabilization in one country can lead to collapse of political stability in neighboring countries, starting a chain reaction of collapse.

East/west divide Geographic separation between the largely democratic and free-market countries of Western Europe and the Americas from the communist and socialist countries of Eastern Europe and Asia.

Electoral College A certain number of electors from each state proportional to and seemingly representative of that state's population. Each elector chooses a candidate believing they are representing their constituency's choice. The candidate who receives a higher proportion of electoral votes within a state receives all the electoral votes for that state.

Electoral vote The decision of a particular state elector that represents the dominant views of that elector's state.

Elongated state A state whose territory is long and narrow in shape.

European Union International organization comprised of Western European countries to promote free trade among members.

Exclave A bounded territory that is part of a particular state but is separated from it by the territory of a different state.

Federalism A system of government in which power is distributed among certain geographical territories rather than concentrated within a central government.

Fragmented state A state that is not a contiguous whole but rather separated parts.

Frontier An area where borders are shifting and weak and where peoples of different cultures or nationalities meet and lay claim to the land.

Geometric boundary Political boundaries that are defined and delimited by straight lines.

Geopolitics The study of the interplay between political relations and the territorial context in which they occur.

Gerrymandering The designation of voting districts so as to favor a particular political party or candidate.

Heartland theory Hypothesis proposed by Halford Mackinder that held that any political power based in the heart of Eurasia could gain enough strength to eventually dominate the world.

Imperialism The perpetuation of a colonial empire even after it is no longer politically sovereign.

International organization An alliance of two or more countries seeking cooperation with each other without giving up either's autonomy or self-determination.

Landlocked state A state that is completely surrounded by the land of other states, which gives it a disadvantage in terms of accessibility to and from international trade routes.

Law of the sea Law establishing states' rights and responsibilities concerning the ownership and use of the earth's seas and oceans and their resources.

Lebensraum Hitler's expansionist theory based on a drive to acquire "living space" for the German people.

Microstate A state or territory that is small in both population and area.

Nation Tightly knit group of individuals sharing a common language, ethnicity, religion, and other cultural attributes.

Nationalism A sense of national pride to such an extent of exalting one nation above all others.

Nation-state A country whose population possesses a substantial degree of cultural homogeneity and unity.

North American Free Trade Agreement Agreement signed on January 1, 1994, that allows the opening of borders between the United States, Mexico, and Canada.

North Atlantic Treaty Organization An international organization that has joined together for military purposes.

North/south divide The economic division between the wealthy countries of Europe and North America, Japan, and Australia and the generally poorer countries of Asia, Africa, and Latin America.

Organic theory The view that states resemble biological organisms with life cycles that include stages of youth, maturity, and old age.

Organization of Petroleum Exporting Countries An international economic organization whose member countries all produce and export oil.

Perforated state A state whose territory completely surrounds that of another state.

Physical boundary Political boundaries that correspond with prominent physical features such as mountain ranges or rivers.

Political geography The spatial analysis of political phenomena and processes.

Popular vote The tally of each individual's vote within a given geographic area.

Prorupted state A state that exhibits a narrow, elongated land extension leading away from the main territory.

Reapportionment The process of a reallocation of electoral seats to defined territories.

Rectangular state A state whose territory is rectangular in shape.

Redistricting The drawing of new electoral district boundary lines in response to population changes.

Rimland theory Nicholas Spykman's theory that the domination of the coastal fringes of Eurasia would provide the base for world conquest.

Self-determination The right of a nation to govern itself autonomously.

State A politically organized territory that is administered by a sovereign government and is recognized by the international community.

States' rights Rights and powers believed to be in the authority of the state rather than the federal government.

Subsequent boundaries Boundary line established after an area has been settled that considers the social and cultural characteristics of the area.

Superimposed boundaries Boundary line drawn in an area ignoring the existing cultural pattern.

Supranational organization Organization of three or more states to promote shared objectives.

Territorial dispute Any dispute over land ownership.

Territorial organization Political organization that distributes political power in more easily governed units of land.

Theocracy A state whose government is either believed to be divinely guided or a state under the control of a group of religious leaders.

United Nations A global supranational organization established at the end of World War II to foster international security and cooperation.

Sample Questions and Answers

Section 2: The Geography of Local and Regional Politics

Multiple-Choice Questions

1. A _____ is a group of people with a common political identity, and a _____ is a country with recognized borders.

   (A) territory . . . federalism
   (B) nation . . . territory
   (C) state . . . nation
   (D) nation . . . state
   (E) territory . . . state

2. _____ governments are organized into a geographically based hierarchy of local government agencies.

   (A) Federal
   (B) Territorial
   (C) Consolidated
   (D) Electoral
   (E) National

3. With its system of regional provinces, Canada is an example of a

(A) microstate.
(B) electoral state.
(C) reapportioned state.
(D) federal state.
(E) nation-state.

4. The drawing of new voting districts is called

(A) reapportionment.
(B) gerrymandering.
(C) reelection.
(D) redrawing.
(E) discretization.

5. When voting districts are redrawn in such a way that they purposely favor a political party, they have been

(A) salamandered.
(B) reapportioned.
(C) redistricted.
(D) gerrymandered.
(E) reelected.

Free-Response Question

1. Describe the difference between territorial organization, federal organization, and electoral voting. What are the advantages of organizing political systems by geographic areas.

Section 3: Territory, Borders, and the Geography of Nations

Multiple-Choice Questions

1. Indonesia is an example of a(n)

(A) elongated state.
(B) microstate.
(C) compact state.
(D) fragmented state.
(E) prorupted state.

2. Which of the following is a landlocked country?

(A) Peru
(B) Germany
(C) Burma
(D) Afghanistan
(E) Colombia

3. In Antarctica, geometric political borders do little to organize a vast

    (A) frontier.
    (B) borderland.
    (C) wasteland.
    (D) tundra.
    (E) territory.

4. _____ forces work to pull countries apart, while _____ forces work to bind them together.

    (A) Centripetal . . . centrifugal
    (B) Centrifugal . . . centripetal
    (C) Communist . . . democratic
    (D) Capitalist . . . socialist
    (E) Socialist . . . centripetal

5. When one country exerts political, economic, or social influence over another without the aid of official government institutions, it is called

    (A) dominance.
    (B) imperialism.
    (C) colonialism.
    (D) federalism.
    (E) territorialism.

6. For many years, French Canadians from Quebec sought _____, or the right to govern themselves and to establish their own independent state.

    (A) nationalism
    (B) self-determination
    (C) anticolonialism
    (D) reapportionment
    (E) colonization

Free-Response Questions

1. Discuss the competing forces that work to bind countries together and pull them apart. Use specific examples.

2. Many explicitly geographic characteristics can work toward or against the political success of a country.

    (a) Discuss how the shape and size of a country might affect the government's ability to govern it effectively.
    (b) Discuss the role different types of boundaries might play in a country's overall political success.

Section 4: International Political Geography

Multiple-Choice Questions

1. Hitler's nationalist/expansionist philosophies drew in part from

    (A) self-determination.
    (B) sound historical evidence.
    (C) organic geopolitical theory.
    (D) rimland theory.
    (E) heartland theory.

2. When countries come together for a common purpose, somewhat limiting their own individual powers, the resulting body is called a(n)

    (A) international organization.
    (B) confederacy.
    (C) supranational organization.
    (D) union.
    (E) national alliance.

3. OPEC is an example of a(n)

    (A) supranational organization.
    (B) commonwealth.
    (C) confederacy.
    (D) international organization.
    (E) national organization.

4. The _____ was based on control of land, markets, and political ideology, whereas the _____ divide is based on wealth and poverty.

    (A) east/west divide . . . north/south divide
    (B) domino theory . . . heartland theory
    (C) north/south divide . . . east/west divide
    (D) organic theory . . . rimland theory
    (E) core/periphery . . . east/west divide

5. _____ boundaries characterize much of Africa as they ignore cultural and tribal differences across space.

    (A) Superimposed
    (B) Subsequent
    (C) Colonial
    (D) Antecedent
    (E) Territorial

Free-Response Question

1. Compare the European Union to the North American Free Trade Agreement. What do they have in common? How are they different?

Answers for Multiple-Choice Questions

Section 2: The Geography of Local and Regional Politics

1. **(D)** Although the terms "nation" and "state" are often used interchangeably, they actually have specific and quite different definitions. Nation connotes a common sense of political identity, while a state has an official government and geographic borders.

2. **(A)** A federal system is a form of territorial, or geographically subdivided, organization in which governments give their constituent territories some degree of autonomy. Federal governments are frequently broken down into states, counties, parishes or other local areas, municipalities, voting districts, and so on, each of which has specific powers within its borders.

3. **(D)** Canada, like the United States and Mexico, has a federally organized government in which power is distributed to local areas, in this case, regional provinces.

4. **(A)** After a census, the demographic data collected is used to form more accurate boundaries around voting districts to ensure fair representation within a political district. This process is called reapportionment or redistricting.

5. **(D)** The purposeful drawing of a political district to favor a political party is called gerrymandering, named both for the first person accused of doing this, and also for the shape of the first gerrymandered district, which resembled the shape of a salamander.

Section 3: Territory, Borders, and the Geography of Nations

1. **(D)** Indonesia consists of about 13,000 islands and islets scattered throughout the giant Malay Archipelago. Because the country is separated into so many small pieces, it is referred to as fragmented. Elongated states, like Chile, are stretched long and thin, and compact states, like Poland, are nearly circular.

2. **(D)** Landlocked countries have no outlet to the ocean. Surprisingly few countries are fully landlocked—Afghanistan is one.

3. **(A)** Several countries have claimed portions of Antarctica as their own; however, these territorial claims have little meaning on the ground. In 1959, twelve countries signed an international treaty establishing large portions of the continent as an international commons, protected for conservation and scientific research.

4. **(B)** Forces such as regionalism are centrifugal, meaning that they work to weaken central authority and cohesiveness, while forces such as nationalism generally work to solidify central authority and bind countries together.

5. **(B)** Colonialism involves official, institutional domination of one group over another; imperialism usually includes unofficial forms of social, cultural, or economic dominance.

6. **(B)** For many years Canadians of French decent have struggled to maintain their political autonomy and cultural heritage. In recent years, separatist movements have waned, but citizens of Quebec still fiercely defend their unique history, language, and traditions.

Section 4: International Political Geography

1. **(C)** Organic geopolitical theory, which held that states must expand their land base in order to grow and maintain viability, influenced many 19th and 20th century nationalist politicians, including Adolph Hitler.

2. **(C)** In supranational organizations member states must give up some dimension of their individual autonomy for some greater cause, such as political or economic security. In international organizations, no such sacrifice is called for.

3. **(D)** In OPEC, petroleum-exporting countries have joined together to regulate and stabilize oil markets around the world. This is an example of an international organization based on economic gain.

4. **(A)** During the Cold War, countries were aligned on either side of an east/west divide, based largely on control of land and political ideology. In the post-Cold War era, the most obvious world axis divides the poorer countries of the south from the wealthier countries of North America and Europe.

5. **(A)** During colonialism, many nations imposed political boundaries designating certain territories for themselves without paying attention to any divisions they may have caused between different tribes. Even after decolonization, these boundaries remain, causing much of the bloodshed that has occurred and will continue to occur on this continent.

Answers for Free-Response Questions

Section 2: The Geography of Local and Regional Politics

1. Main points:
   - Territorial organization implies a geographically based hierarchy of official duties and organizations.
   - In a federal government, the local territories, states, districts, and so on, each has autonomous powers, such as policing, creating local laws, and representing their citizens at the national level.

• The United States has an electoral system of representation in which each political party appoints representatives for each state, and then the party that wins the popular vote within the state gets to cast electoral votes for its candidate. The electoral system can have important implications, as it did in the 2000 presidential election when Al Gore won the popular vote but George W. Bush won the electoral vote.
• Some of the advantages of organizing by geographic areas include more direct representation and accountability of local elected officials, more efficient administration of remote or expansive areas, increased political attention to local or regional issues, and more efficient allocation of public funds and resources.

Section 3: Territory, Borders, and the Geography of Nations

1. Main points:
   • Centrifugal forces work to weaken central authority and cohesiveness, while centripetal forces work to solidify central authority and bind countries together.
   • One example of a country experiencing powerful centrifugal forces was the Soviet Union in the late 1980s. During this period, the USSR had a weak central government and a depressed economy and was composed of increasingly defiant constituent republics. Russia, the Union's central state, could no longer hold the confederacy together, and the USSR disbanded in 1991.
   • During this same period, the Soviet's chief rival, the United States, had a strong central government and a relatively robust economy and was composed of states that were generally deferential to the federal government.

2. Main points:
   • The size of a country can affect the ability for successful governance simply because it is easier to connect all areas of a small space and communicate through those connections, than it is to connect all areas within a large geographic space. Similarly, the shape of a state provides challenges in the government's ability to connect and communicate with all areas of the country. Perforated countries, such as Indonesia, present organizational challenges simply because the nation does not occupy a single, uniform geographical space.
   • It seems that the most ideal boundary system is that of subsequent boundaries. This form designates territories that maintain the spatial clusterings of uniform social and cultural groups. Many formerly colonized states still struggle to unify their populations as the remnants of superimposed boundaries continue to perpetuate cultural and tribal differences.
   • However, it is important to note that the political success of a country is not necessarily determined by its shape or its boundaries. Many successful governments exist in less than ideal territorial and boundary situations.

Section 4: International Political Geography

1. Main points:
   - The EU is a supranational organization, whereas NAFTA is an international agreement.
   - In the EU, member states give up a degree of their individual autonomy in areas such as economic and military policy. The EU now has a central administrative capital in Belgium and a single currency, the Euro. For their sacrifice, member states have become part of a greater, more stable, economic and military power.
   - In NAFTA, the United States, Canada, and Mexico have agreed to open their borders to increased trade. In the process, they have made considerable concessions; however, they have not given up their individual powers in the way the European Union members have.
   - Both the EU and NAFTA are attempts by several states to band together for increased freedom and economic prosperity; however, the states of the European Union have gone much further toward creating a single, unified body, with a sole political identity than the NAFTA countries have.

Additional Resources

Text

Doumitt, Donald P. 1985. *Conflict in Northern Ireland: The History, the Problem, and the Challenge.* New York: P. Lang.

Boyd, Andrew. 1991. *An Atlas of World Affairs (9th ed.)* London: Routledge.

Connor, Walker. 1994. *Ethnonationalism: The Quest for Understanding.* Princeton, New Jersey: Princeton University Press.

Demko, George J., and William B. Wood, eds. 1994. *Reordering the World: Geopolitical Perspective on the 21st Century.* Boulder, Colorado: Westview Press.

Poulsen, Thomas M. 1995. *Nations and States: A Geographic Background to World Affairs.* Englewood Cliffs, New Jersey: Prentice Hall.

Roskin, Michael G., and Nicholas O. Berry. 1997. *The New World of International Relations (3rd ed.).* Upper Saddle River, New Jersey: Prentice-Hall.

Web

Orangenet: *http://www.orangenet.org/*
   This site provides numerous links for investigating further the conflict between the Irish Catholics and the British Protestants in Northern Ireland. As the title implies, it provides information on Protestantism and maintaining statehood with the United Kingdom.

Sinn Fein: *http://sinnfein.ie/index.html*

Sinn Fein is one of the oldest political parties, mostly comprised of Irish Catholics in Northern Ireland. By comparing information from this site with information from the Orangenet site, you can gain a fairly good understanding of the political tensions both currently and historically at work in Northern Ireland.

U.S. Department of State, Office of the Geographer and Global Issues: *http://www.state.gov/www/publications/statemag/statemag_jul99/bom.html*

The department provides a variety of different services that have changed throughout its 75-year history. It began by solving both land and maritime dispute boundaries. While that is still one of its tasks, it also currently investigates many global issues including refugees, expanded UN responsibilities, transnational and subnational ethnic conflicts and recognition of enduring international environmental concerns. Finally, the department not only guides many federal mapping agencies on boundary and foreign name issues but also makes maps for various department publications.

United Nations Systems of Organization: *www.unsystem.org/*

This site provides a catalog of UN system websites linking directly to agencies alphabetically by title, by subject matter, and by a search program. It also contains links to numerous other international organizations.

The World Wide Web Virtual Library page on *International Affairs Resources* at: *http://www.etown.edu/vl/*

This site provides over 2,400 annotated links on a wide range of topics relating to international affairs, international studies, and international relations. The numerous links are organized into four main categories: media sources, organizations, regions and countries, and topics.

The Law of the Sea: *www.oceanlaw.org*

This site is maintained by the Council of Ocean Law and has been designed as a document library and guide to information including an overview and text of the UN Convention on the Law of the Sea as well as reviews of the policies of the United States and other countries.

North Atlantic Treaty Organization: *www.nato.int/*

This site provides information on NATO's structure, documents and library, activities, and links to other international relations sites.

CHAPTER 6
Economic Geography

Summary

Economic geography is the study of the flow of goods and services through space. Economic geographers also study the ways in which people provide for themselves in different places and geographic patterns of inequality at all scales of economic organization. Historically, economic geographers have been profoundly influenced by classical economic theory and capitalism. More recently, the opening of markets and the international character of economic flows, in general, have caused many economic geographers to focus more on international economic alliances, cycles of industrialization, poverty, globalization, and development. In this chapter, we will look at multiple geographic scales in an attempt to better understand this extremely diverse and wide-ranging field.

In This Chapter

- Industrialization
- Models of Development and Measures of Productivity
- Global Economic Patterns
- Location Principles
- Development, Equality, and Sustainability
- Globalization

Key Terms

Agglomeration	Economic backwaters
Ancillary activities	Export-processing zone
Anthropocentric	Fast world
Backwash effect	Footloose firms
Brick-and-mortar business	Fordism
Conglomerate corporation	Foreign investment
Core	Gender equity
Core-periphery model	Globalization
Deglomeration	Gross Domestic Product
Deindustrialization	Gross National Product
Development	Human Development Index
E-commerce	Industrial Revolution

Industrialization
Industrialized countries
Least-cost theory
Least-developed countries
Manufacturing region
Maquiladoras
Net National Product
Offshore financial center
Periphery
Primary economic activities
Productivity
Purchasing Power Parity
Quaternary economic activities
Quinary economic activities
Regionalization

Rostow's stages of development
Rust Belt
Secondary economic activities
Semi-periphery
Service-based economies
Slow world
Spatially fixed costs
Spatially variable costs
Specialty goods
Sustainable development
Tertiary economic activities
Transnational corporation
World cities
World-system theory

Industrialization

Industrialization has always been a major theme in economic geography, and any discussion of the geography of industry must start with the **Industrial Revolution**. When most people talk about the Industrial Revolution, they are usually referring to the profound technological and economic changes that arose in England during the late 18th century and then rapidly spread to other parts of Europe and North America. Modern factories, mass-produced goods, and modern forms of capital investment are all products of this period. Before the Industrial Revolution, most goods were either produced in small shops or out of the home. Many **specialty goods**, which are assembled individually or in small quantities, are still produced to this day, but they are not nearly as dominant as they were before industrialization. By the early 20th century, mass production and assembly lines, first championed by Henry Ford, had replaced many specialty goods. The perfection of standardized mass production, which is in part attributed to Ford, is called **Fordism**. In addition to issues of production and investment, geographers and historians also associate the Industrial Revolution with a set of wide-ranging social changes, which began some time after 1750 and have been unfolding to this day. The rise of wage labor and large-scale urbanization are particularly important examples of the social changes associated with the Industrial Revolution.

For almost 200 years, heavy industry was mostly limited to northern Europe, East Asia, and North America. Britain, France, the United States, Russia, Germany, and Japan remained at the forefront of industrial production and innovation through the middle of the 20th century. These places, which came to be known as the **industrialized countries**, still account for a large portion of the world's total industrial output. However, in recent years, the geography of industrial production has shifted radically. Although the wealthiest countries, where most industrial goods are consumed, still house most major corporations, many firms have relocated their facilities to less-developed countries where it is

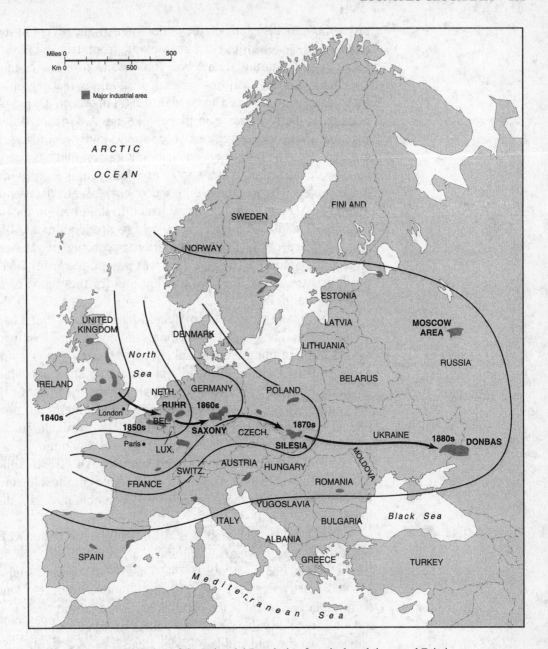

Figure 6.1. Diffusion of the Industrial Revolution from its hearth in central Britain.

cheaper to produce goods. By the 1970s the most highly developed countries, which were once home to the lion's share of industrial facilities, had already started shifting to information and **service-based economies**, which are focused on research and development, marketing, tourism, sales, and telecommunications. This shift has had enormous implications for global economic systems and for the lives of people around the world.

In industrialized countries, this has frequently been a painful transition. The high-tech and service industry jobs that began to dominate these countries' job markets during the 1970s and 1980s generally provide better pay, safer working conditions, less pollution, and a higher standard of living than factory jobs. However, they also require more education and extensive, specialized training from their employees. When companies began to move their production facilities from the older industrialized countries to the newly industrializing countries, such as Mexico, China, and Malaysia, many former factory workers found themselves jobless and with few economic options.

When industrial facilities leave an area, taking that region's economic base with them, it is referred to as **deindustrialization**. Deindustrialization has been particularly extreme in places like the American Midwest and central Britain, where entire regions' economies had previously relied on heavy industry. The Great Lakes is an economic region that has been hit particularly hard by deindustrialization, and Flint, Michigan, is a particularly disheartening example. For decades, Flint's economy revolved around large General Motors (GM) automobile plants located in the town. In the early 1980s GM announced its plans to move the bulk of its production out of Flint to Mexico, which offered cheap labor, flexible environmental regulations, inexpensive land, and enticing tax breaks. This was a good move for GM's shareholders, but it was tragic for the town of Flint and for thousands of factory workers who lost their jobs.

Another interesting aspect of deindustrialization is that it has highly regionalized effects. The entire United States did not suffer directly as a result of the layoffs in Flint, but the Great Lakes region, which is now commonly referred to as the **Rust Belt** for all its idle factories and aging machinery, was debilitated. In the early 1980s so many people were moving out of Flint, to areas of the country where their job prospects were brighter, that moving companies like U-Haul could not keep enough trucks available to supply outgoing demand in the region. When one region's economic gain translates into another's economic loss, it is called a **backwash effect**. Although manufacturing is still a significant part of the economies of most historically industrial regions, many such places have not yet been able to regain their former economic vibrancy and sense of civic pride.

While deindustrialization was debilitating some regions of the developed world, other regions were undergoing a different type of economic revolution—the high-tech boom. Between 1960 and 1990, defense and aerospace contributed greatly to the rapidly growing high-tech industry. During the 1990s, software development and e-commerce rose to prominence. **E-commerce** provides a particularly interesting example of geography's implications in the economy. During the mid and late 1990s, thousands of dot-com companies opened their doors, peddling everything from books, to housewares, to fertilizer. Investors had high hopes for these companies, which many people thought would eventually replace old-fashioned **brick-and-mortar businesses** that operated out of actual stores where people could shop. In the future, all commerce would take place on-line. Today, many people do shop online, however the transformation to e-commerce has been much less spectacular than many expected. In large part, this is because it is simply more efficient and less expensive for some products to be sold out of individual local outlets than to be sold on-line and distributed to individual customers from some centralized location.

On-line grocery stores provide a particularly acute example of this problem. Traditional grocery stores already operate on a razor-thin profit margin, often collecting just a few cents profit on each transaction. On-line grocery stores offered flexible delivery services on top of normal operating costs and, as a result, ended up transporting heavy, bulky, low-cost items such as toilet paper and water across large cities to their customers. Because most prospective clients were not willing to pay much more for their delivery service, and because delivering groceries at their normal retail cost proved to be extremely unprofitable, most on-line grocery stores never ended up making any money. Thus, due to *transaction costs* the on-line grocery stores' business plan ultimately failed. If many of the investors who poured hundreds of millions of dollars into doomed dot-com grocery delivery services had thought more critically about the geography of commerce, then perhaps they would not have lost quite so much money.

Another important feature of today's global economy is the rise of the **transnational corporation**. Transnationals, also referred to as multinational corporations, like General Motors, take advantage of geographic differences in wages, labor laws, environmental regulations, taxes, and the distribution of natural resources by locating various aspects of their production in different countries. A classic example, Nike, has its headquarters in Portland, Oregon, but its factories are located in newly industrialized countries such as Indonesia, where production costs are much lower than in the United States. By taking advantage of Indonesia's low production costs and the relatively low cost of transporting its products back to U.S. markets, Nike can net a greater profit. Nike and General Motors are not unique; in fact, most of the world's large corporations have become transnationals, taking advantage of geographic disparities in the global economy. Most transnationals are also **conglomerate corporations**. Conglomerates are firms that are comprised of many smaller firms that serve different functions. Huge corporations like General Motors, General Electric, and Mitsubishi are actually comprised of many smaller firms, operating all over the world, producing a wide variety of goods and services.

Noticing the advantages of joining the global economy, leaders of many economically developing countries have developed schemes to attract foreign investment. **Export-processing zones**, now common throughout the world, are one example. These zones officially designated for manufacturing, often have accessible distribution facilities, lax environmental restrictions, and attractive tax exemptions for foreign corporations. One prime example is Mexico's system of *maquiladoras,* which dot the United States-Mexico border from the Gulf of Mexico to the Pacific Ocean. *Maquiladoras* are home to dozens of U.S. firms, such as General Motors, which are able to compete better on the global market as a result. In *maquiladora* cities, like Ciudad Juarez, near El Paso, and Tijuana, near San Diego, American companies own large factories that produce and assemble goods for export back to the United States. *Maquiladoras* have grown tremendously during the past decade, resulting in large part from the North American Free Trade Agreement (NAFTA), which removed many of the obstacles that prevented free trade between Mexico, Canada, and the United States. Although *maquiladoras* provide desperately needed jobs for thousands of Mexicans, they are also frequently plagued by extremely high crime rates, corrupt government agencies, and terrible pollution.

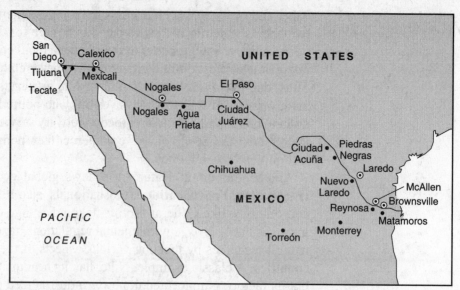

Figure 6.2. Mexico's *maquiladoras,* or industrial export processing zones, are located along the border with the United States.

Some governments have encouraged the establishment of **offshore financial centers** as another strategy for initiating economic growth. Offshore financial centers provide a low-profile way for companies and individuals to conduct financial transactions and to avoid high taxes. Although only some of these centers are actually offshore islands, they all provide conducive environments in which to conduct international business. Examples of offshore financial centers include Panama, Luxembourg, Switzerland, Singapore, the Bahamas, and Kuwait.

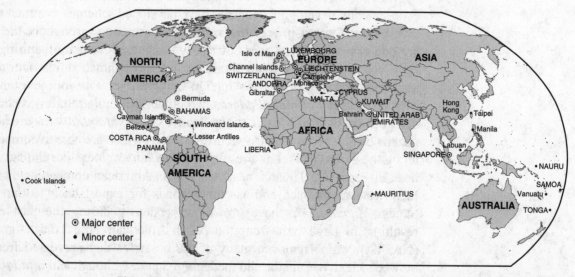

Figure 6.3. Not all offshore financial centers are actually offshore. However, they all provide a variety of incentives for companies to conduct banking and other financial transactions within their borders.

Models of Development and Measures of Productivity

Over the past 200 years, the economies of countries like the United States, Germany, and Great Britain have followed similar paths of economic development. As each of these economies progressed from low levels of economic development and per capita income to higher levels, they tended to rely less on farming, raw materials, and heavy manufacturing, and more on light industry, information, and service-based companies. This evolution traces a path through four economic sectors, each of which is associated with particular types of economic activities.

- **Primary economic activities** are involved with the harvest or extraction of raw materials. Fishing, agriculture, ranching, and mining are all examples of primary economic activities.
- **Secondary economic activities** are generally associated with the assembly of raw materials into goods for consumption. Heavy industries, manufacturing, and textile products are all examples of secondary economic activities.
- **Tertiary economic activities** involve the exchange of goods produced in secondary activities. Retailing, restaurants, and any other basic service job occur in the tertiary sector of the economy.
- **Quaternary economic activities** include research and development, teaching, tourism, and other endeavors having to do with generating or exchanging knowledge.
- **Quinary economic activities** are generally considered a subset of quaternary activities and are those that involve high-level decision making and scientific research.

All countries contain all four types of economic activities. Wealthy countries have extensive tertiary and quaternary sectors, while less-developed countries are dominated by tertiary and secondary activities, and the world's least-developed countries' economies are based almost entirely on primary activities. Switzerland's economy relies on banking, research and development, tourism, and other quaternary activities. Indonesia is extensively industrialized but far less developed than Switzerland; it is currently the site of a vast secondary activity economy, yet it has relatively few advanced quaternary activities. Madagascar, which is one of the world's **least-developed countries**, is in a different situation. Primary economic activities including farming, livestock ranching, nomadic herding, mining, and fishing dominate its economy. The shift from primary and secondary economic sectors to tertiary and quaternary will never achieve absolute completion within a country. Even the most highly developed countries still produce agricultural products and extract raw materials from their lands. Nonetheless, the transition in economically dominant activities within a country indicates the important role technology plays in determining a country's level of development.

In 1960, W. W. Rostow, an American economist and historian, developed these observations into a formal theory called **Rostow's stages of development**. In his research, Rostow argued that countries undergo five stages of economic development. During the first stage, the country's economy is dominated by primary activities—productivity, technological innovation, and per capita incomes remain low. In the second stage, preconditions for economic development arise, including the commercialization of agriculture and increased exploitation of raw materials. In the third stage, **foreign investment** pours in, jumpstarting an economy that was already prepped for growth. An important aspect of the third stage is that a large proportion of foreign investment goes to infrastructure improvements, such as building roads and canals. In the fourth stage, the country develops a broad manufacturing and commercial base. High per capita incomes and high levels of mass consumption characterize the fifth, and final stage.

This model has proven to be a useful tool for students of economic development because it seems to follow the path of European and American history and because we can readily identify countries that, right now, seem to be at each of Rostow's stages. You could say, for instance, that Nepal is at the first stage of economic development, while Denmark is at the fifth. However, Rostow's model has also been criticized for assuming that economies will naturally pass through each of the four stages consecutively. Rostow's model did not explicitly account for factors such as global politics, colonialism, physical geography, war, culture, and ethnic conflict, which may cause countries to follow quite different economic trajectories. Nepal's economy may never look like Denmark's because the two countries' cultures and histories are inherently different. In Saudi Arabia, the presence of oil has created an economic situation that is fundamentally different from either Nepal's or Denmark's. Another problem with Rostow's original model is that it defines the fifth, final, and most highly developed economic stage as being characterized by high mass consumption. Environmentalists and others have criticized Rostow's description of the relationship between development and consumption, claiming that development does not necessarily equal high consumption. For some of these critics, development may mean other things like increased social welfare or ecological sustainability. Finally, the Rostow's stages of development model does not account for deindustrialization. In spite of its many criticisms, Rostow's model is an excellent example of a geographic concept that has made an extremely important contribution, partly because of what it says and partly because of the questions and criticisms that arise from it.

While Rostow was busy trying to model the stages of development, others were busy developing different indices to try and measure development. As it turns out, **development** is a difficult thing to measure because it means so many different things to so many different people. Determining achievable and acceptable levels of development also involves the issue of standard of living. You should be aware of at least a few measures of development, the way different measures characterize standard of living, and the problems associated with each. Generally, indices of development fall into one of two categories: economic measures or noneconomic measures, which usually consist of a specific measure of social welfare. One important economic measure of development that you have probably heard of is the **Gross National Product**, or GNP. The GNP is a measure of all the goods and services produced by a country in a year, including those generated from its investments abroad. Though widely used by economists and reported in the media, the GNP provides a rather broad vision of **productivity**. It assumes that development can

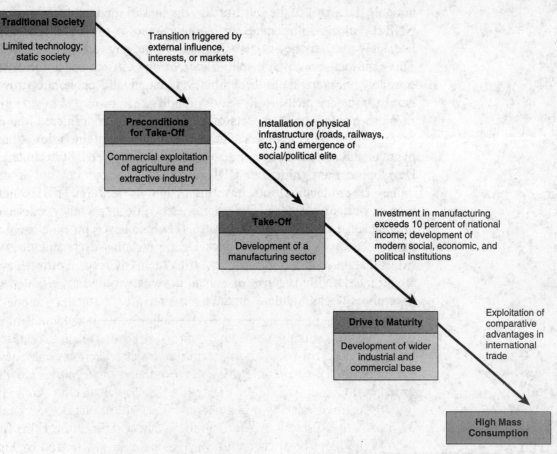

Figure 6.4. Rostow's stages of development model caricatures the development of national economies by depicting them as passing through five stages, from traditional societies to high mass consumption.

be measured simply in monetary terms and that any productivity is good productivity, both of which are highly debatable ideas. First, this value, stated in U.S. dollar terms does not account for the money value of all the goods produced by subsistence economies characteristic of many developing countries. Thus, the GNP systematically reports lower values for productivity in the developing world. To solve this problem, economists have developed a new measure, called **Purchasing Power Parity**, or PPP, which accounts for what money actually buys within different countries. Second, GNP fails to account for capital that is lost through the exploitation of natural resources. **Gross Domestic Product** (GDP) is similar to Gross National Product, except that it omits investments abroad. For a country like Japan, which has extensive investments abroad, the GNP would be significantly larger than the GDP.

Net National Product, or NNP, is a measure of all goods and services produced by a country in a year, including production from its investments abroad *minus* the loss or degradation of natural resource capital as a result of productivity. Let us say that a timber company clear cuts a swath of forest and then sells the timber, earning the company $2 million Using the GNP, this would result in a $2 million input to the national economy. But under the NNP, the country would add $2 million and then subtract for the loss of that timber, which could have been used for a variety of environmental amenities such as open space, water filtration, or wildlife habitat. With NNP, you must consider not only the profit of the sale but also the loss of the forest. The problem with NNP is that the dollar value of standing timber is notoriously hard to calculate. How much money is it worth to have a healthy forest on yonder hillside? This example should give you an idea of how difficult it is for countries to equitably measure their level of development and economic growth with purely monetary measures.

When noneconomic aspects of development are considered, the equation becomes even more complex. The **Human Development Index** is one example of an alternate measure of development. Conceived by the United Nations Development Program, the HDI calculates development not in terms of money or productivity, but in terms of human welfare. The HDI evaluates human welfare based on three parameters: life expectancy, education, and income. On a global scale, the pattern of human development closely matches that of the Gross National Product. One interesting discrepancy between the two is that, in southern Europe, countries such as Greece, Portugal, and Spain are all rated highly in terms of human development but are slightly less high in terms of Gross National Product.

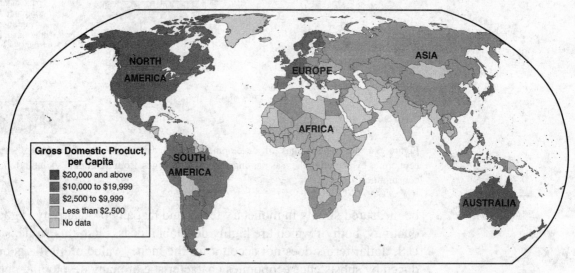

Figure 6.5. Gross National Product by country.

Gender equity is an important measure of human welfare that is not necessarily correlated with GNP. In some of the countries with the highest per capita Gross National Products, gender equity, or women's welfare, lags far behind. Examples of this include Italy, Japan, and Kuwait, where cultural traditions have long discouraged women's achievement in education, government, and business. Fortunately, in countries such as Japan, women have gained much ground in recent years. One fascinating example of this is the growing acceptance of women as sushi chefs. In Japan, women have long been prevented from becoming master sushi chefs, a lucrative, high-status profession that has traditionally been dominated by men. In recent years, more and more women have been accepted as apprentices in the profession, and male customers are even starting to become accustomed to female chefs. This is one of many examples of the complex interface between economics and culture that defines studies of human welfare and economic development.

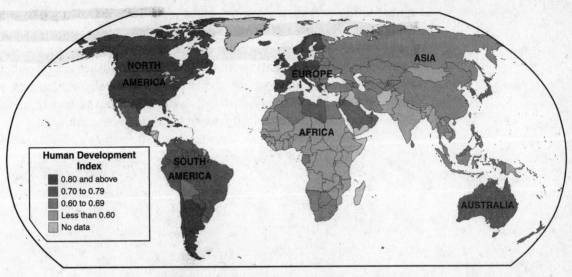

Figure 6.6. Human Development Index by country.

Other economic measures of development include indicators such as per capita energy consumption, the percentage of a country's workforce engaged in certain sectors of the economy, and caloric intake or nourishment levels. While these additional measures may not provide an entirely accurate continuum for judging a country's level of development, they do provide other important clues to a country's economic situation and its people's quality of life.

Global Economic Patterns

One pattern evident in all measures of economic development is the division of the world's countries into a global economic **core**, **semi-periphery,** and **periphery**. This is called the **core-periphery model**. The core—which includes most of Europe, Japan, the United States, Canada, Australia, and New Zealand—is made up of countries with relatively high per-capita incomes and high standards of living. These highly developed countries also contain the great **world cities**, London, Tokyo, and New York, which serve as global centers of economic activity. On the semi-periphery are the newly industrialized countries with median standards of living, such as Chile, Brazil, India, China, and Indonesia. Semi-peripheral countries offer their citizens relatively diverse economic opportunities but also have extreme gaps between rich and poor.

The periphery, the world's less-developed countries, includes Africa, except for South Africa, and parts of South America and Asia. Peripheral states have low levels of economic productivity, low per capita incomes, and generally low standards of living. They also usually lack the infrastructure—paved highways, railroads, sanitation facilities, and telecommunications towers—that would attract foreign investors. Peripheral countries with rapidly growing populations face daunting environmental problems of pollution, deforestation, and topsoil loss, particularly worrisome to subsistence farmers who rely on local timber, water, and crops for their daily needs. Few economic opportunities exists in the peripheral countries, and these places have not benefited significantly from globalization or from the information age. The "**slow world**" of the periphery is often compared to the "**fast world**" of the core, where rapid transit, telecommunications, mass media, and computers have cranked up the pace of life. Surprisingly, the living conditions in the poorest of countries are often better than those of the urban poor in the great, semi-peripheral metropolises, like Sao Paulo, Brazil; Mexico City, Mexico; Jakarta, Indonesia; and Mumbai, India. These people live in some of the worst conditions on earth.

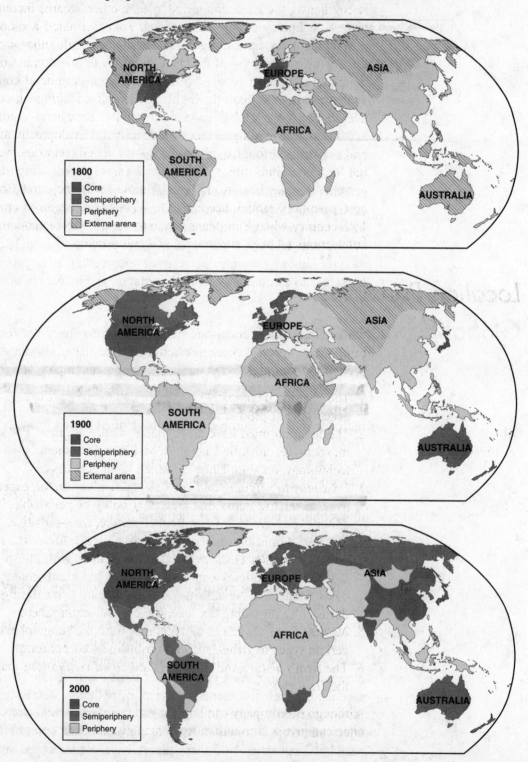

Figure 6.7. The global core, periphery, and semi-periphery by country, 1800 to 2000.

Immanuel Wallerstein's **world-system theory** describes the earth as an interdependent system of countries linked by political and economic competition, similar to the core-periphery model. According to Wallerstein, this network emerged in the late 15th century when European exploration of outside "worlds" began. Increased expeditions stemmed the development of shipbuilding and navigation techniques that began to bind certain places closer together in the 16th century. As these political and economic relations strengthened, the areas connected to each other became increasingly exposed to new technologies and innovations. This facilitated a more rapid path to development for certain regions of the globe, while other areas experienced little to no penetration of the benefits of economic competition. Eventually, the pattern between core, peripheral, and semi-peripheral countries emerged as the network between the highly industrialized European countries continued to dominate global economic activity. Peripheral countries had little access to the technologies that would facilitate development, and semi-peripheral countries, through exploitation by developed countries, were allowed partial entrance into the system. These areas have some dominance over peripheral states but are, in turn, dominated by the core. Consequently, the core-periphery model, according to Wallerstein, began to emerge in the late 15th century when Europeans began to control global economic and political connections through exploration and colonization.

Location Principles

On smaller scales, economic geographers also study the factors that determine where specific economic activities take place. All industries locate their production facilities based on the following geographic factors.

1. The location a company chooses must provide easy *access* to the materials necessary for production.
2. The location must have an adequate *supply of labor*. For some industries, inexpensive, unskilled labor is best, but for others, such as information technology, an abundance of skilled labor is necessary.
3. *Proximity to shipping and markets* is also a key factor, especially for industries producing items that are either bulky or perishable. These items are either expensive to ship or, by their nature, time-sensitive.
4. The site should be chosen to minimize *production costs*. Firms can minimize production costs by locating in a place with cheap land and labor. Government policies can also have an important impact on production costs. States like Nevada have attracted many firms during the past couple decades by providing tax incentives for relocating there.
5. *Natural factors*, such as climate, may limit the geographical distribution of certain types of firms, such as agribusiness corporations.
6. The firm's *history* and its leaders' *personal inclinations* may also influence the final choice.

Although no company can hope to maximize all these factors, an optimal balance can give a firm a distinct advantage over their competition.

Another way of looking at these optimization efforts is **least-cost theory**. According to least-cost theory, which was developed by the economist Alfred Weber, firms locate their production facilities in the place that minimizes transportation costs, agglomeration costs, and labor costs. In terms of transportation costs, Weber believed that companies must take into account the cost of transporting both raw materials and finished products. If the raw materials weigh more than the finished products, then facilities should be closer to the materials and are said to have a material orientation. If the finished products weigh more, then facilities exhibit a market orientation by locating closer to the market than the sources of their raw materials. For example, paper mills transform heavy timber into lightweight paper, making the cost to transport raw materials much greater than the transport of the finished product. Thus, paper mills generally have a material orientation. Tire manufacturers choose a market orientation, since it is significantly more expensive to ship tires a great distance than the various resources used to make tires. An important exception to Weber's theory is that some industries have no real inclination to be located close to either raw materials or primary markets, since their products are so lightweight and valuable. Companies such as this are often called **footloose firms**—the diamond and computer chip markets are excellent examples. For some products, the location of a production facility can determine the cost of products. Some products have **spatially fixed costs**, which do not change despite where the product is assembled, while others have **spatially variable costs**, which change depending on where the products are produced.

Another important component of least-cost theory is **agglomeration**. An agglomeration effect occurs when many companies from the same industry cluster together in a relatively small area to draw from the same set of collective resources. For example, computer companies frequently cluster together in places like Silicon Valley, California, and Austin, Texas, to take advantage of a highly trained labor force. The same is true of fashion designers in

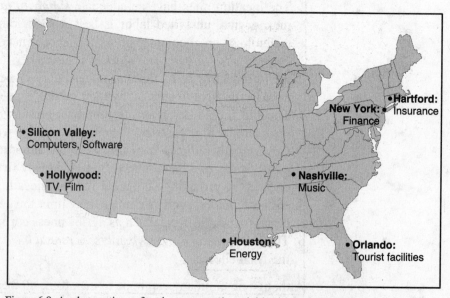

Figure 6.8. Agglomerations of various economic activities in the United States.

Milan, Italy and Paris, France, and of motion picture studios in Los Angeles, California, and Mumbai (Bombay), India. Interestingly, as more firms from the same industry locate in particular areas, even more resources become available. This is called a multiplier effect, and it helps to cement particular regions as centers of certain types of industry. As the Silicon Valley became increasingly known for its high-tech firms, it attracted more and more computer experts. The fact that such a talented labor force existed in this area also encouraged other high-tech firms to locate there. By the late 1990s, the San Francisco Bay Area was poised to take the lead in the information revolution and the dot-com boom in particular. The agglomeration of firms in the Bay Area also spawned a number of **ancillary activities**, which are economic activities that surround and support large-scale industries. Ancillary activities can include everything from shipping to food service. The opposite of agglomeration, **deglomeration**, occurs when firms leave an agglomerated region to start up in a distant, new place. After the dot-com bust, some high-tech firms left San Francisco because the costs of living were so high.

Agglomeration is actually a part of the larger pattern of regionalization processes that occur in every nation's economy. **Regionalization** is the process by which specific regions acquire characteristics that differentiate them from others within the same country. In economic geography, regionalization involves the development of dominant economic activities in particular regions. The primary **manufacturing region** in the United States has historically been the Great Lakes region, which includes Michigan, Illinois, Indiana, Ohio, New

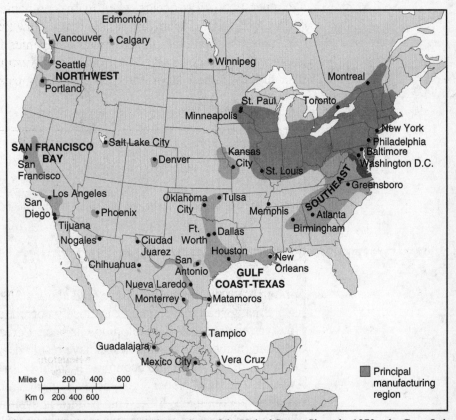

Figure 6.9. Principal manufacturing regions of the United States. Since the 1970s, the Great Lakes, known as the Rust Belt, has lost much of its former economic vitality.

York, and Pennsylvania. Although deindustrialization has eroded the manufacturing core of the Rust Belt, it is still the home of much of the United States' remaining industrial base. Similarly, industrial regions exist in southeastern Brazil and central England. In the United States, certain cities have experienced a regionalization process, and as a result, they are known for particular economic activities. In New York, financial markets are king. Hartford, Connecticut, houses a disproportionate number of insurance companies. San Francisco dominates in shipping and technology, and Houston is home to a number of energy firms.

While some regions experience economic gains from regionalization, others may become **economic backwaters**. As stated earlier, backwash effects occur when one region experiences tremendous economic growth, while others lag behind or even recede. This process can lead to higher levels of outmigration, exodus of investment capital, and shrinking of the local tax base. In China, the vast majority of industry and commerce is located on the eastern coast, while most of the west has little economic activity. In France, a disproportionate amount of economic activity is centered in Paris. Most of Argentina is relatively undeveloped; however, the city of Buenos Aires is a great, albeit somewhat unstable, seat of industry. In the United States, regional economic backwaters include the upper Great Plains, the lower Mississippi Valley, and parts of the Southwest. While the process of regional industrial development creates vibrant centers of production and commerce, it also tends to leave many other areas out of the loop in terms of development and prosperity.

Figure 6.10. The economic core region of China hugs the country's eastern coast.

Development, Equality, and Sustainability

For much of this chapter, you have read about economic development. As you have already seen, development is closely correlated with standard of living. However, the process of developing has been a great struggle for many countries, and many adverse side effects have resulted. Developing countries often contain extreme social and economic inequality. In countries like Mexico and Argentina, a small upper class holds a great amount of wealth, while the majority has relatively little. This pattern is even more extreme in countries like Nigeria, where a small group of people has gained great wealth through their control of land and natural resources, while the vast majority live in abject poverty. Although many people consider such extreme inequality simply a "growing pain" of development, it is uncertain whether the majority of Indians will ever be able to attain the sort of social welfare and security enjoyed by people in highly developed countries like Norway, Sweden, and Canada.

Another problem with development is that, although our economic systems demand growth in order to raise the level of productivity and standard of living, this type of economic growth is probably not sustainable into the distant future. Raw materials, which fuel industry, are generally limited either to nonrenewable stocks or renewable stocks that are frequently harvested at rates far in excess of their rate of natural replacement. This poses a serious problem for firms such as oil companies, which must find new ways to make profits through sustainable energy in the future. If no new oil reserves are tapped, our global supply will probably be depleted in less than 100 years. Other adverse side effects of production, such as air and water pollution, must be contained for people's health and well-being. In some encouraging cases, new technologies have enabled us to increase production while actually decreasing pollution, but truly sustainable development still remains elusive.

Sustainable development is an attempt to address the issues of social welfare and environmental protection within the context of capitalism and economic growth. Sustainable development, which has many definitions, is basically the idea that people living today should be able to meet their needs without prohibiting the ability of future generations to do the same. Implicit in this definition is the idea that you should be able to provide for people today without irreparably harming the environment and thus compromising its ability to provide the things that might be needed in the future. Unfortunately, there are many problems with this vague idea, and many people, without critically analyzing the concept, have used it as a vacuous slogan. In addition, this definition of sustainable development is extremely **anthropocentric**, which means that it focuses specifically on the needs of people—not the needs of myriad other creatures with whom we share the planet or requirements of the ecosystems upon which we depend.

In today's world, where we have not yet reached the absolute limits of the earth's ability to provide for us, economic inequality arises primarily from the inequitable distribution of wealth and resources. In less-developed countries throughout the world, millions of people suffer from malnutrition, lack of clean water and air, and no access to even basic medical care. However, many experiments and initiatives are currently underway for helping people in the less-developed world provide for themselves in a sustainable fashion and for helping people think about economics in different ways. In the tiny Himalayan country of Bhutan, the government's official policy is to measure success through "gross national happiness," not Gross National Product. Although this policy is less than perfect—just ask Bhutan's thousands of refugees or second-class lowland peasants—it represents a way of thinking about welfare and development that diverges sharply from traditional Western thought and may provide important insights for further development efforts in chronically poor countries. Human geography is a particularly well-suited tool for understanding the injustices inherent in global economics and for evaluating options for helping people to create a truly sustainable future.

Globalization

Of all the catch phrases used to explain the world's current political and economic trends, **globalization** is probably the most commonly abused. Globalization is the idea that the world is becoming integrated on a global scale such that smaller scales of political and economic life are becoming obsolete. Some people argue that globalization is knocking down social barriers, decreasing the meaningfulness of space, and rendering geographic diversity a thing of the past. As the world becomes fully globalized, they say, location will lose its meaning, and people everywhere will have the same access to standardized goods, services, and information. This hypothesis, in light of the previous discussion on global inequalities, represents a rather unrealistic scenario for the world's developing countries.

What few people recognize on either side of the issue is that globalization has a long and circuitous history. The world became increasingly interconnected for a time during the Renaissance, when long-distance trade increased markedly between Asia, Europe, and Africa. It was also during this period that European explorers inducted North and South America into the global system. In the 19th century, the Industrial Revolution once again increased global economic integration, as industrializing countries sought raw materials for construction and new markets for their goods. This period of interconnection was interrupted by the wave of economic crises that rocked the world's markets during the 1880s and 1890s. In the beginning of the 20th century, global economic integration once again increased, only to be interrupted by two world wars, the Great Depression, and the Cold War. In many ways, the current period of globalization is simply the most recent manifestation of a trend that seems to be repeating itself over time.

One extremely important factor sets the current time period of increased global interconnectivity apart from similar patterns in world history. The near instantaneous connections that occur across globalized locations resulting from increased telecommunications technology, specifically the Internet, have transformed both the nature of international connections and the space in which these interactions occur. One could argue that cyberspace represents both a new frontier and revolutionary medium for globalization. The increasingly rapid flow of innovations, information, and capital may have profound implications for regulating economic flows across borders and across the world. This argument lends credence to the idea that geographic national boundaries are becoming more permeable, while technology enables the world economy to become increasingly intertwined. But it is also important to note that even the Internet requires a material infrastructure that exists in actual geographic space. This fact alone gives all national governments a certain level of regulation over the activities that occur between globally interconnected nodes.

Others oppose the idea of globalization on the basis of its exclusivity. Although chains like McDonald's and brand names like Nike may seem omnipresent to the international traveler, globalization has not fulfilled its promise of providing standardized, high-quality goods and services, nor has it improved the lives of the world's poorest people, many of whom still remain isolated from economic growth. For them, the benefits of globalization are nothing more than an abstraction. Proponents of antiglobalization movements complain that the forces of globalization, particularly multinational corporations, are tearing at the fabric of local communities and time-honored cultural practices. Many antiglobalization activists also allege that, because multinational corporations have little stake in local communities and ecosystems, globalization also causes environmental destruction. Globalization proponents counter that expansion of the global economic system will give previously marginalized people more economic power, raise the overall standard of living, increase the accountability of governments, and enable greater access to information. Ironically, the awareness that individuals have of the negative effects of this process can often be attributed to the forces they so radically oppose. Protestors use the World Wide Web, one of the biggest features of globalization, and the connection capabilities it allows to spread their messages across the globe. Regardless of whether you are for or against globalization, it is impossible to ignore its effects.

It should be obvious by now that economic geographers have a tremendously difficult yet extremely important job. Understanding spatial patterns of development may be more simple than determining the explanations behind those patterns, but both present crucial challenges. Patterns, trends, regionalizations, and transitions occur continually at all geographic scales, making it extremely difficult to quantitatively measure development levels across the globe. In the face of these challenges, economic geographers must also make viable suggestions for implementing policies to help initiate sustainable economic growth and to improve the lives of people throughout the world.

Key Terms Defined

Agglomeration Grouping together of many firms from the same industry in a single area for collective or cooperative use of infrastructure and sharing of labor resources.

Ancillary activities Economic activities that surround and support large-scale industries such as shipping and food service.

Anthropocentric Human-centered; in sustainable development, anthropocentric refers to ideas that focus solely on the needs of people without considering the creatures with whom we share the planet or the ecosystems upon which we depend.

Backwash effect The negative effects on one region that result from economic growth within another region.

Brick-and-mortar business Traditional businesses with actual stores in which trade or retail occurs; it does not exist solely on the Internet.

Conglomerate corporation A firm that is comprised of many smaller firms that serve several different functions.

Core National or global regions where economic power, in terms of wealth, innovation, and advanced technology, is concentrated.

Core-periphery model A model of the spatial structure of development in which underdeveloped countries are defined by their dependence on a developed core region.

Deglomeration The dispersal of an industry that formerly existed in an established agglomeration.

Deindustrialization Loss of industrial activity in a region.

Development The process of economic growth, expansion, or realization of regional resource potential.

E-commerce Web-based economic activities.

Economic backwaters Regions that fail to gain from national economic development.

Export-processing zone Areas where governments create favorable investment and trading conditions to attract export-oriented industries.

Fast world Areas of the world, usually the economic core, that experience greater levels of connection due to high-speed telecommunications and transportation technologies.

Footloose firms Manufacturing activities in which cost of transporting both raw materials and finished product is not important for determining the location of the firm.

Fordism System of standardized mass production attributed to Henry Ford.

Foreign investment Overseas business investments made by private companies.

Gender equity A measure of the opportunities given to woman compared to men within a given country.

Globalization The idea that the world is becoming increasingly interconnected on a global scale such that smaller scales of political and economic life are becoming obsolete.

Gross Domestic Product The total value of goods and services produced within the borders of a country during a specific time period, usually one year.

Gross National Product The total value of goods and services, including income received from abroad, produced by the residents of a country within a specific time period, usually one year.

Human Development Index Measure used by the United Nations that calculates development not in terms of money or productivity but in terms of human welfare. The HDI evaluates human welfare based on three parameters: life expectancy, education, and income.

Industrial Revolution The rapid economic and social changes in manufacturing that resulted after the introduction of the factory system to the textile industry in England at the end of the 18th century.

Industrialization Process of industrial development in which countries evolve economically, from producing basic, primary goods to using modern factories for mass-producing goods. At the highest levels of development, national economies are geared mainly toward the delivery of services and exchange of information.

Industrialized countries Those countries including Britain, France, the United States, Russia, Germany, and Japan, that were all at the forefront of industrial production and innovation through the middle of the 20th century. While industry is currently shifting to other countries to take advantage of cheaper labor and more relaxed environmental standards, these countries still account for a large portion of the world's total industrial output.

Least-cost theory A concept developed by Alfred Weber to describe the optimal location of a manufacturing establishment in relation to the costs of transport and labor, and the relative advantages of agglomeration or deglomeration.

Least-developed countries Those countries including countries in Africa, except for South Africa, and parts of South America and Asia, that usually have low levels of economic productivity, low per capita incomes, and generally low standards of living.

Manufacturing region A region in which manufacturing activities have clustered together. The major U.S. industrial region has historically been in the Great Lakes, which includes the states of Michigan, Illinois, Indiana, Ohio, New York, and Pennsylvania. Industrial regions also exist in southeastern Brazil, central England, around Tokyo, Japan, and elsewhere.

Maquiladoras Those U.S. firms that have factories just outside the United States/Mexican border in areas that have been specially designated by the Mexican government. In such areas, factories cheaply assemble goods for export back into the United States.

Net National Product A measure of all goods and services produced by a country in a year, including production from its investments abroad, *minus* the loss or degradation of natural resource capital as a result of productivity.

Offshore financial center Areas that have been specially designed to promote business transactions, and thus have become centers for banking and finance.

Periphery Countries that usually have low levels of economic productivity, low per capita incomes, and generally low standards of living. The world economic periphery includes Africa (except for South Africa), parts of South America, and Asia.

Primary economic activities Economic activities in which natural resources are made available for use or further processing, including mining, agriculture, forestry, and fishing.

Productivity A measure of the goods and services produced within a particular country.

Purchasing Power Parity A monetary measurement of development that takes into account what money buys in different countries.

Quaternary economic activities Economic activities concerned with research, information gathering, and administration.

Quinary economic activities The most advanced form of quaternary activities consisting of high-level decision making for large corporations or high-level scientific research.

Regionalization The process by which specific regions acquire characteristics that differentiate them from others within the same country. In economic geography, regionalization involves the development of dominant economic activities in particular regions.

Rostow's stages of development A model of economic development that describes a country's progression which occurs in five stages transforming them from least-developed to most-developed countries.

Rust Belt The manufacturing region in the United States that is currently debilitated because many manufacturing firms have relocated to countries offering cheaper labor and relaxed environmental regulations.

Secondary economic activities Economic activities concerned with the processing of raw materials such as manufacturing, construction, and power generation.

Semi-periphery Those newly industrialized countries with median standards of living, such as Chile, Brazil, India, China, and Indonesia. Semi-peripheral countries offer their citizens relatively diverse economic opportunities but also have extreme gaps between rich and poor.

Service-based economies Highly developed economies that focus on research and development, marketing, tourism, sales, and telecommunications.

Slow world The developing world that does not experience the benefits of high-speed telecommunications and transportation technology.

Spatially fixed costs An input cost in manufacturing that remains constant wherever production is located.

Spatially variable costs An input cost in manufacturing that changes significantly from place to place in its total amount and in its relative share of total costs.

Specialty goods Goods that are not mass-produced but rather assembled individually or in small quantities.

Sustainable development The idea that people living today should be able to meet their needs without prohibiting the ability of future generations to do the same.

Tertiary economic activities Activities that provide the market exchange of goods and that bring together consumers and providers of services such as retail, transportation, government, personal, and professional services.

Transnational corporation A firm that conducts business in at least two separate countries; also known as multinational corporations.

World cities A group of cities that form an interconnected, internationally dominant system of global control of finance and commerce.

World-systems theory Theory developed by Immanuel Wallerstein that explains the emergence of a core, periphery, and semi-periphery in terms of economic and political connections first established at the beginning of exploration in the late 15th century and maintained through increased economic access up until the present.

Sample Questions and Answers

Section 1: Industrialization

Multiple-Choice Questions

1. The Industrial Revolution

   (A) began in Germany in the 16th century.
   (B) was initiated by Henry Ford.
   (C) began in England in the 18th century.
   (D) reached its peak in the 1970s.
   (E) began in the United States in the early 20th century

2. Which of the following are commonly associated with the Industrial Revolution?

(A) Specialty goods
(B) Cottage industries
(C) New forms of capital investment
(D) The printing press
(E) Guild industries

3. Deindustrialization has had a dramatic impact on which of the following regions?

(A) The lower Mississippi Valley
(B) The Great Plains
(C) The Great Lakes
(D) The Pacific Northwest
(E) The Cotton Belt

4. _____ take advantage of geographic differences in wages, labor laws, environmental regulations, taxes, and the distribution of natural resources by locating various aspects of their production in different countries.

(A) Conglomerate corporations
(B) E-businesses
(C) Transnationals
(D) Service industries
(E) Footloose industries

5. Mexico's *maquiladoras* are examples of

(A) offshore financial centers.
(B) transnationals.
(C) brick-and-mortar businesses.
(D) export-processing zones.
(E) ancillary activities.

Free-Response Question

1. Describe the effects of deindustrialization, including the global geography of production that has emerged during the past 30 years and the notion of backwash effects.

Sections 2 and 3: Models of Development and Measures of Productivity and Global Economic Patterns

Multiple-Choice Questions

1. Niger's economy is mostly limited to

   (A) service industries.
   (B) primary economic activities.
   (C) export-processing activities.
   (D) quaternary economic activities.
   (E) nonbasic industry.

2. Rostow's stages of development model predicts that each country's economy will progress from

   (A) high consumption to ecological sustainability.
   (B) low output to high input.
   (C) low per capita incomes to high per capita incomes and high consumption.
   (D) high levels of pollution to efficient resource use.
   (E) low employment in tertiary activities to high employment in primary activities.

3. The _____ is a measure of all goods and services produced by a country in a year, including production from its investments abroad, *minus* the loss or degradation of natural resource capital as a result of productivity.

   (A) Net National Product
   (B) Gross National Product
   (C) Human Development Index
   (D) Intrinsic Productivity Index
   (E) Purchasing Power Parity

4. Gender equity is related to

   (A) Gross National Product.
   (B) cultural traditions.
   (C) education.
   (D) All of the above
   (E) Only (A) and (B)

5. First tier world cities include

   (A) Tokyo, Mexico City, and Sao Paulo.
   (B) Tokyo, London, and New York.
   (C) Paris, Brussels, and Moscow.
   (D) Washington, Moscow, and London.
   (E) Los Angeles, London, and Paris.

Free-Response Question

1. Consider Rostow's stages of development model. What are its assumptions? What evidence would you use to support it? What are its shortcomings? Will all countries eventually conform to the model?

Section 4: Location Principles

Multiple-Choice Questions

1. Firms try to locate their production facilities to

   (A) maximize spatial accessibility.
   (B) maximize visibility and minimize transportation.
   (C) maximize agglomeration.
   (D) minimize costs and maximize profits.
   (E) minimize competition.

2. The clustering of financial firms on Wall Street, in New York, is an example of

   (A) least-cost theory.
   (B) agglomeration.
   (C) deindustrialization.
   (D) ancillary industry.
   (E) central place theory.

3. Mr. Jemstone located his jewelry shop in a place near his home so that he can eat lunch with Mrs. Jemstone every afternoon.

   (A) His locational decision represents a market orientation.
   (B) Since Mr. Jemstone owns his own business, he has chosen an optimal site as he minimizes transport costs to and from work.
   (C) It doesn't matter too much where Mr. Jemstone put his jewelry shop because it is a footloose industry and as long a viable market exists, he can locate pretty much anywhere.
   (D) Because most jewelry shopping occurs on-line, the actual location of the shop is unimportant.
   (E) Mr. and Mrs. Jemstone probably participate in a cottage industry.

4. Economic activities that increase and thereby benefit from agglomerations in particular regions are called

   (A) ancillary activities.
   (B) tertiary activities.
   (C) basic sector services.
   (D) quinary activities.
   (E) footloose industries.

5. Which of the following regions is not an economic backwater?

   (A) Buenos Aires, Argentina
   (B) Western China
   (C) Sao Paolo, Brazil
   (D) Lower Mississippi Valley
   (E) Upper Great Plains

Sections 5 and 6: Development, Equality, and Sustainability and Globalization

Multiple-Choice Questions

1. The idea that resources should be conserved so that people living today can meet their needs without limiting the ability of future generations to do the same is called

   (A) globalization.
   (B) gross national happiness.
   (C) sustainable development.
   (D) environmental conservation.
   (E) subsistence economics.

2. Globalization

   (A) is a new and unique phenomenon.
   (B) has penetrated the entire world.
   (C) is always good for people in the poorest countries.
   (D) has a long and circuitous history.
   (E) does not cause a countermovement of localization.

Free-Response Question

1. Discuss how the spatial patterns of globalization might coincide with levels of development. What are possible explanations for these patterns?

Answers for Multiple-Choice Questions

Section 1: Industrialization

1. **(C)** The Industrial Revolution began in England in the 18th century and then spread to continental Europe, particularly France and Germany, and North America. The Industrial Revolution reached its peak in the 19th and early 20th centuries, but by the 1970s many formerly industrialized regions had lost their manufacturing bases to developing countries such as Mexico and China.

2. **(C)** When most geographers, economists, and historians think about the Industrial Revolution, massive factories, standardized goods, and new forms of capital investment are among the first things to come to mind.

3. **(C)** During the first half of the 20th century, the Great Lakes region, including Ohio, Michigan, and portions of Illinois, Pennsylvania, Indiana, and Wisconsin, became vibrant centers of manufacturing and heavy industry. By the 1970s, that same region had slipped into economic depression, as corporations moved their factories to developing countries and relocated their headquarters to sunbelt states.

4. **(C)** Transnational corporations attempt to maximize their profits by taking advantage of different regulatory and economic situations in different countries. One transnational corporation may have its headquarters in the United States, locate its factories in Mexico and Thailand, and keep its finances at banks in Switzerland and the Cayman Islands.

5. **(D)** *Maquiladoras* are manufacturing areas located along the United States-Mexico border. Products are assembled at *maquiladora* factories and then exported across the border to U.S. markets.

Sections 2 and 3: Models of Development and Measures of Productivity and Global Economic Patterns

1. **(B)** Countries at low levels of economic development, like Niger, have economies that are mostly oriented toward primary activities, such as fishing, farming, and mining.

2. **(C)** Rostow's stages of development model provides a teleological view of economics in which the economies of all nations are headed toward a single ultimate purpose—the attainment of high per capita incomes and high levels of material consumption.

3. **(A)** The Gross National Product computes the value of all goods and services produced by a country in a year, but the Net National Product also subtracts capital lost through the degradation of natural resources.

4. **(D)** Gender equity, or women's welfare, is related to a wide range of cultural and economic issues including, but not limited to, economic productivity, cultural traditions, and education.

5. **(B)** Tokyo, London, and New York are the world's three most important centers of economic activity and are thus categorized as first-tier world cities. Other important centers of government, finance, and popular culture, such as Paris, Washington, Brussels, and Los Angeles are considered to be second-tier world cities.

Section 4: Location Principles

1. **(D)** Firms try to locate their production and distribution facilities in ways that maximize their profit through cutting down on transportation costs.

2. **(B)** Agglomeration occurs when firms find that it is to their advantage to locate close to other firms in the same industry. Advantages include being able to use the same pool of employees and being close to important infrastructure components, such as transportation depots or movie sets.

3. **(C)** Because both the inputs used to make jewelry and the finished product are so lightweight, this type of industry can locate basically anywhere a large enough market exists to make a profit.

4. **(A)** Ancillary activities include all the necessary services to sustain and provide for a local population such as grocery stores, haircutters, and veterinary hospitals. As the population within a region increases, as it does when an area becomes the site for a particular agglomeration, more of the services become necessary. Thus agglomerations have tremendous impacts on the overall economy within a specific region.

5. **(C)** Sao Paolo, Brazil is actually one of the most dominant economic areas in all of South America. Backwaters exist when other regions in a country experience great levels of economic development—like Sao Paolo—and this concentration has negative effects on other regions that cannot generate high levels of economic activity.

Sections 5 and 6: Development, Equality, and Sustainability and Globalization

1. **(C)** Although the term "sustainable development" has many definitions, this one, paraphrased from the Bruntland Report, or "Our Common Future," which was published by the World Commission on Environment and Development in 1987, is the standard that is most frequently quoted.

2. **(D)** During the past 500 years, the world economic system has undergone several periods of greater or less economic integration, or globalization.

Answers for Free-Response Questions

Section 1: Industrialization

1. Main points:
   - Deindustrialization occurs when formerly industrialized regions lose their industrial base.
   - Since the 1970s, deindustrialization has occurred throughout the older manufacturing areas of Britain, continental Europe, and North America.
   - During this time, transnational corporations have geographically reorganized. While most transnationals have maintained their headquarters

in wealthy countries like the United States and Japan, they have moved their production facilities to less-developed countries in Asia and Latin America.

- This shift of industry from the developed to the developing countries can be described in terms of a backwash effect; industrial growth for countries like Mexico and Indonesia is directly linked to industrial decline in North America and Europe.

Sections 2 and 3: Models of Development and Measures of Productivity and Global Economic Patterns

1. Main points:
   - Rostow's stages of development model describes the economic evolution of countries from lower levels of productivity, incomes, and material consumption to higher levels of all three. According to Rostow, along the way, countries will pass through five stages of economic development.
   - Rostow's model makes several basic assumptions. It assumes that (1) all countries will have similar developmental trajectories, (2) intrinsic factors such as natural resources and culture will not affect development, (3) countries that undergo development at different times in history will undergo the same processes, (4) all countries will have the same access to development, and (5) the natural goal, path, and purpose of all economies is to increase productivity and material consumption.
   - Rostow's argument is supported by the observation that some countries actually have undergone similar courses of economic development and that, in the current world economic system, different countries appear to be at different levels in the stages of development model.
   - It is difficult to say whether all countries will eventually conform to Rostow's model. However, it is unlikely that, given all of the simplified assumptions listed here, Rostow's model will be universally applicable.

Sections 5 and 6: Development, Equality, and Sustainability and Globalization

1. Main points:
   - The countries that seem to be the driving forces behind globalization are also those that comprise the highly developed regions of the globe. Additionally, these are the countries that are increasingly relocating to other parts of the world to take advantage of cheap labor and relaxed environmental limitations.
   - Thus the nations that both drive and benefit from globalization are usually those that measure quite well on all indices of economic development. Conversely, the nations that do not benefit from all of globalization's amazing possibilities remain locked in economic dependency on the drivers of this process and continually exhibit poor measures of economic development.
   - It seems that technology continues to widen the gap between the developed and developing nations across the globe. Beginning with the

Industrial Revolution, technology started separating different regions across the globe in terms of productivity and economic dominance on the world market. Our current era of globalization is characterized by powerful technologies that allow for instantaneous connections across the globe. The developing world is still catching up, trying to achieve technological levels characteristic of developed regions during the Industrial Revolution. As such, if the peripheral areas of the world ever achieve the benefits of globalization, it will be a long time in the future, and by then the developed world might be enjoying even greater technologies perpetuating the technology gap that exists between core and peripheral countries.

Additional Resources

Text

Michael Moore. 1989 *Roger & Me* [videorecording]. Dog Eat Dog Films; written, produced, and directed by Michael Moore. Burbank, CA: Warner Home Video.

An excellent documentary film that looks at the effects of deindustrialization in Flint, Michigan. It specifically explores how the relocation of General Motor's firms out of the United States devastated an entire community.

Brown, Lawrence A. 1991. *Place, Migration and Development in the Third World*. New York: Routledge.

In this book, Brown takes a different approach than most discussions on development. He discusses how certain characteristics of places or regions affect human behavior, as well as how human behavior, in the form of migration, affects economic development in certain places.

Fik, T. J. 1997. *The Geography of Economic Development: Regional Changes, Global Challenges*. New York: McGraw-Hill.

This book examines the geography of economic development by looking at how globalization of production, consumption, and exchange has affected different regions' ability to develop. It provides a framework for understanding the implications of regional economic change and for discussing future economic development.

Potter, Robert B., J. A. Binnes, J. A. Elliott, and D. Smith. 1999. *Geographies of Development*. London: Longman.

This is a textbook designed for development classes either in geography or sociology departments. It differs from textbooks covering the same topic by focusing on development ideologies, globalization, modernity, gender, ethnicity, tourism, land degradation and environmental sustainability, whereas other texts generally focus on traditional developmental issues of agriculture, industry, urbanization, trade, and aid.

Seitz, John L. 1995. *Global Issues: An Introduction*. Cambridge, Massachusetts: Blackwell.

An excellent introductory book for many issues discussed in this chapter that are currently affecting the entire globe. The author begins by discussing some of the origins of the disparity that exists between the poor and wealthy nations of the globe. He discusses many environmental and social issues as they relate to this significant distance in wealth, and concludes with suggestions for facilitating discussions of these issues.

Web

Bureau of Economic Analysis: *http://www.bea.doc.gov/*

This organization provides electronic data at several different scales including national data, industry data, international data, and regional data. The national data covers income and product accounts and fixed assets tables, industry data covers input and output values, and the international data contains international transactions accounts. The organization provides regional data on the gross state product, the local area personal income, annual state personal income, and quarterly state personal income.

Businessweek: http://www.businessweek.com/

This site links to the magazine, which contains coverage on both national and international economic news. If you are a teacher, the site would provide you with knowledge of current economic events that you can incorporate into your classroom. If you are a student, the site would allow you to see how some of the concepts you learned in this chapter play out in real life.

Economy.com, *The Dismal Scientist: http://www.economy.com/dismal/*

This is a link to a feature within the economy.com website. The main website, which is definitely worth a visit, provides economic, financial, and industry research to a wide audience. The link to the dismal scientist provides daily updates of the ups and downs of the economy throughout the world. It includes information on different economic indicators, as well as tools for understanding various economic processes such as how the stock market works.

Fortune, Inc.: *http://www.fortune.com*

The website provides access to *Fortune* magazine which basically contains extensive information about different companies and corporations, both big ones and small ones. While providing profiles of numerous different companies, it also discusses current events relating to different businesses within the United States and across the globe.

U.S. Department of Labor: *http://www.dol.gov/*

This comprehensive website provides all kinds of information about being either an employee or employer in the United States including your rights or obligations in terms of health plans, benefits, and unemployment insurance. It also includes information on current and recent labor-related decisions in the U.S. government.

The Wall Street Journal: http://public.wsj.com/home.html

This website links directly to the newspaper, which describes current economic news across the world. You can search for current events by country, or by industry. The site also provides articles describing the most relevant current economic events occurring on a daily basis. This would be an excellent site for understanding how many of the processes introduced in this chapter relate to the real-world economy.

Central Intelligence Agency: *http://www.odci.gov/cia/publications/factbook/*

This site is an excellent source for looking at economic indicators within a particular country. Once you choose a country from the initial page, you can then choose to explore the economics in that country by looking at GDP, GNP, PPP, percent of workforce in different sectors of the economy and many others. It provides an excellent tool for comparing the economic situations between the more- and less-developed countries of the world.

U.S. Agency for International Development: *http://www.usaid.gov/about/resources/*

This site basically houses a directory of development organizations throughout the world and throughout the country, including both government and nongovernment organizations, as well as organizations that investigate the intersection between development, health, and the environment.

World Bank, *World Development Report: http://www.worldbank.org/wdr/*

This link allows you to read both the current and past world development reports. These reports provide current information on the economic, social, and environmental state of the world today, including an analysis of a specific aspect of development which changes with each report but, in the past, included items like transition economies, labor, health, the environment, and poverty.

The Economist: www.economist.com

This link gives access to the current issue, as well as archived stories published within the past few years. These stories provide current information on economic issues around the globe. Similar to the link to the *Wall Street Journal,* this site provides excellent material for understanding the processes discussed in this chapter at work in the world.

What You Need to Know About Economics: *www.economics.about.com*

A website designed for a more general audience; the home page is a useful starting point in locating other economic resources on the Web; it is especially good for understanding the basics of economics.

Women Watch: *www.un.org/womenwatch/*

The website describes a joint venture of UN agencies devoted to women's concerns with interests in the large area of economic and social development.

CHAPTER 7
Agriculture and Rural Geography

Summary

During the past 10,000 years, agriculture has become an endeavor of enormous proportions, with dramatic consequences for the earth's physical and human geography. The first agriculturalists were hunter-gatherers who gradually, over thousands of years, adopted farming as another strategy to ensure their survival. By the beginning of the Colonial Period, agriculture was widespread throughout the world. Four important episodes—the first conscious cultivation of plants, the Industrial Revolution, the Green Revolution, and the Biotechnologic Revolution—have dramatically altered the way farmers work and the way people eat. In many countries, subsistence agriculture and animal husbandry still feed most people; however, large-scale commercial agriculture is an increasingly important endeavor throughout the world. Escalating human populations and unsustainable farming techniques have created a host of social and environmental problems that threaten the potential for future populations to reap sustainable harvests from the land.

In This Chapter

- Historical Geography of Agriculture
- Geography of Modern Agriculture
- Agriculture and the Environment

Key Terms

Agribusiness	Fertile Crescent
Agriculture	Genetically modified organisms
Animal husbandry	Green Revolution
Biotechnology	Hunting and gathering
Capital-intensive agriculture	Industrial Revolution
Commercial agricultural economy	Intensive cultivation
Dairying	Labor-intensive agriculture
Domestication	Livestock ranching
Extensive agriculture	Mechanization
Feedlots	Mediterranean agriculture

Pastoralism	Specialty crops
Pesticides	Subsistence agricultural economy
Planned agricultural economy	Swidden
Plantations	Topsoil loss
Salinization	Transhumance
Shifting cultivation	Urban sprawl
Slash-and-burn agriculture	von Thunen model

Historical Geography of Agriculture

Long ago, when people first began domesticating plants and animals, there was no sign that their actions would dramatically change the face of the earth. However, during the past 10,000 years, **agriculture** has become an endeavor of enormous proportions, with dramatic consequences for the earth's physical and human geography. Agriculture consists of the purposeful planting of crops or raising of livestock for human sustenance. This development has played an important role in the development of human societies, fostering the growth of urban civilizations and initiating global patterns of trade. In fact, it is hard to overestimate the importance of agriculture in human history. Today, changes in agricultural techniques and rural land use are being felt all over the world, as new technologies are introduced, as large corporations gain a greater share of commodity markets, and as traditional areas of **extensive agriculture**, which involve dispersed, widespread ranching and farming, are brought into more **intensive cultivation**, forcing smaller plots to produce greater yields. In some areas, agricultural plots are being lost completely to urban sprawl, and in other areas the soil is rapidly eroding, becoming infertile and thereby decreasing the ability of future farmers to reap a harvest from the land. This chapter examines the problems and challenges of providing for the earth's population while still caring for the land.

If asked where agriculture originated, most Americans would probably say the **Fertile Crescent**. The name "Fertile Crescent" instantly conjures up images of ancient civilizations and bountiful, sun-drenched valleys—an image starkly different from what most people probably have of today's Fertile Crescent, which includes parts of Iraq, Syria, Lebanon, and Turkey. It is true that the Fertile Crescent was an early hearth of agriculture, but it was actually only one of many places where people independently domesticated plants and animals over the past 10,000 years. **Domestication** initially occurred when humans consciously began to manipulate plant and animal species in order to sustain themselves. Other locations of independent domestication include modern-day Peru, central Mexico, East Africa, India, and China. Agricultural innovations diffused far and wide from these early hearths. Although some native peoples never adopted sedentary agriculture, domesticated plants and animals were widespread long before the age of European exploration began, over 500 years ago. It is also worth noting that westerners probably think of the Fertile Crescent as the birthplace of agriculture because Europeans inherited most of their crops and agricultural practices from there, not because it was the most important site of early farming or animal husbandry.

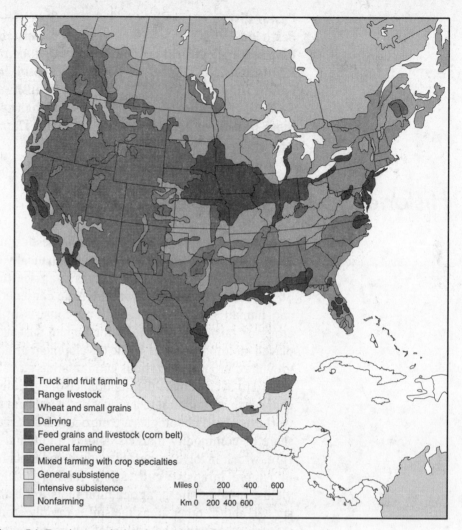

Figure 7.1. Dominant agricultural activities in the United States.

Agriculture was not "invented." It took thousands of years, and many false starts, for people to suitably domesticate plants and animals so that they became useful and dependable. Before the establishment of domesticated crops, all humans were involved in **hunting and gathering**; their diets consisted of animals they captured and wild plants they collected. Even after agriculture became firmly established, most people still hunted and gathered to round out their diet. Only recently, and only in some parts of the world, have the majority of people ceased hunting and gathering altogether. In the early days of agriculture and animal husbandry, domestication was incidental. As hunter-gatherers foraged for their food, they naturally chose the best fruits, nuts, and grains. In doing so they inadvertently spread the seeds of the plants that best suited their purposes, thus selecting for even bigger nuts, even tastier grains, and even juicier fruits. Over thousands of years, some of these plants became domesticated, meaning they had been permanently altered by people for human use. Even when people began to shift slowly to subsistence agriculture, millennia ago, their lives did not necessarily become safer or more secure. It is useful to think of early agriculturalists not as making a conscious decision to shift from hunting and gathering to farming, but as slowly diversifying their survival strategies to provide themselves with a wider range of nutritional sources, and more options if any one strategy failed.

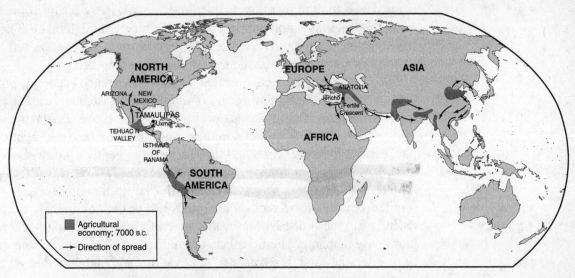

Figure 7.2. The hearths of early agriculture and the initial diffusion of plant and animal domestication.

Three different types of economies have traditionally governed agricultural production and distribution. In **subsistence agricultural economies**, farmers produce goods to provide for themselves and others in the local community. In **commercial agricultural economies**, a competitive market, where farmers freely market their goods with the goal of making a profit, determines agricultural production. Finally, in **planned agricultural economies**, which are associated with communist-controlled countries, the government controls both the supply and the price of goods that are distributed through government agencies. While these three systems seem quite different from one another, very few countries solely abide by one method. Some subsistence farmers produce excess, which they use to trade for goods for themselves and their families. In the United States, commercial farming generally prevails; however, the government does control price and production to some extent by providing subsidies and incentives to farmers across the country. And in many Latin American countries, governments encourage, and sometimes even demand, that farmers produce export commodities.

Once agriculture is categorized according to its economic purposes, further distinctions describe the extent of land under cultivation and the methods used to cultivate that land. These distinctions, described in terms of intensive and extensive cultivation, provide another important distinction for understanding agricultural variation across the globe. Intensive cultivation, whether for personal sustenance or commercial activity, involves a small piece of land with large labor inputs to generate a large amount of produce. Conversely, extensive cultivation usually involves large expanses of land and smaller amounts of labor to generate a specific agricultural product. Generally, population densities are high in intensely cultivated agricultural systems, while extensive systems support only a limited population. Further, a distinction can be made between **capital-intensive agriculture** and **labor-intensive agriculture**: capital-intensive methods use mechanical goods such as machinery, tools, vehicles, and facilities to produce large amounts of agricultural goods, a process requiring very little human labor. Conversely, labor-intensive goods use human hands in large abundance to produce a given amount of output. It is important to note that this distinction is not always a result of the level of technological innovation within a certain country, although that can be a large factor. Some agricultural products by nature must be handpicked such as strawberries, to ensure that the fruit does not get damaged.

The world's first farmers operated under a subsistence economy, producing to support their family and local community. Subsistence farming takes on many different forms in various places across the globe. In **slash-and-burn agriculture**, which is common in the tropics, farmers raze the vegetation in a plot, farm it for a few years and then move on to another plot with fresh soil. Slash-and-burn agriculture is a form of **shifting cultivation,** and land that has been cleared for farming is called **swidden**. The slash-and-burn system allows fragile tropical soils to recover and rainforest vegetation quickly to reoccupy recently farmed plots. However, this type of agriculture usually cannot support dense human populations because individual plots rapidly lose their fertility after the first few years of cultivation, and it takes many years for abandoned plots to regenerate themselves. In the Amazon Basin of Brazil, slashing and burning has been going on for thousands of years. However, in the 1970s and 1980s, the Brazilian government encouraged many of its citizens to move to the interior, and the amount of land being converted increased dramatically. Although the cutting has decreased, large areas of the rainforest have now been converted to livestock grazing.

Pastoralism is another type of subsistence agriculture, based on nomadic **animal husbandry**. Pastoral peoples are found mainly in the dry, mountainous areas of Africa and Asia, where harsh climates render cultivation unfeasible. This type of agricultural activity provides an excellent example of extensive subsistence cultivation as Nomadic livestock herders constantly search for forage to feed their livestock and thus cover a wide range of geographic space. The herders rely solely on their livestock to provide food, clothing, and even shelter. This form of agriculture is currently experiencing rapid decline as various economic, physical, and cultural changes force these people to change their livelihood.

Although subsistence farmers frequently participate in small local markets, the majority of their food is grown on site for local consumption. Because subsistence farmers rarely have much land and are almost always lacking in equipment, fertilizers, and other important agricultural inputs, they frequently lead a precarious existence. Subsistence agriculture—including both farming and animal husbandry—is still the dominant lifestyle and source of food in some areas of the world today, but in general, competitive markets control most of the world's current agricultural activity.

Esther Boserup, an important female agricultural geographer, formalized the transition from extensive subsistence forms of agriculture to more intensive cultivation of the land necessary to support greater populations. In contrast to Thomas Malthus, whose model was discussed in Chapter 3, Boserup viewed population growth as a positive force driving agricultural innovations that could support more people. Her model proposes a five-stage progression in which each stage represents a significant increase in both the intensity of the cultivation system and the number of families it can support. Stage one, called forest-fallow cultivation, involves 20–25 years of letting fields lie fallow after 1–2 years of cultivation. In bush-fallow cultivation, stage two, farmers cultivate the land for 2–8 years followed by a fallow period of 6–10 years. In stage three, the fallow period shortens to just 1–2 years between cultivated periods. In the next stage, farmers begin annual cropping leaving the land fallow for only several months between plantings. And in the final stage, the most intensive system, multicropping the same plot bears several crops a year with little or no fallow period. With each stage, the land can support greater populations, but each transition also involves greater depletion of soil nutrients. While many might argue the unsustainable nature of this system, Boserup argued that the increased levels of productivity would counteract the land being rendered infertile from overuse.

During the modern era, there have been at least four pivotal periods in the history of agriculture. The first key moment in agriculture's history has been mentioned, and it occurred when humans began modifying plant and animal species to sustain themselves. Seed domestication and technology about as advanced as an animal-driven plow actually describes the majority of agricultural history. Up until the late 18th century, most people throughout the world were farmers or hunter-gatherers of some sort. However, the second pivotal moment in agricultural history arrived with the **Industrial Revolution**, which began in the late 1700s in England and rapidly spread to Western Europe and the United States. The effects of this time period dramatically altered the global geography of agriculture.

Three components of the Industrial Revolution were particularly important for the transformation of agriculture in Western Europe and North America. First, during the Industrial Revolution millions of people migrated from rural areas into the cities of France, England, Germany, and the United States. These new urbanities came to cities, such as London, Manchester, Chicago, and New York, looking for jobs in factories and a better way of life. When they arrived, they created enormous *new markets* for the agricultural products produced in adjacent rural areas. Second, *mechanization* replaced human hands with agricultural technology, allowing farmers to produce more crops with less work. Finally, increased access to efficient forms of *transportation*, such as trains and steamboats, allowed farmers to ship their products farther at a lower cost. In fact, increased transportation technology has played a large role in determining which areas of the globe transitioned into commercial agricultural economies. Many isolated spots on the earth's surface remain subsistence economies simply because of their limited access to other parts of the world. Additionally, technological advances like refrigerated boxcars were particularly important because they allowed farmers to ship items great distances to urban consumers. Between 1780 and 1850, these three factors revolutionized farming in the newly industrialized world.

Another important period in the modern history of agriculture came after World War II. Beginning in the late 1940s, the industrialized countries of the northern hemisphere began transferring a great amount of technology, machinery, fertilizers, and other agricultural inputs to the less-developed countries of Africa, Asia, and Latin America. This episode, called the **Green Revolution**, continued into the 1960s, when developed countries finally realized the detrimental effects these new technologies wreaked on the environment. Instead of alleviating hunger, new machinery, "miracle" seeds, elaborate irrigation systems, and potent fertilizers were devastating the land, destroying traditional modes of agricultural production, and shattering ancient social structures. The Green Revolution encouraged rampant land speculation, vast human migrations, and unsustainable farming practices. Agronomists noticed that techniques developed for farming in the temperate climates were often unsuitable for tropical agriculture. And economists watched as multinational corporations began to steer local economies away from producing food for local consumption and toward producing **specialty crops** for export, such as peanuts and pineapples. As with many other well-meaning development projects, the Green Revolution failed largely because proponents did not consider the potential side effects of their actions. Today, many areas once farmed sustainably by local people for local consumption are now planted with specialty crops grown for export to North America and Western Europe.

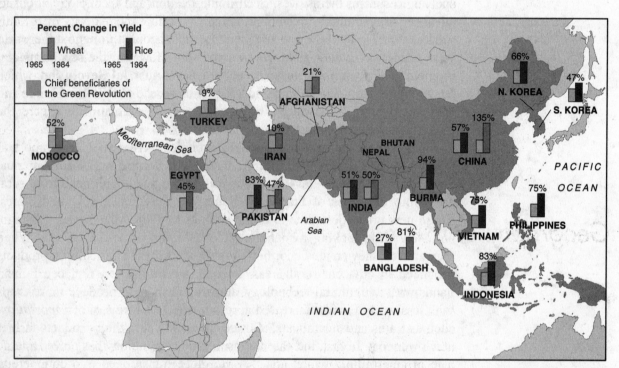

Figure 7.3. This map demonstrates the increases in yields in Asia as a result of the Green Revolution. While increased yields of both wheat and rice certainly helped support expanding populations in these regions, the Green Revolution also forced many local farmers to abandon their farms.

Another agricultural transformation, no less contested than the Green Revolution, currently drives much of the world's agricultural activity. High-tech agriculture, which employs computerized irrigation systems, long-term weather predictions, and genetically modified organisms, is changing agricultural practices throughout the world. Although most people agree that sophisticated irrigation and satellite-based weather predictions can only help farmers, the issue of **genetically modified organisms** is hotly debated. All crops are genetically modified, in the sense that they have been altered from their original genetic state by selection over time for human use. However, today's genetically modified foods are different. Some of these foods are the products of organisms that have had their genes altered in a laboratory for specific purposes, such as disease resistance, increased productivity, or nutritional value. Many agribusiness corporations have embraced the promise of control, predictability, and efficiency that genetically modified organisms represent. Critics say that such products have not been proven safe to people and that their effects on surrounding ecosystems could be devastating. As the debate rages, genetically modified foods are being produced by large corporations and small farmers throughout the world.

Perhaps the most important trend in modern agriculture has been the development of multinational **agribusinesses**. Today, a handful of giant corporations dominate a significant fraction of the world's agricultural markets through their control of land, technology, machinery, shipping, packaging, and marketing, such that the farm no longer maintains its position as the centerpiece of agricultural activity. California, Florida, and Texas gave birth to many agribusiness conglomerates during the first half of the 20th century, and these corporations have since expanded to Africa, Southeast Asia, and Latin America. Although the transformation from small, local farms to integrated agribusiness operations has had some positive effects, it has also had many negative and unintended consequences. One of which, the demise of the American family farm, has forced many traditional farmers into unemployment. During the last 10 years, new movements have arisen to reestablish local food production in both the highly industrialized and the less-developed world. Cooperatives, where money generated benefits the local economy, and local farmer's markets, where family farms can sell their produce, are examples of this grassroots movement to recapture local food production.

Geography of Modern Agriculture

Geographers look at both the spatial variation in agricultural activities and agricultural methods currently in use across the globe. The spatial variation in subsistence agriculture has just been discussed; the global distribution of commercial agriculture also varies across space as climate, soil, the availability of material inputs, and the dominant culture system determines agricultural production within a region. For example, oranges and other citrus fruits cannot thrive outside of tropical climates, sandy desert soils cannot produce tomatoes, and Asians depend on rice as a staple within their diet. These variables, in large part, determine agricultural production across the globe; however, certain technologies, such as greenhouses and hydroponics, have allowed many places to overcome their environmental limitations. For example, Icelanders can produce bananas in simulated tropical environments (greenhouses), and desert dwellers can produce tomatoes thanks to hydroponics, in which plants can grow in nutrient solutions instead of in soil. Thus, it is helpful to think of the global distribution of agricultural practices and products as a constantly shifting mosaic, as specific goods are produced in many different regions by many different methods. However, a few key types of commercial agriculture are worth discussing and mapping out here.

- *Commercial livestock* production takes multiple forms and can be divided up into two major categories: **livestock ranching** and **dairying**. Livestock ranching is widespread throughout much of western North America, South

America, southern Africa, western Asia, and Australia. One interesting practice in livestock ranching is called **transhumance**. Transhumance is the seasonal movement of livestock between different ranges. In many regions, livestock are moved into the mountains in the summer and then down into the valleys in the winter. Dairying is another important form of animal husbandry that is common in northern Europe and the northern United States.

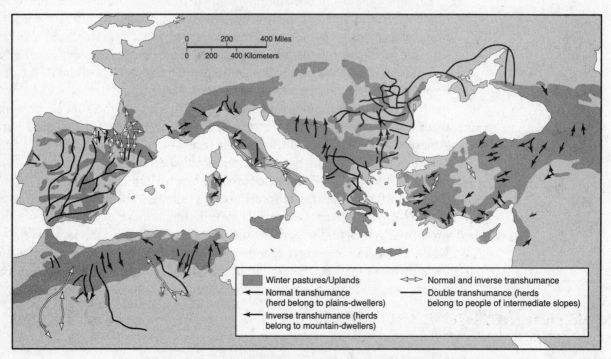

Figure 7.4. Map depicting the routes taken by herders across the globe as they move their flocks from summer to winter pastures for grazing.

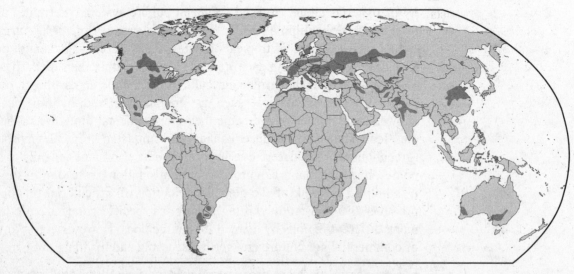

Figure 7.5. The principal wheat growing areas across the globe.

- *Commercial grain farming*, which includes wheat and corn, occurs in the North American Great Plains and in southern Russia. A large component of commercial grain farming goes toward feeding livestock. In fact, in Western Europe, three-fourths of cropland is devoted to grain farming specifically for livestock consumption. In general, the market value of meat from livestock surpasses that of grains, thus many farmers choose to convert their grain into meat by feeding it to livestock.

- *Tropical **plantations*** grow crops such as sugarcane and coffee, and are widespread throughout the tropics, in Central and South America, Africa, Asia, and the Caribbean. Plantations generally have some form of foreign control either through investments, management, or marketing, and often employ people not native to the region. Additionally, while many of the crops grown on plantations are suitable to the tropical environments where they exist, they are not usually native plants to those areas and are almost always exported to other countries rather than consumed locally.

- Finally, *mixed and specialty crop farming* is extremely diverse, and the particular forms it takes depends largely on climate. In the humid, subtropical southeastern United States, citrus fruits, vegetables, and nuts are grown alongside cattle ranches. **Mediterranean agriculture**, practiced in the Mediterranean-style climates of Western Europe, California, and portions of Chile and Australia, consists of diverse specialty crops such as grapes, avocados, olives, and a host of nuts, fruits, and vegetables.

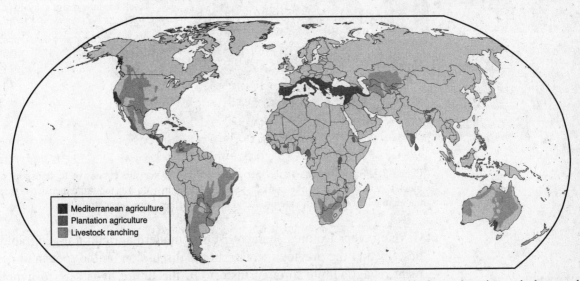

Figure 7.6. The geographic distribution of Mediterranean agriculture, plantation agriculture, and livestock ranching. Ranching tends to occur in midlatitude climates, while Mediterranean agriculture dominates moderate coastal climates, and plantations flourish in tropical coastal regions.

On a smaller scale, the regional distribution of agricultural practices has also been of interest to many geographers. Johann Heinrich von Thunen described one particularly important model of the regional distribution of agriculture during the 19th century. Von Thunen noticed that lands that appeared to have exactly the same physical geography were actually being used for very different agricultural purposes. He explained this phenomenon through the concept of rent. According to the **von Thunen model**, rent, or land value, will decrease the farther one gets away from central markets. Conversely, rent is highest in close proximity to urban markets. Thus, only the agricultural products that use the land intensively, have high transportation costs, and were in great demand would be located close to urban markets. Products that were in lower demand, required more extensive land use, or were less expensive to ship would be found farther away from the markets, where rent was lower. More specifically, von Thunen speculated that dairying and gardening of fruits and vegetables would be located close to the urban market, while extensive cattle ranching, mixed farming, and orchards would be located farther away. Because fruits, vegetables, and dairy products spoil more quickly, require more sensitive forms of transportation, and in general generate higher prices, they can afford to pay the higher price of rent near the market. Although, in real landscapes, this pattern is complicated by many factors, it still describes actual patterns of agricultural land use surrounding many cities.

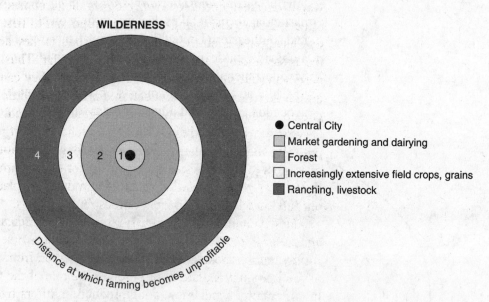

WILDERNESS

● Central City
☐ Market gardening and dairying
☐ Forest
☐ Increasingly extensive field crops, grains
☐ Ranching, livestock

Distance at which farming becomes unprofitable

Figure 7.7. Agricultural activity that generates goods that are expensive to transport or perish quickly occurs closer to the market, whereas goods that do not require expensive transport and maintain a longer shelf life are produced on land farther from the central city.

Many other features characteristic of modern agricultural geography were described in the previous section in the discussion on the roots and development of agriculture through history. In the future, it is safe to hypothesize increasing transitions of extensive agricultural systems into intensive ones that can generate greater amounts of goods on smaller amounts of land. Even activities seemingly impossible to transition, such as livestock ranching, have begun traveling along the path toward intensive cultivation in the form of feedlots. **Feedlots** concentrate the raising of livestock in a small geographic space where they are fed hormones and other fattening grains to prepare them for slaughter at a much more rapid pace and in a much smaller space. Esther Boserup was correct in her observation that increasing population levels necessitate transformations in the world's agricultural systems in order to provide for greater numbers of people. In large part, the technological and biological innovations that have occurred and continue to occur in modern agriculture are responding to the need to produce enough goods to provide for an ever-increasing global population.

Two of the dominant forces of modern agriculture that work to provide maximum yields for greater populations include biotechnology and agribusiness. Both topics were briefly mentioned earlier, but in order to understand the world's current agricultural system, more time must be spent describing these two dramatic shifts in agricultural production. **Biotechnology** involves any techniques used to modify living organisms in such a way that they improve plant and animal species and, in turn, plant and animal production. As mentioned earlier in the discussion of genetically modified foods, these processes allow farmers greater control over the goods they produce, thereby allowing them greater yields. With the development of plants that can resist certain pests and weeds, as well as plants that are clones from the tissues of other plants, the importance of both space and time in agricultural productivity decreases. These forms of technology allow farmers to grow virtually any product anywhere on the globe. However, biotechnology comes with very serious side effects. Before discussing those, it is important to first note that private firms that have patents on the methods and products they achieve develop most of the biotechnology techniques discussed so far. Thus, both countries in the periphery and small farmers lose out because they cannot afford to transition into these new modes of production. Furthermore, little research has been conducted studying the possible effects genetically modified organisms might have on other nonmodified organisms such as butterflies and insects that may pollinate modified plants. Thus, even though the Biotechnologic Revolution may seem to be the answer to providing for future populations, it may be similar to the Green Revolution in that the products are placed on the market without full knowledge of all their various repercussions.

The development of agribusinesses has also radically changed traditional agricultural production. This change evidences itself in several different forms, but the most specific form is a transition from agricultural production to food production, and a transition of the role of the farm as the centerpiece in agricultural production. Food production differs from agricultural production in that it includes an addition of economic value to an agricultural product through canning, refining, packing, or packaging. The modern grocery store provides a perfect example of this process. All the many goods outside of fruits, vegetables, and grains that line the majority of shelves are a result of production processes that process traditional agricultural goods and then package them before they are placed on the shelf in the form of chicken strips or frozen waffles. Additionally, evidence of the rise of the transnational corporation (TNC) within agribusiness also can be seen at most modern grocery stores. The fact that you can get almost any fruit or vegetable from all over the globe at any time of the year implies some level of corporate control over agricultural goods in other parts of the world, usually peripheral countries. In fact, many developing countries encourage TNCs to grow certain goods within their bounds for export in hope that these activities will stimulate their economies. However, this system forces local farmers to abandon traditional methods of agriculture, and a large proportion of the profits generated from these large agribusinesses accrue to the corporation rather than the local economy, thus they do not always provide the economic benefits the host country hopes for. Additionally, they represent a dramatic transition in the control of agricultural activity. The farm used to be the center controlling force, but the business or corporation now holds that place as it controls what seeds are grown where, where goods are packaged or processed, and finally where goods are sold. As the world's need for food continues to expand, agricultural geographers and policy makers will face many sticky issues and difficult challenges regarding sustainable and geographically even food production.

Agriculture and the Environment

Farmers and agricultural engineers have a very difficult job. How can they protect the environment while ensuring a sustainable harvest, providing safe, reliable, and high-quality food for a growing population? Historically, agriculture has had many adverse impacts on the environment. **Pesticides**, such as DDT, the effects of which were made famous by Rachel Carson in the book *Silent Spring*, have harmed wildlife populations; polluted rivers, lakes, and oceans; and worked their way through the food chain all the way up to human beings. **Topsoil loss**, or erosion, is a tremendous problem in areas with fragile soils, steep slopes, or torrential seasonal rains. Because fertile topsoil tends to accumulate very slowly, this essential resource, once lost, could take thousands of years to replace. Another soil conservation issue is salinization. **Salinization** occurs when soils in arid areas are brought under cultivation through irrigation. In arid climates, water evaporates quickly off the ground surface, leaving salty residues and rendering the soil infertile. As a result of these two soil problems, millions of acres of formerly arable land have become infertile. Thus, soil conservation will be essential if the world is to move toward a future of sustainable agricultural production.

Another important environmental issue having to do with agricultural production is rural land use change. In many areas of the United States, **urban sprawl** has overtaken formerly productive agricultural areas, converting fields and orchards to parking lots and subdivisions. Local government planning commissions are attempting to halt this process through agricultural zoning ordinances and tax incentives. However, in places such as California, where land values have risen dramatically over the past quarter century, many farmers find it difficult to pay property taxes and resist the quick financial return associated with developing their land. Unfortunately, some of the lands that are being developed for housing are among the most fertile. Another trend in agricultural land use is the shift from traditional, low-intensity operations, such as ranching, to high-intensity production associated with specialty crops and orchards. These specialty crops frequently offer a greater profit per acre per year; however, they also convert rural landscapes containing diverse habitats to comparatively sterile environments. Interestingly, this pattern has actually reversed itself in New England, where vast areas that were cleared for farms during the 18th and 19th centuries have now reverted back to forest. It is up to local planners, land owners, and voting citizens to decide how to best address the need for housing and services, while preserving traditional landscapes, habitats, and rural lifestyles.

Region	Overgrazing	Deforestation	Agricultural Mismanagement	Other	Total	Degraded Areas as Share of Total Vegetated Land
Asia	197	298	204	47	746	20%
Africa	243	67	121	63	494	22%
South America	68	100	64	12	244	14%
Europe	50	84	64	22	220	23%
North and Central America	38	18	91	71	158	8%
Australia, New Zealand and the South Pacific	83	12	8	0	103	13%
World	679	579	552	155	1,965	17%

(million hectares)

Figure 7.8. The mismanagement of soil has caused massive soil degradation across the globe.

Agricultural geography's complexity should be evident by now as you have explored all the many ways humans have devised to sustain themselves from the land. Throughout human history, agriculture has experienced many dramatic transitions in an effort to support ever-expanding human populations more efficiently. Often, the strategies used to accomplish this goal have unexpected and detrimental consequences on the physical environment. As greater levels of technology and scientific improvements are introduced into agricultural activity, it seems almost that a corresponding negative effect occurs on the natural environment. Agricultural geographers face many challenges in the future as they seek to understand all the various repercussions of modern agricultural techniques, while simultaneously devising methods to improve the earth's yield to accommodate an ever-increasing global population.

Key Terms Defined

Agribusiness The set of economic and political relationships that organize food production for commercial purposes. It includes activities ranging from seed production, to retailing, to consumption of agricultural products.

Agriculture The art and science of producing food from the land and tending livestock for the purpose of human consumption.

Animal husbandry An agricultural activity associated with the raising of domesticated animals, such as cattle, horses, sheep, and goats.

Biotechnology A form of technology that uses living organisms, usually genes, to modify products, to make or modify plants and animals, or to develop other microorganisms for specific purposes.

Capital-intensive agriculture Form of agriculture that uses mechanical goods such as machinery, tools, vehicles, and facilities to produce large amounts of agricultural goods—a process requiring very little human labor.

Commercial agricultural economy All agricultural activity generated for the purpose of selling, not necessarily for local consumption.

Dairying An agricultural activity involving the raising of livestock, most commonly cows and goats, for dairy products such as milk, cheese, and butter.

Domestication The conscious manipulation of plant and animal species by humans in order to sustain themselves.

Extensive agriculture An agricultural system characterized by low inputs of labor per unit land area.

Feedlots Places where livestock are concentrated in a very small area and raised on hormones and hearty grains that prepare them for slaughter at a much more rapid rate than grazing; often referred to as factory farms.

Fertile Crescent Area located in the crescent-shaped zone near the southeastern Mediterranean coast (including Iraq, Syria, Lebanon, and Turkey), which was once a lush environment and one of the first hearths of domestication and thus agricultural activity.

Genetically modified foods Foods that are mostly products of organisms that have had their genes altered in a laboratory for specific purposes, such as disease resistance, increased productivity, or nutritional value allowing growers greater control, predictability, and efficiency.

Green Revolution The development of higher-yield and fast-growing crops through increased technology, pesticides, and fertilizers transferred from the developed to developing world to alleviate the problem of food supply in those regions of the globe.

Hunting and gathering The killing of wild animals and fish as well as the gathering of fruits, roots, nuts, and other plants for sustenance.

Industrial Revolution The rapid economic changes that occurred in agriculture and manufacturing in England in the late 18th century and that rapidly spread to other parts of the developed world.

Intensive cultivation Any kind of agricultural activity that involves effective and efficient use of labor on small plots of land to maximize crop yield.

Labor-intensive agriculture Type of agriculture that requires large levels of manual labor to be successful.

Livestock ranching An extensive commercial agricultural activity that involves the raising of livestock over vast geographic spaces typically located in semi-arid climates like the American West.

Mechanization In agriculture, the replacement of human labor with technology or machines.

Mediterranean agriculture An agricultural system practiced in the Mediterranean-style climates of Western Europe, California, and portions of Chile and Australia, in which diverse specialty crops such as grapes, avocados, olives, and a host of nuts, fruits, and vegetables comprise profitable agricultural operations.

Pastoralism A type of agricultural activity based on nomadic animal husbandry or the raising of livestock to provide food, clothing, and shelter.

Pesticides Chemicals used on plants that do not harm the plants, but kill pests and have negative repercussions on other species who ingest the chemicals.

Planned agricultural economy An agricultural economy found in communist nations in which the government controls both agricultural production and distribution.

Plantation A large, frequently foreign-owned piece of agricultural land devoted to the production of a single export crop.

Salinization Process that occurs when soils in arid areas are brought under cultivation through irrigation. In arid climates, water evaporates quickly off the ground surface, leaving salty residues that render the soil infertile.

Shifting cultivation The use of tropical forest clearings for crop production until their fertility is lost. Plots are then abandoned, and farmers move on to new sites.

Slash-and-burn agriculture System of cultivation that usually exists in tropical areas where vegetation is cut close to the ground and then ignited. The fire introduces nutrients into the soil, thereby making it productive for a relatively short period of time.

Specialty crops Crops including items like peanuts and pineapples, which are produced, usually in developing countries, for export.

Subsistence agricultural economy Any farm economy in which most crops are grown for nearly exclusive family or local consumption.

Swidden Land that is prepared for agriculture by using the slash-and-burn method.

Topsoil loss Loss of the top fertile layer of soil is lost through erosion. It is a tremendous problem in areas with fragile soils, steep slopes, or torrential seasonal rains.

Transhumance The movements of livestock according to seasonal patterns, generally lowland areas in the winter, and highland areas in the summer.

Urban sprawl The process of urban areas expanding outwards, usually in the form of suburbs, and developing over fertile agricultural land.

von Thunen model An agricultural model that spatially describes agricultural activity in terms of rent. Activities that require intensive cultivation and cannot be transported over great distances pay higher rent to be close to the market. Conversely, activities that are more extensive, with goods that are easy to transport, are located farther from the market where rent is less.

Sample Questions and Answers

Section 1: Historical Geography of Agriculture

Multiple-Choice Questions

1. The first agriculturalists were

   (A) commercial farmers.
   (B) European entrepreneurs.
   (C) also hunter-gatherers.
   (D) also ranchers.
   (E) most likely males.

2. Slash-and-burn agriculture is

   (A) not sustainable.
   (B) practiced in high, mountainous regions.
   (C) typical for tropical forests.
   (D) a relatively new invention.
   (E) always completely sustainable.

3. The Industrial Revolution transformed Western agriculture

   (A) through mechanization and the creation of new markets.
   (B) with biotechnology.
   (C) through technological and religious change.
   (D) by eliminating agricultural pests.
   (E) by eliminating plant hybridization.

4. The Green Revolution greatly increased crop production in some countries

   (A) without adverse side effects.
   (B) as a replacement for deindustrialization.
   (C) with some adverse side effects.
   (D) by encouraging the cultivation of local crop varieties.
   (E) by introducing organic agricultural methods.

5. Which of the following was not a location of independent plant and animal domestication?

   (A) India
   (B) Iraq
   (C) California
   (D) China
   (E) Peru

6. Ranching is a good example of which type of agricultural system?

   (A) Intensive subsistence cultivation
   (B) Extensive commercial cultivation
   (C) Labor-intensive agriculture
   (D) Capital-intensive agriculture
   (E) Controlled agriculture

Free-Response Question

1. Discuss the effects of the Industrial Revolution on modern agriculture.

Section 2: The Geography of Modern Agriculture

Multiple-Choice Questions

1. The modern global geography of agriculture is determined by

   (A) climate.
   (B) soil.
   (C) cultural traditions.
   (D) All of the above
   (E) Only (A) and (B)

2. According to von Thunen, the regional geography of agriculture is determined by

   (A) land area.
   (B) rent.
   (C) urban marketing.
   (D) availability of material inputs.
   (E) climate.

3. _____ is (are) widespread in semiarid climates throughout the world.

   (A) Ranching
   (B) Tropical plantations
   (C) Dairying
   (D) Slash-and-burn agriculture
   (E) Rice paddies

4. The effects of biotechnology

   (A) are positive because it allows for much greater agricultural yields.
   (B) are negative because its expense limits its availability to all farmers across the globe.
   (C) are unknown because very little research has been conducted on them.
   (D) All of the above
   (E) None of the above

5. Agribusiness has had all of the following effects on agriculture, except

   (A) the farm is no longer the center of agricultural activity.
   (B) TNCs often control agricultural activity abroad.
   (C) family farmers, through increasing technology, are producing goods for the global economy.
   (D) agriculture has become a multilevel process of production, processing, marketing, and consumption.
   (E) Some corporations essentially dictate agricultural production in other countries besides their own.

Free-Response Question

1. Describe some of the driving forces behind the world's current agricultural systems using some of their benefits and disadvantages.

Section 3: Agriculture and the Environment

Multiple-Choice Questions

1. In arid climates, like southern California and the Middle East, _____ can cause the soil to become salty and infertile.

   (A) erosion
   (B) topsoil loss
   (C) salinization
   (D) saltation
   (E) droughts

2. _____ is a common cause of decreasing farmland in rapidly growing urban areas.

   (A) Urban sprawl
   (B) Topsoil loss
   (C) Loss of material inputs
   (D) Industrialization
   (E) Agribusiness

3. DDT is an example of a _____ that has had negative effects all the way through the food chain.

   (A) herbicide
   (B) pesticide
   (C) bacteria
   (D) fungicide
   (E) genetically modified organism

4. Soil specialists must work to overcome the negative effects of _____ associated with agricultural production.

   (A) fertilization and salinization
   (B) pesticides and fertilization
   (C) salinization and topsoil loss
   (D) topsoil loss and gentrification
   (E) the Green Revolution and agribusiness

Free-Response Question

1. Discuss the environmental impacts of modern agriculture.

Answers for Multiple-Choice Questions

Section 1: Historical Geography of Agriculture

1. **(C)**   Hunter-gatherers were the first individuals to domesticate plants and animals. Even after domesticating certain species, most hunter-gatherers continued hunting and gathering to round out their diet.

2. **(C)**   Slash-and-burn agriculture is an agricultural method that introduces nutrients into the soil through burning of organic matter. It occurs mostly in tropical forests where the soil is rather nutrient poor as a way to increase soil productivity. Slash and burn can be unsustainable if farmers who practice it do not allow the land enough time to regenerate itself. Generally, the system of shifting cultivation can be quite sustainable if managed sensibly.

3. **(A)**   During the Industrial Revolution, many people migrated from rural areas to large urban centers generating a great need for agricultural goods within those centers. Furthermore, the technology characteristic of the Industrial Revolution transformed agricultural production as mechanization allowed for much more rapid cultivation of greater expanses of land.

4. **(C)**   The Green Revolution brought technology, miracle seeds, fertilizer, and other inventions of the developed world into developing nations to stimulate agricultural growth. While certainly these new inputs led to increased agricultural productivity, they carried with them detrimental implications for the local natural environment.

5. **(C)** Although many people associate the Fertile Crescent with the first site of agricultural activity, in reality, several other places across the globe independently began domesticating plants and animals for human sustenance at around the same time. California, although currently an extremely important location of agricultural activity, was not one of these first hearths.

6. **(B)** Ranching is an agricultural activity that takes place over large expanses of land and as such is a good representative of an extensive commercial agricultural activity. Additionally, it does not require either large amounts of human labor or capital inputs.

Section 2: Geography of Modern Agriculture

1. **(D)** Geographers are concerned with what is grown where on the earth's surface. Both currently and historically, climate, soil, and cultural traditions determine this pattern. With increasing technology, these factors are losing their potency, but they still remain the dominant forces in the world's current agricultural mosaic.

2. **(B)** According to the von Thunen model, the land located nearest the market will have the highest rent. Generally, agricultural activities that occur in this region are those that are expensive to transport and require intensive cultivation.

3. **(A)** Ranching takes place in the drier climates across the globe where wide expanses of land that are not very good for cultivation exist. Both tropical plantations and slash-and-burn agriculture exist in warm, moist climates, and dairying usually exists in cooler climates such as northern Europe and the northern United States.

4. **(D)** While the effects of biotechnology have not been critically investigated, it still is affecting global agricultural production allowing for much greater yields of certain products. Because the processes of biotechnology are patented by private companies, only large agribusinesses can afford them, thereby limiting their use.

5. **(C)** Agribusiness has largely contributed to the demise of the family farm. As agriculture becomes increasingly controlled by large corporations that have the technology to mass produce goods without much human capital, it loses its need for human labor. Furthermore, the agricultural activities that require large amounts of labor have been relocated to parts of the globe where human labor is cheaper.

Section 3: Agriculture and the Environment

1. **(C)** Salinization occurs when arid environments use irrigation to provide enough moisture for plant production. When the water evaporates, it leaves a salty residue, which eventually causes the soil's infertility.

2. **(A)** As urban areas continue to expand outward, usually in the form of suburbs, the development often takes over agricultural land.

3. **(B)** The effects of DDT, made popular by Rachel Carson in *Silent Spring,* demonstrate all the various effects pesticide use has all the way through the food chain. All the other options may too have effects through the food chain, but DDT is a pesticide specifically designed to eliminate insects, or pests, that threaten certain agricultural products.

4. **(C)** Chemical fertilizers may cause negative effects on the soil, but some forms of fertilizers are organic, meaning that they use natural products rather than chemicals to stimulate plant growth and, therefore, do not harm the soil. Both salinization and topsoil loss destroy the soil's properties and must be overcome by soil scientists if they want the land to remain fertile.

Answers for Free-Response Questions

Section 1: Historical Geography of Agriculture

1. Main points:
    - The impacts on agriculture as a result of the Industrial Revolution can be categorized into three main areas: rural to urban migrations, mechanization, and transportation.
    - With the Industrial Revolution came many new factory jobs in large urban areas. This stimulated a mass rural-to-urban migration specifically in France, Germany, the United Kingdom, and the United States. These large population centers generated a great need for agricultural products from the surrounding rural areas. Thus, the Industrial Revolution, created a giant market for agricultural products.
    - Second, mechanization of certain agricultural activities radically transformed the amount of agricultural output in relation to input of human labor. The introduction of tractors and combines slowly began to transform agricultural activity in the developed regions of the globe.
    - Finally, increased transportation technology allowed farmers to ship their goods greater distances for smaller costs, allowing them to grow more than they could traditionally as they had greater access to distant markets. Additionally, refrigerated transportation technology allowed the more time-sensitive products to extend their geographical market.

Section 2: Geography of Modern Agriculture

1. Main points:
    - First, the driving forces behind the current agricultural system are responding to an increasing need to provide enough food for an ever-expanding global population. As such, scientists, economists, business people, and policy makers have had to devise products, processes, and plans to accommodate such a large population.

- Two of the main forces in use to provide greater agricultural yields are biotechnology and the rise of agribusinesses.
- Biotechnology is the use of organisms to improve other organisms. These technological processes have improved agricultural production through the development of pest- and disease-resistant plants and the technology for cloning specific plant species. However, biotechnology is expensive and patented within the private sector, limiting its use to agribusinesses that can afford to profit from it. Furthermore, the environmental impacts have not been thoroughly investigated. Most of the European community has banned the sale of genetically modified foods because they have not been proven safe and many are suspicious of their effects on other species including humans.
- Agribusiness has transformed agricultural production into a global food chain of production, processing, and consumption. Corporations have replaced farms as the driving force behind agriculture and have expanded production capabilities dramatically such that almost any individual in the developed world can obtain any agricultural good at any time of the year. Because corporations have overtaken local agricultural production, they have displaced many family farmers and disrupted many agricultural traditions. Furthermore, often large-scale agricultural production involves the use of chemicals to ensure specific yields in turn dramatically affecting the natural environment.

Section 3: Agriculture and the Environment

1. Main points:
   - Modern forms of agriculture wreak many forms of destruction on the land. Common destroying forces include pesticide use, salinization, loss of topsoil, and urban sprawl.
   - Pesticide use introduces certain chemicals into soil mixtures that are ingested into plants and other organisms and eventually make their way up the food chain, into humans. These chemicals have varying effects on different species. For example, when birds ingest too much DDT, a pesticide popular not too long ago, their egg shells no longer harden, killing many birds before they even have a chance to hatch.
   - Both salinization and topsoil loss, if not counteracted, can render the soil infertile. Salinization occurs in arid areas that use irrigation to water plants. When water evaporates in these environments, it leaves a salty residue, which over time destroys the soil's chemical and biological makeup. Topsoil loss occurs through erosion, which may be the result of overcultivation, or when steep slopes are cultivated. When topsoil loss occurs, the most nutrient-rich layer of soil disappears, dramatically affecting the soil's ability to be productive.
   - With urban sprawl, certain fertile lands are being paved over, thus arable land is not being used for its best purpose. When this process occurs, it necessitates the need for intensive cultivation systems elsewhere, and these levels of intensity can have very negative effects on the environment.

Additional Resources

Text

Anderson, Sarah. 2000. *Views from the South: The Effects of Globalization and the WTO on Third World Countries.* Chicago: Food First Books.

Bowler, Ian R., ed. 1992. *The Geography of Agriculture in Developed Market Economies.* Harlow, Essex: Longman Scientific & Technical.

Lanegran, David. 2000. "Modern Agriculture in Advanced Placement Human Geography." *Journal of Geography* 99: 120–131.

Tarrant, John. ed. 1991. *Food and Farming.* New York: Oxford University Press.

Web

Food and Agricultural Organization (FAO): *http://www.fao.org/*

This is an excellent website for understanding agriculture both within the United States and across the world. Once you get to the main page of the Food and Agricultural Organization, you can choose from a wide variety of options, including "Agriculture." After you navigate to this page, you will be presented with all types of options that lead to interesting information. On the main page, you can investigate headline stories from across the world relating to agriculture, or you can investigate the agricultural divisions of the FAO, or a wide variety of agricultural subjects, including biotechnology. An excellent source of information exists under the heading "Interdisciplinary Action." Here you can explore such topics as integrated production systems, organic agriculture, food for cities, and conservation agriculture. It is extremely easy to navigate this website. As you do, you will find much useful and interesting information.

Food First: *http://www.foodfirst.org*

Food first is a non-profit, non-government organization that works toward making food a fundamental human right across the globe. On the site, you can explore the reasons why both biotechnology and genetically modified organisms are such hotly contested issues; you can also look at different literature exploring the problems with the current food distribution system and how Food First works to change distribution patterns from the bottom up.

Tremblay, Genevieve. *Agromedia: http://collections.ic.gc.ca/highway/english/global/index.html*

Once you get to this page, you need to go to the bottom and click on the link labeled "Agromedia." From here, you are presented with an excellent educational website relating to all the many facets of agricultural production. With accompanying illustrations you can explore both the extensive agricultural process as well as many of the various environmental implications of intensive land use by exploring one of these nine options: soil and water conservation, biotechnology, animal welfare, costs of producing food, environmental impact, globalization, pesticides, nonfood products, and energy use.

Shiva, Vandana. The Threat of the Globalization of Agriculture: *http://www. hartford-hwp.com/archives/25a/007.html*

Vandana Shiva looks at the impact of global agriculture in terms of food security and farmers' rights.

The United States Department of Agriculture: *www.usda.gov/*

This is a comprehensive website that gives you detailed information regarding the latest news and developments within the United States Department of Agriculture. It also contains useful links to other government agencies concerned with agriculture, both within the United States and across the globe.

Yahoo Science: Agriculture: *www.yahoo.com/Science/Agriculture/*

This site is an excellent starting point if you are generally interested in agriculture. It contains numerous links organized by topic, i.e. Agribusiness, Biotechnology, Migrant Farmworkers, etc. Virtually every term defined within this chapter can be found on their list of topics, and thus the website proves to be an excellent resource for obtaining more in-depth knowledge of the subjects discussed in this chapter.

CHAPTER 8
Urban Geography

Summary

Urban geographers study all aspects of the world's cities, from their historical development, to their spatial organization, to the ways that they interact with the regions surrounding them, to their importance in the world economic system. The first cities arose thousands of years ago in regions where agriculture had gained an early foothold. By the beginning of the Colonial Period, large, prosperous cities existed on every continent except Australia. During the 19th century, the Industrial Revolution fundamentally changed both the way that cities were built and their basic economic and cultural functions. Since then, a variety of architectural movements and transportation innovations have profoundly shaped the urban environment. Many of today's cities still retain much of their historical architecture and layout, but they also represent dynamic products of constantly changing social and cultural forces. A few such places have managed to establish themselves as world centers of economic, cultural, or administrative power. The impoverished and rapidly expanding megacities of the developing world provide a stark contrast to these prosperous world centers.

In This Chapter

- Historical Geography of Urban Environments
- Culture and Urban Form
- The Spatial Organization of Urban Environments
- Urban Planning

Key Terms

Action spaces
Beaux arts
Central business district
Central place theory
City Beautiful movement
Colonial city
Concentric zone model
Edge city
European cities
Exurbanite

Feudal city
Gateway city
Gentrification
Ghettoization
Hinterland
Industrial Revolution
Inner city decay
Islamic cities
Latin American cities
Medieval city

Megacities
Megalopolis
Metropolitan areas
Modern architecture
Multiple nuclei model
Node
Postmodern architecture
Primate city
Rank-size rule

Sector model
Segregation
Squatter settlements
Suburb
Urban growth boundaries
Urban revitalization
Urban sprawl
World City

Historical Geography of Urban Environments

Where do you think the world's first cities arose? If you said "in the same places that were hearths of early agriculture," then you were right. In fact, the growth of early cities was only possible after people had developed sedentary agriculture to the point when farmers began producing surplus crops, or more food than their family alone could eat. When this happened—in places like the Middle East, China, Peru, and the Mississippi Valley—some people were able to quit farming and take up other occupations, such as carpenter, merchant, artisan, scholar, priest, and doctor. The flowering of these different occupations fueled the growth of cities and increased demand for more agricultural products. Thus, early cities were closely linked to their adjacent agricultural regions.

Although the first urban settlements date back several thousand years, urbanism actually spread very slowly, with many fits and starts. In Europe, a few Mediterranean cities, such as Athens and Rome, grew markedly during the Classical Period. However, the Middle Ages, or "dark ages," interrupted the blossoming of urban life in Europe, and Western culture lapsed into a stagnant period of few intellectual advances or cultural endeavors. The feudal system, which dominated most of Europe during this time, discouraged urbanism and confined most people to lives as uneducated peasant-farmers. Most European **feudal cities** lacked diversity, cultural vibrancy, and active trade and served mainly as centers of military or religious power. Interestingly, during the period we normally think of as the dark ages, great cities outside of Europe, in the Middle East, Far East, Indian subcontinent, Mesoamerica, and South America were prospering.

During the Renaissance Period, which lasted from about 1350 to 1650, European culture was reborn and cities became vibrant centers of learning. Urban growth accelerated dramatically after the Hundred Years War, which ended in 1453, and dozens of new towns began to spring up out of the countryside. The great **European cities** that first emerged during this period include Dublin, Madrid, Prague, Vienna, Amsterdam, and Barcelona. It was only during this period that the cities of northern and Western Europe began to compete, in size, wealth, and complexity, with those of the Middle East, Asia, and the Americas.

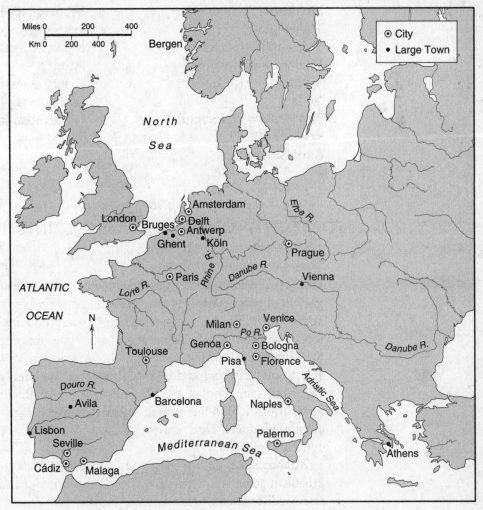

Figure 8.1. The towns and cities of Europe in 1350.

The Colonial Period, which began during the Renaissance and lasted through the 19th century, represented a new time for the world's cities. During this period, European colonial powers sent their explorers to every corner of the globe in the name of God and gold. At the beginning of the Colonial Period, some of the world's greatest cities—and most sophisticated cultures—were located in the Americas. When Cortez and his ragtag troops first stumbled into the Aztec capital of Tenochtitlan, it was probably the largest and richest city on earth. But when the local leaders fell victim to Cortez' fiendish trickery, superior armaments, and alien diseases, the city was reduced to a shadow of its former glory, smaller communities broke off from the larger alliance, and the people of central Mexico became subjects of the Spanish crown. Such was the fate of many native peoples in Africa and the Americas that eventually fell under some sort of European colonial rule. Many of the old Native American cities later became **colonial cities**, and served as regional administrative centers for the European powers. Current-day Mexico City, with its picturesque colonial architecture, sprawls outward from the ancient site of Tenochtitlan. Consequently, although the Colonial Period was a time of vigorous trade, diversification, and growth for European cities, it was also a time of calamitous decline and chaotic transformation for cities in many other parts of the world.

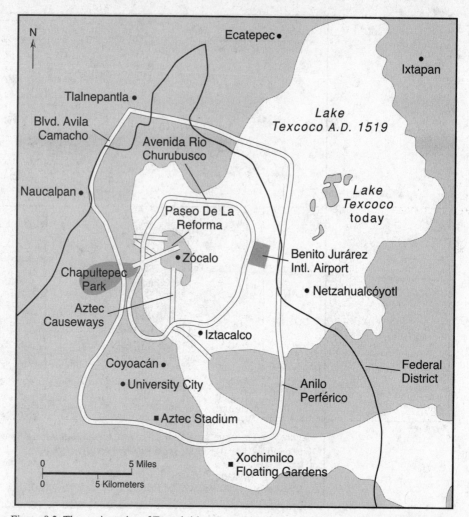

Figure 8.2. The ancient city of Tenochtitlan once existed as a world center of wealth and culture, it deteriorated after colonization and now houses one of the world's most populous and polluted cities—Mexico City. The ancient city was built on an island in Lake Texcoco, which has become a landfill, currently housing most of the poor population of Mexico City.

It was not until the 18th century that urbanism really exploded on a global scale. The Industrial Revolution, which, as we have already seen, began in England during the 18th century and spread rapidly to Western Europe and North America, propelled much urban growth during this period. The **Industrial Revolution** stimulated tremendous population growth in cities such as Manchester and Chicago, which became centers for processing, manufacturing, shipping, and finance. Chicago, which became a central hub for railroads carrying wheat, beef, timber, and other commodities, grew from a small village in 1840, to a city of 1 million in 1900. By 1930 Chicago had over 3 million inhabitants, qualifying it as one of the world's fastest-growing industrial centers.

In cities like Chicago, urban growth posed important social problems. In the 19th century, immigrants flooded into the city by the thousands, making it a center of both cultural diversity and urban unrest. In the beginning of the 20th century, African-Americans from Mississippi, Louisiana, and elsewhere also migrated en masse to Chicago, hoping to flee the oppressively racist

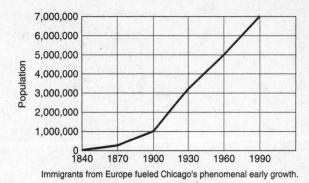

Immigrants from Europe fueled Chicago's phenomenal early growth.

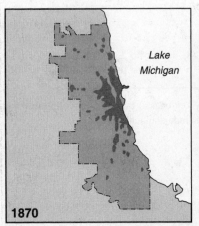

1870

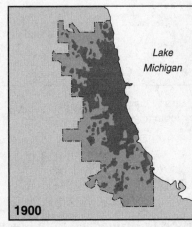

1900

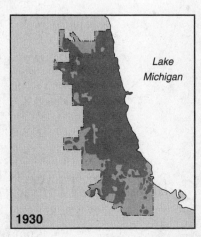

1930

Figure 8.3. The rapid growth of Chicago's population from 1870 to 1930. As seen on the graph, the city continued its pattern of rapid growth even after 1930.

South and to take advantage of new opportunities in urban factories. What many of these new Chicagoans found was an environment where competition for homes and jobs led to suspicion and prejudice. These tensions culminated in the Chicago race riots of 1919. Many of Chicago's ghettos that were formed over 100 years ago, and were hubs of civil unrest in 1919, are still poverty-stricken and continue to be dominated by recent immigrants and people of other races.

During this period, some cities also grew rapidly because of the strategic economic advantages owing to their locations. For example, New York and San Francisco both grew tremendously in the 19th century, in large part because of their proximity to raw materials and markets, their excellent natural harbors, and their position as gateway cities. **Gateway cities** act as ports of entry and distribution centers for large geographic areas. San Francisco, which, like St. Louis, has frequently been called "the gateway to the West," experienced a population explosion after gold was discovered in California's Sierra Nevada Mountains, in 1849. Similarly, for the millions of European immigrants that entered the United States through Ellis Island, between 1892 and 1954, the New York harbor represented an open door to a new life with endless opportunity. New York's highly symbolic urban landscape, which includes monuments to freedom like the Statue of Liberty, emphasizes the values and opportunities that so many immigrants sought when they came to America.

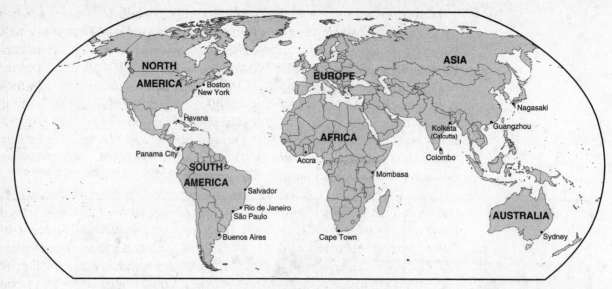

Figure 8.4. Gateway cities almost exclusively occupy key coastal positions providing tremendous ports of entry for immigrants, as well as corridors for trade and distribution.

Culture and Urban Form

From Brussels to Beijing and from London to Lima, the urban geography of today's cities is incredibly diverse. Geographers, architects, historians, and planners have devised a variety of ways of describing, categorizing, and comparing these varied urban environments. The following paragraphs provide a basis for understanding the geography of contemporary urban environments. However, it is worth noting that all cities are, to some extent, products of their own unique histories, and as a result, each comprises a distinctive and unique cultural landscape.

Comparing cities in different regions provides a great way for understanding the structures of urban environments. On a regional or even continental scale, cities are frequently products of similar cultures and related histories, and this provides a basis for insightful comparisons. One example of a region characterized by comparable urban environments is Europe. European cities take many forms, however, many of Europe's great cities matured during the Medieval Period and still retain characteristics that were typical of cities of that time. Typical **medieval cities** are extremely densely packed with narrow buildings and winding streets, contain an ornate church that prominently marks the city center, and are surrounded by high walls that provided defense against attack. This type of urban organization harkens back to a time when rival city-states vied for regional dominance, religious leaders held the balance of power, and transportation was limited to horses and foot traffic. In the centuries since, many such cities have jumped their walls and spread out into the surrounding countryside. However, some are still intact, and many large European cities still contain a central medieval core. Excellent examples of intact medieval cities include Montepulciano, Assisi, and the dozens of other quaint hilltop towns that dot the Italian countryside.

Islamic cities, such as Mecca in Saudi Arabia, owe their distinctive urban geographies to the teachings of Muslim faith. As in medieval European cities, Islamic cities contain mosques at their center and walls guarding their perimeter. However, Islamic cities have distinctive features, such as bustling open-air markets, courtyards surrounded by high walls, and dead-end streets, which limit foot traffic in residential neighborhoods. Although many features of the traditional, Middle Eastern Islamic city are related to Muslim values and religious practices, some are also adaptations to the hot and dry desert climate in which they exist. Light-colored surfaces reflect sunlight, and roofs are designed to capture and recycle rainwater efficiently.

In Asia, Africa, and Latin America, cities represent complex expressions of native culture, colonial dominance, industrial aspirations, and widespread poverty. In places like China, cities frequently contain cultural monuments related to Buddhism and communism. Other common features include colonial buildings, factories, and squatter settlements surrounding a symbolic city center or port. African cities, such as Nairobi, Kenya, owe most of their urban form to colonialism, 20th century industrial expansion, and rapid, unplanned population growth. **Latin American cities,** though generally more developed than their African counterparts, owe much of their urban form to the same sorts of causes. In many Latin American cities, distinctive sectors of industrial or residential development radiate out like the spokes of a wheel from the **central business district**, where most industrial and financial activity occurs. Mexico City, with its grand boulevards originating in the city center, is an excellent example of the Latin American metropolis.

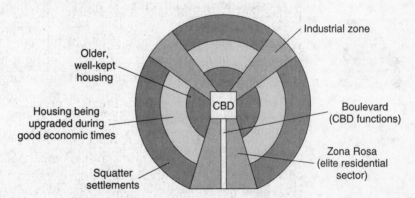

Figure 8.5. Typical Latin American cities contain a central business district at their core, with both rings and sectors segregating a variety of residential and commercial activities.

Environmental design can have profound impacts on the forms that urban areas take and on the various arrangements of cities. Although an in-depth discussion of urban design would require many volumes, a few key concepts are worth mentioning here because they have so profoundly affected many of today's largest and most important cities. In the 19th century, European city planners struggled to respond to the lessons of the French and American Revolutions within the context of their new industrial societies. The **beaux arts** school, centered in Paris and Vienna, had profound implications for planning in a number of European cities, by stressing the marriage of older, classical forms with newer, industrial ones. Beaux arts planners designed wide thoroughfares, spacious parks, and civic monuments that stressed progress, freedom, and national unity. The **City Beautiful movement**, which has found important expressions in the United States, drew directly from the beaux arts school. Architects from this movement strove to impart order on hectic, industrial centers by creating urban spaces that conveyed a sense of morality and civic pride, which many feared was absent from the frenzied new industrial world. The classic example of City Beautiful design is Chicago, where, following the fire that ravaged the city in 1871, architects and planners created a new urban environment with expansive parks, extravagant monuments, and an orderly street plan. Their goal was primarily to impose a sense of piety and organization on what had previously been a chaotic urban mass.

In the mid-20th century, **modern architecture** reigned supreme. From the modernist's perspective, cities and buildings should act like well-oiled machines, with little energy spent on frivolous details or ornate designs. Instead, efficient, geometrical structures made of concrete and glass dominated urban forms for half a century. Perhaps the world's greatest expression of modernist planning and architecture is Brasilia, the capital of Brazil, which was comprehensively planned and designed by Oscar Niemeyer. Located in what had previously been a sparsely populated Amazonian interior, Brasilia's fantastic modern architecture conveys a sense of futuristic order, scientific progress, and industry. Although many consider modernist buildings, such as those found in Brasilia, to be stark and impersonal, they represent just one expression of the trust in scientific efficiency that captivated the world for much of the 20th century. Modernist structures also dominate many of the American cities that grew so quickly during the mid-20th century.

Postmodern architecture is quickly becoming familiar to many Americans, Europeans, and Australians. Largely a reaction to the feeling of sterile alienation that many people get from modern architecture, postmodernism uses older, historical styles and a sense of light-heartedness and eclecticism. Post-modern buildings combine pleasant-looking forms and playful colors, although they may feel a bit artificial; these architectural forms appropriate old architectural themes in order to convey new ideas, and to create spaces that are more people-friendly than their modernist predecessors.

No two cities on the globe look the same or feel the same or smell the same. Cities are results of a wide variety of political decisions, economic possibilities, geographic opportunities, design initiatives, and a multitude of other factors that contribute to the dynamic processes occurring in every city across the globe, every day. As already discussed, some cities display relics of their history, some of their religious beliefs, and some of their economic activities. Additionally, throughout history, cities have served as palettes for architects and urban designers and display all the various trends and philosophies fading in and out of these fields over time. As such, cities always represent eclectic environments serving all sorts of different functions in different buildings to different kinds of people. Beyond understanding the various dynamics that make cities unique, geographers also strive to explain the layout of urban environments in terms of the spatial organization of all the many activities taking place within a city on a daily basis.

The Spatial Organization of Urban Environments

One of the fundamental aims of urban geography is to understand how cities are organized. To do this, geographers have developed models that explain and categorize cities in terms of their internal spatial organization. Three main models of urban environments—the concentric zone model, the multiple nuclei model, and the sector model—are particularly worthy of consideration. The **concentric zone model** applies to cities that have rings of development emanating outward from a core, or central business district. In theory, each ring contains different types of development and economic activities. This is because the value of land decreases as you go farther out from the central core. Many geographers cite Chicago as an excellent example of the concentric zone model. The **multiple nuclei model** applies to a city that lacks a strong central core, but instead has numerous "**nodes**" of business and cultural activity. A classic example of this model is Los Angeles, which has a relatively small downtown business district but contains many independent nodes of high land value and vigorous business activity, such as Santa Monica, Hollywood, Westwood, and Pasadena. Cities that conform more to the **sector model** tend to have corridors of different types of development that radiate outward like spokes from the central business district. These corridors often follow long-standing transportation routes, such as wide boulevards, train tracks, or waterways, which affect land values and lend themselves to certain types of development. Some Latin American cities, such as Mexico City, conform to this model. It is worth pointing out, however, that no city matches any model perfectly and that each city's urban organization is tied to both to its unique history and physical geography.

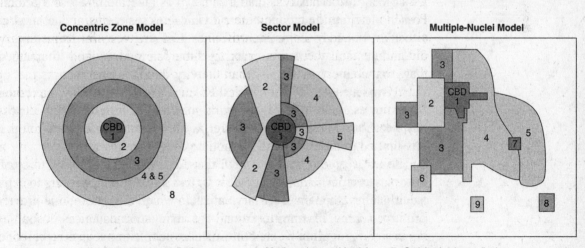

| Concentric Zone Model | Sector Model | Multiple-Nuclei Model |

1. Central business district
2. Wholesale, light manufacturing
3. Low-class residential
4. Medium-class residential
5. High-class residential
6. Heavy manufacturing
7. Outlying business district
8. Residential suburb
9. Industrial

Figure 8.6. Three different models urban geographers have developed to explain the variety of forms urban environments can take in terms of the locations of different urban activities.

Inner cities frequently surround the central business district and contain dynamic urban geographies. During much of the 20th century, the trend in the United States and Europe was toward the **ghettoization** of inner cities. Many inner cities became dilapidated centers of poverty as affluent whites moved out to the **suburbs,** or residential communities on the outskirts of urban areas, and immigrants and people of color vied for scarce jobs and resources in the declining urban center. In the United States, **inner city decay** was particularly extreme in northern cities that had formerly been centers of heavy industry, such as Detroit, Michigan, and Pittsburgh, Pennsylvania. Interestingly, in places like Pittsburgh and Baltimore this pattern has now reversed itself; the inner cities have revived much of their former vibrancy and economic opportunity. **Urban revitalization,** which usually includes the construction of new shopping districts, entertainment venues, and cultural attractions, has enticed young urban professionals, or "yuppies," back into the cities where nightlife and culture are more accessible. The process by which inner city neighborhoods turn into expensive and fashionable urban districts is called **gentrification**. Although urban revitalization may seem like a great idea, higher-cost living frequently squeezes out the low-income residents who have made these places their homes for many years.

Perhaps the most important factor affecting the development of contemporary cities is transportation. A quick look at a few of the United States' most prominent cities shows why this is the case. Manhattan Island, the heart of New York City, was largely developed during the 19th century, at a time when horse-drawn buggies and pedestrians dominated urban streets. People's mobility was limited by their transportation options; as a result, Manhattan came to be characterized by densely packed high-rise buildings and narrow cobblestone streets. Unlike New York, Chicago's development was closely related to its role as a railroad hub. Even today, most people who commute into downtown Chicago's central business district, known as "the loop," do so via trains that branch out from the city center, and Chicago's many distinct urban neighborhoods are linked by commuter rail lines. Los Angeles was planned around the automobile. Today, LA is a sprawling suburban metropolis, with clogged freeways that connect distant nodes of activity, and far-flung suburbs that operate largely independent of each other. Relatively few Angelinos, or residents of Los Angeles, walk to school or work, the city has little unifying identity and, despite efforts to establish commuter rail lines, public transportation is generally limited to buses that must negotiate congested city streets.

The exact type of urban sprawl that Los Angeles has come to symbolize now plagues many American cities. **Urban sprawl**, which refers to expansive suburban development over large areas in which the automobile provides the primary source of transportation, has many consequences. Urban sprawl increases **segregation** by enabling affluent people to live in ethnically homogenous suburbs, increases pollution caused by long car commutes, degrades a sense of community that people who live close to the places where they work tend to have, and gobbles up open spaces important for public recreation and wildlife habitat. People who have left the inner city and moved to outlying suburbs or rural areas are called **exurbanites**.

In some places, urban sprawl has taken the form of edge cities. **Edge cities**, which are located on the outskirts of larger cities, serve many of the same functions of urban areas, but in a sprawling, decentralized suburban environment. The classic example of the edge city is Tyson's Corner, Virginia, located near the intersection of several highways outside of Washington, D.C. In this case, Americans would probably do well to learn from Europeans and Canadians who have managed to limit urban sprawl through long-range planning, efficient public transportation, and the establishment of **urban growth boundaries**. Toronto, Canada, is one example of a city that has used smart growth policies, efficient transportation networks, and a consolidated regional government to create a livable and sustainable urban environment. Although some cities in the United States, such as Portland, Oregon, have attempted to adopt this model, it has met with intense controversy and mixed results.

Urban geographers also study the roles that cities play in their larger regions. It is clear that cities have profound influences on the communities surrounding them. In fact, the U.S. Census Bureau defines cities in large part by their **metropolitan areas**, which includes the central city and all the surrounding communities that have "a high degree of social and economic integration with that core." According to this definition, the city is not solely contained within its spatially defined city limits; it is more accurately conceived of in terms of social and economic relationships within its region. For example, the Tulsa, Oklahoma, metropolitan area is composed of five counties: Creek, Osage, Rogers, Tulsa, and Wagoner.

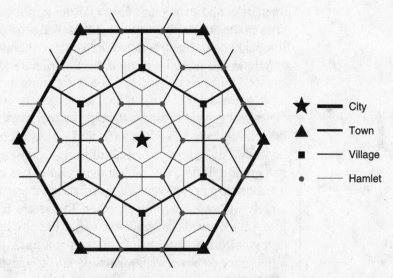

Figure 8.7. The star at the center represents the center of a city, which has the greatest market area or hexagon encompassing its bounds. Moving down in geographic scale, each type of center requires a smaller population to be economically sustainable. Thus, at the level of the hamlet, an economic function such as a gas station may by profitable, whereas the city's market area can support higher-order activities such as professional sporting events.

Metropolitan areas are in part based on **central place theory,** which provides a more explicit framework for looking at the relationship between cities and their surrounding communities, based on people's demand for goods and services. According to the central place theory, large cities serve as the economic hubs of their regions because they provide a great variety of goods and services that are not available in smaller communities. In this view, a region is defined as an area with one central place, or large city, surrounded by increasingly smaller towns and hamlets, each of which contain fewer goods and services than the central place. Thus, people in small towns must occasionally travel to the central place to take advantage of big-city amenities like professional sports events, museums, and a diversity of stores, music, and food that is simply not available in the **hinterlands**. Geographers have also noticed that, in any given region, there should be many small hamlets, some towns, and a few small cities, but only one central city.

The proportion of small towns to large cities is called the **rank-size rule,** and it applies both to regions and to the world as a whole. The rank-size rule says that there is a specific relationship between the relative abundance of settlements of different sizes, and that the smallest settlements should always be the most abundant. More specifically, the rank-size rule states that the population of any given town should be inversely proportional to its rank in the country's or world's hierarchy of cities. Thus, the second largest city should be half the population of the largest city within a certain country. In a global perspective, there are very few cities as big as Tokyo or Sao Paulo, but there are hundreds of cities the size of Cincinnati or Nashville, and there are literally thousands of small cities and little towns throughout the world. Many countries, especially in the developed world, do not display this kind of pattern in terms of their city's populations. Many of these countries have one **primate city** that overwhelmingly dominates the urban concentration within a country. Seoul, South Korea, contains over one-third of the country's urban population and over one-quarter of the entire country's population! Primate cities in the developing world are largely a relic of their colonial history when European colonizers concentrated all economic, transportation, and trade activity in one place, leaving the infrastructure in place after decolonization.

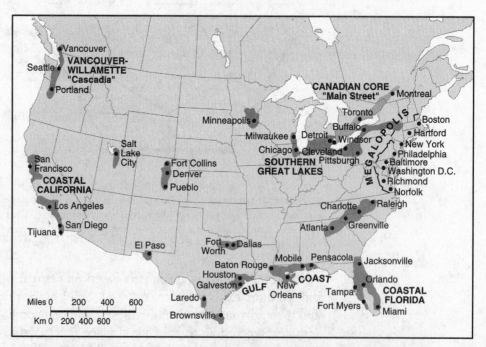

Figure 8.8. The United States demonstrates the megalopolis phenomenon in several areas as neighboring metropolitan areas continually spread out and form an even larger urban complex.

In some regions, many towns and cities have grown together and merged over time, creating a **megalopolis**. A megalopolis is an entire region that has become highly urbanized. In North America, megalopolises include the Boston-New York-Philadelphia-Baltimore-Washington, D.C. urban mass along the eastern seaboard and the Los Angeles-Orange County-San Diego-Tijuana megalopolis in southern California and Baja, Mexico. Other, global examples of megalopolises include Sao Paulo-Rio de Janeiro, in Brazil and Tokyo-Osaka in Japan.

Megacities are different from megalopolises. Megacities are increasingly a phenomenon of the developing world, where high population growth and migration has caused some urban areas to explode in population since World War II. All megacities are plagued by chaotic, unplanned growth, terrible pollution, and widespread poverty. A ubiquitous feature of these megacities is the **squatter settlements** that cluster on hillsides and near waterways, and that crop up, seemingly, overnight. Usually constructed of scrap materials, such as aluminum siding and plywood, these makeshift neighborhoods exemplify the tragedy of urban squalor in the less-developed world.

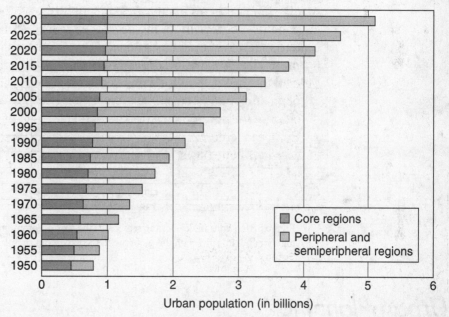

Figure 8.9. Since World War II, most of the world's urban growth can be attributed to peripheral and semi-peripheral regions where the majority of the world's megacities expand their numbers on a daily basis.

The counterpoint to the chaotic megacity is the world city. World cities are centers of economic, cultural, or political activity, and thus have an influence felt worldwide. World cities are commonly categorized into several tiers indicating the extent of their influence, but all world cities enjoy a significant amount of economic influence and prosperity. Top-tier world cities include the economic and cultural powerhouses of New York, London, and Tokyo. Second-tier world cities include seats of government, such as Moscow, Paris, Washington, D.C., and Brussels, Belgium; centers of popular culture, such as Los Angeles and Mumbai, India; and centers of industry, such as Mexico City and Sao Paulo, Brazil. It is interesting to note that, in economic terms, the world's most populous cities are not its most powerful. Indeed, all the most prominent world cities are located in the wealthy and highly industrialized countries.

1950	Population	1980	Population	2010	Population
New York	12.3	Tokyo	21.9	Tokyo	28.8
London	8.7	New York	15.6	Mumbai (Bombay)	23.7
Tokyo	6.9	Mexico City	13.9	Lagos	21.0
Paris	5.4	São Paulo	12.1	São Paulo	19.7
Moscow	5.4	Shanghai	11.7	Mexico City	18.7
Shanghai	5.3	Osaka	10.0	New York	17.2
Essen	5.3	Buenos Aires	9.9	Karachi	16.7
Buenos Aires	5.0	Los Angeles	9.5	Dhaka	16.7
Chicago	4.9	Kolkata (Calcutta)	9.0	Shanghai	16.6
Kolkata (Calcutta)	4.4	Beijing	9.0	Kolkata (Calcutta)	15.6
Osaka	4.1	Paris	8.7	Delhi	15.2
Los Angeles	4.0	Rio de Janeiro	8.7	Beijing	14.3
Beijing	3.9	Seoul	8.3	Los Angeles	13.9
Milan	3.6	Moscow	8.2	Manila	13.7
Berlin	3.3	Mumbai (Bombay)	8.0	Buenos Aires	13.5
Mexico City	3.1	London	7.8	Cairo	13.2
Philadelphia	2.9	Tianjin	7.7	Seoul	12.9
St. Petersburg	2.9	Cairo	6.9	Jakarta	12.7
Mumbai (Bombay)	2.9	Chicago	6.8	Tianjin	12.4
Rio de Janeiro	2.9	Essen	6.7	Istanbul	11.7
Detroit	2.8	Jakarta	6.4	Rio de Janeiro	11.4
Naples	2.8	Metro Manila	6.0	Osaka	10.6
Manchester	2.5	Delhi	5.5	Guangzhou	10.3
São Paulo	2.4	Milan	5.4	Paris	9.7
Cairo	2.4	Tehran	5.4	Hyderabad	9.4
Tianjin	2.4	Karachi	5.0	Moscow	9.3
Birmingham	2.3	Bangkok	4.8	Teheran	9.2
Frankfurt	2.3	St. Petersburg	4.7	Lima	8.8
Boston	2.2	Hong Kong	4.5	Bangkok	8.8
Hamburg	2.2	Lima	4.4	Lahore	8.6

Source: Data, United Nations, *World Urbanization Prospects*. New York: U.N. Department of Economic and Social Affairs, 1998.

Figure 8.10. Cities in developing regions of the world, commonly megacities, will soon be the most highly populated cities on the globe, with the exception of Tokyo.

Urban Planning

A discussion on urban planning provides a unifying medium for understanding how the many aspects of cities discussed so far fit together, and it also provides an avenue for considering the future of the world's cities. Earlier in the chapter, the topic of urban planning was touched on in the discussion of urban form. This section mostly emphasized urban design and how certain overarching architectural trends and philosophies have historically dictated the many forms a city may take. However, the job of the urban planner is usually more complex. Many human geographers enter the field of urban planning, as it provides them with a way to apply their understanding of different human spatial activities within a specific job field. Urban planners consider individuals' perceptions and feelings within urban environments, both specifically and generally, to ensure that the cities they work for provide a comfortable and enjoyable living environment for their citizens.

Urban planners work together with behavioral geographers to understand and predict human behavior in urban environments. Together, they have discovered that urban spatial behavior is, in large part, determined by individual perceptions of the specific urban environments they interact with. Additionally, these perceptions, when generalized, often determine how cities are rated in terms of whether or not they are good places to live. Kevin Lynch in his famous book, *Image of the City,* published in 1960, studied individual's perceptions of urban environments to determine the *legibility* of urban spaces. How well an individual could, in effect, read a landscape depended on both the city's physical structure as well as the individual's orientation. Both of these factors contribute to an individual's comfort level and confidence in successfully navigating through that city. Lynch classified the geographical contents of cities into five main elements: paths, edges, districts, nodes, and landmarks. Paths consist of channels of movement such as highways, sidewalks, or transit lines, with dominant paths ideally containing concentrations of activities. Edges mark the boundaries between two areas and come in the form of rivers, rail lines, large walls, or forested spaces. Areas that the individual both enters and leaves within a city are called districts, and they can be both mental and physical. Physical districts include the central business district, or industrial areas, whereas mental or emotional districts include spaces such as dangerous neighborhoods or wealthy areas that may have more well-defined boundaries in the individual's mind than in the actual landscape. Nodes are any focal points within the city such as the junction of paths, and, similar to landmarks, highly visible structures enhance their image. Finally, landmarks are any point references external to the observer, usually used for directional cues within a city. All of these factors, according to Lynch, work together to form a legible or illegible city. If these factors do not cohesively form a legible landscape, individuals do not believe that they can orient themselves within that city, and their mobility, in turn, is severely limited.

Another important collaboration between planners and behavioral geographers comes through the investigation of individual **action spaces**. These spaces comprise all the parts of a city in which daily movement occurs. In small towns, an individual's action space could cover the entire town, but in large cities, it's more likely that an individual's action space covers just a portion of the city's geographic space. Generally, five rules apply to people's daily spatial behavior:

1. *People tend to make many more short trips than long trips.* For example, although you probably go to school or to work every day, you go on longer trips to see distant relatives much less frequently.
2. *People tend to worry little about distance when moving around very close to home, but when the trip requires you to venture farther away from home, distance becomes an important factor in deciding whether or not to go.* Running down to the corner store is not something you give very much thought, but going on a trip to Europe might require many months of planning.
3. *The longest trips tend to be work-related.* Although this probably does not apply to you, it might apply to your parents if their work requires them to make business trips to other states or countries.
4. *Transportation limits some spatial behaviors.* Are you old enough to drive? If you are, can you remember how hard it was to get around when your

transportation options were more limited? If you are not old enough to have a license, or if you do not have access to a car, then you know exactly what this rule is all about.

6. *People tend to avoid perceived hazards, whether or not those hazards pose a real threat.* Are there certain parts of town that you avoid? Do you hate going over tall bridges? These are both perceived hazards that could affect your daily travel.

While all of these rules do not explicitly apply to urban spatial behavior, they provide important insights for planners in terms of how people conceive of space and time. Thus, they can help planners make informed decisions when thinking about transportation planning, urban design, and the location of various facilities such as schools, grocery stores, and banks.

Urban planning can be an extremely difficult job because planners must deal with the highly dynamic nature of the city in working to provide for all the city's diverse inhabitants. Additionally, planners must always keep future growth in mind, and consider all the implications increasing populations might have on sewage treatment needs, health services, education services, utilities, social welfare programming, and many other services cities provide their inhabitants. Furthermore, as planners devise plans for cities to better serve community needs, they often meet with opposition from many different forces. As they formulate new plans, they must consider all possible avenues and arguments and seek development initiatives that accommodate all different kinds of needs and opinions. At times, it seems almost impossible!

Cities, with all their many dynamic forces and opportunities, house the majority of the world's population. Every day, they draw tourists, immigrants, young and opportunistic college graduates, and people of different ethnic groups into their bounds. Urban geographers investigate all the many forces at work within a city contributing to its unique character, unique set of opportunities, and unique problems and social ills. By generalizing some city characteristics across the globe, geographers have developed models to generally explain both the spatial distribution of cities across the globe and the spatial distribution of activities within a city. Furthermore, by collaborating with behavioral geographers, urban planners have a greater understanding of how individuals perceive and behave within urban environments. All of these observations and tools will become increasingly necessary for urban geographers and urban planners as they strive to design policies to provide services for ever-increasing urban populations.

Key Terms Defined

Action space The geographical area that contains the space an individual interacts with on a daily basis.

Beaux arts This movement within city planning and urban design that stressed the marriage of older, classical forms with newer, industrial ones. Common characteristics of this period include wide thoroughfares, spacious parks, and civic monuments that stressed progress, freedom, and national unity.

Central business district The downtown or nucleus of a city where retail stores, offices, and cultural activities are concentrated; building densities are usually quite high; and transportation systems converge.

Central place theory A theory formulated by Walter Christaller in the early 1900s that explains the size and distribution of cities in terms of a competitive supply of goods and services to dispersed populations.

City Beautiful movement Movement in environmental design that drew directly from the beaux arts school. Architects from this movement strove to impart order on hectic, industrial centers by creating urban spaces that conveyed a sense of morality and civic pride, which many feared was absent from the frenzied new industrial world.

Colonial city Cities established by colonizing empires as administrative centers. Often they were established on already existing native cities, completely overtaking their infrastructures.

Concentric zone model Model that describes urban environments as a series of rings of distinct land uses radiating out from a central core, or central business district.

Edge city Cities that are located on the outskirts of larger cities and serve many of the same functions of urban areas, but in a sprawling, decentralized suburban environment.

European cities Cities in Europe that were mostly developed during the Medieval Period and that retain many of the same characteristics such as extreme density of development with narrow buildings and winding streets, an ornate church that prominently marks the city center, and high walls surrounding the city center that provided defense against attack.

Exurbanite Person who has left the inner city and moved to outlying suburbs or rural areas.

Feudal city Cities that arose during the Middle Ages and that actually represent a time of relative stagnation in urban growth. This system fostered a dependent relationship between wealthy landowners and peasants who worked their land, providing very little alternative economic opportunities.

Gateway city Cities that, because of their geographic location, act as ports of entry and distribution centers for large geographic areas.

Gentrification The trend of middle- and upper-income Americans moving into city centers and rehabilitating much of the architecture but also replacing low-income populations, and changing the social character of certain neighborhoods.

Ghettoization A process occurring in many inner cities in which they become dilapidated centers of poverty, as affluent whites move out to the suburbs and immigrants and people of color vie for scarce jobs and resources.

Hinterland The market area surrounding an urban center, which that urban center serves.

Industrial Revolution Period characterized by the rapid social and economic changes in manufacturing and agriculture that occurred in England during the late 18th century and rapidly diffused to other parts of the developed world.

Inner city decay Those parts of large urban areas that lose significant portions of their populations as a result of change in industry or migration to suburbs. Because of these changes, the inner city loses its tax base and becomes a center of poverty.

Islamic cities Cities in Muslim countries that owe their structure to their religious beliefs. Islamic cities contain mosques at their center and walls guarding their perimeter. Open-air markets, courtyards surrounded by high walls, and dead-end streets, which limit foot traffic in residential neighborhoods, also characterize Islamic cities.

Latin American cities Cities in Latin America that owe much of their structure to colonialism, the rapid rise of industrialization, and continual rapid increases in population. Similar to other colonial cities, they also demonstrate distinctive sectors of industrial or residential development radiating out from the central business district, where most industrial and financial activity occurs.

Medieval cities Cities that developed in Europe during the Medieval Period and that contain such unique features as extreme density of development with narrow buildings and winding streets, an ornate church that prominently marks the city center, and high walls surrounding the city center that provided defense against attack.

Megacities Cities, mostly characteristic of the developing world, where high population growth and migration have caused them to explode in population since World War II. All megacities are plagued by chaotic and unplanned growth, terrible pollution, and widespread poverty.

Megalopolis Several, metropolitan areas that were originally separate but that have joined together to form a large, sprawling urban complex.

Metropolitan area Within the United States, an urban area consisting of one or more whole county units, usually containing several urbanized areas, or suburbs, that all act together as a coherent economic whole.

Modern architecture Point of view, wherein cities and buildings are thought to act like well-oiled machines, with little energy spent on frivolous details or ornate designs. Efficient, geometrical structures made of concrete and glass dominated urban forms for half a century while this view prevailed.

Multiple nuclei model Type of urban form wherein cities have numerous centers of business and cultural activity instead of one central place.

Node Geographical centers of activity. A large city, such as Los Angeles, has numerous nodes.

Postmodern architecture A reaction in architectural design to the feeling of sterile alienation that many people get from modern architecture. Postmodernism uses older, historical styles and a sense of lightheartedness and eclecticism. Buildings combine pleasant-looking forms and playful colors to convey new ideas and to create spaces that are more people-friendly than their modernist predecessors.

Primate city A country's leading city, with a population that is disproportionately greater than other urban areas within the same country.

Rank-size rule Rule that states that the population of any given town should be inversely proportional to its rank in the country's hierarchy when the distribution of cities according to their sizes follows a certain pattern.

Sector model A model or urban land use that places the central business district in the middle with wedge-shaped sectors radiating outwards from the center along transportation corridors.

Segregation The process that results from suburbanization when affluent individuals leave the city center for homogenous suburban neighborhoods. This process isolates those individuals who cannot afford to consider relocating to suburban neighborhoods and must remain in certain pockets of the central city.

Squatter settlements Residential developments characterized by extreme poverty that usually exist on land just outside of cities that is neither owned nor rented by its occupants.

Suburb Residential communities, located outside of city centers, that are usually relatively homogenous in terms of population.

Urban growth boundary Geographical boundaries placed around a city to limit suburban growth within that city.

Urban revitalization The process occurring in some urban areas experiencing inner city decay that usually involves the construction of new shopping districts, entertainment venues, and cultural attractions to entice young urban professionals back into the cities where nightlife and culture are more accessible.

Urban sprawl The process of expansive suburban development over large areas spreading out from a city, in which the automobile provides the primary source of transportation.

World City Centers of economic, culture, and political activity that are strongly interconnected and together control the global systems of finance and commerce.

Sample Questions and Answers

Section 1: Historical Geography of Urban Environments

Multiple-Choice Questions

1. The first cities arose in

   (A) ancient Greece.
   (B) hearths of early agriculture.
   (C) the Indian subcontinent.
   (D) central Mexico.
   (E) near the equator.

2. Some prominent Native American cities later became

   (A) manufacturing hubs.
   (B) agricultural distribution centers.
   (C) gateway cities.
   (D) colonial cities.
   (E) export processing zones.

3. The Industrial Revolution

   (A) had little impact on urban areas.
   (B) spawned vast manufacturing centers.
   (C) began in the Great Lakes region.
   (D) made factory workers obsolete.
   (E) caused an urban to rural migration.

4. _____ is an important gateway city.

   (A) Oslo, Norway,
   (B) Perth, Australia,
   (C) Nairobi, Kenya,
   (D) Honolulu, Hawaii,
   (E) Denver, Colorado,

5. During the Middle Ages, _____ dramatically slowed the growth of urban areas.

(A) feudalism
(B) colonialism
(C) Black Death
(D) Renaissance
(E) the Industrial Revolution

Free-Response Question

1. Describe the historical evolution of the city and how it has historically varied in form and function across the globe.

Section 2: Culture and Urban Form

Multiple-Choice Questions

1. Classic _____ cities have narrow, winding streets, open-air markets, many dead-ends, and courtyards surrounded by high walls.

(A) medieval European
(B) Hindu
(C) Latin American
(D) Islamic
(E) colonial

2. Architects and planners from the _____ strove to introduce beauty and impose order on chaotic industrial cities.

(A) postmodern school
(B) modernist tradition
(C) City Beautiful movement
(D) beaux arts school
(E) classical movement

3. Modernist architecture

(A) stressed efficiency and geometrical order.
(B) uses eclectic and classic forms.
(C) stressed the ornate.
(D) is limited to newer American cities.
(E) is characterized by skyscrapers.

4. Asian, African, and South American cities

(A) contain dominant centers, usually surrounding something of religious significance.
(B) contain strong manufacturing and industrial sectors within the city.
(C) display mostly modern forms of architecture as they are recently developing themselves after colonialism.
(D) contain many structural relics from colonialism.
(E) usually have a church at the center of the city.

5. Medieval European cities usually contain all the following characteristics except

(A) winding streets and tall narrow buildings.
(B) large, ornate cathedrals.
(C) walls surrounding the city for defense purposes.
(D) wide streets to accommodate large military troops.
(E) a high density of buildings.

Free-Response Question

1. If you were traveling in a new city, what kinds of evidence would you look for to symbolize each of the following trends in urban design: beaux arts, City Beautiful movement, modernism, and postmodernism?

Section 3: The Spatial Organization of Urban Environments

Multiple-Choice Questions

1. Los Angeles provides an excellent example of

(A) the Beaux Arts tradition.
(B) a central business district.
(C) the multinucleated metropolis.
(D) the concentric zone model.
(E) disagglomeration.

2. Many Latin American cities conform more or less to the

(A) theory of ghettoization.
(B) the sector model.
(C) the multinode model.
(D) inner city decay theory.
(E) the concentric zone model.

3. In cities like Baltimore, inner-city revitalization has transformed _____ into gentrified urban neighborhoods.

(A) suburbs
(B) central business districts
(C) edge cities
(D) ghettos
(E) agglomerations

4. Which of the following cities exemplifies an urban geography defined by railroads?

(A) Boston
(B) Mexico City
(C) Chicago
(D) San Francisco
(E) Los Angeles

5. Which of the following best describes edge cities?

(A) They are located along freeways on the outskirts of major cities.
(B) They are usually found in Europe and Asia.
(C) They are small, isolated communities.
(D) They are designed in the Beautiful City tradition.
(E) They are gentrified communities.

6. According to the central place theory,

(A) small communities bind regions together.
(B) most people live in mid-sized cities.
(C) large cities serve as economic hubs.
(D) regions are impossible to define.
(E) there are more large cities than small cities.

7. The coastal southern California and northern Baja, Mexico region can be described as a

(A) central place.
(B) artificial construction.
(C) megacity.
(D) megalopolis.
(E) agglomeration.

Free-Response Question

1. Describe the influence of transportation on modern American cities.

Section 4: Urban Planning

Multiple-Choice Questions

1. Which of the following was not one of the main elements contributing to a city's legibility according to Kevin Lynch?

   (A) Landmarks
   (B) Nodes
   (C) Links
   (D) Edges
   (E) Districts

2. Action space consists of

   (A) recreational facilities in an urban area.
   (B) the space in which individual daily activity occurs.
   (C) spaces within a city designated for transportation.
   (D) a diagrammatic representation of the amount of time it takes to travel between activities on a particular day.
   (E) the area surrounding the interactions a central place has with the surrounding community.

3. Individual spatial behavior on a daily basis

   (A) generally involves more shorter trips than longer trips.
   (B) can be described as that individual's action space.
   (C) can be limited by transportation possibilities.
   (D) mostly involves work-related travel.
   (E) All of the above

Free-Response Question

1. Discuss why it might be important for urban planners to consult behavioral geographers when making planning decisions.

Answers for Multiple-Choice Questions

Section 1: Historical Geography of Urban Environments

1. **(B)** The first cities only developed after sedentary agriculture advanced to the point at which crop surpluses allowed some people to take up professions other than farming, such as brick laying and carpentry. When and where this occurred, the first cities arose.

2. **(D)** Mexico City is just one example of a great Native American city (Tenochtitlan) that eventually became a center of colonial government administration and military might. Colonial powers used these cities as bases from which to dominate people in the surrounding countryside.

3. **(B)** Chicago is the classic example of a city that was born during the Industrial Revolution and then experienced tremendous growth, becoming a great center of manufacturing, processing, and transportation.

4. **(D)** Honolulu's extremely strategic location, isolated in the center of the Pacific Ocean, has made it an important gateway for travelers heading both east and west. As a result of its position, Honolulu has become an important shipping hub and military base. The city has also attracted an extremely diverse population of people from around the Pacific Rim.

5. **(A)** Feudalism fostered a system of dependence between landholders and lowly peasants that worked the land. During the Middle Ages, this system prevailed, and because of the lack of opportunity imbedded within it, urban areas experienced a period of stagnation.

Section 2: Culture and Urban Form

1. **(D)** Islamic cities are complex landscapes that incorporate both symbolic expressions of the Muslim faith and adaptations to hot desert climates. Muslim cities outside the Middle East—in places like Indonesia—lack desert adaptations but retain traditional Muslim design and architecture.

2. **(C)** Both the beaux arts and City Beautiful movements were attempts to create urban spaces that reflected changing social values while harkening back to classical forms. The City Beautiful movement, which is well-represented in cities like Chicago and Washington, D.C., was, more specifically, an effort to give new industrial spaces—which lacked the ancient history and sense of place of the older European cities—beauty, order, and a sense of civic identity.

3. **(A)** Boxy, geometrical structures built of concrete and glass typify the modernist movement. Modernist architects tried to convey a sense of futuristic order and scientific rationality on urban spaces. Many such spaces would later be thought of as sterile and impersonal.

4. **(D)** The majority of cities in each of these three areas, at one time, were colonial cities. As such, this extremely devastating historical process has largely determined their spatial organization.

5. **(D)** Medieval streets are generally narrow and winding. The only forms of transportation that traversed them were people on foot or horses, neither of which necessitated wide streets.

Section 3: The Spatial Organization of Urban Environments

1. **(C)** Although Los Angeles has a central industrial core, its downtown area is not nearly as dominant of a city center as, say, Chicago's loop. Instead, Los Angeles is a vast metropolis with many "centers," or nodes of commercial and industrial activity.

2. (B) The sector model of urban geography describes cities in which different types of development—residential, commercial, industrial—radiate out from the city center like the spokes of a wheel. These spokes often follow avenues of transportation, such as grand boulevards, riverways, or railroads. Mexico City's Paseo de la Reforma is one example.

3. (D) Ghettos are economically depressed inner-city neighborhoods often populated by ethnic minorities. During the past 20 years, many American cities have successfully revitalized their inner cities by luring young urban professionals back into funky urban neighborhoods. However, many long-time residents of these former ghettos have been forced to move owing to increasing costs of living. Other cities, such as Detroit, have had much less success at transforming their urban cores.

4. (C) Historically, Chicago has been a city of railroads. Chicago has served as the railroad hub of the West since the 1870s and, within the city itself, many people travel by light rail. The "el," or elevated train system moves hundreds of thousands of people per day around the tightly packed urban area.

5. (A) Edge cities serve the same functions as many urban areas but, for many, are conveniently located just outside of urban areas, usually on important corridors or freeway systems.

6. (C) Large cities, because they generally have a large population, have a much greater economic base and thus can support and provide a greater variety of economic and cultural opportunities.

7. (D) This region consists of a conurbation of linked cities such that, as you drive north or south along the coast in this region, you will always be driving through urban areas. These cities, at one time, were probably very geographically separate from one another but, because they have been increasingly expanded, have molded together into a megalopolis.

Section 4: Urban Planning

1. (C) According to Kevin Lynch, the five main elements contributing to a city's legibility include: paths, edges, districts, landmarks, and nodes. Links may exist in cities in the form of transportation systems, but they do not exist as one of the fundamental units that make cities more easily readable for their inhabitants and first-time visitors.

2. (B) Action spaces are used by behavioral geographers to analyze individuals' daily spatial activities. They describe all the typical interactions individuals have with their environment on any given day, and thus can provide insightful information for urban planners in making decisions on transportation routes and locations of various facilities within a city.

3. (E) Behavioral geographers have analyzed numerous people's action spaces to draw general conclusions about human spatial behavior on a daily basis. In general, this kind of behavior conforms to five rules: people take many more shorter trips than longer trips, most trips tend to be work-related, trips of greater distances require more thought and planning, travel decisions can be quite limited by transportation, and, people tend to avoid perceived hazards when going about their daily activities.

Answers for Free-Response Questions

Section 1: Historical Geography of Urban Environments

1. Main points:
   - The first cities arose in areas of early agriculture. As agricultural systems became increasingly developed, farmers were able to grow more than they needed of certain products. These excesses generated a trading system between farmers. Soon, not as many farmers were needed to produce the same amount of goods, and some began specializing in other functions that also served the community, such as carpentry, metalwork, and education.
   - These first urban areas experienced a period of relative stagnation during the Middle Ages when a feudal system prevailed, and most cities remained centers of religious and military power rather than centers of culture and education.
   - During the Renaissance, cities once again flourished and became cultural and learning centers. Also, during this period, many European countries began colonizing various parts of Africa and South America, establishing colonial cities of administrative powers, usually overtaking the already existing infrastructure of established native cities.
   - The Industrial Revolution sparked dramatic changes in urban areas across the developed world. The job opportunities in manufacturing, processing, and finance, which urban areas now represented, drew thousands of people in from rural areas.

Section 2: Culture and Urban Form

1. Main points:
   - Evidence of the beaux arts influence and the City Beautiful movement might be difficult to distinguish from each other as both stressed a sense of order and placed an emphasis on civic pride. Clues such as wide thoroughfares and spacious parks give evidence to beaux arts, and monuments and spaces dedicated to fostering civic identity and pride exemplify the influence of the City Beautiful movement.
   - Relics of modern architecture might manifest themselves in buildings that appear to be extremely functional rather than beautiful. Buildings that are extremely geometrical and made of concrete and glass, would provide evidence of modernist influence on a city.
   - Finally, postmodernism would show itself in landscapes of eclecticism where different agricultural forms and colors are combined to be more inviting and unexclusive.

Section 3: The Spatial Organization of Urban Environments

1. Main points:
   - The layout of cities across the United States can largely be attributed to the dominant form of transportation available to that city at its period of most-rapid development.
   - For example, comparing two of the major cities in California—Los Angeles and San Francisco—provides an example of the effects of transportation on both the organization and geographical spread of the city. San Francisco developed before the automobile and most individuals traversed the city on its famous form of transportation, the trolley car. As such, San Francisco is much more compactly developed, with narrow, windy streets that now cause tremendous congestion for automobile traffic. Conversely, Los Angeles developed after the invention of the automobile, and the mobility offered by the car allowed the area to extend geographically into an extremely large metropolitan area. As such, Los Angeles has no real center, just numerous nodes that are quite geographically spread out from one another.
   - Other examples that illustrate the effects of transportation on city design include two other great American cities: Chicago and New York. New York, as one of the first American cities, developed before the automobile, thus limiting its boundaries. As such, Manhattan is an extremely dense city with small streets, also now extremely congested, because they weren't initially planned for automobile traffic. Chicago was a city dominated by rail. Today, Chicago's center, or the loop, is located just at the edge of Lake Michigan and spokes, or rail lines, radiate outside of that hub bringing people in and out of the city on a daily basis.

Section 4: Urban Planning

1. Main points:
   - Behavioral geographers are very interested in how individuals perceive different environments and, in turn, how those perceptions affect both their feelings towards those environments and behavior within them. As such, urban planners can gain much insightful information regarding how individuals perceive urban environments and the types of factors that contribute to greater comfort levels within a city.
   - One such tool urban planners and behavioral geographers can use to understand individual behavior within urban environments is a record of their action spaces. These records generally depict all of the various interactions an individual has within the urban environment on a daily basis. They can provide insights on commonly used places, commonly avoided places, dominant forms of transportation, and utility of other services within the city.
   - Additionally, urban planners have benefited from other research by behavioral geographers on factors in the city that contribute to a city's legibility. If a city is well-organized, containing a diversity of unique landmarks, individuals generally feel a greater sense of orientation, contributing to their overall comfort level and confidence to venture out into places that may not be extremely familiar.

Additional Resources

Text

Dear, Michael J. 2000. *The Postmodern Urban Condition*. Malden, Massachusetts: Blackwell.

First, the text provides a general introduction to cities and urbanism in the postmodern world. Then, Dear analyzes how concepts of postmodernism and urban space have led to the genesis of the "postmodern urban condition." He investigates the intellectual, moral, and political consequences of postmodernism and looks at the role of space and place in contemporary social theory and philosophy.

Ford, Larry R. 1994. *Cities and Buildings*. Baltimore: Johns Hopkins University Press.

Larry Ford is an urban geographer who writes about "real" American cities and buildings. He looks at architectural and social history as well as fundamental spatial patterns and processes to understand the architectural makeup of many of the world's cities.

Garreau, Joel. 1991. *Edge City: Life on the New Frontier*. New York: Doubleday.

In this book, Garreau traces the genesis of edge cities, discussing both suburbanization and the rise of the American mall, and how these phenomena lead to the development of areas just outside of cities that end up being larger than the central cities they surround. He looks at several specific examples of edge cities within the United States and some of the social and economic effects this type of location has on the surrounding community.

Knox, Paul L. 1994. *Urbanization: An Introduction to Urban Geography*. Englewood Cliffs, New Jersey: Prentice-Hall.

This is an urban geography textbook that looks at how urbanization processes have changed through history and the various outcomes of these changing processes. It looks at how the interlocking processes of urbanization contribute to ever-changing urban geographies both within the United States and across the globe.

Web

Official City Websites: *http://www.officialcitysites.com/*

This fun website allows you to link to numerous cities around the world. Unfortunately, many cities are not available, but if you are interested in exploring some interesting details for numerous cities in the United States, Australia, Canada, France, Germany, Japan, Netherlands, New Zealand, or the United Kingdom, you should be able to access the official websites for most large cities within these countries.

University of California, Downtown Los Angeles Walking Tour: *http://www. usc.edu/dept/geography/losangeles/lawalk/*.

This extremely interesting website allows you to explore downtown Los Angeles. You can choose from several main districts of downtown Los Angeles, such as the historic core or Chinatown, and once you arrive to those pages you can explore that area through pictures and descriptions. A very well-presented website that allows you to learn more about the history and architecture of one of the world's great cities.

The United Nations Human Settlements Programme: *www.unhabitat.org/*

The site reports on the programme's work all over the globe, mainly building or rebuilding homes in poverty-stricken or devastated areas. It also contains links to both the World Summit on Sustainable Development and the annual seminar on Learning from Best Practices.

International City Profiles: *www.un.org/Pubs/CyberSchoolBus/special/habitat*

This is an excellent website for both students and teachers. It comes from the United Nations CyberSchool Bus tour and it's called the "Cities of Today, Cities of Tomorrow" project. On the first page, you can choose from four categories: About, Units, Activities, and Resources. The "About" section tells you more about the project, the "Units" section provides six complete teaching units on urbanization, the "Activities" section provides several general activities along with an activity for each of the six units, and the "Resources" section gives background information on nine different topics including, "Women, homes, and communities," and "Is there a right to housing?" Along with a section called "Doing Good," which provides 105 ways to deal with urbanization, it also outlines 21 profiles of the world's largest cities and finally provides a bibliography of resources used in the project.

Center for Urban Policy Research, Rutgers University: *www.policy.rutgers. edu/cupr*

The center performs research on a multiplicity of urban-geography-related issues: affordable housing, land use policy, the arts and cultural policy, development impact analysis, the costs of sprawl, transportation information systems, environmental impacts, and community economic developments. Additionally, the site houses a *State of the Nation's Cities* database on 77 American cities and suburbs, which contains various economic and demographic measures for each of the 77 cities.

"Modules in Urban and Economic Geography": *www.utexas.edu/depts/ grg/virtdept/contents.html*

After you get to the title page, click on "Urban and Economic Geography." This link contains a directory of lesson plans or modules, compiled by title, written by different professors all across the country, each relating to different issues in urban geography and community planning. It provides an excellent resource for teachers looking for ideas for teaching certain topics relating to urban geography.

Practice Test 1

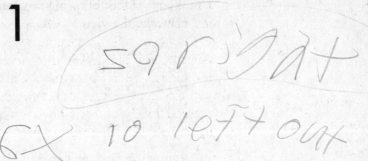

Test

Multiple-Choice Questions

Directions: Read each question carefully and choose the correct response. If you are unsure of the correct answer, be careful of guessing wildly—a ¼-point penalty is given for each incorrect answer.

1. The word "geography" literally means

    (A) the study of space.
    (B) earth study.
    (C) people and nature.
    (D) earth writing.
    (E) human ground.

2. New York City is divided into five _____, in order to better organize social services for millions of people.

    (A) counties
    (B) voting precincts
    (C) town councils
    (D) school districts
    (E) boroughs

3. In which of the following countries would you expect to find the highest rate of population growth?

    (A) Canada
    (B) Namibia
    (C) Sweden
    (D) Chile
    (E) United States

4. In distance decay models, the slope of the decay function illustrates

    (A) the type of interaction.
    (B) the nature of the network.
    (C) the influence of "friction of distance."
    (D) topography.
    (E) net dispersion.

5. Which of the following projections places the North or South Pole at the center of the view?

(A) Azimuthal
(B) Choropleth
(C) Pole view
(D) Fuller's
(E) Mercator

6. Rap music first appeared in New York in the 1970s. Later, it spread to large cities with vibrant African-American populations—such as Los Angeles, Oakland, Chicago, and Detroit—without being absorbed by the smaller cities and rural areas in-between. This type of spatial diffusion is called

(A) relocation diffusion.
(B) hierarchical diffusion.
(C) contagious diffusion.
(D) cultural diffusion.
(E) indeterminant diffusion.

7. Cartography is the art and science of

(A) demographics.
(B) map-making.
(C) spatial orientation.
(D) cognitive imagery.
(E) spatial decision making.

8. Which of the following is false regarding slash-and-burn agriculture?

(A) It occurs mainly in tropical environments.
(B) It is associated with deforestation in Brazil.
(C) It is part of the Green Revolution.
(D) It was practiced sustainably by indigenous peoples.
(E) It is uncommon in the temperate latitudes.

9. A population pyramid

(A) shows the age and sex structure of a population.
(B) cannot be used to compare two different countries.
(C) demonstrates the demographic transition model.
(D) only accurately depicts declining populations.
(E) is most useful in illustrating social upheaval.

10. The Pleistocene overkill theory argues that

    (A) hearths of early agriculture resulted from environmental conditions.
    (B) geographers have overemphasized the importance of environmental conditions in human history.
    (C) poor environmental management resulted in the ecological collapse of the Fertile Crescent.
    (D) current human geography is not a product of the distant past.
    (E) hunter-gatherers caused the extinction of many species after the end of the last ice age.

11. In an address to the 1994 United Nations International Conference on Population and Development, India argued that, although population growth has placed pressure on the world's natural resources, _____ by industrialized nations has also had extreme consequences for environmental quality.

    (A) fiscal policy
    (B) material consumption
    (C) tourism
    (D) international aid
    (E) racism

12. Geographical research that applies only to one place or region is

    (A) nomothetic.
    (B) denominational.
    (C) idiographic.
    (D) nonscientific.
    (E) cultural studies.

13. Approximately how long did it take for Eurasian hunter-gatherers to reach the tip of South America after their initial arrival in Alaska?

    (A) 500 years
    (B) 2,000 years
    (C) 5,000 years
    (D) 20,000 years
    (E) 40,000 years

14. The demographic accounting equation computes future population as a function of current population:

    (A) + births − infant mortality + cohort
    (B) + births − deaths × life expectancy
    (C) + births − deaths + immigration − emigration
    (D) births / deaths − immigration + emigration
    (E) + immigration − emigration × demographic transition

15. Which of the following models of urban geography best describes this map?

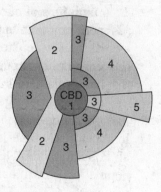

(A) central place theory
(B) rank-size rule
(C) Von Thunen's concentric ring theory
(D) Sector model of urban development
(E) Multinucleated model of urban development

16. Longitude is

(A) the angular distance north or south of the prime meridian.
(B) the angular distance east or west of Greenwich, England.
(C) the angular distance north or south of the equator.
(D) useful in determining relative location.
(E) useful in describing a place's situation.

17. The idea that our impressions and experiences of the world around us are filtered through the lens of our culture and our individual experiences, which critiques the sort of scientific, universalist grand theories offered by modernists is called

(A) postmodernism.
(B) ecofeminism.
(C) consumptionism.
(D) reductionism.
(E) possitivism.

18. The religious practices of some Native American groups combine elements both from their traditional religion and from Christianity. This is an example of

(A) a cultural complex.
(B) a cultural confluence.
(C) a counter culture.
(D) a diametric culture.
(E) a cultural syncretism.

19. The demographic transition model posits that

(A) advanced industrialized countries will have rapid population growth.
(B) pre-industrial states will have both low birth and death rates.
(C) countries with high levels of economic production will have lower birth rates.
(D) underdeveloped countries cannot become developed.
(E) time is the dominant force behind population change.

20. One important consequence of cultural extinction is

(A) decreasing population.
(B) increased poverty in peripheral regions.
(C) loss of genetic diversity.
(D) loss of indigenous knowledge about ecosystems.
(E) increasing population.

21. _____ maps work well for locating and navigating between places, while _____ maps display one or more variables across a specific space.

(A) Reference . . . thematic
(B) Thematic . . . reference
(C) Spatial . . . cartographic
(D) Cartographic . . . spatial
(E) Topologic . . . choropleth

22. Which of the following religions originated in northern India and then spread across central and southeast Asia, Indonesia, and Japan?

(A) Hinduism
(B) Buddhism
(C) Islam
(D) Taoism
(E) Judaism

23. States with federal forms of government must also have

(A) territorial organization.
(B) fascist regimes.
(C) social-democracies.
(D) proportional representation.
(E) congressional oversight.

24. In the world systems model, the core nations of the world are

(A) situated in the present-day Middle East.
(B) located in the prosperous southern continents.
(C) located mainly in Europe and North America.
(D) located in the former Soviet republics.
(E) located in the heartland, not the rimland.

25. The study of the interaction between human cultures and natural ecosystems is called

  (A) cultural ecology.
  (B) semiotics.
  (C) cognitive science.
  (D) linguistics.
  (E) sociobiology.

26. Which of the following is not a potential cause of Balkanization?

  (A) Ethnic divisions
  (B) Varying levels of economic development within a country
  (C) External pressures
  (D) Centripetal forces
  (E) A strong central government

27. In the following distance decay function,

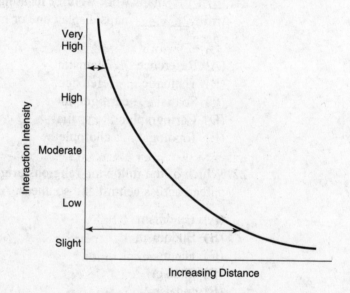

  (A) the friction of distance has little effect on connectivity.
  (B) connectivity is related to the position of a central place.
  (C) distance imposes a significant barrier to spatial interactions.
  (D) topological space acts independently of distance.
  (E) absolute decay is different than relative decay.

28. Which of the following is true about language extinctions?

  (A) They happen suddenly and without warning.
  (B) They are usually the result of genocide.
  (C) There could be several thousand over the next century.
  (D) They are increasingly rare.
  (E) They are unrelated to cultural imperialism.

29. _____ involves the economic and political domination of one state by another, while _____ includes official, institutionalized government rule.

(A) Regionalism . . . sectionalism
(B) Sectionalism . . . regionalism
(C) Imperialism . . . colonialism
(D) Colonialism . . . imperialism
(E) Nationalism . . . isolationism

30. Sources of forced migration include

(A) complementarity and individual choice.
(B) economic opportunities and religious freedom.
(C) political unrest and ecological degradation.
(D) the draw of a pleasant climate.
(E) familial ties in another country.

31. In a 1995 plebiscite, the Canadian province of Quebec sought which of the following?

(A) Electoral reapportionment
(B) Economic freedom
(C) Unitary standing
(D) Self-determination
(E) Membership in the United Nations

32. The disproportionate siting of power plants and waste disposal facilities in African-American and Latino neighborhoods—independent of other economic and historical factors—is an example of

(A) postmaterialism.
(B) environmental racism.
(C) deindustrialization.
(D) environmental justice.
(E) ecological inferiority.

33. Advanced economic countries, like the United States, may produce more pollution than less economically advanced countries because

(A) they consume more resources.
(B) they are less concerned about the environment.
(C) they desire global domination.
(D) they have more resources to begin with.
(E) they lack waste management technology.

34. Latitude is

(A) the angular distance north or south of the prime meridian.
(B) the angular distance east or west of Greenwich, England.
(C) the angular distance north or south of the equator.
(D) useful in determining relative location.
(E) a measure of social or political freedom.

35. Primary economic activities involve

(A) the transformation and assembly of raw materials.
(B) the sale and exchange of goods and services.
(C) the handling and processing of information.
(D) research and development.
(E) the direct extraction or harvest of natural resources.

36. According to Thomas Malthus, _____ grows arithmetically, but _____ grows geometrically.

(A) population . . . food production
(B) passion between the sexes . . . willingness to have sex
(C) food production . . . population
(D) technology . . . environmental impact
(E) population . . . technology

37. Since 1960, the difference between per capita Gross National Products of the world's wealthiest countries and the world's poorest countries has

(A) remained about the same.
(B) decreased somewhat.
(C) decreased dramatically.
(D) increased dramatically.
(E) increased slightly.

38. In the gravity model of spatial interaction, population and distance

(A) are inversely related.
(B) are directly related.
(C) each have multiple measures.
(D) do not affect the final solution.
(E) vary significantly.

39. Core-periphery patterns exist within countries as well as among them. In the United States, economic peripheries include

(A) New England and the Great Basin.
(B) southern Appalachia and the lower Mississippi Valley.
(C) the northern Rockies and Pacific Northwest.
(D) the Desert Southwest and Great Lakes.
(E) the Rust Belt.

40. Agricultural techniques developed in the temperate latitudes are frequently inappropriate for wet tropical climates because rainforest soils tend to be

(A) poorly drained.
(B) nutrient-rich.
(C) nutrient-poor.
(D) salinized.
(E) sandy.

41. All choropleth maps use

(A) shading and coloring.
(B) isolines.
(C) dots.
(D) graphs and charts.
(E) the Mercator projection.

42. Hearths of early Eurasian agriculture were generally located

(A) in Mediterranean climates.
(B) on the moist, windward side of mountain ranges.
(C) in fertile river valleys.
(D) along the coast.
(E) at high latitudes and altitudes.

43. The aggregate measure of economic development that accounts for the depreciation of capital and natural resources is called the

(A) Gross National Product.
(B) Gross Domestic Product.
(C) Net National Product.
(D) Human Development Index.
(E) Gender Empowerment Index.

44. The Kurds are an example of an ethnic group that

(A) has a stable and prosperous nation.
(B) has recognized an antecedent boundary between Iraq and Jordan.
(C) has historical homelands spanning many national borders.
(D) does not want to live in an independent country.
(E) has disappeared due to cultural extinction.

45. Which of the following is an example of an edge city?

(A) Anchorage, Alaska
(B) Seattle, Washington
(C) Boston, Massachusetts
(D) Tyson's Corner, Virginia
(E) Las Vegas, Nevada

46. Hearth regions of early agriculture included present-day

(A) China, India, Turkey, and Mexico.
(B) China, India, Sudan, and Malaysia.
(C) India, Ethiopia, Greece, and Morocco.
(D) Anatolia, Peru, Borneo, and Hanalee.
(E) California, Illinois, New Brunswick, and Ireland.

47. Von Thunen's model of rural land use is based on which of the following premises?

    (A) Land values decrease farther from the urban center.
    (B) Land values increase farther from the urban center.
    (C) Perishable goods are least valuable.
    (D) Railroads provide fixed transportation costs.
    (E) Vegetarianism is socially beneficial.

48. Washington D.C.'s Lincoln Memorial and Mall, with their dramatic neoclassical architecture and symbolic references to democracy and populism, are associated with

    (A) modernism.
    (B) revisionism.
    (C) pluralism.
    (D) postmodernism.
    (E) the City Beautiful movement.

49. The theory that explains the regional organization of urban areas, based on their functions and the goods and services they offer, is called

    (A) metropolitan area theory.
    (B) sector theory.
    (C) central place theory.
    (D) urban matrix theory.
    (E) the rank-size rule.

50. The city of San Francisco is known for which of the following?

    (A) Beaux arts architecture
    (B) Early 20th century modernism
    (C) 19th century Victorian architecture
    (D) Its balmy climate
    (E) Postmodern architecture

51. The geographic differentiation between the colonizing countries of Europe, North America, and eastern Asia and the colonized states of Africa and South America has been called

    (A) the north/south divide.
    (B) the iron curtain.
    (C) the east/west divide.
    (D) the thin red line.
    (E) the western front.

52. Which city's dense urban core became the "birthplace of the skyscraper"?

   (A) New York
   (B) Tokyo
   (C) Sao Paulo
   (D) Paris
   (E) Chicago

53. The greatest concentration of linguistic diversity on earth is in

   (A) Amazonia.
   (B) the Congo.
   (C) Madagascar.
   (D) New Guinea.
   (E) Mexico.

54. By 2020, most of the world's biggest cities will be located in

   (A) Western Europe.
   (B) Russia.
   (C) South America.
   (D) Asia.
   (E) Africa.

55. _____ is strategically located on the border between two continents, and at the intersection of many cultures and religions.

   (A) Istanbul, Turkey,
   (B) Lagos, Nigeria,
   (C) Mexico City, Mexico,
   (D) Karachi, Pakistan,
   (E) Berlin, Germany,

56. Cartographic scale refers to

   (A) the size of an object in the real world.
   (B) the number of different objects depicted on the map.
   (C) the projection.
   (D) the relation between a distance on a map and distance on the ground.
   (E) angular distance from the equator.

57. Which of the following factors is most responsible for the dramatic demographic collapse of Native Americans during the Colonial Period?

   (A) The slave trade
   (B) Eurasian diseases
   (C) The hacienda system
   (D) Language extinction
   (E) Civil war

58. Primate cities are those that

(A) are the seats of ecclesiastical power in a nation.
(B) are the national capitals.
(C) are disproportionately larger than other cities in a nation.
(D) were the first to be established in a new colony.
(E) are inhabited by monkeys and apes.

59. The term _____ describes a group of people with a common ethnic identity that is spread out over a large geographic area.

(A) "caste"
(B) "sect"
(C) "diaspora"
(D) "race"
(E) "cultural complex"

60. The National Geographic Society uses the Robinson projection for many of its maps because

(A) it is the only perfectly proportioned projection.
(B) it fits on the pages.
(C) it is versatile and aesthetically pleasing.
(D) it orients the United States in the center of the world.
(E) it sells at the newsstands.

61. Which of the following does *not* qualify as a Protestant denomination?

(A) Presbyterianism
(B) Methodism
(C) Catholicism
(D) Southern Baptist
(E) Lutheran

62. During the 1980s and 1990s, Santa Monica, California, became significantly wealthier and more expensive. This process is referred to as

(A) escalation.
(B) gentrification.
(C) urban zonation.
(D) reallotment.
(E) reification.

63. Which of the following regions experienced rapid industrial growth during the early 20th century, followed by a severe decline and difficult period of economic readjustment?

(A) The mid-Atlantic
(B) The Great Plains
(C) South Florida
(D) The Great Lakes
(E) The Great Plains

64. Which of the following qualifies as a primate city?

    (A) Toronto, Canada
    (B) Cape Town, South Africa
    (C) Jerusalem, Israel
    (D) Mexico City, Mexico
    (E) Phoenix, Arizona

65. Geographic information systems use _____ to display multiple spatial data sets.

    (A) thematic layers
    (B) cartograms
    (C) remotely sensed images
    (D) dot maps
    (E) isolines

66. Break-of-bulk points are

    (A) places where natural hazards prohibit spatial interaction.
    (B) uniform throughout space and time.
    (C) hindrances to global economic development.
    (D) sites where goods are transferred for continued shipping.
    (E) cities that offer the largest markets for any given good or service.

67. The process by which one ethnic group becomes integrated into a larger culture is called

    (A) articulation.
    (B) ossification.
    (C) assimilation.
    (D) syncretism.
    (E) a melting pot.

68. The _____ will increase over the next decade, as baby boomers reach old age and are no longer able to work and provide for themselves.

    (A) poverty line
    (B) population pyramid
    (C) arithmetic density
    (D) dependency ratio
    (E) doubling time

69. When the crude birth rate is higher than the crude death rate, the difference between the two is called the

    (A) total fertility rate.
    (B) replacement rate.
    (C) natural increase.
    (D) natural decrease.
    (E) life expectancy.

70. Maps like the one shown here are referred to as

(A) perceptual regions.
(B) false maps.
(C) nodes.
(D) cognitive maps.
(E) functional regions.

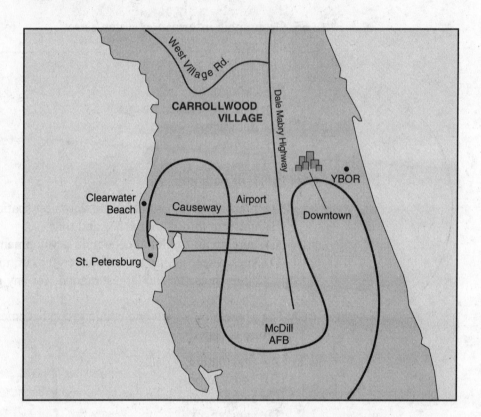

71. In Rostow's stages of development model, economic maturity is characterized by

(A) sustainability.
(B) high mass consumption.
(C) gender empowerment.
(D) high per capita incomes.
(E) gross national happiness.

72. According to public opinion polls, more than 80% of Americans consider themselves "environmentalists." Which of the following could you logically conclude from this information?

(A) The American environment is on the verge of collapse.
(B) Americans are poorly informed on scientific issues.
(C) Americans are becoming increasingly liberal in their political views.
(D) Most Americans consider environmental issues to be important.
(E) On average, Americans are more politically liberal than Europeans.

73. Which of the following is true based on the map of global voluntary migration flows shown here?

(A) Europe is experiencing significant out migration.
(B) Colombians are leaving their homeland.
(C) Climate is a significant pull factor.
(D) Asians from a variety of countries are moving to the United States.
(E) Australians are global wanderers.

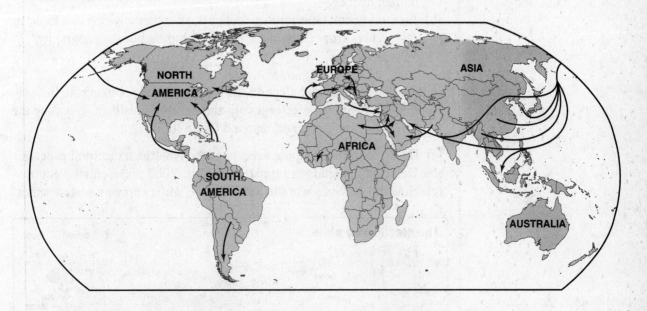

74. Religious fundamentalism

(A) appears to be on the rise in many parts of the world.
(B) is limited to the Middle East.
(C) is limited to the Deep South.
(D) is decreasing globally.
(E) is a serious political issue in Western Europe.

75. Which of the following is not correct regarding the great metropolises of the developing world?

(A) They contain both great wealth and tremendous poverty.
(B) Many retain architectural elements of their colonial past.
(C) Most have squatter settlements on their outskirts.
(D) Because their economies are less developed, they rarely suffer from significant pollution.
(E) They house an increasing proportion of the world's population.

Free-Response Questions

Directions for free-response questions: Read each question carefully and write your essays on standard composition paper. At the actual exam, you will be given a bound booklet containing lined pages for your free-response essays.

1. Consider the concept of environmental determinism.

    (a) What implications does this theory have for the role of geography in human history?

    (b) Environmental determinism has been an extremely divisive topic for researchers from many disciplines, including human geography. Why is this so?

2. In the 2000 presidential election, Al Gore won the popular vote but George Bush won the electoral vote and became president. Examine the following electoral map and respond to the following:

    (a) Describe the geographic aspects of the American electoral process.

    (b) Describe national voting patterns in the 2000 presidential election.

    (c) How did Al Gore win the popular vote while carrying so few states?

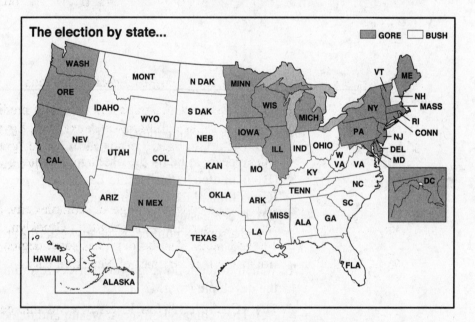

3. Deindustrialization occurs at the national level, the regional level, and even on the scale of individual neighborhoods as businesses move their operations to unincorporated suburbs and edge cities.

    (a) Give examples of deindustrialization at each of these three geographic scales and discuss the social and economic consequences of each.

    (b) What factors caused the deindustrialization of the American Rust Belt?

Answers and Explanations

Answers for Multiple-Choice Questions

1. D	16. B	31. D	46. A	61. C
2. E	17. A	32. B	47. A	62. B
3. B	18. E	33. A	48. E	63. D
4. C	19. C	34. C	49. C	64. D
5. A	20. D	35. E	50. C	65. A
6. B	21. A	36. C	51. A	66. D
7. B	22. B	37. D	52. E	67. C
8. C	23. A	38. A	53. D	68. D
9. A	24. C	39. B	54. D	69. C
10. E	25. A	40. C	55. A	70. D
11. B	26. E	41. A	56. D	71. B
12. C	27. C	42. C	57. B	72. D
13. B	28. C	43. C	58. C	73. D
14. C	29. C	44. C	59. C	74. A
15. D	30. C	45. D	60. C	75. D

Explanations for Multiple-Choice Questions

1. **(D)** The word geography is generally credited to Eratosthenes, who served as the head librarian at Alexandria, Egypt, during the third century B.C. The prefix "geo" means earth, while "graphy" means writing. Photography is a similar word, which literally means "writing with light."

2. **(E)** As an extremely large and complex city, New York has been divided into five boroughs—Manhattan, Brooklyn, the Bronx, Queens, and Staten Island. Each borough has some degree of autonomy in local governance, yet all are part of New York City.

3. **(B)** Countries at low levels of economic development, where women have few opportunities to become educated or participate in the government or economy, tend to have the highest growth rates. Namibia is an excellent example.

4. **(C)** Distance decay functions show how the connectivity between two places decreases with distance. The slope of the line on a distance decay function tells us how each unit of distance affects connectivity. Thus, if the friction of distance is strong, then small increases in distance will significantly affect overall connectivity and the slope of the function will be steep. If the friction of distance is weak, then each extra unit of distance separating the two places will have only a minor effect on connectivity, and the slope of the function will be shallow.

5. **(A)** An azimuthal perspective of the earth is one in which the viewer looks down directly on one of the poles.

6. **(B)** Hierarchical diffusion occurs when something is transmitted from one place to another because the two places have some common characteristic. In this case, Los Angeles, Oakland, Chicago, and Detroit all have large African-American populations that, early on, were highly receptive to rap music and hip hop culture in general. In relocation diffusion, someone brings something with them when they move from one place to another. This is also different from contagious diffusion, whereby something is passed from one person to another simply because they are in proximity to each other.

7. **(B)** Although cartographers may also study various aspects of human geography, such as demographics or spatial behavior, cartography is the art and science of map-making.

8. **(C)** Slash-and-burn agriculture was, historically, practiced in a sustainable manner by native people in tropical regions across the globe. However, it has now become associated with population growth, migration, and tropical deforestation, in Brazil and elsewhere. It is not part of the Green Revolution, in which scientists and government officials sought to increase crop yield through state-of-the-art irrigation systems, new crop strains, and other technological advances. As you may recall, the Green Revolution has had mixed results, and a variety of unintended consequences.

9. **(A)** Population pyramids consist of two sides: a male side and a female side. They tell us the proportion of males and females at a given age, the overall age structure of the population, and the total population, but they can also give us hints as to the population history of the area being depicted.

10. **(E)** The Pleistocene overkill theory is one explanation for the fact that, at about the same times that Eurasian hunter-gatherers invaded Australia, North America, and the various Pacific Islands, large numbers of animals went extinct. In North America, these animals include saber-toothed tigers, woolly mammoths, giant ground sloths, and other members of, what paleontologists call, the Pleistocene megafauna.

11. **(B)** Population is certainly a growing problem that puts direct pressure on the earth's ecosystems and natural resources. However, overconsumption by some wealthy countries, particularly the United States, also drives environmental degradation. While the United States has only a few percent of the world's population, it consumes approximately one-fifth of its resources.

12. (C) Idiographic information applies to one place. The prefix "idio" implies uniqueness, just as in the word "idiosyncratic." Nomothetic information is universally applicable.

13. (B) Although 2,000 years may seem like a short time to traverse the entire western hemisphere from north to south, it only amounts to a few miles of expansion each year. The Eurasian invasion of North America was rapid, dramatic, and comprehensive.

14. (C) The demographic accounting equation takes into account both intrinsic factors (natural increase) and extrinsic factors (immigration and emigration), to compute overall population change in a particular place.

15. (D) This map depicts a city that conforms to the sector model, in which various sectors radiate out from the center city like the spokes of a wheel. This type of urban organization contrasts with cities that have concentric rings of specific types of development emanating out from the center, like Chicago, and with cities that have many distinct nodes of activity within the larger urban area, like Los Angeles.

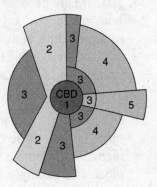

16. (B) Lines of longitude, which all converge at the North and South Poles, measure angular distance east and west in the same way that lines of latitude measure distance north and south. If you were to go to the center of the earth and measure the angle looking outward to any place on the surface of the earth, either east or west of the prime meridian, then you would get that location's longitude. The prime meridian is at 0° longitude and the International Date Line is centered on 180° longitude, on the opposite side of the earth. Interestingly, the International Date Line wavers back and forth a bit in the Pacific Ocean in order to circumvent political boundaries and important physical features.

17. **(A)** Postmodernism is an incredibly complex and diverse movement that generally speaks out against the rationalistic modernism so prevalent in art, design, philosophy, and social theory throughout the first half of the 20th century. Postmodernists tend to bring the human factor back to such pursuits and to resist monolithic, overarching explanations in favor of a myriad of different, and sometimes discordant, voices.

18. **(E)** A cultural syncretism occurs when two or more different cultures or cultural traits converge to form something new.

19. **(C)** In the demographic transition model, countries go through a series of stages, from extremely low levels of economic production and low rates of population growth, to higher levels of economic production and extremely high levels of population growth, to very high levels of economic production, high per capita incomes, and low levels of population growth. In the middle phase, birth rates dramatically outpace death rates, while in the first and second phases, birth rates and death rates are more closely aligned with each other.

20. **(D)** Many geographers, ecologists, and medical researchers have noted that indigenous knowledge about nature can be extremely helpful in understanding ecosystems and in locating potential organisms for biomedical research. However, with decreasing cultural diversity, such knowledge is inevitably being lost.

21. **(A)** Another way to think about cartographic representation is to divide maps up into those used for reference and those that focus on a specific theme. An example of a reference map would be a road map or even a globe. An example of a thematic map would be a dot map that shows instances of petty crimes in the London metropolitan area.

22. **(B)** Buddhism, one of the three great world religions, began in the Indian subcontinent and then spread across central and eastern Asia.

23. **(A)** Federalism implies territorial organization. In territorial organization, national governments divide up their land base into smaller units, such as states and counties. These smaller units assume some level of autonomy in issues of local governance and representation.

24. **(C)** The world's core nations include the wealthy nations of the north, including Japan, while the peripheral and semiperipheral countries are mostly located in Asia, South America, and Africa.

25. (A)   Cultural ecology is a general term that applies to a wide variety of research in many different fields, including geography, history, anthropology, sociology, and others. In general, cultural ecologists work to understand the relationship between people and their environments, over both space and time.

26. (E)   The term "balkanization" refers to the breakup of a state into its smaller constituents for any reason, including ethnic divisions, varying levels of economic development, external pressure, or other centripetal forces.

27. (C)   The curve of this distance decay function is steep, indicating that connectivity decreases significantly with distance. If the line were perfectly horizontal, there would be no friction associated with distance, and if the line were vertical, then there would be complete friction and no interaction over any measurable space. In reality, all distance decay functions fall within these two extremes.

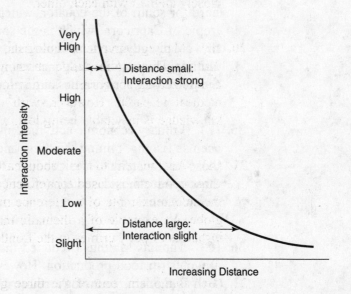

28. (C)   Language extinctions can result from cultural imperialism or genocide; however, the single most important fact about the current geography of language is that diversity is being lost at a rapid rate.

29. (C)   A country need not have official rule over another in order to dominate it. Imperialism can include cultural, political, or any other form of external control. Colonialism includes official, organized political and military rule.

30. (C)   In forced migration, people leave an area for reasons beyond their own choice. Other, more-specific examples include religious persecution, ethnic cleansing, and drought.

31. **(D)** The Canadian province of Quebec stands out because of its heritage of French language and culture. As a result, many of Quebec's citizens have sought to establish their own French-speaking state. Since 1995, this movement has waned considerably.

32. **(B)** Environmental racism is any activity that causes people of a particular racial or ethnic group to be purposefully disproportionately exposed to environmental hazards or pollution, or for such a group to have decreased access to environmental amenities, such as clean water or open space.

33. **(A)** It is important to remember that, although economic productivity is an important indicator of human welfare, consumption of resources associated with such activities also produces pollution that can be damaging both to the environment and to human health.

34. **(C)** Lines of latitude, which are all parallel, measure angular distance north or south of the equator, which is at 0° latitude. For example, the tropic of Capricorn, which is the southernmost point at which the sun's rays are directly overhead during the course of a year, is located at 23.5°S latitude. This implies that, measuring from the center of the earth's core, the tropic of Capricorn lies at an angle 23.5°S of the equator.

35. **(E)** Primary economic activities involve only the most basic endeavors, such as fishing, mining, hunting, and farming. Secondary activities turn those raw materials into product. Tertiary activities transport and sell those products, and quaternary activities involve services, research, and development.

36. **(C)** Thomas Malthus predicted that population growth would eventually outstrip food production. However, he failed to account for factors such as modern technology, redistribution of food resources, and voluntary birth control.

37. **(D)** In the past 40 years, the richest countries have gotten considerably richer, while the poorest countries have gotten poorer.

38. **(A)** In the gravity model, two places are increasingly "attracted" (connected), the bigger they are and the closer together they are to each other. Rio de Janeiro and Sao Paulo, Brazil, are two extremely large cities that are located very close to each other, thus they are very tightly connected, in terms of economics, politics, and so on. New York and Los Angeles are much farther away; however they are both extremely large and thus highly connected. In its most basic form, the gravity model does not take into account national borders, language, or other political, cultural, or physical boundaries.

39. (B) Southern Appalachia and the lower Mississippi Valley are both regional economic peripheries. Their economies are relatively sluggish and both areas failed to benefit from the growth of the Sun Belt or from expanding service and high-tech economies.

40. (C) Although the poor quality of many rainforest soils has been known for hundreds of years, it has been frequently ignored by farmers, politicians, and others who have attempted to impose technological innovations from the north on a tropical ecosystem.

41. (A) Choropleth maps all use shading and coloring to depict geographic information. Such information is represented as being uniform over some defined space, such as a county or voting precinct. Isolines are common on topographic maps, weather maps, and other types of maps where data values vary continually over space. Dot maps depict individual occurrences, while graphs and charts associate specific data values with geographic areas.

42. (C) Examples include early agricultural civilizations in the Fertile Crescent, the Nile River Valley, India, and China.

43. (C) Whereas the Gross National Product only measures the economic benefits of production, the Net National Product takes into account the depreciation of natural capital associated with such production. For example, when a forest is clear-cut, the GNP counts the money made from the sale of the timber as an economic benefit, but the NNP attempts to also calculate the capital lost by no longer having those trees in the forest to provide things like clean air and water, store carbon, promote wildlife habitat, and grow larger for future harvest.

44. (C) People of Kurdish descent live in Iraq, Turkey, Iran, and Syria, yet the Kurdish people do not have their own country. Peoples such as the Kurds, who have a unified political identity but who lack self-determination, are often referred to as nations without states.

45. (D) In the book *Edge City*, Joel Garreau described Tyson's Corner, Virginia, as an example of the new urban environment—a sprawling, unincorporated suburban area on the outskirts of a major city, in this case, Washington, D.C.

46. (A) China, India, Turkey, and Mexico were among the first areas to develop independently sedentary, agricultural societies.

47. (A) In Von Thunen's model, agricultural land use changes the farther away from the city center you get, primarily due to land and commodity values. Expensive, perishable commodities are grown closer to urban markets, while less expensive, more expansive (in terms of the land area necessary for production) agricultural industries are located farther from the city center.

48. (E) Another example of the City Beautiful movement, which is characterized by grand neoclassical architecture, monuments, and dramatically organized open spaces, is Chicago. Chicago is centrally planned, with a vast system of parks, museums, and public open space areas along the Lake Michigan shore.

49. (C) The central place theory describes the organization of urban areas in a region or country. According to this theory, there should be a few large centers that provide a wide range of goods and services surrounded by a matrix of smaller cities, towns, and hamlets that offer increasingly fewer products and enticements. The central place is the large area that dominates the region and that people travel to for a variety of needs.

50. (C) Although many of San Francisco's older Victorian structures were destroyed during the 1906 earthquake and fire, many survived, and some were rebuilt. Ornate and playful residential architecture was quite popular at the time and still remains attractive today.

51. (A) The north/south divide is largely an economic one, brought about by underdevelopment in the southern countries of Asia, Africa, and Latin America and a legacy of northern colonial and imperial domination.

52. (E) During the late 19th and early 20th century, Chicago became known as the birthplace of the skyscraper. Architects designed Chicago's great skyscrapers using new materials such as concrete and steel beams in an attempt to demonstrate the city's role as the imperial center of the western United States and its central place in western commerce, culture, and financial markets.

53. (D) Cultural traditions, mores, physical geography, isolation, and other factors have all contributed to the island of New Guinea's extreme linguistic diversity.

54. (D) By 2020, rapidly growing Asian megacities such as Beijing, China; Mumbai, India; and Karachi, Pakistan, will be among the biggest in the world.

55. **(A)**   The city of Istanbul, and Turkey in general, is located at a strategic position between Europe, Asia, and the Middle East. As a result, it is a city of great historical importance and cultural diversity. During the next century, it will also become one of the world's largest cities.

56. **(D)**   There are two types of scale. Cartographic scale is the ratio of units on a map to units on the earth's surface. A typical U.S. Geological Survey Quadrangle is drawn at a scale of 1:24,000, meaning that one unit on the map equals 24,000 units on the earth's surface. Geographic scale refers to a hierarchy of places that geographers describe based on their observations of the real world. One example of such a hierarchy occurs in urban geography, where a neighborhood is generally smaller than a town, which is smaller than a city, which is smaller than a metropolis, which is smaller than a megalopolis.

57. **(B)**   During the Colonial Period, native people throughout the western hemisphere were exposed to virulent diseases that had previously been limited to Europe, Africa, and Asia. In many places, diseases such as small pox eliminated up to 95% of the precontact native population.

58. **(C)**   Excellent examples of primate cities include London, Paris, Tokyo, and Lagos, Nigeria. New York is also a primate city, although Los Angeles, Chicago, San Francisco, and Washington, D.C., each claim a significant share of national power.

59. **(C)**   An example of a diaspora is the community of Jews that are spread throughout the world.

60. **(C)**   All projections are a compromise between distortions in area, shape, distance, and direction. Some projections are more appropriate for some uses; for example, the Mercator projection maintains accurate compass direction and, as a result, it is useful for navigation. The Robinson projection balances various distortions to create a map that is well proportioned and aesthetically pleasing.

61. **(C)**   During the 16th century, attempts to reform the Catholic Church led to political and social strife throughout Europe and resulted in the formation of Protestantism. Protestantism has been evolving ever since and now includes dozens of denominations throughout the world.

62. **(B)**   Gentrification is the process by which older neighborhoods become more attractive, increase in cost of living, and attract wealthier individuals and families. This was common throughout the United States in the 1990s, as older urban neighborhoods became more attractive for young professionals. Other examples of recently gentrified neighborhoods include Evanston, Illinois, on the north side of Chicago; Ybor City in Tampa, Florida; and Brooklyn in New York City.

63. (D)   The Great Lakes region boomed with heavy industry during the first half of the twentieth century. During this period, cities such as Detroit, Michigan, and Gary, Indiana, became models of industrial growth and success. However, by the late 1980s, such places had become part of the Great Lakes Rust Belt, a deindustrialized, economically depressed region full of vacant factories and stalled assembly lines. With the exception of a few cities, like Chicago, the region has never fully recovered.

64. (D)   Mexico City, like other primate cities, is by far the largest, most important, most productive, and most powerful city in its parent country. Other primate cities include Paris, Tokyo, and London.

65. (A)   Each thematic layer includes a different set of data, such as roads, topography, per capita income, or instances of violent crime. When all of the layers are combined, they form a rich and complex map that can tell us a great deal about the relationship between a variety of different geographic variables.

66. (D)   For example, Chicago has historically been an important break of bulk point for commodities such as beef, timber, and wheat that were grown or harvested in the western states and are being sold and prepared for shipment to the eastern seaboard.

67. (C)   Assimilation is frequently confused with syncretism, which is when two cultures merge to form something new. The term "melting pot" was popular in the United States in the early part of 20th century to describe the process by which many cultures become assimilated into a larger, generic American culture. This notion has now been replaced by the "alphabet soup" metaphor, which reminds us that many different cultures persist inside the United States without becoming subsumed by the larger culture.

68. (D)   The dependency ratio refers to the percentage of people in a population who are either too old or too young to work, and thus must rely on the productive labor of others to meet their needs.

69. (C)   The term "natural increase" refers to the difference between the crude birth rate and crude death rate. Natural increase includes only factors that are internal to the population. It does not include immigration or emigration.

70. (D)   Cognitive maps are expressions of people's perceptions of place. In this figure, someone familiar with the city of Tampa drew a map that reflects his own ideas of that place, including important landmarks, barriers, and transportation routes.

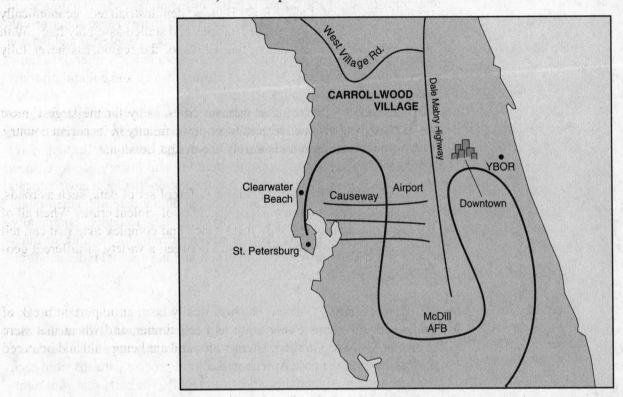

71. (B)   In Rostow's model, countries evolve from low levels of economic productivity and mass consumption, through several stages of investment and development, to a state of high productivity, high per capita incomes, and high mass consumption.

72. (D)   The other answers may be true or false; the question provided has not given us any information either way. However, we know that public opinion polls indicate that most Americans do call themselves environmentalists and are concerned about environmental problems.

73. (D)   Numerous arrows from Southeast Asia, central Asia, the Korean peninsula, and the Indian subcontinent all converge on the United States, indicating significant migration.

74. (A)   Religious fundamentalism is indeed on the rise in many areas throughout the world and is no way solely limited to Islam or the Middle East.

75. (D)   Great metropolises of the developing world, such as Sao Paulo, Brazil; Jakarta, Indonesia; Lagos, Nigeria; and Mumbai, India, all suffer from terrible pollution.

Answers for Free-Response Questions

1. Environmental determinism is the idea that cultures and the events of history are determined by natural factors. For example, environmental determinists might argue that, because of the climates and landscapes of Western Europe, superior cultures developed there. These superior cultures were then able to colonize and dominate people throughout the world who, because of their environments, were innately inferior to Europeans. This theory basically reduces human history and cultural diversity to being determined by physical geography.

   Because environmental determinism has so many derogatory racial and cultural undertones, and because it is frequently associated with racist totalitarian regimes, such as the Nazis, most intellectuals have discredited it as a way of explaining culture and history. However, new theories, such as possibilism, which is the notion that local environments to some extent place limits on societies but do not determine their qualities, have gained considerable support in the academic community. Within the field of geography, the notion of human-environment interactions has become especially important and has revived older subdisciplines such as cultural ecology.

2. The United States has a federal system of government. This means that the country is divided up into smaller territories that have some degree of political autonomy. In the American electoral process, citizens from each state vote for a presidential candidate and party. The party that wins nominates a set of electors who have pledged to cast a ballot for that party's candidate. Each state chooses its own electors, the number of which are based on that state's population.

   In the 2000 presidential election, Al Gore barely won the popular vote by capturing significant majorities in many of the most populated states, in particular New York and California. Although more populous states also have more electoral votes, Gore fell just a few hundred votes short of capturing Florida, and thus lost all that state's electoral votes and the presidency itself. George W. Bush won most of the smaller, more rural states, including every southern state.

   This outcome has significant implications for the American electoral system. Many people were upset that, although Gore won the popular vote, Bush won the presidency. In addition, the fact that the margin of victory was so close in Florida, yet when Bush won he took all of Florida's electoral votes exposed another potential problem in the system. It is unlikely that the American electoral system will change any time soon. However, the 2000 election showed Americans, and people throughout the world, some of the potential problems associated with various forms of geographic representation.

3. Deindustrialization can occur at a variety of geographic scales. At the national level, deindustrialization has plagued countries such as Great Britain, which led the Industrial Revolution in the 18th and 19th centuries, but by the mid-20th century had lost much of its heavy industry to countries where production costs were lower. Britain's current economy is geared more toward tertiary and quaternary economic activities; however, many blue collar workers still struggle to make ends meet in the new economy. At the regional level, the Great Lakes region of the United States was one of the world's foremost industrial centers during the early and mid-20th century. During the 1970s and 1980s the area lost much of its industrial activities to developing countries like Mexico. This resulted in widespread unemployment and spurred outward migration of midwesterners to Sun Belt states, where more opportunity awaited. Finally, at the local level, many industrial facilities have left their former locations in the inner city and moved to outlying suburbs, rural locations, and edge cities. In cities like Chicago, this has caused unemployment in the inner city, changed transportation patterns, and caused suburban sprawl.

Deindustrialization in the American Rust Belt occurred in the late 1970s and early 1980s when multinational corporations, like General Motors, began moving their facilities to countries with lower production costs, like Mexico. Multinational corporations, such as GM, exploit economic and political differences between countries in order to lower production costs and increase profits. Mexico's lower costs were largely the result of financial incentives and low wages. Deindustrialization caused an economic boom in some Mexican manufacturing towns but led to the decline of America's former industrial heartland.

Practice Test 2

Test

Multiple-Choice Questions

Directions: Read each question carefully and choose the correct response. If you are unsure of the correct answer, be careful of guessing wildly—a ¼-point penalty is given for each incorrect answer.

1. The Demographic Transition Theory states that, as a nation develops economically

   (A) birth rates decrease, then death rates decrease, and population increases.
   (B) death rates decrease, then birth rates decrease, and population levels off.
   (C) birth rates and death rates both increase simultaneously.
   (D) birth rates decrease while all else remains constant.
   (E) birth and death rates remain constant over time.

2. The center and place of origin of a cultural tradition is called a

   (A) culture center.
   (B) cultural complex.
   (C) cultural trait.
   (D) culture hearth.
   (E) cultural genesis.

3. Demographic information from the U.S. Census affects the political process by

   (A) determining the amount of electoral votes given to each state.
   (B) determining the amount of congressional delegates given to each state.
   (C) determining the amount of federal aid given to various political jurisdictions.
   (D) All of the above
   (E) None of the above

4. Multinational corporations take advantage of geographic differences in

(A) wage rates.
(B) labor laws.
(C) the distribution of natural resources.
(D) relaxed environmental standards.
(E) all of the above.

5. Swidden agriculture can have negative environmental impacts if

(A) the period of fallow is too short for proper nutrient regeneration.
(B) the human population becomes too low in a region.
(C) the practice is combined with livestock raising.
(D) All of the above
(E) None of the above, swidden agriculture is environmentally benign

6. Which of the following U.S. regions has seen the most population growth since 1945?

(A) The Black Belt
(B) The Sun Belt
(C) The Rust Belt
(D) The Citrus Belt
(E) The Cotton Belt

7. Increased air pollution, segregation, habitat destruction, inner-city decay, and loss of productive farmlands are all caused by

(A) climate change.
(B) urban sprawl.
(C) postmodernism.
(D) ozone depletion.
(E) gentrification.

8. The Italian language varies significantly between Milan, Rome, Naples, and Palermo. These varieties are examples of

(A) pidgins.
(B) lingua franca.
(C) language groups.
(D) dialects.
(E) idioms.

9. In a spatial context, multinational corporations tend to

(A) have localized headquarters and dispersed production centers.
(B) be situated in many countries.
(C) move production centers quite quickly.
(D) situate themselves to minimize costs and maximize influence.
(E) All of the above

10. Which of these figures demonstrates the largest dependency ratio?

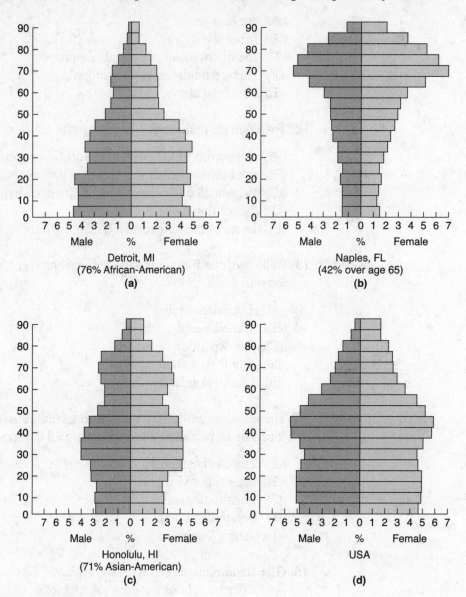

(A) Figure a
(B) Figure b
(C) Figure c
(D) Figure d
(E) Not enough information to answer the question

11. Isolines are common on which of the following?

    (A) Globes
    (B) Atlases
    (C) Cartograms
    (D) Topographical maps
    (E) Dot maps

12. The term "transhumance" refers to

    (A) nomadic pastoralism that is seasonal.
    (B) slash-and-burn agriculture.
    (C) the mobility of an advanced economic society.
    (D) the movement of liquid in plants.
    (E) the movement of soil on a hillside.

13. Religious practices, language, and dietary preferences, when combined, form a

    (A) cultural complex.
    (B) cultural hearth.
    (C) dialect.
    (D) idiom.
    (E) cultural trait.

14. These makeshift neighborhoods, constructed of scrap materials, are found in all of the world's large peripheral cities.

    (A) Squatter settlements
    (B) Edge cities
    (C) Swidden lands
    (D) Regional centers
    (E) Gentrified districts

15. Globalization involves

    (A) an ever-widening spatial scale of economic and social activities.
    (B) increased systems of linkages between places and people.
    (C) a parallel, localization effect.
    (D) (A) and (B)
    (E) (A), (B), and (C)

16. Which of the graphs depicts Malthus' hypothesis regarding food production?

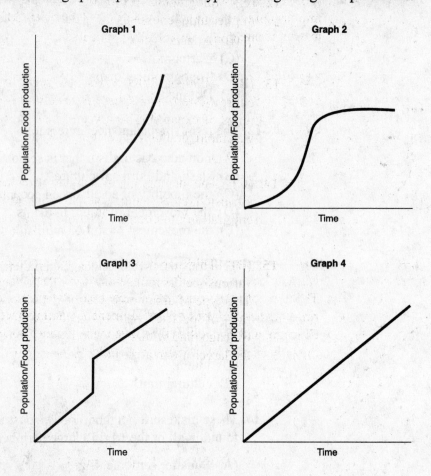

(A) Graph 1
(B) Graph 2
(C) Graph 3
(D) Graph 4
(E) None of the graphs represents Malthus' view of food production.

17. The language family spoken by the most people on earth today is

(A) Germanic.
(B) English.
(C) Indo-European.
(D) Sino-Tibetan.
(E) Latin.

18. Nomadic herding is associated with

(A) pastoralism.
(B) swidden.
(C) agribusiness.
(D) deindustrialization.
(E) dairying.

19. Which of the following is an example of a nation without a state?

    (A) Israel
    (B) Palestine
    (C) Texas
    (D) Jamaica
    (E) Yugoslavia

20. In the pre-industrial phase of urban settlement in the United States, the economy was dominated by:

    (A) tertiary activities.
    (B) quaternary activities.
    (C) primary activities.
    (D) secondary activities.
    (E) (A) and (D)

21. Based on this map of Los Angeles which urban model does it most closely correspond to?

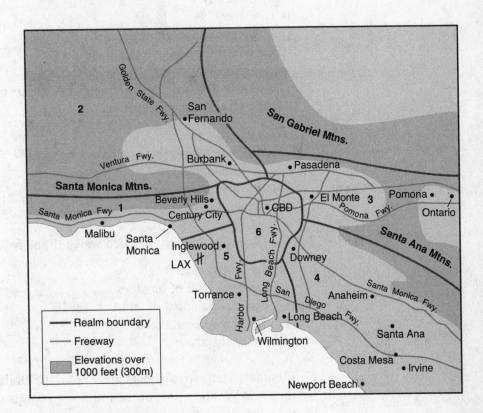

    (A) Multiple-nuclei model
    (B) Sector model
    (C) Concentric zone model
    (D) Mixed land use model
    (E) Urban corridor model

22. Gentrification can be described as

(A) a revitalizing force against urban decay.
(B) a segregating force between rich and poor.
(C) a cohesive force uniting urban activities.
(D) (A), (B), and (C)
(E) (A) and (B)

23. The nomothetic view of geography suggests that

(A) universal laws guide all spatial patterns in the world.
(B) similarities between places can be explained using universal laws.
(C) individual places can be sufficiently explained with models.
(D) individual places are unique.
(E) all spatial scales can be modeled equally well.

24. Which of the following could qualify as a barrier to spatial diffusion?

(A) An ocean
(B) A freeway
(C) A river
(D) An affluent neighborhood
(E) All of the above

25. The weakly defined political boundary regions of Antarctica and the Amazon Basin are examples of

(A) *maquiladoras.*
(B) regional backwaters.
(C) cultural cohorts.
(D) frontiers.
(E) functional regions.

26. The Green Revolution included which of the following?

(A) Irrigation projects
(B) Increased use of biocides
(C) The development of "miracle seeds"
(D) Hybridization methods
(E) All of the above

27. If both you and your parents grew up in the United States, and your dad fought in WWII, which of the following cohorts do you probably belong to?

(A) Generation X
(B) Generation Y
(C) the Beatnik generation
(D) Baby boom
(E) Baby bust

28. Which of the following represents the forced migration event pictured on the map?

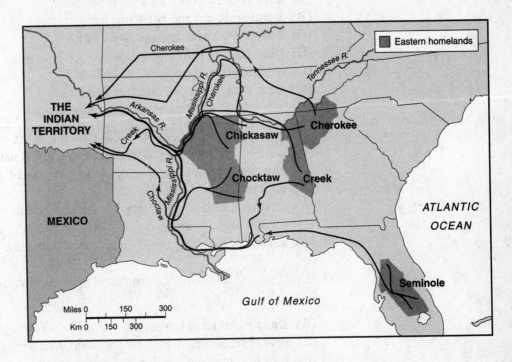

(A) Caribbean-American walk of shame
(B) Trail of Tears
(C) The Great Oakie dustbowl migration
(D) French natives forced out of Louisiana in 1829
(E) African-Americans forced to move north to work industrial jobs in the late 1800s

29. Mexico's *maquiladoras* are located within

(A) offshore financial centers.
(B) developmental conglomerates.
(C) export-processing zones.
(D) ecotourism destinations.
(E) the United States, just along the United States-Mexico border.

30. The United Nations is a(n)

(A) confederacy.
(B) international organization.
(C) supranational organization.
(D) disorganization.
(E) transnational organization.

31. The three world cities that exercise the greatest degree of global economic dominance are

    (A) London, Paris, and Moscow.
    (B) Tokyo, Mexico City, and Sao Paulo.
    (C) New York, London, and Tokyo.
    (D) Los Angeles, New York, and Madrid.
    (E) New York, Chicago, and Los Angeles.

32. Overgrazing, deforestation, and agricultural mismanagement are all significant causes of

    (A) crop failure.
    (B) nationalism.
    (C) urban growth.
    (D) topsoil loss.
    (E) salinization.

33. Which of the following statements is false concerning human spatial behavior?

    (A) Daily patterns of movement are fairly predictable.
    (B) People frequently travel far for basic necessities.
    (C) People's movement is limited by the available transportation.
    (D) People tend to avoid perceived hazards.
    (E) People tend to move around more in their local environment.

34. The degree of connectedness between places is referred to as

    (A) isoline scale.
    (B) topological space.
    (C) diffusion potential.
    (D) deep space.
    (E) topographic space.

35. Which of the following is a problematic characteristic of most definitions of sustainable development?

    (A) They are anthropocentric and only focus on future human needs.
    (B) They focus solely on the earth's future well being without considering growing human populations.
    (C) They focus only on certain resources, failing to neglect preservation of all the earth's stocks.
    (D) They encourage only subsistence economies, neglecting development initiatives for commercial economies.
    (E) They ignore developing country's population problems.

36. Mecca represents the geographical focal point of which religion?

(A) Judaism
(B) Hinduism
(C) Buddhism
(D) Taoism
(E) Islam

37. Which of the following is not an example of a frontier?

(A) Antarctica
(B) Pacific Ocean
(C) Historical American West
(D) Amazon Basin
(E) Lake Michigan

38. A Pakistani man moves his entire family to a predominantly Pakistani neighborhood in London where he and his community maintain many of their cultural traditions. This describes

(A) diorama.
(B) diaspora.
(C) multicultural enclave.
(D) Pakistani ghetto.
(E) gentrified community.

39. Which of the following initiatives help a city fight urban sprawl?

(A) Efficient transportation policies
(B) Urban growth boundaries
(C) Economic incentives for locating in downtown areas
(D) All of the above
(E) Only (A) and (B)

40. Which of the following does not represent an extensive commercial agricultural activity?

(A) Ranching
(B) Plantation farming
(C) Dairying
(D) Nomadic herding
(E) Feeder grain production

41. In 1926, the famous geographer Ellsworth Huntington came back from traveling with his friend, Raphael Pumpelly, in southwestern Asia. Based on his investigations, Huntington promoted in his textbooks the idea that cultural changes were strongly influenced by climatic change. Huntington's ideas represent the philosophy of

(A) possibilism.
(B) positivism.
(C) environmental determinism.
(D) cultural determinism.
(E) postmodernism.

42. Transnational corporations generally locate facilities outside of national boundaries to take advantage of

(A) cheaper labor.
(B) proximity to local markets.
(C) relaxed environmental standards.
(D) both (A) and (C)
(E) (A), (B), and (C)

43. After the 2000 Census, lines were redrawn around districts to ensure maximum political fairness. When districts are drawn specifically to favor a particular political party or voting block, it is called

(A) salamandering.
(B) reapportionment.
(C) gentrification.
(D) gerrymandering.
(E) pork bellying.

44. The von Thunen model describes agricultural activity as it takes place in relation to the market. Which of the following statements generally represents the agricultural landscape according to the model?

(A) Agricultural activity is solely determined by the longevity of the agricultural product; thus things that don't last long grow near the market.
(B) Goods that are expensive to transport and spoil quickly must be located closer to the market.
(C) Smaller agricultural goods like beans, herbs, and berries will be grown closer to the market than bigger goods like pumpkins.
(D) Animals will be located closer to the market, like grazing cattle and hens, because they are difficult to move.
(E) Dairy products like milk, eggs, and cheese will be far from the market as they do not cost much to transport.

45. Kevin Lynch's book has had a dramatic impact on urban planners as it provided

(A) a framework for understanding the legibility of urban environments.

(B) maps of activity spaces for individuals from different cities across the country.

(C) descriptions of the best methods for encouraging use of mass forms of transportation.

(D) survey results from people from all sorts of different cities on architectural preferences.

(E) study results from a test researching woman's fear of urban environments.

46. According to the gravity model, distance may not greatly affect level of interaction if:

(A) populations are extremely large.

(B) populations are extremely small.

(C) distance is extremely large.

(D) (B) and (C)

(E) None of the above

47. Which of the following statements is not an accurate description of globalization?

(A) Antiglobalization proponents argue that it tears the fabric weaving local communities together.

(B) Globalization has encouraged a counter-process of localization.

(C) The Internet is a driving force behind current patterns of globalization.

(D) Many argue that it's nothing new but rather a process that's been occurring over the last several centuries.

(E) It encourages economic development across the entire globe.

48. Which of the following does not represent an international organization?

(A) NAFTA

(B) EU

(C) OPEC

(D) NATO

(E) CIA

49. This form of agriculture takes place in each of the highlighted regions on the map

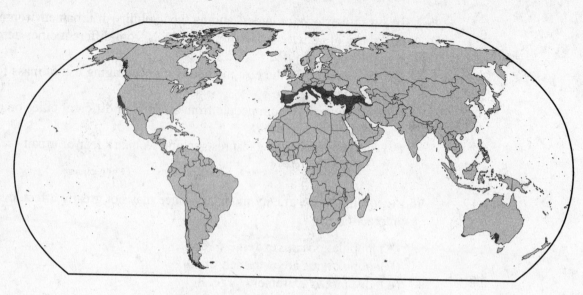

(A) Intensive subsistence agriculture
(B) Mediterranean agriculture
(C) Organic grape farming
(D) Intensive aquaculture
(E) Livestock raising in feedlots

50. Two mountain towns with unique languages develop a new simple language, understood by both groups, for trade purposes. What is this called?

(A) Trade dialect
(B) Lingua franca
(C) Linguistic diaspora
(D) Threat to language extinction
(E) Both (A) and (C)

51. Many European cities characterized by narrow winding streets and an ornate church inherited their organization from which type of cities

(A) Renaissance
(B) Medieval
(C) Industrial
(D) Baroque
(E) Classical

52. Developing countries generally demonstrate dominance in which economic sector?

(A) Quaternary sector
(B) Basic sector
(C) Tertiary sector
(D) Primary sector
(E) Nonbasic sector

53. Which of the following best describes the shape of the state of Thailand?

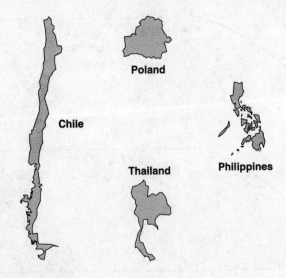

(A) Prorupted
(B) Rectangular
(C) Elongated
(D) Compact
(E) Perforated

54. Hearth regions of early agriculture included present-day

(A) China, India, Peru, and Mexico.
(B) China, India, Sudan, and Malaysia.
(C) India, Ethiopia, Greece, and Morocco.
(D) Anatolia, Peru, Borneo, and Hanalee.
(E) California, Illinois, New Brunswick, and Ireland.

55. Which of the following is not descriptive of spatial patterns of literacy?

(A) It was a powerful tool contributing to colonial dominance.
(B) It is often used as a means to limit educational opportunities for women by tyrannical governments.
(C) The historical development of alphabets largely explains dominant languages across the globe today.
(D) Literacy rates vary little between developed and developing nations.
(E) In general, literacy rates are increasing across the globe.

56. The ratio between distance on a map and distance on the earth's surface is called the

(A) projection.
(B) resolution.
(C) scale.
(D) isoline.
(E) proruption.

57. Which of the following represent a synonymous relationship?

    (A) Nation : state
    (B) State : country
    (C) Territory : nation
    (D) Country : nation
    (E) Frontier : territory

58. The dark regions on this map would describe high rates for all of the following indicators of development except?

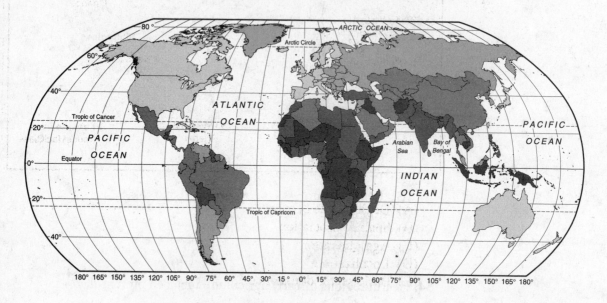

    (A) infant mortality rates.
    (B) growth rates.
    (C) infectious diseases.
    (D) literacy rates.
    (E) total fertility rates.

59. Which of the following processes often results from irrigation use in arid environments?

    (A) Topsoil loss
    (B) Salinization
    (C) Desertification
    (D) Gentrification
    (E) Alluviation

60. When several large urban areas essentially merge together to form an even larger urban complex, it's called a(n)

    (A) urban agglomeration.
    (B) megacity.
    (C) city conglomerate.
    (D) megolopolis.
    (E) megatropolis.

61. This map depicts the location of various economic activities across the United States. Based on your observations, which pattern emerges?

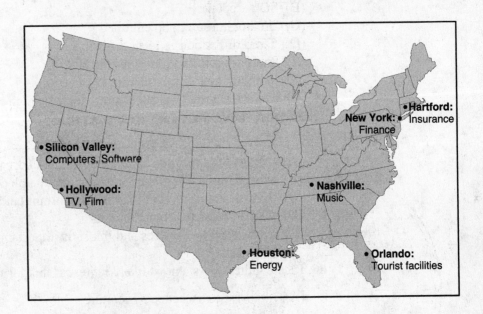

(A) Deglomerate economy
(B) Spatial association
(C) Agglomeration
(D) Localization
(E) Basic sector dominance

62. Total fertility rate is not closely correlated with which of the following?

(A) Industrial output
(B) Gender empowerment
(C) Education
(D) Economic development
(E) Literacy rates

63. Which of the following statements is not an accurate description of agribusiness?

(A) It has removed the family farm from its traditional role in agriculture.
(B) It has transformed agricultural production dramatically in terms of where and how agricultural goods are produced, marketed, and sold.
(C) It affects only the United States as one of the world's major agricultural producers.
(D) It allows for crossings of national boundaries in the production process.
(E) It has introduced more steps into what was once a more simple economic activity.

64. Elements of _____change rapidly over time, but not space, whereas elements of _____change very little over time, but dramatically over space.

(A) folk culture . . . pop culture
(B) rapid diffusion . . . local diffusion
(C) the fast world . . . the slow world
(D) pop culture . . . folk culture
(E) youth culture . . . elite culture

65. A cognitive map tells us

(A) the absolute location of features in the landscape.
(B) everything that someone knows about the place they live.
(C) the precise location of the most important landmarks.
(D) which projection to use.
(E) what someone believes and thinks is important about a place.

66. Rice paddies in Asia most likely represent this form of agriculture.

(A) Intensive-subsistence agriculture
(B) Extensive-commercial agriculture
(C) Planned agriculture on a community farm
(D) Capital-intensive agriculture
(E) Extensive-subsistence agriculture

67. You are a furniture maker and use pinewood to make tables and chairs. It costs about the same to ship the pinewood to your factory as it does to bring your furniture to the market as both have close to the same weight. Where do you put your factory in relation to the pine forest and the market to minimize transportation costs?

(A) Closer to the market
(B) Closer to the forest
(C) Anywhere you want in between them
(D) Closest to the nearest waste facility to minimize transportation costs of waste
(E) Farthest away from the other furniture maker to ensure maximum market

68. According to the rank-size rule, a city that has a rank of three

(A) would be the second city closest to that country's primate city.
(B) won third place in a country's survey of its inhabitants favorite cities.
(C) would contain approximately one-third of the urban amenities generally provided within that country.
(D) would contain one-third of the country's total urban population.
(E) would contain one-third the population of the country's largest city.

69. According to the United Nations Population Division, world population will reach 7 billion by

   (A) 2013.
   (B) 2045.
   (C) 2076.
   (D) It has already reached 7 billion
   (E) 2150.

70. An example of a basic economic occupation is

   (A) a supermarket clerk.
   (B) an automobile assembler.
   (C) a firefighter.
   (D) a city official.
   (E) a restaurateur.

71. A model is useful in that it

   (A) conveys the whole truth about a phenomenon.
   (B) eliminates the complexity associated with the world.
   (C) provides a comprehensible and limited view of a phenomenon.
   (D) relies completely on empirical data for confirmation or refutation.
   (E) eliminates the need to use math or quantify phenomena.

72. An example of a city that conforms to the concentric zone model of urban growth is

   (A) Los Angeles.
   (B) Chicago.
   (C) Calgary.
   (D) Boston.
   (E) Toronto.

73. These types of religions actively seek new members or believers

   (A) monotheistic religions.
   (B) ethnic religions.
   (C) global religions.
   (D) universalizing religions.
   (E) polytheistic religions.

74. Which of the following would not be characterized as a pull factor in a migration decision?

   (A) Educational opportunity.
   (B) Employment.
   (C) Agreeable climate.
   (D) Affordable housing.
   (E) Economic recession.

75. Economic activities that increase and thereby benefit from agglomerations in particular regions are called

(A) Ancillary activities.
(B) tertiary activities.
(C) basic sector services.
(D) quinary activities.
(E) specialty services.

Free-Response Questions

Directions for free-response questions: Read each question carefully and write your essays on standard composition paper. At the actual exam, you will be given a bound booklet containing lined pages for your free-response essays.

1. Agriculture has experienced dramatic changes throughout its history. Describe these transitions in terms of:

   (a) The areas where agriculture originated and some of the factors leading to this development.
   (b) The impacts of the Industrial Revolution, the Green Revolution, and the Biotechnologic Revolution.
   (c) The spatial implications of agribusiness.

2. Based on the information from this table

1950	Population	1980	Population	2010	Population
New York	12.3	Tokyo	21.9	Tokyo	28.8
London	8.7	New York	15.6	Mumbai (Bombay)	23.7
Tokyo	6.9	Mexico City	13.9	Lagos	21.0
Paris	5.4	São Paulo	12.1	São Paulo	19.7
Moscow	5.4	Shanghai	11.7	Mexico City	18.7
Shanghai	5.3	Osaka	10.0	New York	17.2
Essen	5.3	Buenos Aires	9.9	Karachi	16.7
Buenos Aires	5.0	Los Angeles	9.5	Dhaka	16.7
Chicago	4.9	Kolkata (Calcutta)	9.0	Shanghai	16.6
Kolkata (Calcutta)	4.4	Beijing	9.0	Kolkata (Calcutta)	15.6
Osaka	4.1	Paris	8.7	Delhi	15.2
Los Angeles	4.0	Rio de Janeiro	8.7	Beijing	14.3
Beijing	3.9	Seoul	8.3	Los Angeles	13.9
Milan	3.6	Moscow	8.2	Manila	13.7
Berlin	3.3	Mumbai (Bombay)	8.0	Buenos Aires	13.5
Mexico City	3.1	London	7.8	Cairo	13.2
Philadelphia	2.9	Tianjin	7.7	Seoul	12.9
St. Petersburg	2.9	Cairo	6.9	Jakarta	12.7
Mumbai (Bombay)	2.9	Chicago	6.8	Tianjin	12.4
Rio de Janeiro	2.9	Essen	6.7	Istanbul	11.7
Detroit	2.8	Jakarta	6.4	Rio de Janeiro	11.4
Naples	2.8	Metro Manila	6.0	Osaka	10.6
Manchester	2.5	Delhi	5.5	Guangzhou	10.3
São Paulo	2.4	Milan	5.4	Paris	9.7
Cairo	2.4	Tehran	5.4	Hyderabad	9.4
Tianjin	2.4	Karachi	5.0	Moscow	9.3
Birmingham	2.3	Bangkok	4.8	Teheran	9.2
Frankfurt	2.3	St. Petersburg	4.7	Lima	8.8
Boston	2.2	Hong Kong	4.5	Bangkok	8.8
Hamburg	2.2	Lima	4.4	Lahore	8.6

Source: Data, United Nations, *World Urbanization Prospects*. New York: U.N. Department of Economic and Social Affairs, 1998.

The World's Largest Metro Areas Ranked by Population Size 1950, 1980, and 2010.

(a) Describe how the general geographic spread of the world's major cities changes from 1950 until 2010.

(b) Discuss some of the possibilities for why the distribution has changed over this rather short period of time.

(c) Describe some of the issues geographers and policy makers will face in the future in terms of growth.

3. The geographic implications of colonialism surface throughout the many subareas of human geography.

(a) Discuss the geographic implications of colonialism in terms of language.

(b) Discuss the geographic implications of colonialism in terms of urban areas.

(c) Finally, discuss how colonialism might explain the core, semi-peripheral, and peripheral countries in terms of economic development.

Answers and Explanations

Answers for Multiple-Choice Questions

1. B	16. D	31. C	46. A	61. C
2. D	17. C	32. D	47. E	62. A
3. D	18. A	33. B	48. E	63. C
4. E	19. B	34. B	49. B	64. D
5. A	20. C	35. A	50. B	65. E
6. B	21. A	36. E	51. B	66. A
7. B	22. E	37. E	52. D	67. C
8. D	23. B	38. B	53. A	68. E
9. E	24. E	39. D	54. A	69. A
10. B	25. D	40. D	55. D	70. B
11. D	26. E	41. C	56. C	71. C
12. A	27. D	42. D	57. B	72. B
13. A	28. B	43. D	58. D	73. D
14. A	29. C	44. B	59. B	74. E
15. E	30. C	45. A	60. D	75. A

Explanations for Multiple-Choice Questions

1. **(B)** The demographic transition theory explains how a country's population changes through time as death and birth rates decrease. Initially country exhibits both high birth and death rates and experiences lit population growth. As death rates drop, the population beings to gr rapidly. Later, birth rates drop, and the population eventually stabilize

2. **(D)** A cultural hearth is the area where a particular cultural traditi originated. An agricultural hearth describes places where agriculture fi took place.

3. **(D)** The U.S. Census provides information critical to the electoral process, since state populations determine the allocation of electoral votes and the number of representatives each receives in the House of Representatives. In addition, allocation of federal aid is often based on demographic information collected in the census.

4. **(E)** Multinational corporations, also known as transnational corporations, locate production facilities overseas to cut costs in the manufacturing process. The availability of cheap labor and more relaxed environmental and labor laws, along with greater access to natural resources, makes locating in these areas much more economically beneficial than locating in the country where the corporation is headquartered.

5. **(A)** Swidden agriculture, also know as slash-and-burn agriculture, can be sustainable if the soil is allowed enough time to regenerate itself. Swidden agriculture depends on nutrient addition to the soil through the burning of vegetation. Consequently, short fallow periods do not allow enough time for a substantial amount of vegetation to grow in previously cultivated plots to provide adequate nutrients for the next round of cultivation. As this process continues, the plot is eventually rendered infertile.

6. **(B)** Since 1945, the Sun Belt—including Florida, Georgia, Tennessee, North Carolina, and areas of the Southwest including parts of Texas, Arizona, and southern California—has attracted more and more people with its pleasant climate, affordable housing, and jobs in new high-tech industries.

7. **(B)** As cities increasingly spread outward from their urban cores, productive agricultural land and habitat for certain species succumb to development, while the congestion between suburban areas and the downtown area causes increased air pollution. Sprawl frequently occurs when affluent individuals leave older downtown areas, causing both segregation and inner-city decay. Sprawl is an enormous problem in the United States, where planners are often unable to deal with rapid residential and commercial growth in outlying areas.

8. **(D)** All the individuals from these cities speak Italian. However, variations in the ways they pronounce their words, and in the use of different vocabulary to describe the same objects signal the existence of several different local dialects.

9. **(E)** Multinational corporations locate their facilities in several different countries in order to lower costs and maximize profits. This strategy allows them to increase their profits by taking advantage of cheap labor, relaxed environmental standards, and access to natural resources where they exist. Headquarters for these corporations generally exist in developed countries, such as the United States, where corporate leaders make decisions that affect workers across the globe.

10. **(B)** The dependency ratio is determined by the number of individuals who are either too young or too old to support themselves, and who depend on economically productive individuals to support them. A small dependency ratio indicates that there are many productive individuals available to support the economically unproductive population within a country. Figure b, with its bulge in the middle of the pyramid and its rather small percentages of both young and old individuals, illustrates this situation.

11. **(D)** Topographical maps portray changes in elevation with isolines. An isoline is a line on a map that represents a constant value. For example, an isoline on a topographical map might represent the 10,000-foot elevation level. If you followed that isoline in the actual landscape, then you would be always be walking at ten thousand feet.

12. **(A)** Transhumance refers to livestock raising that varies in geographic location depending on the season. Generally, nomadic herders allow their livestock to graze in the mountains during the summer and move to the valleys during winter.

13. **(A)** A cultural complex describes the unique traits or characteristics of a particular culture. Those traits can include language, religious practices, dress, food, and art, among others.

14. **(A)** All the world's developing cities contain squatter settlements. Many of the people residing in these settlements are rural migrants who have been displaced from their land and come to the city seeking economic opportunity. As more and more individuals follow these rural-urban migration paths, squatter settlements continue to expand. Squatter settlements are among the poorest areas in the world.

15. **(E)** Globalization describes the increasing connections, both economic and social, occurring across national boundaries. While parts of the world become increasingly "globalized," many other areas have been left out entirely. Anti-globalization activists reject mass consumerism and advocate smaller, localized economies.

16. **(D)** Malthus determined that food production grew arithmetically through the addition of new fields into cultivation. This type of growth most accurately follows the curve depicted by the straight line in graph 4. He also believed that population grew geometrically, and that at some point population growth would surpass food production, causing widespread starvation and "negative checks." We now know that food production does not follow the curve in graph 4. Technological advances have allowed for increases in food production to support ever-increasing populations. In fact, inefficient distribution, not a lack of production, is the primary cause of world hunger today.

17. **(C)** Although the Sino-Tibetan language family contains Chinese, which has the most primary speakers across the globe, the number of people who speak English, Spanish, and French is actually much greater. These languages fall in the Indo-European family, making this the most popular language family on the globe today.

18. **(A)** Pastoralism involves the raising of livestock by nomadic groups or tribes that travel seasonally to find forage for their herds.

19. **(B)** Palestine is the only nation listed that does not have politically recognized national boundaries.

20. **(C)** Primary activities are those that deal directly with the extraction of the earth's natural resources through mining, agriculture, hunting, fishing, or forestry.

21. **(A)** Los Angeles, unlike many urban areas, contains several nodes, or centers of urban activity, other than downtown Los Angeles. These include Pasadena, Santa Monica, Beverly Hills, and Westwood. Los Angeles is an excellent example of the multiple-nuclei model of urban areas.

22. **(E)** Gentrification is the process whereby wealthy individuals colonize formerly poor neighborhoods. Gentrification does work to revitalize the city by generating wealth from upper-class residents; however, it creates new forms of segregation as the wealthy elite displace the urban poor.

23. **(B)** The nomothetic approach to geography parallels a systematic approach in which methods, models, theories, and processes can be applied universally across space. One way of ensuring this uniformity is by comparing the similarities of different places across the globe and formalizing them into a particular model or law. This contrasts with the idiographic approach, in which places are studied purely to uncover their unique characteristics.

24. **(E)** A barrier to spatial diffusion prevents a phenomenon from diffusing between two places. Physical barriers are actual physical elements in the landscape that prohibit interaction and diffusion. All four examples can serve as barriers to the diffusion of particular phenomena.

25. **(D)** Frontiers are defined as places where several competing peoples lay claim to the land. Both Antarctica and the Amazon Basin contain boundaries supposedly corresponding to a different state's ownership; however, these boundaries carry little significance on the ground.

26. **(E)**   The Green Revolution involved the use of new kinds of agricultural technologies to produce greater yields. During the Green Revolution, the developed world imposed these technologies on the developing world to provide more food and stimulate economic activity.

27. **(D)**   After World War II, the United States enjoyed a time of economic prosperity. During this time, the United States also experienced a high growth rate. Current population pyramids for the United States, show a bulge in the cohorts representing American males and females who are now in their fifties, illustrating the baby boom that occurred in the late 1940s and 1950s.

28. **(B)**   This map depicts an event that took place in the 1830s when the U.S. Congress, under the direction of President Andrew Jackson, passed the Indian Removal Act, which forced about 100,000 Cherokees, Chickasaws, Choctaws, Creeks, and Seminoles to move west of the Mississippi.

29. **(C)**   After NAFTA was signed, the U.S. corporations took advantage of the free trade zone in northern Mexico. They located numerous factories called *maquiladoras* just outside the border in an export-processing zone that allows for quick export of goods back into the United States.

30. **(C)**   Supranational organizations unite together three or more countries that share a common objective; in this case, the objective involves maintaining international security and cooperation across the globe.

31. **(C)**   Tokyo, London, and New York are the world's three most important centers of economic activity and are thus categorized as first-tier world cities. Other important centers of government, finance, and popular culture, such as Paris, Washington, Brussels, and Los Angeles are considered to be second-tier world cities.

32. **(D)**   Overgrazing, deforestation, and agricultural mismanagement can all cause the top, nutrient-rich layer of soil to erode, rendering the soil infertile.

33. **(B)**   People's daily spatial activities tend to occur very near their home. People travel the shortest distances to get things like milk, eggs, and gasoline, and are willing to travel farther to obtain specialty items like cars, jewelry, clothing, and concert tickets.

34. **(B)**   Topological space accounts for the relative distance between places, in terms of connectivity. Often places that are farther apart in absolute distance may actually be highly connected socially, culturally, or economically. Thus, a description of topological space may provide a more accurate measure of the cultural distance between two places.

35. **(A)** Most definitions of sustainable development involve using the earth's current resources in such as way as to avoid jeopardizing resources for future human populations. Many of these definitions concern themselves with the relationship between diminishing resources and human needs, and thus neglect the plight of nonhuman organisms.

36. **(E)** Mecca represents an extremely sacred space for the adherents of Islam. No matter where they live, Muslims face Mecca each time they pray. In addition, many Muslims make a pilgrimage to the holy city at least once during their lifetime. This photograph illustrates the thousands of people that enter this holy city on a daily basis.

37. **(E)** A frontier generally connotes an area where borders are shifting and weak, and where peoples of different nationalities lay claim to the land. Currently, Antarctica, the world's oceans, and the Amazon basin contain many claims of ownership that do not have much political significance. Lake Michigan is the only option where political ownership is clearly undisputed.

38. **(B)** "Diaspora" is a term used to describe places where people of certain ethnicities, living outside of their country of origin, establish a community and maintain many of the traditions of their cultural heritage. In many cities across the globe, especially the larger ones, ethnic neighborhoods can be distinguished by their unique cultural traditions including music, dress, cuisine, and religious practices. The word, which was originally applied to Jews, may also refer to the broad distribution of a people with a common identity from their cultural hearth or place of origin.

39. **(D)** Urban sprawl results from an increasing number of individuals and corporations locating on the outskirts of urban areas, where land values are cheaper and where highways and single-family homes dominate the landscape. Sprawl can lead to development of previously fertile agricultural lands, traffic, and pollution, as suburbanites commute back and forth from suburbs to central cities. To counteract this problem, urban planners develop strategies to keep people in the heart of the city and to limit the negative effects of sprawl. Efficient public transportation can limit the traffic and auto-related environmental problems of sprawl, while initiatives curbing urban growth and encouraging the revitalization of downtown areas work to draw families and corporations back into older urban cores.

40. **(D)** Nomadic herding is practiced for subsistence by only a few remaining cultures around the world today. Most nomadic herders live in high-altitude or semiarid regions of Africa and Asia.

41. **(C)** Environmental determinism is the idea that the specific environment humans inhabit determines their cultural system. Huntington's explorations, in his mind, demonstrated that climatic change dictated cultural changes; therefore, by studying the physical environment of different cultural groups he could determine why certain traits, unique to that group, developed in that particular environment. Possibilism argues that humans have agency and although environmental factors constrain certain possibilities, human cultures and qualities are not determined by natural factors.

42. **(D)** Many transnational corporations with corporate headquarters in the United States or other developed countries often choose to locate their manufacturing facilities outside of their home country in order to take advantage of cheaper labor and more relaxed environmental standards available elsewhere.

43. **(D)** Gerrymandering involves the illegal redistricting or reapportionment of voting districts to include or exclude a certain population, and to favor one political party over another.

44. **(B)** According to von Thunen's model, land will cost more the closer it is to the market. Thus, producers who choose to locate near the market must justify their decision in terms of rents and transportation costs. Goods that are grown close to markets tend to be those that are expensive and spoil quickly.

45. **(A)** Kevin Lynch's book, *Image of the City,* used data from surveys of urban inhabitants to determine the features in the urban landscape that contributed to a particular city's legibility or lack thereof. Lynch described five features that make a city more readable for both its inhabitants and for visitors: paths, landmarks, nodes, edges, and districts. The organization of these features, in large part, determines peoples' ability to navigate urban environments. Thus, Lynch's research has provided helpful structural guidelines for urban planners.

46. **(A)** In predicting the level of interaction between New York and London, the two very large numbers multiplied together in the numerator (population) will counteract the distance measure in the denominator. Thus, although New York and London are far away from each other in absolute distance, they still have a high degree of interaction, in part due to their large populations.

47. **(E)** Globalization shows an extremely uneven distribution of its benefits. While a few highly developed nations enjoy the economic benefits of globalization, few of these benefits trickle down to other parts of the economically peripheral world.

322 PRACTICE TEST 2

48. (E) All four of the acronyms except the CIA represent an international alliance between two or more countries.

49. (B) Each of the areas highlighted on the map experience a Mediterranean climate characterized by mild, ocean-regulated temperatures; cool, wet winters; and warm, dry summers. Agriculturally, these areas tend to specialize in grapes, olives, avocados, and other fruits and nuts.

50. (B) A lingua franca is a language that is used by two groups who usually speak different languages to successfully complete economic transactions. Lingua francas are usually quite simple, containing just enough mutually comprehensible words for the two groups to communicate and conduct trade.

51. (B) Medieval cities have large, ornate cathedrals at their center, narrow and winding streets, and high walls that protected the city from attack. These types of cities served as precursors to many current European cities, which explains the presence of such remnant features in those cities today.

52. (D) As a country becomes increasingly developed economically, it generally transitions through the four economic sectors discussed in Chapter 6. The developed countries of the world demonstrate high levels of both tertiary and quaternary activities, while developing countries generally demonstrate dominance in primary and secondary activities. To transition between sectors, countries need to develop the infrastructure necessary to participate in the activities associated with each of the sectors. Since developing countries lack much of the industrial and technological infrastructure to participate in secondary, tertiary, and quaternary activities, their economies usually depend on agriculture or the extraction of natural resources.

53. (A) Thailand has a long thin arm jutting out from the rest of its territory into the Malay Peninsula, thus it is referred to as a prorupted state.

54. (A) Early agricultural hearths existed in lush, river valleys. Recall from Chapter 7 that these places included China, India, Peru, Mexico, Africa, and the Fertile Crescent region of the Middle East.

55. (D) Human welfare indexes, or social indicators of economic development, use literacy rates to evaluate a country's level of development. Many developing countries across the globe exhibit literacy rates much lower than those in developed countries. Furthermore, literacy rates sometimes differ significantly between the sexes in many developing countries, with girls and women often lagging behind.

56. (C)   A map's scale tells you how a unit on a map compares to units on the ground. For example, if your map scale says 1:24,000 this means that one unit on the map represents 24,000 of those same units in reality.

57. (B)   The only two terms that connote a politically recognized bounded territory are "state" and "country." Neither nations nor territories have internationally recognized political boundaries.

58. (D)   For most indicators, less-developed countries are worse off than developed countries. Indicators such as infant mortality, growth, fertility, number of births, and number of deaths are quite high in developing regions of the globe; similarly illiteracy and other human welfare indicators tend to be quite high in these regions.

59. (B)   When irrigation is used to make arid environments more agriculturally productive, excess water evaporates leaving a salty residue. This residue seeps into the soil making it more acidic and less productive; the entire process is called salinization.

60. (D)   A megalopolis refers to any area on the globe where large urban areas have merged, forming a gigantic urban complex. The most commonly used example of this phenomena is the megalopolis that exists along the Atlantic coast of the United States running from Boston to Washington, D.C. Another example is the Rio de Janeiro and Sao Paulo megalopolis in Brazil.

61. (C)   This map depicts economic activities that have agglomerated in certain cities in the United States. Similar industries often locate near each other in order to share a similar infrastructure and labor pool. For example, Los Angeles houses a large proportion of actors, makeup artists, stuntpeople, screenwriters, directors, and producers. These people provide an anchor, keeping the entertainment industry firmly grounded in Los Angeles.

62. (A)   High total fertility rates are generally typical of developing regions across the globe. A lack of gender empowerment often associated with a lack of access to education and political power for women leads to higher fertility rates. Many developing regions' economies focus on either primary or secondary activities.

63. (C)   Agribusiness increasingly characterizes much of agricultural activity occurring across the globe today. It involves the mass production of agricultural goods and all the marketing and processing involved when agricultural activities become massive in scale and highly integrated. Transnational corporations increasingly control agribusiness operations throughout the world.

64. (D)   Popular culture looks fairly similar throughout the world; however, the popular elements describing this culture change quite rapidly as trends and fads come and go. Conversely, folk cultures represent the unique characteristics of a particular group and thus change significantly over space. Folk cultures are very slow to adapt new innovations, causing their cultural system to remain fairly constant through time.

65. (E)   Cognitive maps contain specific information individuals assimilate from their environment to help them navigate. Usually they include items like landmarks or other prominent features in the landscape that individuals perceive to be important for understanding and navigating within different environments.

66. (A)   Rice farming is an extremely intensive agricultural activity; both the land's productivity per area and the amount of labor needed per area are higher than many other agricultural goods. Rice provides a staple for many Asian countries and still remains a subsistence form of agriculture in these parts of the world.

67. (C)   According to Weber's material index, discussed in Chapter 6, industries will locate their facilities to minimize transportation costs. Location is determined by the weight of raw material versus the weight of finished product. If the weight of the raw material is greater, the factory will have a resource orientation and will locate near the raw materials. If the finished product weighs more, the factory will exhibit a market orientation, minimizing transportation costs between the factory and the market. In this case, both the raw materials and the finished product weigh the same, enabling the furniture maker to locate anywhere between them, since transportation costs will be the same in both directions.

68. (E)   According to the rank-size rule, cities within a country follow a particular pattern in terms of the sizes of their populations. Each city will have a population total that corresponds to its rank. The second largest city should be one-half the size of the first; the third, one-third of the first; the fourth, one-quarter of the first.

69. (A)   In 1999, the world passed the 6 billion-population marker. As this large number exponentially increases, the time it takes to add another billion people to the population will become significantly smaller. The world will have 7 billion people by about the year 2013.

70. (B)   Basic activities within a local economy generate money from sources outside of the community, whereas the nonbasic sector provides services to the community, keeping that wealth circulating within the local area. Because automobile factories produce goods for consumption by individuals outside of the local area, they generate wealth from outside sources for the community or city. In addition, because people working basic jobs need services provided by the nonbasic sector, an increase in basic jobs leads to an increase in nonbasic jobs, thereby providing a significant economic stimulus for the entire community.

71. (C)   Models provide geographers and other scientists with ways of simplifying reality, while identifying the essential components necessary to describe a particular phenomenon. Because models usually apply to more than one place, it is impossible to include every factor of a particular phenomenon. However, by using the important elements of a process, geographers can use models to provide a comprehensible view of a particular process or phenomenon.

72. (B)   The concentric zone model applies to cities that have rings of development emanating outward from a core, or central business district. In theory, each ring contains different types of development and economic activities. This is because the value of land decreases as you go farther out from the central core. Many geographers cite Chicago as an excellent example of the concentric zone model.

73. (D)   Universalizing religions can appeal to people across the globe, independent of their location. Often, universalizing religions are also global, but not all global religions, such as Buddhism, are evangelical, seeking to actively recruit new believers.

74. (E)   Pull factors are positive forces that pull migrants to a new destination; push factors are negative forces that push individuals out of a particular area or country. Common pull factors include new job and educational opportunities, better climate, and affordable housing. Push factors include an economic recession or loss of job, religious or ethnic persecution, and environmental degradation.

75. (A)   Ancillary activities include all the necessary services to sustain and provide for a local population, such as grocery stores, barbers, and veterinary hospitals. As the population within a region increases, as it does when an area becomes the site for a particular agglomeration, more of these services become necessary. Thus agglomerations have tremendous impacts on the overall economy within a specific region.

Answers for Free-Response Questions

1. Agricultural production has changed dramatically from its early beginnings when hunter-gatherers began domesticating plants for consumption by local populations. It now exists on a massive scale as agribusiness increasingly governs agricultural activity across the globe.

The first agriculturalists lived in places like Turkey, Peru, China, and Mexico where the lush environment facilitated agricultural production. These societies originally subsisted on hunting and gathering. Through time, as gatherers collected the best fruits and nuts, they scattered the seeds for those plants, and gradually the nuts and fruits of their diet became domesticated. As this process continued and expanded, different agricultural innovations have allowed for many varieties of products to be grown all across the globe.

The Industrial Revolution dramatically changed agricultural production in two ways. Mechanization allowed for machines to replace human labor, encouraging both cheaper and larger agricultural yields. Additionally, as industries drew population from rural areas to cities for jobs, the increased population generated a large market for agricultural goods in those areas. The Green Revolution introduced several innovations, many still in use, to encourage greater yields across the globe. Chemical herbicides, pesticides, and fungicides, as well as "miracle seeds" produced from plant hybridization, all designed in the developed world, disseminated to developing nations to encourage greater production. However, many of the chemicals introduced wreaked havoc on the land to such an extent that the full effects have not yet been determined. Finally, the technology developed during the Green Revolution encouraged scientists to develop even more extensive technologies that use plants to modify other plants. The development of these methods began the Biotechnologic Revolution, which led to the production of genetically modified organisms that can withstand certain environmental limitations or provide even greater nutrients than the unmodified varieties. Similar to the Green Revolution, the full effects of these biotechnological innovations have yet to be realized, but many people are skeptical of genetically modified foods. Europe banned the import and sale of any foods that have been genetically modified.

Current agricultural production differs remarkably from its historical roots as evidenced most convincingly by the rise of agribusiness. Agribusiness has transformed agricultural production such that family farms no longer exist as the centerpiece of production. Rather, a network of producers, marketers, corporate managers, and consumers dictate and necessitate agricultural production on a massive scale. Agribusiness uses the technology developed in each of the three revolutions to, in turn, revolutionize agricultural production such that agricultural goods have become one of the many commodities produced, marketed, and consumed on a global scale.

Agricultural production has changed dramatically from when it first developed thousands of years ago. While during its inception, agriculturists used primarily human labor to support a small number of people, now extensive inputs, including various chemicals, biological innovations, and increased technology, allow for agricultural production to exist on a global scale to support an ever-increasing global population.

2. In 1950, the world's biggest cities were mostly located in developed countries. Since then, the geographic distribution of population has shifted dramatically from developed regions to developing regions, and from rural areas to cities. This has been caused by a combination of population growth and migration. As these cities continue to grow, they will face a myriad of difficult social and environmental problems.

During the past few centuries, the world's largest cities were located in Europe, eastern Asia, and North America; however, rapidly growing cities in peripheral countries, particularly in South America, and Southeast Asia, are beginning to take the lead as the world's most populated urban areas. In looking at historical population growth, rates for developing countries dramatically increased right around 1950. Increased medical access has allowed the death rate to drop and the birth rate to remain high, increasing the distance between them, and thus allowing for rapid exponential growth. Additionally, as more economic opportunities concentrate in urban areas, these countries experience droves of rural migrants moving to their cities on a daily basis. With this many people both migrating and being born into these cities every day, it is easy to understand why they took the population lead so quickly.

Many cities in the developing world have difficulty adequately supplying the needs of their original population. Thus, they are essentially unable to provide services for ever increasing numbers of people. Squatter settlements surround the outskirts of all peripheral cities and, in many, extend for miles, as more individuals settle on the rims every day. The pollution, disease, and other environmental problems that arise from so many people crowded in such a small space without access to sanitation and other health benefits present numerous health and well-being problems for both geographers and policy makers. Geographers and policy makers must rapidly devise plans for helping these cities better accommodate increasing populations, both for their own sake and for the sake of the entire globe, as many of the environmental repercussions of these overcrowded cities will soon be felt across the earth.

3. The effects of colonialism during the last 500 years are hard to underemphasize. Colonialism has been used to explain many of the global disparities present across the earth's surface today. Specifically, the dominance of colonial languages, along with the development of colonial cities, and economic structures developed during colonial times have dramatically impacted geographic patterns and processes across space.

When colonizing countries took over vast amounts of land in Africa and South America, they brought their alphabets and language systems with them. As these became the standard of economic and political activity, many native groups were essentially forced to adopt the new languages, losing their native tongue. Linguistic acculturation during the Colonial Period largely explains the mass extinction of so many of the world's native languages along with the geographic dominance of European tongues.

Furthermore, when colonizing countries took over new lands, they often designated one area to serve as the focal point of all economic and political activity. These cities grew and developed at the expense of cities and towns in the rest of the country. Even after decolonization, these cities remained the core area within those countries explaining why many states in the developing world contain primate cities where the majority of the urban population resides. Some of these cities currently house a good proportion of the world's total urban population presenting numerous welfare and environmental issues for both the local area and the entire earth.

Finally, many argue that colonialism fostered a dependency relationship between colonizing countries, or the European core, and colonized countries, or the African, Asian, and South American periphery. In other words, the core develops at the expense of the periphery. The political and economic relationships established during colonialism set in place a system whereby the developing regions of the globe depend on developed nations for any chance at economic success. Considering the presence of numerous multinational corporations in developing areas of the world, the argument is probably well founded. Unfortunately, the periphery has become so economically dependent on the core that it will be hard for them to transcend these patterns established during colonial times. Thus, the effects of colonialism on the colonized will not soon be overcome.

Index